STEPS TO
WRITING WELL

Jean Wyrick, Director of Composition at Colorado State University

"This fourth edition of Steps to Writing Well was written and revised for teachers of composition who have had trouble finding a text that is accessible to their students. While there are many methods of teaching composition, Steps to Writing Well tries to help inexperienced writers by offering a clearly defined approach to writing the short essay. By presenting simple, practical advice directly to the students, this text is intended to make the demanding jobs of teaching and learning the basic principles of composition easier and more enjoyable for everyone."

—Jean Wyrick

Also by Jean Wyrick:
Steps to Writing Well with Additional Readings
The Rinehart Reader
Discovering Ideas, 2/e

STEPS TO WRITING WELL

WITH ADDITIONAL READINGS

JEAN WYRICK
Colorado State University

Holt, Rinehart and Winston, Inc.

Fort Worth   Chicago   San Francisco   Philadelphia
Montreal   Toronto   London   Sydney   Tokyo

Publisher   Charlyce Jones Owen
Acquisition Editor   Michael Rosenberg
Production Manager   Kenneth A. Dunaway
Design and Composition   Publications Development Company
Cover Artist   Bill Reed
Cover Design Supervisor   Vicki McAlindon Horton

Address Orders to: 6277 Sea Harbor Drive, Orlando, FL 32887
   1-800-782-4479, or 1-800-433-0001 (in Florida)

Address Editorial Correspondence to: 301 Commerce Street, Suite 3700, Fort Worth, TX 76102

Note: This work is derived from STEPS TO WRITING WELL, Fourth Edition by Jean Wyrick, copyright © 1989 by Holt, Rinehart and Winston, Inc.

Printed in the United States of America

Library of Congress Cataloging-in-Publication Data

Wyrick, Jean.
    Steps to writing well with additional readings.

    Includes bibliographical references.
    1. English language—Rhetoric.   2. College readers.
I. Title.
PE1408.W94   1990   808'.042   89-26900
ISBN   0-03-030812-7

0 1 2 3   039   9 8 7 6 5 4 3 2 1

Holt, Rinehart and Winston, Inc.
The Dryden Press
Saunders College Publishing

This book is dedicated to DAVID
and to SARAH, KATE, and AUSTIN

To the Teacher

Steps to Writing Well is written for teachers of composition who have had trouble finding a text that is accessible to their students. Too many texts on today's market, these teachers rightfully complain, are still unnecessarily complex, sophisticated, or massive for the majority of students. Written simply in an informal, straightforward style and addressed to the student, this text is designed to provide a clear step-by-step guide to writing a variety of 500-to-800 word essays. The combination of concise, practical advice, a number of student and professional samples, and a brief handbook should provide more than enough helpful information for students enrolled in a one-semester or one-quarter course without intimidating them with more material than they can possibly master.

The book is organized into four parts. Part One offers advice on "The Basics of the Short Essay"; Part Two discusses the "Modes and Strategies"; Part Three presents "A Concise Handbook"; Part Four contains "Additional Readings." The text begins with the essay "To the Student," which not only argues that students can learn to write better with practice and dedication but also gives them a number of practical reasons why they *should* learn to write better.

Part One, containing seven chapters, moves students sequentially through the process of writing the short essay. Chapter 1, on prewriting, stresses finding the proper attitude ("the desire to communicate") and presents over a half-dozen helpful suggestions for selecting and focusing a subject. In addition, a section on using the journal explains more than a dozen ways students may improve their skills by writing a variety of nonthreatening—and even enjoyable—assignments. The section on audience should help student writers identify their particular readers and communicate more effectively with them.

After finding a topic and identifying their audience, students are then ready for Chapter 2, devoted almost entirely to a discussion of the thesis statement. This chapter first explains the role of the "working thesis" in early drafts and then clearly outlines what a good thesis is and isn't by presenting a host of examples to illustrate the advice. Also included in this chapter is explanation of the "essay map," an organizational tool that can help students shape their essays and plan their body paragraphs.

Chapter 3 discusses in detail the requirements of good body paragraphs: topic sentences, unity, order and coherence, adequate development, use of specific detail, and logical sequence. Over forty paragraphs illustrate both strengths and weaknesses of student writing. These paragraphs are not complex literary or professional excerpts but rather well-designed, precise examples of the principles under examination, written on subjects students can understand and appreciate. Moreover, this chapter twice provides the opportunity for students to see how a topic may progress from a working thesis statement to an informal essay outline, which, in turn, helps produce well-developed paragraphs in the body of an essay. To complete the overview of the short essay, Chapter 4 explains, through a number of samples, how to write good introductions, conclusions, and titles.

Chapter 5, "Revising Your Writing," is one of the most important in this text. Because too many students still think of "revision" as merely proofreading their essays rather than as an essential recursive activity, this chapter is devoted to explaining the revision process and to stressing the necessity of revision in all good writing. These pages guide the students through the various stages of revision, carefully cautioning novice writers against trying to analyze and revise too many parts of their papers at once. The chapter also includes hints for overcoming writer's block, a checklist for essays, a special note for writers with word processors, and two student essays for revision practice.

Chapter 6, on effective sentences, emphasizes the importance of clarity, conciseness, and vividness, with nearly one hundred and fifty sample sentences illustrating the chapter's advice. Chapter 7, on word choice, presents practical suggestions for selecting accurate, appropriate words that are specific, memorable, and persuasive. This chapter also contains sections on avoiding sexist language and "bureaucratese."

Each chapter in Part One contains numerous samples and exercises. "Practicing What You've Learned" exercises follow each major section in each chapter so that both teacher and students may quickly discover if particular material needs additional attention. Moreover, by conquering small steps in the writing process, one at a time, the students should feel more confident and should learn more rapidly. Assignments, which also follow each major section in these chapters, suggest class activities and frequently emphasize "peer teaching," a useful method that asks students to prepare appropriate exercises for classmates and then to evaluate the results. Such assignments, operating under the premise that "you don't truly learn a subject until you teach it," provide engaging classroom activity for all the students and may also remove from the teacher some of the burden of creating exercises. In addition, throughout the chapters in Part One, activities called "Applying What You've Learned to *Your* Writing" follow the exercises and assignments. Each of these activities encourages students to "follow through" by incorporating into a current draft the skill they have just read about and practiced. By following a three-step procedure—reading the advice in the text, practicing the advice through the exercises, and then applying the advice directly to their own prose—students should improve their writing processes. Finally, each of the chapters in Part One concludes with a summary, designed to help students review the important points in the material under study.

Part Two concentrates on the four rhetorical modes: exposition, argumenta-tion, description, and narration. Chapter 8 on exposition is divided into separate discussions of the expository strategies: example, process, comparison/contrast, definition, division and classification, and causal analysis. Each discussion in Chapter 8 and each of the chapters on argument, description, and narration fol-lows a similar format by offering the students (a) a clear definition of the mode (or strategy), explained with familiar examples; (b) practical advice on developing each essay; (c) warnings against common problems; (d) suggested essay topics on subjects that appeal to students' interests and capabilities; (e) a sample student essay with marginal notes; (f) a professional essay followed by questions on con-tent, structure, and style, and a vocabulary list; (g) a revision worksheet to guide student writers through their rough drafts. The advice on developing the essay and the section on common problems are both explained in easy-to-understand language accompanied by numerous examples. The ten student essays should en-courage student writers by showing them that others in their situation can indeed compose organized, thoughtful essays. The student essays that appear here are not perfect, however; consequently, teachers may use them in class to generate suggestions for still more revision.

The ten professional essays presented in Part Two were selected to spur class discussion and to illustrate the rhetorical principles discussed in the text. While each of the modes and strategies are illustrated by a professional essay, Chapter 9, on argumentation, contains two professional essays so that students may see writers arguing different sides of a current controversy. This chapter also presents two advertisements that directly counter each other, again offering students an opportunity to compare and contrast argumentative approaches.

Chapter 12, "Writing the Research Paper," shows students how to use the library, take notes, and incorporate source material into their essays. Examples are provided to help students understand the difference between summary and paraphrase and between plagiarism in its various forms and proper documenta-tion. The chapter contains information on the current MLA parenthetical docu-mentation format and samples of the most often used bibliographic entries, as well as a "problem-solving" student essay that uses research material to sup-port its points. It also includes discussion of the APA style of documentation and samples of the most frequently used entries.

Part Three contains a concise handbook with non-technical explanations and easy-to-understand examples showing how to correct the most common er-rors in grammar, punctuation, and mechanics. This part also includes nine sets of exercises over the grammar and punctuation rules. Instead of following each and every rule with five or ten simplistic sentences containing the error in question, this text offers a series of exercises systematically placed so that the students may practice applying several rules at one sitting, just as they must do when they write their own prose. A brief section on spelling hints may offer some limited relief to students who suffer from the malady of being poor spellers.

Part Four gives teachers the opportunity to choose among twenty-seven additional professional essays. These essays—some serious, some humorous, some familiar, some new—also illustrate the modes and strategies discussed in

Part Two and offer a variety of ideas, structures, and styles to consider. By assigning some of these readings, in addition to the ten in Part Two, teachers may show students different organizational patterns found within the same strategy. For example, students studying comparison/contrast may see several essays developed by the "block" method and others developed by the "point-by-point" method. Similarly, students writing process analysis papers may study both directional and informational models; students studying causal analysis may see some essays that primarily focus on the causes of something and others, on the effects; and so on. Studying the professional essays presented here should help novice writers as they make their own rhetorical choices.

One minor note: readers of this text may discover an occasional attempt at humor. The lighthearted tone of some samples and exercises is the result of the author's firm belief that while learning to write is serious business, solemn composition classrooms are not always the most beneficial environments for anxious beginning writers. The author takes full responsibility (and all of the blame) for the bad jokes and even worse puns.

Finally, an Instructor's Manual, which includes suggestions for teaching the text, answers to the exercises and Part Two's essay questions, and questions for the essays in Part Four, is available. For a free copy, write the English Editor; Holt, Rinehart and Winston Publishers; Suite 3700, 301 Commerce Street; Ft. Worth, TX, 76102.

While there are many methods of teaching composition, *Steps to Writing Well* tries to help inexperienced writers by offering a clearly defined sequential approach to writing the short essay. By presenting simple, practical advice directly to the students, this text is intended to make the demanding jobs of teaching and learning the basic principles of composition easier and more enjoyable for everyone.

ACKNOWLEDGMENTS

I wish to thank Charlyce Jones Owen, Publisher for Humanities, for her continued support for my projects. I am especially grateful to English Acquisitions Editor Michael Rosenberg, who guided the book with intelligence and care; to Laurie Runion, Editorial Assistant, who improved the manuscript in numerous ways; and to Nancy Marcus Land at Publications Development Company, who managed the book's production. In addition, I appreciate the advice of colleagues across the country who offered many excellent suggestions: Sandra Clark, Anderson University; Louis Emond, Dean Junior College; Virginia Hudgens, Memphis State University; James O'Neil, Edison Community College; Jill Sessoms, University of South Carolina-Coastal Carolina College; Russell E. Ward, Aims Community College.

And, as always, my love and thanks to the most special people in my life for their patience and understanding: my husband, David Hall, and our children, Sarah, Kate, and Austin.

To the Student

FINDING THE RIGHT ATTITUDE

If you agree with one or more of the following statements, we have some serious myth-killing to do before you begin this book:

1. I'm no good in English—never have been, never will be.
2. Only people with natural talent for writing can succeed in composition class.
3. My composition teacher is a picky, comma-hunting liberal/conservative/ hippie freak/old fogey/whatever, who will insist I write just like him or her.
4. I write for myself, not for anyone else, so I don't need this class or this book.
5. Composition classes are designed to put my creativity in a straitjacket.

The notion that good writers are born, not made, is a widespread myth that may make you feel defeated before you start. But the simple truth is that good writers *are* made—simply because *effective writing is a skill that can be learned*. Despite any feelings of insecurity you may have about composition, you should realize that you already know many of the basic rules of good writing; after all, you've been writing since you were six years old. What you need now is some practical advice on composition, some coaching to sharpen your skills, and a strong dose of determination to practice those skills until you can consistently produce the results you want. Talent, as the French writer Flaubert once said, is nothing more than long patience.

Think about learning to write well as you might consider your tennis game. No one is born a tennis star. You first learn the basic rules and movements and then go out on the court to practice. And practice. No one's tennis will improve if he or she stays off the court; similarly, you must write regularly and receive feedback to improve your composition skills. Try to see your teacher not as Dr. Frankenstein determined to reproduce his or her style of writing in you, but rather as your coach, your loyal trainer, who wants you to do the very best you can. Like any good coach, your teacher will point out your strengths and weaknesses; she or he will often send you to this text for practical suggestions for improvement. And while there are no quick, magic solutions for learning to write well, the most important point to remember is this: with this text, your own common sense, and determination, *you can improve your writing.*

WHY WRITE?

"OK," you say, "so I can improve if I try—but why should I bother? Why should I write well? I'm not going to be a professional writer."

In the first place, writing helps us explore our own thoughts and feelings. Writing forces us to articulate our ideas, to discover what we really think about an issue. For example, let's suppose you're faced with a difficult decision and that the arguments pro and con are jumbled in your head. You begin to write down all the pertinent facts and feelings, and, suddenly, you begin to see that you do, indeed, have stronger arguments for one side of the question than the other. Once you "see" what you are thinking, you may then scrutinize your opinions for any logical flaws or weaknesses and revise your argument accordingly. In other words, writing lays out our ideas for examination, analysis, and thoughtful reaction. Thus when we write, we (and the world at large) see who we are, and what we stand for, much more clearly. Moreover, writing can provide a record of our thoughts that we may study and evaluate in a way that conversation cannot. In short, writing well enables us to see and know ourselves—our feelings, ideas, and opinions—better.

On a more practical level, we need to write effectively to communicate with others. While a part of our writing is done solely for ourselves, the majority of it is created for others to share. In this world, it is almost impossible to claim that we write only for ourselves. We are constantly asked to put our feelings, ideas, and knowledge in writing for others to read. In four years of college, no matter what your major, you will repeatedly be required to write essays, tests, reports, and exercises (not to mention letters home). Later, you may need to write formal letters of application for jobs or graduate training. And on a job you may have to write numerous kinds of reports, proposals, analyses, and requisitions. To be successful in any field, you must make your correspondence with business associates and co-workers clearly understood; remember that enormous amounts of time, energy, and profit have been lost because of a single unclear office memo.

There's still a third—more cynical—reason for studying writing techniques. Once you begin to improve your ability to use language, you will become more aware of the ways others write and speak. Through today's mass media, we are continually bombarded with words from politicians, advertisers, scientists, preachers, and teachers. We need to understand and evaluate what we are hearing, not only for our benefit but also for self-protection. Language is frequently manipulated to manipulate us. For example, years ago some government officials on trial preferred us to see Watergate as an "intelligence information gathering mission" rather than as simple breaking and entering, and today some politicians claim to merely "misspeak themselves" when caught in lies. Similarly, military officers and CIA members may discuss the "neutralization" of their enemies, possibly through the use of weapons with names such as "Peacekeeper," designed to obscure their potential for our total destruction. (In 1988, the National Council of Teachers of English gave their Doublespeak Award to the U.S. officers who, after accidentally shooting down a plane of civilians, reported that the plane didn't crash—rather, it had "uncontrolled contact with the ground.") Advertisers frequently try to sell us "authentic art reproductions" that are, of course, fakes all the same; the television networks treat us to "encore presentations" that are the same old summer reruns. And "fenestration engineers" are still window cleaners; "environmental superintendents" are still janitors; "drain surgeons" are still plumbers.

By becoming better writers ourselves, we can learn to recognize and reject the irresponsible, cloudy, and dishonest language of others before we become victims of their exploitation.

A GOOD PLACE TO START

If improving writing skills is not only possible but important, it is also something else: hard work. H. L. Mencken, American critic and writer, once remarked that "for every difficult and complex problem, there is an obvious solution that is simple, easy and wrong." No composition text can promise easy formulas guaranteed to improve your writing overnight. Nor is writing always fun for anyone. But this text can make the learning process easier, less painful, and more enjoyable than you might anticipate. Written in plain, straightforward language addressed to you, the student, this book will suggest a variety of practical ways for you to organize and write clear, concise prose. Because each of your writing tasks will be different, this text cannot provide a single, simple blueprint that will apply in all instances. Later chapters, however, will discuss some of the most common methods of organizing essays, such as development by example, definition, classification, causal analysis, comparison/contrast, and argument. As you become more familiar with, and begin to master, these patterns of writing, you will find yourself increasingly able to assess, organize, and explain the thoughts you have about the people, events, and situations in your own life. And while it may be true that in learning to write well there is no free ride, this book, along with your own willingness to work and improve, can start you down the road with a good sense of direction.

J.W.

Contents

To the Teacher   vii

To the Student   xi

PART ONE   THE BASICS OF THE SHORT ESSAY

1 Prewriting   3

Getting Started (Or Soup-Can Labels Can
   Be Fascinating)   3
Selecting a Subject   4
Finding Your Essay's Purpose and Focus   5
After You've Found Your Focus   15
   Practicing What You've Learned   15

Discovering Your Audience   16
How to Identify Your Readers   17
   Practicing What You've Learned   20

Keeping a Journal (Talking to Yourself *Does* Help)   22

Chapter 1 Summary   26

2 The Thesis Statement   27

After Selecting Your Subject   27
What Does a Thesis Do?   27
What Is a "Working" Thesis?   28
What Is a Good Thesis?   28
Avoiding Common Errors in Thesis Statements   33
   Practicing What You've Learned   35
   Assignment   36

Using the Essay Map   36
   Practicing What You've Learned   38
   Assignment   39

Chapter 2 Summary   40

3 The Body Paragraphs   41

Planning the Body of Your Essay   41
Organizing the Body Paragraphs   44
The Topic Sentence   45
   Practicing What You've Learned   49
   Assignment   52
   Applying What You've Learned to *Your* Writing   52

Paragraph Development   52
Paragraph Length   56
   Practicing What You've Learned   57
   Assignment   57
   Applying What You've Learned to *Your* Writing   58

Paragraph Unity   58
   Practicing What You've Learned   60
   Applying What You've Learned to *Your* Writing   61

Paragraph Coherence   62
   Practicing What You've Learned   68

Paragraph Sequence   71
Transitions between Paragraphs   72
   Applying What You've Learned to *Your* Writing   73

Chapter 3 Summary   73

4 Beginnings and Endings   74

How to Write a Good Lead-In   74
Avoiding Errors in Lead-Ins   77
   Practicing What You've Learned   78

How to Write a Good Concluding Paragraph   78
Avoiding Errors in Conclusions   80
   Practicing What You've Learned   80

How to Write a Good Title   81
   Assignment   81
   Applying What You've Learned to *Your* Writing   82

Chapter 4 Summary   82

5 Revising Your Writing   **83**

    Preparing the First Draft   84
    Revising the First Draft   84
    Revising the Second Draft   85
    Revising the Third Draft   87
    The Final Touches   87
    A Special Note for Writers with Word
      Processors   88
    Some Last Advice: How to Play with Your
      Mental Blocks   89
    A Checklist for Your Essay   91
      Practicing What You've Learned   92
      Assignment   94

    Chapter 5 Summary   94

6 Effective Sentences   **95**

    Develop a Clear Style   96
    Develop a Concise Style   102
      Practicing What You've Learned   107
      Assignment   109

    Develop a Lively Style   109
      Practicing What You've Learned   112
      Assignment   113

    Develop an Emphatic Style   114
      Practicing What You've Learned   117
      Assignment   119
      Applying What You've Learned to *Your* Writing   120

    Chapter 6 Summary   120

7 Word Logic   **121**

    Selecting the Correct Words   121
      Practicing What You've Learned   127

    Selecting the Best Words   128
      Practicing What You've Learned   137
      Assignment   139
      Applying What You've Learned to *Your* Writing   141

    Chapter 7 Summary   141

    The Basics of the Short Essay: Part One
      Summary   141

PART TWO   MODES AND STRATEGIES

8 Exposition   145

The Strategies of Exposition   145

Strategy One: Development by Example   146
Essay Topics   151
Sample Student Essay   152

Professional Example Essay: "So What's So Bad
about Being So-So?"   154
The drive for perfection is preventing too many people
from enjoying sports and hobbies, says author Lisa
Wilson Strick (who proudly plays the piano badly but
with great pleasure).

A Revision Worksheet for Your Example Essay   157

Strategy Two: Development by Process
Analysis   157
Essay Topics   161
Sample Student Essay   161

Professional Process Essay: "To Bid the World
Farewell"   164
By describing the embalming process in vivid, step-by-step
detail, social critic and author Jessica Mitford questions
the value—and necessity—of the entire procedure.

A Revision Worksheet for Your Process Essay   170

Strategy Three: Development by Comparison and
Contrast   170
Essay Topics   174
Sample Student Essay   175

Professional Comparison/Contrast Essay: "Grant
and Lee: A Study in Contrasts"   177
Noted historian Bruce Catton compares and contrasts
the two great generals of the Civil War, concluding that
their roles at Appomatox made possible "a peace of
reconciliation."

A Revision Worksheet for Your Comparison/Contrast
Essay   181

Strategy Four: Development by Definition   181
Essay Topics   185
Sample Student Essay   186

Professional Definition Essay: "The Androgynous Male" 188

Columnist Noel Perrin defines a new class of men and argues that they may have more freedom than those who imitate the he-man, all-American-who-loves-football male stereotype.

A Revision Worksheet for Your Definition Essay   192

Strategy Five: Development by Division and Classification   192
Essay Topics   195
Sample Student Essay   196

Professional Classification Essay: "The Sound of Music: Enough Already"   198

Contemporary satirist Fran Lebowitz classifies the bad music she hears everywhere into five categories so that "music might more clearly see the error of its ways."

A Revision Worksheet for Your Classification Essay   201

Strategy Six: Development by Causal Analysis   201
Essay Topics   204
Sample Student Essay   205

Professional Causal Analysis Essay: "The Great American Cooling Machine"   207

America's addiction to air conditioning may have altered our technology and personal habits more than we might think, according to magazine editor Frank Trippett, whose essay notes both positive and negative effects of the popular twentieth-century invention.

A Revision Worksheet for Your Causal Analysis Essay   211

9 Argumentation   213

Developing Your Essay   213
Common Logical Fallacies   222
Practicing What You've Learned   225
Assignment   226
Essay Topics   227
Sample Student Essay   228

Professional Argument Essays: "Should There Be A Uniform Poll-Closing Time?" Yes/No 232

Announcing the winners of national elections before people in some parts of the country have voted presents problems that could be avoided if we had a uniform poll-closing policy, argues Congressional representative Al Swift. But former political science professor Robert Gillmore maintains that a uniform poll-closing policy is a bad solution that would infringe on our rights.

Pro/Con Advertising: "I'm the NRA" and "A $29 Handgun Shattered My Family's Life" 233
A Revision Worksheet for Your Argumentative Essay 236

10 Description **237**

How to Write Effective Description 237
Essay Topics 242
Sample Student Essay 243
Professional Description Essay: "The Discus Thrower" 245

Surgeon Richard Selzer describes the last hours of a terminally-ill patient—a man who is vigorously following the poet Dylan Thomas's advice: "Do not go gentle into that good night."

A Revision Worksheet for Your Descriptive Essay 248

11 Narration **250**

How to Write Effective Narration 250
Essay Topics 253
Sample Student Essay 254
Professional Narration Essay: "Shame" 256

Civil rights activist Dick Gregory recounts a painful lesson he learned in school, one that had nothing to do with academics.

A Revision Worksheet for Your Narrative Essay 259

12 Writing the Research Paper **261**

Searching for Your Topic 261
Taking Notes 264
Distinguishing Paraphrase from Summary 265

Choosing Your Sources   267
Incorporating Your Source Material   268
Avoiding Plagiarism   271
   Practicing What You've Learned   273
   Assignment   274

Choosing the Documentation Style for
   Your Essay   275
Sample Student Paper Using MLA Style   285

PART THREE   A CONCISE HANDBOOK

13 Major Errors in Grammar   **293**

Errors with Verbs   293
   Practicing What You've Learned   298

Errors with Nouns   298
Errors with Pronouns   299
   Practicing What You've Learned   302

Errors with Adverbs and Adjectives   303
Errors in Modifying Phrases   304
   Practicing What You've Learned   305

Errors in Sentences   306
   Practicing What You've Learned   309

14 A Concise Guide to Punctuation   **311**

The Period   311
The Question Mark   312
The Exclamation Point   312
The Comma   312
   Practicing What You've Learned   317

The Semicolon   318
The Colon   318
   Practicing What You've Learned   319

The Apostrophe   320
Quotation Marks   321
   Practicing What You've Learned   323

Parentheses   323
Brackets   325
The Dash   325
The Hyphen   326

Italics   327
The Ellipsis Mark   328
   Practicing What You've Learned   328

15 A Concise Guide to Mechanics   **330**

Capitalization   330
Abbreviations   331
Numbers   332
   Practicing What You've Learned   333

Spelling   334

PART FOUR   ADDITIONAL READINGS

16 Exposition: Development by Example   **339**

"Clever Animals" by Lewis Thomas   339
"Why Don't We Complain?" by William F.
   Buckley, Jr.   341
"A Dying Art: The Classy Exit Line" by
   Lance Morrow   346

17 Exposition: Process Analysis   **349**

"Oranges" by John McPhee   349
"Attitude" by Garrison Keillor   354
"How to Write an 'F' Paper: Fresh Advice for Students
   of Freshman English" by Joseph C. Pattison   357

18 Exposition: Comparison/Contrast   **359**

"Two Ways of Viewing the River" by
   Samuel Clemens   359
"That Lean and Hungry Look" by Suzanne Britt   361
"The Good Scythe" by Wendell Berry   363

19 Exposition: Definition   **366**

"In Praise of the Humble Comma" by Pico Iyer   366
"The Santa Ana" by Joan Didion   368
"What Are Manners?" by Michael Korda   371

20 Exposition: Division/Classification   **373**

"Friends, Good Friends, and Such Good Friends"
   by Judith Viorst   373

"The Plot Against People" by Russell Baker   377
"College Pressures" by William Zinsser   379

21 Exposition: Casual Analysis   **385**

"Why Do Women Work?" by Gloria Steinem   385
"The Violence Is Fake, the Impact Is Real"
   by Ellen Goodman   389
"The Effects of a Nuclear Explosion" by
   Jonathan Schell   391

22 Argumentation   **394**

"Teenagers Work Too Soon" by Neal Peirce   394
"Animals in Research: The Case for
   Experimentation" by Frederick A. King   396
"I Have a Dream" by Martin Luther King, Jr.   400

23 Description   **404**

"Pictures of My Parents" by Maxine Hong
   Kingston   404
"Ode to Thanksgiving" by Michael J. Arlen   407
"The Man in the Water" by Roger Rosenblatt   410

24 Narration   **413**

"38 Who Saw Murder Didn't Call the Police"
   by Martin Gansburg   413
"A Hanging" by George Orwell   416
"Beauty: When the Other Dancer Is the Self"
   by Alice Walker   420

Index   **427**

PART ONE

The Basics of the Short Essay

The first section of this text is designed to move you through the writing process as you compose a short essay, the kind you are most likely to encounter in composition class and in other college courses. Chapters 1 and 2, on prewriting and the thesis statement, will help you find a topic, purpose, and focus for your essay. Chapter 3, on paragraphs, will show you how to plan, organize, and develop your ideas; Chapter 4 will help you complete your essay. Chapter 5 will offer suggestions for revising your writing, and Chapters 6 and 7 will present additional advice on selecting your words and composing your sentences.

1

Prewriting

GETTING STARTED (OR SOUP-CAN LABELS CAN BE FASCINATING)

For many writers, getting started is the hardest part. You may have noticed that when it is time to begin a writing assignment, you suddenly develop an enormous desire to defrost your refrigerator, water your plants, or sharpen your pencils for the fifth time. If this situation sounds familiar, you may find it reassuring to know that many professionals undergo these same strange compulsions before they begin writing. Jean Kerr, author of *Please Don't Eat the Daisies,* admits that she often finds herself in the kitchen reading soup-can labels—or anything—in order to prolong the moments before taking pen in hand. John C. Calhoun, vice-president under Andrew Jackson, insisted he had to plow his fields before he could write; and Joseph Conrad, author of *Lord Jim* and other novels, is said to have cried on occasion from the sheer dread of sitting down to compose his stories.

In order to spare you as much hand-wringing as possible, this chapter presents some practical suggestions on how to begin writing your short essay. Although all writers must find the methods that work best for them, you may find some of the following ideas helpful.

But no matter how you actually begin putting words on paper, it is absolutely essential to maintain two basic ideas concerning your writing task. Before you write a single sentence, you should always remind yourself that

1. you have some valuable ideas to tell your reader, and
2. more than anything, you want to communicate those ideas to your reader.

These reminders may seem obvious to you, but without a solid commitment to your own opinions as well as to your reader, your prose will be lifeless and boring. If *you* don't care about your subject, you can't very well expect anyone else to. Have confidence that your ideas are worthwhile and that your reader genuinely wants, or needs, to know what you think.

Most importantly, however, you must have a strong desire to tell others exactly what you are thinking. The single most serious mistake inexperienced writers make is writing for themselves only. The very act of composing an essay demonstrates that you have ideas about your subject; the point is to communicate your opinions to others clearly and persuasively. Whether you wish to inform your readers, change their minds, or stir them to action, you cannot accomplish your purpose by writing so that only you understand what you mean. Remember that the burden of communicating your thoughts falls on *you*, not the reader, who is under no obligation at all to struggle through confused, unclear prose, paragraphs that begin and end for no apparent reason, sentences that come one after another with no more logic than lemmings following one another into the sea. Therefore, before you begin writing, commit yourself to becoming more sensitive to the feelings of your reader. Ask yourself as you revise your writing, "Am I making myself clear to others, or am I merely jotting down a conversation with myself?" Other chapters in this book will give you concrete advice on ways to make your writing clearer, but for now, at the jumping-off point in the writing process, the goal is to become *determined to communicate with your readers*.

SELECTING A SUBJECT

Once you have decided that communicating with others is your primary goal, you are ready to select the subject of your essay. Here are some suggestions on how to begin:

Start early. Writing teachers since the earth's crust cooled have been pushing this advice, and for good reason. It's not because teachers are egoists competing for the dubious honor of having the most time-consuming course; it is because few writers, even experienced ones, can do a good job when rushed. You need time to mull over ideas, organize your thoughts, revise and polish your sentences. Rule of thumb: always give yourself twice as much time as you think you'll need to avoid the two-A.M.-why-did-I-come-to-college panic.

Select something in which you currently have a strong interest. If the essay subject is left to you, think of something fun, fascinating, or frightening you've done or seen lately, something perhaps you've already told a friend about. The subject might be the pleasure of a new hobby, the challenge of a recent book or movie, or even the harassment of registration—anything in which you are personally involved. If you aren't enthusiastic enough about your subject to want to spread the word, pick something else. Bored writers write boring essays.

Don't feel you have nothing from which to choose your subject. Your days are full of activities, people, joys, and irritations. Essays do not have to be written on lofty intellectual or poetic subjects—in fact, some of the world's best essays have been written on such subjects as china teacups, roast pig, and chimney sweeps. Think: what have you been talking or thinking about lately? What have you been doing that you're excited about? Or what about your past? Reflect a few moments on some of your most vivid memories—special people, vacations, holidays, childhood hideaways, your first job or first date—all of which are possibilities.

If a search of your immediate or past personal experience doesn't turn up anything inspiring, you might try looking in the campus newspaper for stories that arouse your strong feelings; don't skip the "Letters to the Editor" column. What are the current topics of controversy on your campus? How do you feel about open admissions? Dorm hours and restrictions? Compulsory class attendance? Consider the material you are studying in your classes—information on spies during the Civil War might lead to a thought-provoking essay comparing nineteenth-century espionage to the modern methods of the CIA or FBI. Finally, your local newspaper or national news magazine might suggest essay topics to you on local, national, or international affairs that affect your life.

In other words, when you're stuck for an essay topic, take a closer look at your environment: your own life, past, present, and future; your hometown; your college town; your state; your country; and your world. You'll probably discover more than enough subjects to satisfy the assignments in your writing class.

Narrow a large subject. Once you've selected a general subject to write on, you may find that it is too broad for effective treatment in a short essay; therefore, you may need to narrow it somewhat. Suppose, for instance, you like to work with plants and have decided to make them the subject of your essay. The subject of "plants," however, is far too large and unwieldy for a short essay, perhaps even for a short book. Consequently, you must make your subject less general. "Houseplants" is more specific, but, again, there's too much to say. "Minimum-care houseplants" is better, but you still need to pare this large, complex subject further so that you may treat it in depth in your short essay. After all, there are many houseplants that require little attention. After several more tries, you might arrive at more specific, manageable topics such as "houseplants that thrive in dark areas" or "the easy-care Devil's Ivy."

Then again, let's assume you are interested in sports. A 500–800-word essay on "sports" would obviously be superficial, since the subject covers so much ground. Instead, you might divide the subject into categories such as "sports heroes," "my years on the high school tennis team," "the new role of women in sports," "my love of jogging," and so forth. Perhaps several of your categories would make good short essays, but after looking at your list, you might decide that your real interest at this time is jogging and that it will be the topic of your essay.

FINDING YOUR ESSAY'S PURPOSE AND FOCUS

Even after you've narrowed your large subject to a more manageable topic, you still must find a specific *purpose* for your essay. Why are you writing about this topic? Do your readers need to be informed, persuaded, entertained? What do you want your writing to accomplish?

After you know your purpose, you must also find a clear *focus* or direction for your essay. You cannot, for example, inform your readers about every aspect of jogging. Instead, you must decide on a particular part of the sport and then determine the main point you want to make. If it helps, think of a camera: you see a sweeping landscape you'd like to photograph but you know you can't get it all into one picture, so you pick out a particularly interesting part of the scene. Focus in an essay works in the same way; you zoom in, so to speak, on a particular part of your topic and make that the focus of your paper.

Sometimes part of your problem may be solved by your assignment; your teacher may choose the focus of your essay for you by asking for certain specific information or by prescribing the method of development you should use (compare jogging to aerobics; explain the process of jogging properly; analyze the effects of daily jogging, and so forth). But if the purpose and focus of your essay are decisions you must make, you should always allow your interest and knowledge to guide you. Often a direction or focus for your essay will surface as you narrow your subject, but don't become frustrated if you have to discard several ideas before you hit the one that's right. For instance, you might first consider writing on how to select running shoes and then realize that you know too little about the shoe market, or you might find that there's just too little of importance to say about jogging paths to make an interesting 500-word essay.

Let's suppose for a moment that you have decided on a topic for your essay, but now you're stuck—you simply don't know what you want to say about your topic or what your paper's purpose or focus might be.

At this point you may profit from trying more than one prewriting exercise, designed to help you generate some ideas about your topic. The exercises described next are, in a sense, "pump-primers" that will get your creative juices flowing again. Since all writers compose differently, not all of those exercises will work for you—in fact, some of them may lead you nowhere. Nevertheless, try all of them at least once or twice; you may be surprised to discover that some pump-primer techniques work better with some topics than with others.

1. LISTING

Try jotting down all the ideas that pop into your head about your topic. Free associate; don't hold back anything. Try to brainstorm for at least ten minutes.

A quick list on jogging might look like this:

fun	races
healthy	both sexes
relieves tension	any age group
no expensive equipment	running with friend or spouse
shoes	too much competition

poor shoes won't last

shin splints

fresh air

good for heart

jogging paths vs. streets

hard surfaces

muscle cramps

going too far

going too fast

sense of accomplishment

great expectations

good for lungs

improves circulation

firming

no weight loss

warm-ups before run

cooling-downs after

getting discouraged

hitting the wall

marathons

As you read over the list, look for connections between ideas or one large idea that encompasses several small ones. In this list you might first notice that many of the ideas focus on improving health (heart, lungs, circulation), but you discard that subject because a "jogging improves health" essay is too obvious; it's a topic that's been done too many times to say anything new. A closer look at your list, however, turns up a number of ideas that concern how *not* to jog or reasons why someone might get discouraged and quit a jogging program. You begin to think of friends who might have stuck with jogging as you have if only they'd warmed up properly beforehand, chosen the right places to run, paced themselves more realistically, and so on. You decide, therefore, to write an essay telling first-time joggers how to start a successful program, how to avoid a number of problems from shoes to track surfaces that might otherwise defeat their efforts before they've given the sport a chance.

2. FREEWRITING

Some people simply need to start writing to find a focus. Take out several sheets of blank paper, give yourself at least ten to fifteen minutes, and begin writing whatever comes to mind on your subject. Don't worry about spelling, punctuation, or even complete sentences. Don't change, correct, or delete anything. If you run out of things to say, write "I can't think of anything to say" until you can find a new thought. At the end of the time period you may discover that by continuously writing and writing you will have written yourself into an interesting, focused topic.

Here's a sample of freewriting from a student given ten minutes to write on the general topic of "Television Today."

> Television is the pits. I can't stand to watch all the dumb sitcoms and police shows. So many of my friends are hooked on weekly programs that they can't study or go out or anything on those nights. Soap operas too—yeach. Even my little brother is hooked. After school he's glued to the tube watching these violent outer space cartoon fantasy shows where the characters change into supermen (and superwomen!) to fight evil forces. They always

win, of course. One interesting thing though is that these shows often have a "moral" at the end that one of the characters talks to the kids about. Cartoons when I was growing up sure didn't have that. They were pretty much violence but it was the cat chases the mice and gets banged over the head by the mice or by their friend the bull dog or the coyote runs off the cliff for the hundredth time. Sort of sadistic, really. At least today's cartoons are putting the violence into some kind of good triumphs over evil story. People are always complaining about the effects of violence on T.V. on kids. I wonder if today's kids ———→ out of time

This student quickly found himself thinking about the difference in the kinds of violence in today's cartoons as opposed to the cartoons of his childhood. More thinking (and maybe more freewriting) on this subject might lead him to an interesting argument paper (today's T.V. cartoons aren't harmful to children) or perhaps a research paper (studies on the effects of today's new brand of cartoon violence) or a contrast paper (changes in cartoon violence in the last ten years).

3. LOOPING*

Looping is a variation on freewriting that works amazingly well for many people, including those who are frustrated rather than helped by freewriting.

Let's assume you've been assigned that old standby "My Summer Vacation." Obviously you must find a focus, something specific and important to say. Again, take out several sheets of blank paper and begin to freewrite, as described above. Write for at least ten minutes. At the end of this period read over what you've written and try to identify a central idea that has emerged. This idea may be an important thought that occurred to you in the middle or at the end of your writing, or perhaps it was the idea you liked best for whatever reason. It may be the idea that was pulling you onward when time ran out. In other words, look for the thought that stands out, that seems to indicate the direction of your thinking. Put this thought or idea into one sentence called the "center-of-gravity sentence." You have now completed loop one.

To begin loop two, use your center-of-gravity sentence as a jumping-off point for another ten minutes of freewriting. Stop, read what you've written, and complete loop two by composing another center-of-gravity sentence. Use this second sentence to start loop three. You should write at least three loops and three center-of-gravity sentences. At the end of three loops, you may find that you have focused on a specific topic that might lead to a good essay. If you're not satisfied with your topic at this point, by all means try two or three more loops until your subject is sufficiently narrowed and focused.

Here's an example of one student's looping exercise:

* This technique is suggested by Peter Elbow in *Writing Without Teachers* (New York: Oxford University Press, 1975).

Summer Vacation

Loop One

I think summer vacations are very important aspects of living. They symbolize getting away from daily routines, discovering places and people that are different. When I think of vacations I think mostly of traveling somewhere too far to go, say, for a weekend. It is a chance to get away and relax and not think about most responsibilities. Just have a good time and enjoy yourself. Vacations can also be a time of gathering with family and friends.

Center-of-gravity
sentence

Vacations are meant to be used for traveling.

Loop Two

Vacations are meant for traveling. Last summer my family and I drove to Yellowstone National Park. I didn't want to go at first. I thought looking at geysers would be dumb and boring. I was really obnoxious all the way up there and made lots of smart remarks about getting eaten by bears. Luckily, my parents ignored me and I'm glad they did, because Yellowstone turned out to be wonderful. It's not just Old Faithful—there's lots more to see and learn about, like these colorful boiling pools and boiling patches of mud. I got interested in the thermodynamics of the pools and how new ones are surfacing all the time, and how algae make the pools different colors.

Center-of-gravity
sentence

Once I got interested in Yellowstone's amazing pools, my vacation turned out great.

Loop Three

Once I got interested in the pools, I had a good time, mainly because I felt I was seeing something really unusual. I knew I'd never see anything like this again unless I went to Iceland or New Zealand (highly unlikely!). I felt like I was learning a lot, too. I liked the idea of learning a lot about the inside of the earth without having to go to class and study books. I really hated to leave— Mom and Dad kidded me on the way back about how much I'd griped about going on the trip in the first place. I felt pretty dumb. But I was really glad I'd given the Park a closer look instead of holding on to my view of it as a boring bunch of water fountains. I would have had a terrible time, but now I hope to go back someday. I think the experience made me more open-minded about trying new places.

Center-of-gravity
sentence

My vacation this summer was special because I was willing to put aside my expectations of boredom and learn some new ideas about the strange environment at Yellowstone.

At the end of three loops, this student has moved from the general subject of "summer vacation" to the more focused idea that her willingness to learn about a new place played an important part in the enjoyment of her vacation. Although her last center-of-gravity sentence still contains some vague words ("special," "new ideas," "strange environment"), the thought stated here may eventually lead to an essay that will not only say something about this student's vacation but may also persuade the readers to reconsider their approach to taking trips to new places.

4. CLUSTERING

Another excellent technique is clustering (sometimes called "mapping"). Place your general subject in a circle in the middle of a blank sheet of paper and begin to draw other lines and circles that radiate from the original subject. Cluster those ideas that seem to fall together. At the end of ten minutes see if a topic emerges from any of your groups of ideas.

Ten minutes of clustering on the subject of "A Memorable Holiday" might look like the drawing on page 11.

This student may wish to brainstorm further on the Christmas he spent in the hospital with a case of appendicitis or perhaps the Halloween he first experienced a house of horrors. By using clustering, he has recollected some important details about a number of holidays that may help him focus on an occasion he wants to describe in his paper.

5. CUBING

Still another way to generate ideas is cubing. Imagine a six-sided cube that looks something like this:

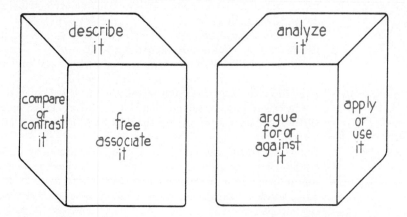

Mentally, roll your subject around the cube and freewrite the answers to the questions that follow. Write whatever comes to mind for ten or fifteen minutes; don't concern yourself with the "correctness" of what you write.

    a. *Describe it:*   What does your subject look like? What size, colors, textures does it have? Any special features worth noting?

    b. *Compare or contrast it:*   What is your subject similar to? What is your subject different from? In what ways?

    c. *Free associate it:*   What does this subject remind you of? What does it call to mind? What memories does it conjure up?

    d. *Analyze it:*   How does it work? How are the parts connected? What is its significance?

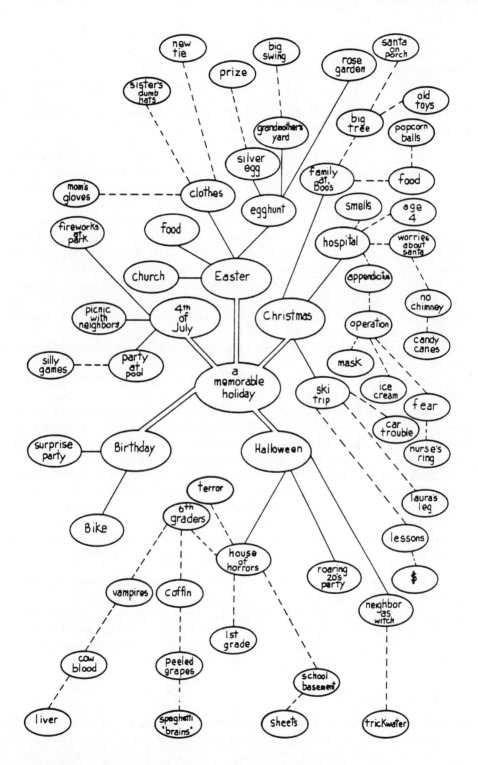

e. *Argue for or against it:* What arguments can you make for or against your subject? What advantages or disadvantages does it have? What changes or improvements should be made?

f. *Apply it:* What are the uses of your subject? What can you do with it?

If you had recently attended a Bruce Springsteen concert, your responses might look like this:

a. *Describe it:* The concert was at Red Rocks, an outdoor concert hall built into a natural setting. So beautiful as the sun went down behind the mountains. A real contrast to the trash we saw at the concert's ending. The backdrop on stage was a big American flag—appropriate for some of Springsteen's songs.

b. *Compare or contrast it:* The Springsteen concert was so different from the Willie Nelson concert a couple of weeks before. Willie's fans look mellow and fairly normal but the Boss's fans are louder and more excited and some are punker types with weird hairdos. More electricity at Springsteen's.

c. *Free associate it:* I guess I associate the concert with the Springsteen tapes I listen to. Often in the car. Makes me think of last summer's drive from Florida to Texas. Long stretches of highway, small towns, lots of fields. Driving too fast to match the beat of the music! Got to watch that.

d. *Analyze it:* What's Springsteen's appeal? He writes about regular people with everyday problems. No, he's sexy! So much energy, vitality, animal magnetism, whatever that is. He seems real, a likable guy, approachable by fans. Often donates money to needy groups.

e. *Argue for or against it:* I was so irritated with the stupid way the tickets were sold! First you had to camp out 48 hours in advance outside the Mall where the record store is located. It was freezing and we all had visions of being run over in the parking lot at night in our sleeping bags. Then the tickets didn't show up on time causing another delay. I missed a lot of work. You couldn't buy reserve seats either so that meant another wait and then crush at the concert. Then the big stampede through the gates—really dangerous. Must be a better way.

f. *Apply it:* How to use a concert? I'm not sure I can go anywhere with this one. Except to say that everyone needs to blow off some steam occasionally and a concert like Springsteen's is a great way to relax and party!

After you've written your responses, see if any one approach to your subject gives you an idea for a topic to write a paper on. The student who wrote about the Springsteen concert, for instance, decided she wanted to do an essay suggesting a better, safer way to distribute and sell the tickets for the rock concert series in her town. Cubing helped her realize that she had something to say about the concert that she might not have thought of otherwise.

6. INTERVIEWING

Another way to find a direction for your paper is through interviewing. Ask a classmate or friend to discuss your subject with you. Let your thoughts range over your subject as your friend asks you questions that arise naturally in the conversation. Or your friend might try asking what are called "reporter's questions" as she or he "interviews" you on your subject:

Who?	When?
What?	Why?
Where?	How?

Listen to what you have to say about your subject. What were you most interested in talking about? What did your friend want to know? Why? By talking about your subject, you may find that you have talked your way into an interesting focus for your paper. If, after the interview, you are still stumped, question your friend: if he or she had to publish an essay based on the information from your interview, what would that essay focus on? Why?

7. SKETCHING

Sometimes when you have found or been assigned a general subject, the words to explain or describe it just won't come. While listing or freewriting or one of the other methods suggested here work well for some people, other writers find these techniques intimidating or unproductive. Some of these writers are visual learners—that is, they respond better to pictorial representations of material than they do to written descriptions or explanations. If, on occasion, you are stuck for words, try drawing or sketching or even cartooning the pictures in your mind.

You may be surprised at the details that you remember once you start sketching. For example, you might have been asked to write about a favorite place or a special person in your life or to compare or contrast two places you have lived or visited. See how many details you can conjure up by drawing the scenes or the people; then look at your details to see if some dominant impression or common theme has emerged. Your Aunt Sophie's insistence on wearing two pounds of costume jewelry might become the focus of a paragraph on her sparkling personality, perhaps, or the many details you recalled about your grandfather's barn might lead you to a paper on the hardships of farm life. For some writers, a picture can be worth a thousand words—especially if that picture helps them begin putting those words on paper.

8. DRAMATIZING THE SUBJECT

Some writers find it helpful to visualize their subject as if it were a drama or play unfolding in their minds. Kenneth Burke, a thoughtful writer himself, suggests that writers might think about human action in dramatists' terms and then see what sorts of new insights arise as the "drama" unfolds. Burke's dramatists' terms might be adapted for our use here and pictured in this way:

Just as you did in the cubing exercise, try mentally rolling your subject around the star above and explore the possibilities that emerge. For example, suppose you want to write about your recent decision to return to college after a long period of working, but you don't know what you want to say about your decision. Start thinking about this decision as a drama and jot down brief answers to such questions as

Action: What happened?
         What were the results?
         What is going to happen?

Actors: Who was involved in the action?
         Who was affected by the action?
         Who caused the action?
         Who was for it and who was opposed?

Motive: What were the reasons behind the action?
         What forces motivated the actors to perform as they did?

Method: How did the action occur?
         By what means did the actors accomplish the action?

Setting: What was the time and place of the action?
         What did the place look like?
         What positive or negative feelings are associated with this time
         or place?

These are only a few of the dozens of questions you might ask yourself about your "drama." (If it helps, think of your "drama" as a murder mystery and answer the questions the police detective might ask: what happened here? to whom? who did it? why? with what? when? where? and so on.)

You may find that you have a great deal to write about the combination of actor and motive but very little to say in response to the questions on setting or method. That's fine—simply use the "dramatists' approach" to help you find a specific topic or idea you want to write about.

> If at any point in this stage of the writing process, you are experiencing *Writer's Block,* you might turn to the suggestions for overcoming this common affliction, which appear on pp. 89–91 in Chapter 5. You might also find it helpful to read the section on *Keeping a Journal,* pp. 22–25 in this chapter, as writing in a relaxed mood on a regular basis may be the best long-term cure for your writing anxiety.

AFTER YOU'VE FOUND YOUR FOCUS

Once you think you've found the focus of your essay, you may be ready to compose a *working thesis statement,* an important part of your essay discussed in great detail in the next chapter. And if you've used one of the prewriting exercises outlined in this chapter, by all means hang onto it. The details and observations you generated as you focused your topic may be useful to you as you begin to organize and develop your body paragraphs.

PRACTICING WHAT YOU'VE LEARNED

A. Some of the subjects listed below are too broad for a 500–800-word essay. Identify those topics that might be treated in short papers and those that still need to be narrowed.

1. The role of the modern university
2. My first (and last) experience with cross-country skiing
3. The characters of William Shakespeare
4. Nuclear accidents
5. Collecting baseball cards
6. Gun-control laws
7. Down with throwaway bottles
8. Computers

9. The best teacher I've ever had

10. Selecting the right bicycle

B. Select two of the large subjects below and, through looping or listing details or another prewriting technique, find focused topics that would be appropriate for essays of 500–800 words.

1. music
2. cars
3. education
4. jobs
5. television commercials
6. politics
7. drugs
8. childhood
9. pollution
10. athletics

DISCOVERING YOUR AUDIENCE

Once you have a focused topic and perhaps some ideas about developing your essay, you need to stop a moment and consider your *audience*. Before you can begin to decide what information needs to go in your essay and what should be omitted, you must know who will be reading your paper and why. Knowing your audience will also help you determine what *voice* you should use to achieve the proper tone in your essay.

Suppose, for example, you are attending a college organized on the quarter system, and you decide to write an essay arguing for a switch to the semester system. If your audience is composed of classmates, your essay will probably focus on the advantages to the student body, such as better opportunities for in-depth study in one's major, the ease of making better grades, and the benefits of longer mid-winter and summer vacations. On the other hand, if you address the Board of Regents, you might emphasize the power of the semester system to attract more students, cut registration costs, and use professors more efficiently. If your audience is composed of townspeople who know little about either system, you will have to devote more time to explaining the logistics of each one and then discuss the semester plan's advantages to the local merchants, realtors, restauranteurs, etc. *In other words, such factors as the age, education, profession, and interests of your audience can make a difference in determining which points of your argument to stress or omit, which ideas need additional explanation, and what kind of language to adopt.*

HOW TO IDENTIFY YOUR READERS

To help you analyze your audience before you begin writing your working thesis statement and rough drafts, here are some steps you may wish to follow:

1. First, check to see if your writing assignment specifies a particular audience (editors of a journal in your field or the Better Business Bureau of your town, for example) or a general audience of your peers (your classmates or readers of the local newspaper, for instance). Even if your assignment does not mention an intended audience, try to imagine one anyway. Imagining specific readers will help you stick to your goal of communicating with others. Forgetting that they have an audience of real people often causes writers to address themselves to their typing paper, a mistake that usually results in dull or unclear prose.

2. If a specific audience is designated, ask yourself some questions about their motivation or *reasons for reading* your essay.

- What do these readers want to learn?
- What do they hope to gain?
- Do they need your information to make a decision? Formulate a new plan? Design a new project?
- What action do you want them to take?

The answers to such questions will help you find both your essay's purpose and content. If, for example, you're trying to persuade an employer to hire you for a particular job, you certainly would write your application in a way that stresses the skills and training the company is searching for. You may have a fine hobby or wonderful family, but if your prospective employer-reader doesn't need to hear about that particular part of your life, toss it out of this piece of writing.

3. Next, try to discover what *knowledge* your audience has of your subject.

- What, if anything, can you assume that your readers already know about your topic?
- What background information might they need to know to clearly understand a current situation?
- What facts, explanations, examples will best present your ideas? How detailed should you be?
- What terms need to be defined? Equipment explained?

Questions like these should guide you as you collect and discard information for your paper. An essay written to your colleagues in electrical engineering, for instance, need not explain commonly used technical instruments; to do so might even insult your readers. But the same report read by your composition classmates would probably need more detailed explanation in order for you to make yourself understood. Always put yourself in your reader's place and ask: What else do I need to know to understand this point completely?

4. Once you have decided what information is necessary for your audience, dig a little deeper into your readers' identities. Pose some questions about their *attitudes* and emotional states.

- Are your readers already biased for or against your ideas in some way?
- Do they have positive or negative associations with your subject?
- Are they fearful or anxious, reluctant or bored?
- Do they have radically different expectations or interests?

It helps enormously to know the emotional attitudes of your readers toward your subject. Let's suppose you were arguing for the admission of a child with AIDS into a local school system, and your audience was the parent-teacher organization. Some of your readers might be frightened or even hostile; knowing this, you would wisely begin your argument with a disarming array of information showing that no cases of AIDS have developed from the casual contact of schoolchildren. In other words, the more you know about your audience's attitudes before you begin writing, the more convincing your prose, because you will make the best choices about both content and organization.

5. Last, think of any *special qualities* that might set your audience apart from any other.

- Are they older or younger than your peers?
- Do they share similar educational experiences or training?
- Are they from a particular part of the world or country that might affect their perspective? Urban or rural?
- Are they in positions of authority?

Knowing special facts about your audience makes a difference, often in your choice of words and tone. You wouldn't, after all, use the same level of vocabulary addressing a group of fifth-graders as you would writing to the children's teacher or principal. Similarly, your tone and word choice probably wouldn't be as formal in a letter to a friend as in a letter to the telephone company protesting your most recent bill.

Without question, analyzing your specific audience is an important step to take before you begin to shape your rough drafts. And before you move on to writing a working thesis, here are a few tips to keep in mind about *all* audiences, no matter who your readers are or what their reasons for reading your writing.

1. Readers don't like to be bored. Grab your readers' attention and fight to keep it. Remember the last dull movie you squirmed—or slept— through? How much you resented wasting not only your money but your valuable time as well? How you turned it off mentally and drifted away to someplace more exciting? As you write and revise your drafts, keep imagining readers who are as intelligent—and busy—as you are. Put yourself in their place: would you find this piece of writing stimulating enough to keep reading?

2. Readers hate confusion and disorder. Can you recall a time when you tried to find your way to a party, only to discover that a friend's directions were so muddled you wound up hours later out of gas cursing in a cornfield? Or the afternoon you spent trying to follow a friend's notes for setting up a chemistry experiment, with explanations that twisted and turned like a wandering gypsy? Try to relive such moments of intense frustration as you struggle to make *your* writing clear and direct.

3. Readers want to think and learn (whether they realize it or not). Every time you write, you strike a bargain of sorts with your readers: in return for their time and attention, you promise to inform and interest them, to tell them something new or show them something familiar in a different light. You may enlighten them or amuse them or even try to frighten them—but they must feel, in the end, that they've gotten a fair trade. As you plan, write, and revise, ask yourself, "What are my readers learning?" If the honest answer is "nothing important," then you may be writing only for yourself. (If you yourself are bored re-reading your drafts, you're probably not writing for anybody at all.)

4. Readers want to see what you see, feel what you feel. Writing that is vague keeps your readers from fully sharing the information or experience you are trying to communicate. Clear, precise language—full of concrete details and specific examples—lets your readers know that you understand your subject and that you want them to understand it, too. Even a potentially dull topic such as tuning a car can become engaging to a reader if the right details are provided in the right places: your terror as blue sparks leap under your nose when the wrong wire is touched, the depressing sight of the screwdriver squirming from your greasy fingers and disappearing into the oil pan, the sudden shooting pain when the wrench slips and turns your knuckles to raw hamburger. Get your readers involved and interested—and they'll listen to what you have to say. (Details also persuade your reader that you're an authority on your subject; after all, no reader likes to waste time listening to someone whose tentative, vague prose style announces "I only sort-of know what I'm talking about here.")

5. Readers are turned off by writers with pretentious, phony voices. Too often inexperienced writers feel they must sound especially scholarly, scientific, or sophisticated for their essays to be convincing. In fact, the contrary is true. When you assume a voice that is not yours, when you pretend to be someone you're not, you don't sound believable at all—you sound phony. Your readers want to hear what *you* have to say, and the best way to communicate with them is in a natural voice. You may also believe that to write a good essay it is necessary to use a host of unfamiliar, unpronounceable, polysyllabic words gleaned from the pages of your thesaurus. Again, the opposite is true. Our best writers agree with Mark Twain, who once said, "Never use a twenty-five-cent word when a ten-cent word will do." In other words, avoid pretension in your writing just as you do in everyday conversation. Select simple, direct words you know and use frequently; keep your voice natural, sincere, and reasonable. (For additional help on choosing the appropriate words and the level of your diction, see Chapter 7.)

Don't ever forget your readers!
Thinking about them both before and as you write will help you choose your ideas, organize your information effectively, and select the best words.

PRACTICING WHAT YOU'VE LEARNED

The article that follows appeared in newspapers across the country some time ago. Read about the new diet called "Breatharianism" and then write the assignments that follow the article.

THE ULTIMATE IN DIET CULTS: DON'T EAT ANYTHING AT ALL

CORTE MADERA, Calif.—Among those seeking enlightenment through diet cults, Wiley Brooks seemed to have the ultimate answer—not eating at all. He called himself a "Breatharian" and claimed to live on air, supplemented only by occasional fluids taken to counteract the toxins of urban environments.

"Food is more addictive than heroin," the tall, gaunt black man told hundreds of people who paid $500 each to attend five-day "intensives," at which he would stand before them in a camel velour sweatsuit and talk for hours without moving, his fingers meditatively touching at their tips.

Brooks, 46, became a celebrity on the New Age touring circuit. ABC-TV featured him in October, 1980, as a weight lifter; he allegedly hoisted 1,100 pounds, about 10 times his own weight. He has also been interviewed on radio and in newspapers.

Those who went to his sessions during the past six months on the West Coast and in Hawaii were not just food faddists, but also physicians and other professionals who—though not necessarily ready to believe—thought this man could be onto something important. Some were convinced enough by what they saw to begin limiting their own diets, taking the first steps toward Breatharianism.

In his intensives, Brooks did not recommend that people stop eating altogether. Rather, he suggested they "clean their blood" by starting with the "yellow diet"—24 food items including grapefruit, papaya, corn products, eggs, chicken, fish, goat's milk, millet, salsa piquante (Mexican hot sauce) and certain flavors of the Haagen Dazs brand ice cream, including "rum raisin." These foods, he said, have a less toxic effect because, among other things, "their vibrational quality is yellow."

Last week, however, aspirants toward Breatharianism were shocked by reports that Brooks had been eating—and what's more, eating things that to health food purists are the worst kind of junk.

Word spread that during an intensive in Vancouver, Brooks was seen emerging from a 7-Eleven store with a bag of groceries. The next morning there were allegedly room service trays outside his hotel room, while inside, the trash basket held empty containers of chicken pot pie, chili and bisquits.

Kendra Wagner, regional Breatharian coordinator, said she herself had seen Brooks drinking a Coke. "When I asked him about it he said, 'That's how dirty the air is here,' she explained. "We (the coordinators) sat down with Wiley after the training and said, 'We want you to tell us the truth.' He denied everything. We felt tricked and deceived."

As the rumors grew, some Breatharians confronted their leader at a lecture in San Francisco. Brooks denied the story and said that the true message of Breatharianism did not depend on whether he ate or not, anyway.

The message in his promotional material reads that "modern man is the degenerate descendant of the Breatharian," and that "living on air alone leads to perfect health and perfect happiness." Though followers had the impression Brooks has not eaten for 18 years, his leaflets merely declare that "he does not eat, and seldom drinks any fluid. He sleeps less than seven hours a week and is healthier, more energetic and happier than he ever dreamed possible."

In a telephone interview, Brooks acknowledged that this assertion is not quite correct. "I'm sure I've taken some fruit, like an apple or an orange, but it's better in public to keep it simple." He again staunchly denied the 7-Eleven story.

Among those who have been on the yellow diet for months is Jime Collison, 24, who earlier tried "fruitarianism," fasting and other special regimens, and moved from Texas to the San Francisco Bay area just to be around the Breatharian movement. "Now I'm a basket case," he said. "My world revolved around Wiley's philosophy." He had thought Wiley "made the jump to where all of us health food fanatics were going," Collison said.

Other Brooks disciples, though disappointed, feel they nevertheless benefitted from their experience. Said a physician who has been on the yellow diet for four months: "I feel very good. I still don't know what the truth is, but I do know that Wiley is a good salesman. So I'll be patient, keep an open mind and continue to observe."

"Breatharianism is the understanding of what the body really needs, not whether Wiley eats or doesn't," said James Wahler, 35, who teaches a self-development technique called "rebirthing," in Marin County. "I'm realizing that the less I eat the better I feel." He also suggested that Brooks may have lied for people's own good, to get them to listen.

"Everyone has benefitted from what I'm saying," Brooks said. "There will be a food shortage and a lot of unhappy people when they realize that I was trying to save their lives."

Each of the assignments listed below is directed to a different audience, none of whom know much about Breatharianism. What information does each audience need to know? What kinds of details will be the most persuasive? What sort of organization will work best for each purpose and audience?

1. Write a brief radio advertisement for the five-day intensives. What appeals will persuade people to pay $500 each to attend a seminar to learn to eat air?

2. Assume you are a regional Breatharian coordinator. Write a letter to your City Council petitioning for a parade permit that will allow members of your organization to parade down your main street in support of this diet and its lifestyle. What do Council members need to know and understand before they vote for such a permit?

3. You are a former Breatharian who is now unhappy with the diet and its unfulfilled promises. Write a report for the Vice Squad calling for an investigation into the organization. Convince the investigators that the organization is defrauding local citizens and should be stopped.

After writing these assignments, you might exchange them with those written by some of your classmates. Which ads, petitions, and reports were the most persuasive and why?

KEEPING A JOURNAL (TALKING TO YOURSELF *DOES* HELP)

Many professional writers carry small notebooks with them so they can jot down ideas and impressions for future use. Other people have kept daily logs or diaries for years to record their thoughts for their own enjoyment. In your composition class, you may find it useful to keep a journal that will help you with your writing process, especially in the early stages of prewriting. Journals can also help you to prepare for class discussions and to remember important course material.

You may have kept a journal in another class. There, it may have been called a daybook or learning log or some other name. While the journal has a variety of uses, it frequently is assigned to encourage you to record your responses to the material read or discussed in class as well as your own thoughts and questions. Most often the journal is kept in a notebook of some kind (spiral is fine, although you may find a prong or ring notebook more convenient because it will allow you to add or remove pages where and when you wish). Even if a journal is not an assigned part of your composition class, it is still a useful notebook for you to keep.

Writers who have found journal writing effective advise trying to write a minimum of three entries a week, with each entry at least a half-page. To keep your entries organized, you might start each new entry on a new page and date each entry you write. You might also leave the backs of your pages blank so that you could return and respond to an entry at a later date if you wished.

USES OF THE JOURNAL

Here are some suggested uses for your journal as you begin and move through the writing process. You may want to experiment with a number of these suggestions to see which are the most productive for you.

1. Use the journal, especially in the first weeks of class, to confront your fears of writing, to conquer the blank page. Write anything you want to—thoughts, observations, notes to yourself, letters home, anything at all. Best your enemy by writing down that witty retort you thought of later and wished you said. Write about your ideal job, vacation, car, or home. Write a self-portrait or make a list of all the subjects that you are an "authority" on. The more you write, the easier writing becomes—or at least, the easier it is to begin writing because, like a sword swallower, you know you have accomplished the act before and lived to tell about it.

2. Improve your powers of observation. Record interesting snippets of conversations you overhear or catalog noises you hear in a given ten-minute period in a crowded place such as your student center, a bookstore, or a mall. Eat something with multiple layers (a piece of fruit such as an orange) and list all the tastes, textures, and smells you discover. Look around your room and write down a list of everything that is yellow. By becoming sensitive to the sights, sounds, smells, and textures around you, you may find that your powers of description and explanation will expand, enabling you to help your reader "see" what you're talking about in your next essay.

3. Save your own brilliant ideas. Jot down those bright ideas that might turn into great essays. Or save those thoughts you have now for the essay you know is coming later in the semester so you won't forget them. Expand or elaborate on any ideas you have; you might be able to convert your early thoughts into a paragraph when it's time to start drafting.

4. Save other people's brilliant ideas. Record interesting quotations, facts, and figures from other writers and thinkers. You may find some of this

information useful in one of your later essays. It's also helpful to look at the ways other writers made their words emphatic, moving, arresting, so you can try some of their techniques in your own prose. (Important: don't forget to note the source of any material you record, so if you do quote any of it in a paper later, you will be able to document properly.)

5. Be creative. Write a poem or song or story or joke. Parody the style of someone you've heard or read. Become an inanimate object and complain to the humans around you (for example, what would a soft drink machine like to say to those folks constantly beating on its stomach?). Become a little green creature from Mars and convince a human to accompany you back to your planet as a specimen of Earthlings (or be the invited guest and explain to the creature why you are definitely not the person to go). The possibilities are endless, so go wild.

6. Prepare for class. If you've been given a reading assignment (an essay or article or pages from a text, for instance), try a split-page entry. Draw a line down the middle of a page in your journal and on the left side of the page write a summary of what you've read or perhaps list the main points. Then on the right side of the same page, write your responses to the material. Your responses might be your personal reaction to the content (what struck you hardest? why?), or it might be your agreement or disagreement with a particular point or two. Or the material might call up some long-forgotten idea or memory. By thinking about your class material both analytically and personally, you almost certainly will remember it for class discussion. You might also find that a good idea for an essay will arise as you think about the reading assignments in different ways.

7. Record responses to class discussions. A journal is a good place to jot down your reactions to what your teacher and your peers are saying in class. You can ask yourself questions ("What did Megan mean when she said . . . ") or note any confusion ("I got mixed-up when . . . ") or record your own reactions ("I disagree with Jason when he argued that . . . "). Again, some of your reactions might become the basis of a good essay.

8. Focus on a problem. You can restate the problem or explore the problem or solve the problem. Writing about a problem often encourages the mind to range over the information in ways that allow discoveries to happen. Sometimes, too, we don't know exactly what the problem is or how we feel about it until we write about it (you can see the truth of this statement almost every week if you're a reader of advice columns such as "Dear Abby"—invariably someone will write a letter asking for help and end by saying "Thanks for letting me write; I know now what I should do").

9. Practice audience awareness. Write letters to different companies, praising or panning their product; then write advertising copy for each product. Become the third critic on a popular movie-review program and show the other two

commentators why your review of your favorite movie is superior to theirs. Thinking about a specific audience when you write will help you plan the content, organization, and tone of each writing assignment.

10. Describe your own writing process. It's helpful sometimes to record how you go about writing your essays. How do you get started? How much time do you spend getting started? On drafting? How do you revise? Do you write multiple drafts? Do you cut and paste? These and many other questions may give you a clue to the problems you may experience as you write your next essay. If, for example, you see that you're having trouble again and again with conclusions, you can turn to Chapter 4 for some extra help. Sometimes it's hard to see that there's a pattern in our writing process until we've described it several times.

11. Write a progress report. List all the skills you've mastered as the course progresses. You'll be surprised at how much you have learned. Read the list over when you're feeling down, and take pride in your growth.

12. Become sensitive to language. Keep a record of jokes and puns that play on words. Record people's weird-but-funny uses of language (overheard at the dorm cafeteria: "She was so skinny she was emancipated" and "I'm tired of being the escape goat"). Rewrite some of today's bureaucratic jargon or retread a cliché. Come up with new images of your own. Playing with language in fun or even silly ways may make writing tasks seem less threatening.

13. Write your own textbook. Make notes on material that is important for you to remember. For instance, make your own grammar or punctuation handbook with only those rules you find yourself referring to often. Or keep a list of spelling rules that govern the words you misspell frequently. Writing out the rules in your own words and having a convenient place to refer to them may help you teach yourself quicker than studying any textbook (including this one!).

These suggestions are some of the many uses you may find for your journal once you start writing in one on a regular basis. Obviously, not all of the suggestions here will be appropriate for you, but some might be, so you might consider using a set of divider tabs to separate the different functions of your journal (one section for class responses, one section for your own thoughts, one for your own handbook, and so on).

You may find, as some students have, that the journal is especially useful to you during the first weeks of your writing course when putting pen to paper is often hardest. Many students, however, continue to use the journal throughout the entire course, and others adapt their journals to record their thoughts and responses to their other college courses and experiences. Whether you continue using a journal beyond this course is up to you, but consider trying the journal for at least six weeks. You may find that it will improve your writing skills more than anything else you have tried before.

CHAPTER 1 SUMMARY

Here is a brief summary of what you should know about the prewriting stage of your writing process:

1. Before you begin writing anything, remember that you have valuable ideas to tell your readers.

2. Moreover, it's not enough that these valuable ideas are clear to you, the writer. Your single most important goal is to clearly communicate those ideas to your readers, who cannot see what's in your mind until you tell them.

3. Whenever possible, select a subject to write on that is of great interest to you and always give yourself more time than you think you'll need to work on your essay.

4. Try a variety of prewriting techniques to help you find your essay's purpose and a narrowed, specific focus.

5. Review your audience's knowledge of and attitudes toward your topic before you begin your first draft; ask yourself questions such as "Who needs to know about this topic, and why?"

6. Consider keeping a journal to help you explore good ideas and possible topics for writing in your composition class.

2

The Thesis Statement

AFTER SELECTING YOUR SUBJECT

The famous American author Thomas Wolfe had a simple formula for beginning his writing: "Just put a sheet of paper in the typewriter and start bleeding." For a few writers, the "bleeding" method works fine. Some of us, however, need a more structured approach. Without a clear notion of our essay's main purpose or a definite plan of how to begin and where to go, we may often find ourselves drifting aimlessly through ideas, starting with "x," trudging through "y," and concluding with several layers of wadded paper balls strewn about our feet. To avoid the problem of roaming from one unrelated idea to another, you first need to formulate a *working thesis statement*.

WHAT DOES A THESIS DO?

The thesis statement declares the main point or controlling idea of your entire essay. Frequently located near the beginning of a short essay, the thesis briefly answers the questions "What is my opinion on subject 'x'?" and "What am I going to argue (or illustrate or define or explain) in this essay?"

The essay on jogging discussed in Chapter 1, for instance, might contain the working thesis statement "Before beginning a successful jogging program, novice runners should learn a series of warm-up and cool-down exercises." The freewriting exercise on cartoons might lead to a working thesis such as "The television cartoons of today are less harmful to small children than the violent shows of ten years ago." Such a thesis states an opinion about the essay topic (less harmful to children) and suggests what the essay will do (show why modern cartoons are better than the earlier ones).

A working thesis statement, prepared if possible before you begin your first rough draft, is perhaps your single most useful organizational tool. Once you know your essay's main point, you can arrange the rest of your paper to explain and back up your thesis statement. In other words, *everything in your essay should support your thesis.* Consequently, if you write your thesis statement at the top of your first draft and refer to it often, your chances of drifting away from your purpose should be reduced.

WHAT IS A "WORKING" THESIS?

It's important for you to notice at this point that there may be a difference between the working thesis that appears in your rough drafts and your final thesis. As you begin your first rough draft, you may have one main idea in mind that surfaced from your prewriting activities. But as you write, you discover that what you really want to write about is slightly different. That's fine—*writing is an act of discovery*—and frequently we don't know exactly what we think or what to say until we write it. Don't hesitate to change or modify your working thesis if your rough draft has taken a new, better direction. A working thesis is there to help you focus and organize your essay, but it's not carved in stone. Just remember that if you do change your paper's topic or purpose, revise your thesis so that it is consistent with the body of your essay and so that it will guide your readers rather than confuse them.

WHAT IS A GOOD THESIS?

To help you prepare a useful thesis statement, here are some guidelines.

A good thesis states the writer's clearly defined opinion on some subject. You must tell your reader what you think. Don't dodge the issue; present your opinion specifically and precisely. For example, if you were asked to write a thesis statement expressing your position on the national law that designates twenty-one the legal minimum age to purchase or consume alcohol, the first three theses listed below would not be acceptable:

Poor   Many people have different opinions on whether people under twenty-one should be able to drink alcohol, and I agree with some of them. [The writer's opinion on the issue is not clear to the reader.]

Poor   The question of whether we need a national law governing the minimum age to drink alcohol is a controversial issue in many states. [This statement might introduce the thesis, but the writer has still avoided stating a clear opinion on the issue.]

Poor   I want to give my opinion on the national law that sets twenty-one as the legal age to drink alcohol and the reasons I feel this way. [What is the writer's opinion? The reader still doesn't know.]

Better   To reduce the number of highway fatalities, our country needs to en-
force the national law that designates twenty-one as the legal minimum age to purchase and consume alcohol. [The writer clearly states
an opinion that will be supported in the essay.]

Better   The legal minimum age for purchasing alcohol should be eighteen
rather than twenty-one. [Again, the writer has asserted a clear position on the issue that will be argued in the essay.]

A good thesis asserts one main idea. Many essays drift into confusion
because the writer is trying to explain or argue two different, large issues in one
essay. You can't effectively ride two horses at once; pick one main idea and
explain or argue it in convincing detail.

Poor   The proposed no-smoking ordinance in our town will violate a number
of our citizens' civil rights, and no one has proved secondary smoke is
dangerous anyway. [This thesis contains two main assertions—the ordinance's violation of rights and secondary smoke's lack of danger—
that require two different kinds of supporting evidence.]

Better   The proposed no-smoking ordinance in our town will violate our civil
rights. [This essay will show the various ways the ordinance will infringe on personal liberties.]

Better   The most recent U.S. Health Department studies claiming that secondary smoke is dangerous to nonsmokers are based on faulty research.
[This essay will also focus on one issue: the validity of the studies on
secondary smoke danger.]

Poor   High school athletes shouldn't have to maintain a certain grade-point
average to participate in school sports, and the value of sports is often
worth the lower academic average. [Again, this essay moves in two
different directions.]

Better   High school athletes shouldn't have to maintain a certain grade-point
average to participate in school sports. [This essay will focus on one
issue: reasons why a particular average shouldn't be required.]

Better   For some students, participation in sports is often more valuable than
achieving a high grade-point average. [This essay will focus on why
the benefits of sports may sometime outweigh those of academics.]

Incidentally, at this point you may recall from your high school days a
rule about always expressing your thesis in one sentence. Writing teachers often
insist on this rule to help you avoid the double-assertion problem discussed
above. While not all essays have one-sentence theses, many do, and it's a good
habit to strive for at this early stage of your writing.

A good thesis has something worthwhile to say. Although it's true that almost any subject can be made interesting with the right treatment, some subjects are more predictable and therefore more boring than others. Before you write your thesis, think hard about your subject: does your position lend itself to trite, shallow, or overly obvious ideas? For example, most readers would find the theses below tiresome unless the writers had some original method of developing their essays:

Poor Dogs have always been man's best friends. [This essay might be full of ho-hum clichés about dogs' faithfulness to their masters.]

Poor Friendship is a wonderful thing. [Again, watch out for tired truisms that restate the obvious.]

Poor Food in my dorm is horrible. [While this essay might be enlivened by some vividly repulsive imagery, the subject itself is ancient.]

Frequently in composition classes you will be asked to write about yourself; after all, you are the world's authority on that subject, and you have many significant ideas and interests to talk about whose subject matter will naturally intrigue your readers. However, some topics that you may consider writing about won't necessarily appeal to other readers because the material is simply too personal or restricted to be of general interest. In those cases, it often helps to universalize the essay's thesis so your readers can also identify with, or learn something about, the general subject, while learning something about you at the same time:

Poor The four children in my family have completely different personalities. [This statement may be true, but would anyone but the children's parents really be fascinated with this essay topic?]

Better Birth order can influence children's personalities in startling ways. [The writer is wiser to offer this controversial statement, which is of more interest to readers than the one above because most readers have brothers and sisters of their own; the writer can then illustrate her claims with examples from her own family, and from other families, if she wishes.]

In other words, try to select a subject that will interest, amuse, challenge, persuade, or enlighten your readers; if your subject itself is commonplace, try to find a unique approach or an unusual, perhaps even controversial, point of view. If your subject is intensely personal, ask yourself if the topic alone is enough to interest readers; if not, think about universalizing the thesis to include your audience. Remember that a good thesis should encourage readers to read on with enthusiasm rather than invite groans of "not this again" or shrugs of "so what."

A good thesis is limited to fit the assignment. Your thesis should show that you've narrowed your subject matter to an appropriate size for your essay. Don't allow your thesis to promise more of a discussion than you can adequately deliver in a short essay. You want an in-depth treatment of your subject, not a superficial one. Certainly you may take on important issues in your essays; don't feel you must limit your topics to local or personal subjects. But one simply cannot re-fight Vietnam or effectively defend U.S. foreign policy in Central America in five to eight paragraphs. Focus your essay on an important part of a broader subject that interests you. (For a review of ways to narrow and focus your subject, see pp. 4–15.)

Poor Nuclear power should be banned as an energy source in this country. [Can the writer give the broad subject of "nuclear power" a fair treatment in three to five pages?]

Better Because of its poor safety record over the past two years, the Collin County nuclear power plant should be closed. [This writer could probably argue this focused thesis in a short essay.]

Poor The parking permit system at this university should be completely revised. [An essay calling for the revision of the parking permit system would probably involve discussion of permits for various kinds of students, faculty, administrators, staff, visitors, delivery personnel, disabled persons, and so forth. Therefore, the thesis is probably too broad for a short essay.]

Better Because of the complicated application process, the parking permit system at this university penalizes disabled students. [This thesis is focused on a particular problem and could be argued in a short paper.]

Poor Black artists have contributed much to American culture. ["Black artists," "culture," and "much" cover more ground than can be dealt with in one short essay.]

Better Scott Joplin was a major influence in the development of the uniquely American music called ragtime. [This thesis is more specifically defined.]

A good thesis is clearly stated in specific terms. More than anything, a vague thesis reflects lack of clarity in the writer's mind and almost inevitably leads to an essay that talks around the subject but never makes a coherent point. Try to avoid words whose meanings are imprecise or those that depend largely upon personal interpretation, such as "interesting," "good," and "bad."

Poor The Women's Movement has been good for our country. [How is it good? For whom?]

Better   The Women's Movement has worked to ensure the benefits of equal pay for equal work for both male and female Americans. [This tells who will benefit and how—clearly defining the thesis.]

Poor   Registration is a big hassle. [No clear idea is communicated here. How much trouble is a "hassle"?]

Better   Registration's alphabetical fee-paying system is inefficient. [The issue is specified.]

Poor   Living in an apartment for the first time can teach you many things about taking care of yourself. ["Things" and "taking care of yourself" are both too vague—what specific ideas does the writer want to discuss? And who is the "you" the writer had in mind?]

Better   By living in an apartment, freshmen can learn valuable lessons in financial planning and time management. [The thesis is now clearly defined and directed.]

A good thesis is clearly located, often in the first or second paragraph. Many students are hesitant to spell out a thesis at the beginning of an essay. To quote one student, "I feel as if I'm giving everything away." Although you may feel uncomfortable "giving away" the main point so soon, the alternative of waiting until the last page to present your thesis can seriously weaken your essay.

Without an assertion of what you are trying to prove, your reader does not know how to assess the supporting detail your essay presents. For example, if your roommate comes home one afternoon and points out that the roof on your apartment leaks, the rent is too high, and the closet space is too small, you may agree but you may also be confused. Does your roommate want you to call the owner, or is this merely a gripe session? How should you respond? On the other hand, if your roommate first announces that he or she wants to move to a new place, you can put the discussion of the roof, rent, and closets into its proper context and react accordingly. Similarly, you write an essay to have a specific effect on your readers. You won't have a chance of producing this effect unless the readers understand what you are trying to do.

Granted, there are some essays whose position is unmistakably obvious from the outset that can get by with a strongly *implied thesis,* and it's true that some essays, often those written by professional writers, are organized to build dramatically to a climax. But if you are an inexperienced writer, the best choice at this point still may be to give a clear statement of your main idea. It is, after all, your responsibility to make your purpose clear, with as little expense of time and energy on the readers' part as possible. Readers should not be forced to puzzle out your essay's main point—it's your job to tell them.

Remember: an essay is not a detective story, so don't keep your readers in suspense until the last minute. Until you feel comfortable with more sophisticated patterns of organization, plan to put your clearly worded thesis statement near the beginning of your essay.

Important:

Many times writers "discover" their real thesis near the end of their first draft. That's fine—consider that draft a prewriting or focusing exercise and begin another draft using the newly discovered thesis as a starting point.

AVOIDING COMMON ERRORS IN THESIS STATEMENTS

Here are five mistakes to avoid when forming your thesis statements:

1. Don't make your thesis merely an announcement of your subject matter or a description of your intentions. State an attitude toward the subject.

Poor   The subject of this theme is my experience with a pet boa constrictor. [This is an announcement of the subject, not a thesis.]

Poor   I'm going to discuss boa constrictors as pets. [This represents a statement of intention, but not a thesis.]

Better   Boa constrictors do not make healthy indoor pets. [The writer states an opinion that will be explained and defended in the essay.]

Better   My pet boa constrictor, Sir Pent, was a much better bodyguard than my dog, Fang. [The writer states an opinion that will be explained and illustrated in the essay.]

2. Don't clutter your thesis with expressions such as "in my opinion," "I believe," and "in this essay I'll argue that . . ." These unnecessary phrases weaken your thesis statement because they often make you sound timid or uncertain. This is your essay; therefore, the opinions expressed are obviously yours. Be forceful; speak directly, with conviction.

Poor   My opinion is that the federal government should devote more money to solar energy research.

Poor   My thesis states that the federal government should devote more money to solar energy research.

Better   The federal government should devote more money to solar energy research.

Poor   In this essay I will give you lots of reasons why horse racing should not be legalized in Texas.

Better   Horse racing should not be legalized in Texas.

3. Don't be unreasonable. Making irrational or oversimplified claims will not persuade your reader that you have a thorough understanding of the issue. Don't insult any reader; avoid irresponsible charges, name calling, and profanity.

Poor Radical religious fanatics across the nation are trying to impose their right-wing views by censoring high school library books. [Words such as "radical," "fanatics," "right-wing," and "censoring" will antagonize many readers immediately.]

Better Only local school board members—not religious leaders or parents—should decide which books high school libraries should order.

Poor Too many corrupt books in our high school libraries selected by liberal or atheistic educators are undermining the morals of our youth. [Again, some readers will be offended.]

Better In order to ensure that high school libraries contain books that reflect community standards, parents should have a voice in selecting new titles.

4. Don't merely state a fact. A thesis is an assertion of opinion that leads to discussion. Don't select an idea that is self-evident or dead-ended.

Poor Child abuse is a terrible problem in our country. [Yes, of course; who wouldn't agree that child abuse is terrible?]

Better Child-abuse laws in this state are too lenient for repeat offenders. [This thesis will lead to a discussion in which supporting arguments and evidence will be presented.]

Poor Advertisers often use sex in their ads to sell products. [True. But how could this essay be turned into something more than a description of one ad after another?]

Better A number of liquor advertisers, well known for using pictures of sexy models to sell their products, are now using special graphics to send subliminal sexual messages to their readers. [This claim is controversial and will require persuasive supporting evidence.]

Better Although long criticized for their sexist portrayal of women in television commercials, the auto industry is just as often guilty of stereotyping men as brainless idiots unable to make a decision. [This thesis makes a point that may lead to an interesting discussion.]

5. Don't express your thesis in the form of a question, unless the answer is already obvious to the reader.

Poor Why should every college student have to take two years of foreign language?

Better Math majors should be exempt from the foreign language requirement.

PRACTICING WHAT YOU'VE LEARNED

A. Identify each of the following thesis statements as adequate or inadequate. If the thesis is weak or insufficient in some way, explain the problem.

1. I think *Star Wars* was the most interesting movie of its decade.
2. Which car is a better value, the Chevy or the Ford?
3. Some people think that college entrance examinations are biased against women and minorities.
4. My essay will tell you how to apply for a college loan with the least amount of trouble.
5. During the fall term, final examinations should be given before the Christmas break, not after the holidays as they are now.
6. Raising the cost of tuition will be a terrible burden on the students and won't do anything to help the quality of education at this school.
7. Bicycle riding is my favorite exercise because it's so good for my body.
8. Defeat of this year's nuclear test-ban treaty will lead to the world's ultimate destruction.
9. Persons over 75 should be required to renew their driver's licenses every year.
10. Having a close friend you can talk to is very important.

B. Rewrite the sentences below so that each one is a clear thesis statement. Be prepared to explain why you changed the sentences as you did.

1. Applying for a job can be a negative experience.
2. Skiing is a lot of fun, but it can be expensive and dangerous.
3. There are many advantages and disadvantages to the county's new voting machines.
4. The deregulation of the telephone system has been one big headache.
5. In this paper I will debate the pros and cons of the controversial motorcycle helmet law.
6. We need to do something about the billboard clutter on the main highway into town.
7. The gun-control laws in this country need to be rewritten.
8. Prayer in the schools is a hot issue today.
9. In my opinion, Santa Barbara is a fantastic vacation spot.
10. The Civil Rights Movement of the 1960s had a tremendous effect on this country.

ASSIGNMENT

Narrow the subject and write one good thesis sentence for five of the following topics:

1. A political or social issue
2. College or high school
3. Family
4. A hobby or pastime
5. A recent book or movie
6. Vacations
7. Fast-food restaurants
8. A current fad or fashion
9. A job or profession
10. A rule, law, or regulation

USING THE ESSAY MAP *

Many thesis sentences will benefit from the addition of an *essay map,* a brief statement in the introductory paragraph introducing the major points to be discussed in the essay. Consider the analogy of beginning a trip by checking your map to see where you are headed. Similarly, an essay map allows the readers to know in advance where you, the writer, will be taking them in the essay.

Let's suppose you have been assigned the task of praising or criticizing some aspect of your campus. You decide that your thesis will be "The campus bookstore is the worst place in town to buy textbooks." While your thesis does take a stand ("worst place"), your reader will not know why the bookstore is so poor or what points you will cover in your argument. With an essay map added, the reader will have a brief but specific idea where the essay is going and how it will be developed:

Essay map (underlined)

> Thesis: The campus bookstore is the worst place in town to buy textbooks. The unreasonable prices, the lack of qualified employees, and the constant book shortages discourage all but the most loyal customers.

Thanks to the essay map, the reader knows that the essay will discuss the store's prices, employees, and book shortages.

---

* I am indebted to Professor Susan Wittig for this useful concept, introduced in *Steps to Structure: An Introduction to Composition and Rhetoric* (Cambridge, MA: Winthrop Publishers, Inc., 1975), pp. 125–126.

Here's another example—this time let's assume you decided to praise your school's Study Skills Center:

Essay map (underlined)

Thesis: The University's Study Skills Center is an excellent place for freshmen to receive help with basic courses. <u>The Center's numerous free services, well-trained tutors, and variety of supplementary learning materials can often mean the difference between academic success and failure for many students.</u>

After reading the introductory paragraph, the reader knows the essay will discuss the center's services, tutors, and supplementary learning aids. In other words, the thesis statement defines the main purpose of your essay, and the essay map indicates the route you will take to accomplish that purpose.

The essay map is often inserted after the thesis, but it can also appear before it. It is, in fact, frequently tacked onto the thesis statement itself, as illustrated in the following examples:

Thesis with underlined essay map

<u>Unreasonable prices, unqualified employees, and constant shortages</u> make the campus bookstore a terrible place to buy texts.

Thesis with underlined essay map

Because of its <u>free services, well-trained tutors, and useful learning aids,</u> the Study Skills Center is an excellent place for freshmen seeking academic help.

Thesis with underlined essay map

For those freshmen who need extra help with their basic courses, the Study Skills Center is one of the best resources <u>because of its numerous free services, well-trained tutors, and variety of useful learning aids.</u>

In addition to suggesting the main points of the essay, the map provides two other benefits. It will provide a set of guidelines for organizing your essay, and it will help keep you from wandering off into areas only vaguely related to your thesis. A clearly written thesis statement and essay map provide a skeletal outline for the sequence of paragraphs in your essay, with one body paragraph frequently devoted to each main point mentioned in your map. (Chapter 3, on paragraphs, will explain in more detail the relationships among the thesis, the map, and the body of your essay.) Note that the number of points in the essay map may vary, although three or four may be the number found most often in 500–800-word essays. (More than four main points in a short essay may result in underdeveloped paragraphs; see pp. 52–56 for additional information.)

One important warning: avoid a tendency to make your essay map sound too repetitive or mechanical; try to link the thesis and map as smoothly as possible.

Poor   The Campus Bookstore is a bad place to buy texts for three reasons. The reasons are high prices, unqualified employees, and book shortages.

Better   Unreasonable prices, unqualified employees, and book shortages combine to give the Campus Bookstore its well-deserved reputation as the worst place in town to buy texts.

If you feel your essay map is too obvious or mechanical, try using it only in your rough drafts to help you organize your essay. Once you're sure it isn't necessary to clarify your thesis or to guide your reader, you might consider dropping it out of your final draft.

Practicing What You've Learned

A. Identify the thesis and the essay map in the following sentences by underlining the map.

1. *Citizen Kane* deserves to appear on a list of "Top Movies of All Times" because of its excellent ensemble acting, its fast-paced script, and its innovative editing.
2. Our state should double the existing fines for first-offense drunk drivers. Such a move would lower the number of accidents, cut the costs of insurance, and increase the state revenues for highway maintenance.
3. To guarantee sound construction, lower costs, and personalized design, more people should consider building their own log cabin home.
4. Apartment living is preferable to dorm living because it's cheaper, quieter, and more luxurious.
5. Not everyone can become an astronaut. To qualify, a person must have intelligence, determination, and training.
6. Through unscrupulous uses of propaganda and secret assassination squads, Hitler was able to take control of an economically depressed Germany.
7. Because it builds muscles, increases circulation, and burns harmful fatty tissue, weight lifting is a sport that benefits the entire body.
8. The new tax bill will not radically reform the loophole-riddled revenue system: deductions on secondary residences will remain, real estate tax shelters are untouched, and nonprofit health organizations will be taxed.
9. Avocados make excellent plants for children. They're inexpensive to buy, easy to root, quick to sprout, and fun to grow.
10. His spirit of protest and clever phrasing blended into unusual musical arrangements have made Bob Dylan a recording giant for over twenty years.

B. Review the thesis statements you wrote for the Assignment on page 36. Write an essay map for each thesis statement. You may place the map before or after the thesis, or you may attach it to the thesis itself. Identify which part is the thesis and which is the essay map by underlining the map.

ASSIGNMENT

Use one of the quotations below to help you think of a subject for an essay of your own. Don't merely repeat the quotation itself as your thesis statement, but, rather, allow the quotation to lead you to your subject and a main point of your own creation that is appropriately narrowed and focused. Don't forget to designate an audience for your essay, a group of readers who need or want to hear what you have to say.

1. "You can never get enough of what you don't need"—Eric Hoffer, writer and social observer
2. "Few things are harder to put up with than the annoyance of a good example"—Mark Twain, writer and humorist
3. "Though familiarity may not breed contempt, it takes the edge off admiration"—William Hazlitt, writer
4. "In this world there are only two tragedies. One is not getting what one wants, and the other is getting it"—Oscar Wilde, writer
5. "Noncooperation with evil is as much a moral obligation as is cooperation with good"—Martin Luther King, Jr., statesman and civil rights activist
6. "It is never too late to be what one might have been"—George Eliot, writer
7. "Happiness is not something you experience; it's something you remember"—Oscar Levant, writer
8. "People change and forget to tell each other"—Lillian Hellman, writer
9. "Nobody can make you feel inferior without your consent"—Eleanor Roosevelt, stateswoman
10. "When a person declares that he's going to college, he's announcing that he needs four more years of coddling before he can face the real world"—Al Capp, creator of the *Li'l Abner* cartoon
11. "The mass of men lead lives of quiet desperation"—Henry Thoreau, writer and naturalist
12. "The mass of Americans lead lives of diet desperation"— J. C. Wheeler, writer
13. "Family jokes are the bond that keeps most families alive"—Stella Benson, writer

14. "Nobody ever went broke underestimating the intelligence of the American public"—H. L. Mencken, writer and critic

15. "Even if you are on the right track, you will get run over if you just sit there"—Will Rogers, humorist and author

---

CHAPTER 2 SUMMARY

Here's a brief review of what you need to know about the thesis statement:

1. A thesis statement declares the main point of your essay; it tells the reader what clearly defined opinion you hold.

2. Everything in your essay should support your thesis statement.

3. A good thesis statement asserts one main idea, narrowed to fit the assignment, and is stated in clear, specific terms.

4. A good thesis statement makes a reasonable claim about a topic that is of interest to its readers as well as to its writer.

5. A good thesis statement is clearly presented near the beginning of the essay, usually in the first or second paragraph, or is so strongly implied that readers cannot miss the writer's main point.

6. A "working" or trial thesis statement is an excellent organizing tool to use as you begin writing your first draft because it will help you decide which ideas to omit or include.

7. Because writing is an act of discovery, you may find that you will write yourself into a better thesis statement by the end of your first draft. Don't hesitate to begin a new draft with the new thesis statement.

8. Some writers may profit from using an essay map, a brief statement accompanying the thesis that introduces the supporting points to be discussed in the body of the essay.

3

The Body Paragraphs

PLANNING THE BODY OF YOUR ESSAY

The middle or *body* of your essay is composed of paragraphs that support the thesis statement. By presenting details, explaining causes, offering reasons, and citing examples in these paragraphs, you supply enough specific evidence to persuade your reader that the opinion expressed in your thesis is a sensible one. Each paragraph in the body usually presents and develops one main point in the discussion of your thesis. Generally, but not always, a new body paragraph signals another major point in the discussion.

To plan the body of your essay, look at your introduction. The main points mentioned in your essay map will frequently provide the basis for the body paragraphs of your essay.

For example, recall, from Chapter 2, the thesis and essay map praising the Study Skills Center (p. 37): "Because of its free services, well-trained tutors, and useful learning aids, the Study Skills Center is an excellent place for freshmen seeking academic help." Your plan for developing the body of your essay might look like this:

Body paragraph one: discussion of free services
Body paragraph two: discussion of tutors
Body paragraph three: discussion of learning aids

At this point you may wish to sketch in some of the supporting examples and details you will include in each paragraph. You might find it helpful to go back to your prewriting activities (listing, looping, freewriting, mapping, cubing, and so on) to see what ideas surfaced then. Adding some examples and supporting details might make a scratch outline appear this way:

I.   Free Services

    A. Mini-course on improving study skills

    B. Tutoring ⟨composition / math⟩

    C. Weekly seminars ⟨stress management / test anxiety / building vocabulary⟩

    D. Testing for learning disabilities

II. Tutors

    A. Top graduate students in their fields

    B. Experienced teachers

    C. Some bilingual

    D. Have taken training course at Center

III. Learning Aids

    A. Supplementary texts

    B. Workbooks

    C. Audiovisual aids

Notice that the sketch above is an *informal* or *scratch outline* rather than a *formal outline*—that is, it doesn't have strictly parallel parts nor is it expressed in complete sentences. Unless your teacher requests a formal sentence or topic outline, don't feel you must make one at this early stage. Just consider using the scratch outline to plot out a tentative plan that will help you start your first draft.

Here's an example of a scratch outline at work: let's suppose you have been asked to write about your most prized possession—and you've chosen your 1966 Mustang, a car you have restored. You already have some ideas but they're scattered and too few to make an interesting, well-developed essay. You try a scratch outline, jotting down your ideas thus far:

I.   Car is special because it was a gift from Dad

II. Fun to drive

III. Looks great—new paint job

IV. Engine in top condition

V. Custom features

VI. Car shows—fun to be part of

After looking at your scratch outline, you see that some of your categories overlap and could be part of the same discussion. For example, your thoughts about the engine are actually part of the discussion of "fun to drive" and "custom features" are what make the car look great. Moreover, the outline may help you discover new ideas—custom features could be divided into those on the interior as well as those on the exterior of the car. The revised scratch outline might look like this:

I.   Gift from Dad

II. Fun to drive

    A. Engine

    B. Steering

III. Looks great

    A. New paint job

    B. Custom features

        1. exterior

        2. interior

IV. Car shows

You could continue playing with the scratch outline, even moving big chunks of it around; for example, you might decide that what really makes the car so special is that it was a graduation gift from your Dad and that is the note you want to end on. So you move "I. Gift from Dad" down to the last position in your outline.

The important point to remember about a scratch or working outline is that it is there to help you—not control you. The value of a scratch outline is its ability to help you see logical connections between your ideas and to help you see obvious places to add new ideas and details. Don't be intimidated by the outline!

Here's one more sample scratch outline, this time for the thesis and essay map on the campus bookstore, from Chapter 2:

> Thesis-Map: "Unreasonable prices, unqualified employees, and book shortages combine to give the Campus Bookstore its well-deserved reputation of the worst place in town to buy texts."

I.   Unreasonable Prices

    A. Too expensive compared to other stores

    B. Sudden mark-ups

    C. Cheap buy-back policy

II. Unqualified Personnel

    A. Clerks with little knowledge of prices or book orders

    B. Untrained cashiers

III. Book Shortages

    A. Too few books ordered

    B. Wrong books ordered

    C. Wrong edition ordered

    D. Late orders

Of course, you may have more than three points to make in your essay. And, on occasion, you may need more than one paragraph to discuss a single point. For instance, you might discover that you need two paragraphs to explain fully the services at the Study Skills Center (for advice on splitting the discussion of a single point into two or more paragraphs, see p. 56). At this stage, you needn't bother trying to guess whether you'll need more than one paragraph per point; just use the outline to get going. Most writers don't know how much they have to say before they begin writing—and that's fine because writing itself is an act of discovery and learning.

When you feel you have a plan in mind or are comfortable with the number of ideas you have generated, you may be ready to start drafting your essay. (By the way, the scratch outline is handy to keep around in case you're interrupted for a long period while you're drafting; you can always check the outline to see where you were and where you were going when you stopped.) Before you begin writing, however, you might review the hints on pp. 84–85 in Chapter 5 for composing the first draft; remember, too, that Chapter 5 contains suggestions for beating Writer's Block, should this condition arise while you are drafting some part of your essay.

ORGANIZING THE BODY PARAGRAPHS

There are many ways to develop body paragraphs. Paragraphs developed by such common patterns as example, comparison, definition, and so forth will be discussed in specific chapters in Part Two; at this point, however, here are some comments about the general nature of all good paragraphs that should help you write the first draft of your essay.

Most of the body paragraphs in your essay will profit from a focused *topic sentence*. In addition, every paragraph should have adequate *development, unity, and coherence.*

THE TOPIC SENTENCE

Most body paragraphs present one main point in your discussion, expressed in a *topic sentence*. The topic sentence of a body paragraph has three important functions:

1. It supports the thesis by clearly stating a main point in the discussion.
2. It announces what the paragraph will be about.
3. It controls the subject matter of the paragraph. The entire discussion—the examples, details, explanations—in a particular paragraph must directly relate to and support the topic sentence.

Think of a body paragraph (or a single paragraph) as a kind of mini-essay in itself. The topic sentence is, in a sense, a smaller thesis. It too asserts one main idea on a limited subject that the writer can explain or argue in the rest of the paragraph. Like the thesis, the topic sentence should be stated in as specific language as possible.

To see how a topic sentence works in a body paragraph, study this sample:

Essay Thesis: The Study Skills Center is an excellent place for freshmen who need academic help.

Topic Sentence
1. The topic sentence supports the thesis by stating a main point (one reason why the Center provides excellent academic help).
2. The topic sentence announces the subject matter of the paragraph (a variety of free services that improve basic skills).
3. The topic sentence controls the subject matter (all the examples—the mini-course, the tutoring, the seminars, and the testing—support the claim of the topic sentence).

The Center offers students a variety of free services designed to improve basic skills. Freshmen who discover their study habits are poor, for instance, may enroll in a six-week mini-course in study skills that offers advice on such topics as how to read a text, take notes, and organize material for review. Students whose math or writing skills are below par can sign up for free tutoring sessions held five days a week throughout each semester. In addition, the Center presents weekly seminars on special topics such as stress management and overcoming test anxiety for those students who are finding college more of a nerve-wracking experience than they expected; other students can attend evening seminars in such worthwhile endeavors as vocabulary building or spelling tips. Finally, the Center offers a series of tests to identify the presence of any learning disabilities, such as dyslexia, that might prevent a student from succeeding academically. With such a variety of free services, the Center could help almost any student.

Here's another example from the essay on the bookstore:

Essay Thesis: The campus bookstore deserves its reputation as the worst place in town for students to buy their texts.

Topic Sentence
1. The topic sentence supports the thesis by stating a main point (one reason why the store is a bad place to buy texts).
2. The topic sentence announces the subject matter of the paragraph (unreasonable pricing policies).
3. The topic sentence controls the subject matter (all the examples—the high prices, the mark-ups, and the refund problems—support the claim of the topic sentence).

The campus bookstore's unreasonable pricing policies discourage potential customers. In the first place, the store's prices are, on the average, far higher than those of the other two bookstores that carry college texts. For instance, while the basic text required for Intro to Biology costs $18.95 at both other stores, it's marked up to $21.98 at the campus store. Similarly, the required freshman math book is $16.95 at the campus store whereas it's $14.50 elsewhere. Moreover, the prices at the store don't remain constant during the book-buying period. One day a book might be $11.95 and the next day it's $13.95. The campus store management defends this policy by noting it reflects "shifting overhead costs," but it's bothersome for the students who are trying to plan their tight budgets. And if high, fluctuating prices aren't bad enough, the campus store's buy-back policy is terrible. The refund on returned books is ten percent lower than that at the other stores, and the semester's refund period is but three days, often too brief a time for students to finish arranging their class schedules. Policies such as these often drive customers to the store's competitors.

Always be sure your topic sentences actually support the particular thesis of your essay. For example, the second topic sentence listed below doesn't belong in the essay promised by the thesis:

Thesis   Elk hunting should be permitted because it financially aids people in our state.

Topic Sentences

1. Fees for hunting licenses help pay for certain free, state-supported social services.
2. Hunting helps keep the elk population under control.
3. Elk hunting offers a means of obtaining free food for those people with low incomes.

While topic sentence 2 is about elk and while it may be true, it doesn't support the thesis's emphasis on financial aid and therefore should be tossed out of this essay.
    Here's another example:

Thesis   In the past fifty years, movie stars have often tried to change the direction of America's politics.

Topic Sentences

1. During World War II stars sold liberty bonds to support the country's war effort.
2. Many stars refused to cooperate with the blacklisting of their colleagues in the 1950s.
3. Some stars were actively involved in protests against the Vietnam War.
4. More recently, stars have appeared in Congress criticizing the lack of legislative help for struggling farmers.

Topic sentences 2, 3, and 4 all show how stars have tried to effect a change. But topic sentence 1 only says that stars sold bonds to support, not change, the political direction of the nation. Although it does show stars involved in politics, it doesn't illustrate the claim of this particular thesis.

Sometimes a topic sentence needs only to be rewritten or slightly recast to fit:

Thesis The recent tuition hike will discourage students from attending our college.

Topic Sentences

1. Students already pay more here than at other in-state schools.
2. Out-of-state students would have to pay an additional "penalty" to attend.
3. Tuition funds should be used to give teachers raises.

As written, topic sentence 3 doesn't show why students won't want to attend the school. However, a rewritten topic sentence does support the thesis:

3. Because the tuition money will not be used for teachers' salaries, many top professors may take job offers elsewhere, and their best students may follow them there.

In other words, always check carefully to make sure that *all* your topic sentences clearly support your thesis's assertion.

FOCUSING YOUR TOPIC SENTENCE

A vague, fuzzy, or unfocused topic sentence most often leads to a paragraph that touches only on the surface of its subject or that wanders away from the writer's main idea. On the other hand, a topic sentence that is tightly focused and stated precisely will not only help the reader to understand the point of the paragraph but will also help you select, organize, and develop your supporting details.

Look, for example, at these unfocused topic sentences and their revisions:

Unfocused	Too many people treat animals badly in experiments. (What people? Badly how? What kinds of experiments?)
Focused	The cosmetic industry often harms animals in unnecessary experiments designed to test their products.
Unfocused	Grades are an unfair pain in the neck. (Again, the focus is so broad: all grades? Unfair how?)
Focused	Course grades based solely on one term paper don't accurately measure a student's knowledge of the subject.
Unfocused	Getting the right job is important and can lead to rewarding experiences. (Note both vague language and a double focus—"important" and "can lead to rewarding experiences.")
Focused	Getting the right job can lead to an improved sense of self-esteem.

Before you practice writing focused topic sentences, you may wish to review pages 27–34, the advice on composing good thesis statements, as the same rules generally apply.

PLACING YOUR TOPIC SENTENCE

While the topic sentence most frequently occurs as the first sentence in the body paragraph, it also often appears as the second or last sentence. A topic sentence that directly follows the first sentence of a paragraph usually does so because the first sentence provides an introductory statement or some kind of a "hook" to the preceding paragraph. A topic sentence frequently appears at the end of a paragraph that first presents particular details and then concludes with its central point. Here are two paragraphs in which the topic sentences do not appear first:

Introductory Sentence

Topic Sentence

Millions of Americans have watched the elaborate Rose Bowl Parade televised nationally each January from Pasadena, California. *Less well known, but growing in popularity, is Pasadena's Doo Dah Parade, an annual parody of the Rose Bowl spectacle, that specializes in wild-and-crazy participants.* Take this year's Doo Dah Precision Drill Team, for instance. Instead of marching in unison, the members cavorted down the avenue displaying—what else—a variety of precision electric drills. In heated competition with this group was the Synchronized Briefcase Drill Team, whose male and female members wore gray pinstripe suits and performed a series of tunes by tapping on their briefcases. Another crowd-pleasing entry was the Citizens for the Right to Bare Arms, whose members sang while carrying aloft unclothed mannequin arms. The zany procession, led this year as always by the All-Time Doo Dah Parade Band, attracted more than 150,000 fans and is already preparing for its twelfth anniversary celebration next January 1.

In the previous paragraph, the first sentence serves as an introduction leading into the topic sentence; in the following paragraph, the writer places the topic sentence last to make a general comment about the importance of VCRs.

Topic Sentence

> Because of VCRs, we no longer have to miss a single joke on our favorite sitcom. Sporting events can be recorded in their entirety even though we may have to go to work or class after the fifth inning or second quarter. Even our dose of television violence does not have to be postponed forever just because a popular special is on another channel at the same time. Moreover, events of historical significance can be captured and replayed for future generations even if Aunt Tillie keeps us eating tacos until after the show begins. *In but a few years, VCRs have radically changed America's television viewing habits.*

As you can see, the position of topic sentences largely depends on what you are trying to do in your paragraph. However, if you are a beginning writer, you may want to practice putting your topic sentences first for a while to help you organize and unify your paragraphs.

Some paragraphs with a topic sentence near the beginning also contain a concluding sentence that makes a final general comment based on the supporting details. The last sentence below, for example, sums up and restates the main point of the paragraph.

Topic Sentence

Concluding
Sentence

> *Of all nature's catastrophes, tornadoes cause the most bizarre destruction.* Whirling out of the sky at speeds up to three hundred miles per hour, tornadoes have been known to drive broom handles through brick walls and straws into tree trunks. In one extreme case, a Kansas farmer reported that his prize rooster had been sucked into a two-gallon distilled-water bottle. More commonly, tornadoes lift autos and deposit them in fields miles away or uproot trees and drop them on lawns in neighboring towns. One tornado knocked down every wall in a house but one—luckily, the very wall shielding the terrified family. *Whenever a tornado touches the earth, spectacular headlines are sure to follow.*

Practicing What You've Learned

A. Point out the topic sentences in the following paragraphs; identify those paragraphs that also contain concluding sentences.

Denim is one of America's most widely used fabrics. It was first introduced during Columbus's voyage, when the sails of the Santa Maria were made of the strong cloth. During our pioneer days, denim was used for tents, covered wagons, and the now-famous blue jeans. Cowboys found denim an ideal fabric for protection against sagebrush, cactus, and saddle sores. World War II also gave denim a boost in popularity when sailors were issued jeans as part of their dress code. Today, denim continues to be in demand as more and more casual clothes are cut from the economical fabric. Because of its low cost and durability, manufacturers feel that denim will continue as one of America's most useful fabrics.

Cooking in a microwave oven has simplified my hectic life. Instead of having to wait the interminable ten minutes for my morning coffee, I can place my cup in the micro and have hot coffee in seconds. I no longer have to decide in the foggy morning what ingredients must be defrosted for the evening meal. I can now come home at 5 P.M., decide what I feel like eating, and have it defrosted in a matter of minutes. The shortened cooking time means I can have full-course meals that once took me hours to cook. The microwave also makes cleanup much easier because the dish I cook in is the dish I eat in. Microwaves may be expensive, but the time and effort they save is worth a million to those of us with too-busy lives.

You always think of the right answer five minutes after you hand in the test. You always hit the red light when you're already late for class. The one time you skip class is the day of the pop quiz. Back-to-back classes are always held in buildings at opposite ends of campus. The one course you need to graduate will not be offered your last semester. If any of these sound familiar, you've obviously been a victim of the "Murphy's Laws" that govern student life.

Want to win a sure bet? Then wager that your friends can't guess the most widely sold musical instrument in America today. Chances are they won't get the answer right—not even on the third try. In actuality, the most popular instrument in the country is neither the guitar nor the trumpet, but the lowly kazoo. Last year alone, some three and one-half million kazoos were sold to music lovers of all ages. Part of the instrument's popularity arises from its availability, since kazoos are sold in variety stores and music centers nearly everywhere; another reason is its inexpensiveness—it ranges from the standard thirty-nine-cent model to the five-dollar gold-plated special. But perhaps the main reason for the kazoo's popularity is the ease with which it can be played by almost anyone—as can testify the members of the entire Swarthmore College marching band, who have now add a marching kazoo number to their repertoire. Louie Armstrong, move over!

You know the scenario: Dad won't stop the car to ask directions, despite the fact that he's been hopelessly lost for over forty-five minutes. Mom keeps nagging Dad to slow down and finally blows up because your little sister suddenly remembers she's left her favorite doll, the one she can't sleep without, at the rest stop we left over an hour ago. Your legs are sweat-glued to the vinyl seats, you need desperately to go to the bathroom, and your big brother has just kindly acknowledged that he will relieve you of your front teeth if you allow any part of your body to extend over the imaginary line he has drawn down the back seat. The wonderful institution known as the "family vacation" has begun.

B. Rewrite these topic sentences so that they are clear and focused rather than fuzzy or too broad.

1. My personality has changed a lot in the last year.
2. His blind date turned out to be really great.
3. The movie's special effects were incredible.
4. The Memorial Day celebration was more fun than ever before.
5. The evening with her parents was an unforgettable experience.

C. Add topic sentences to the following paragraphs:

Famous inventor Thomas Edison, for instance, did so poorly in his first years of school that his teachers warned his parents that he'd never be a success at anything. Similarly, Henry Ford, the father of the auto industry, had trouble in school with both reading and writing. But perhaps the best example is Albert Einstein, whose parents and teachers suspected that he was retarded because he responded to questions so slowly and in a stuttering voice. Einstein's high school record was poor in everything but math, and he failed his college entrance exams the first time. Even out of school the man had trouble holding a job—until he announced the theory of relativity.

A 1950s felt skirt with Elvis's picture on it, for example, now sells for $150, and Elvis scarves go for as much as $200. Elvis handkerchiefs, originally 50 cents or less, fetch $150 on today's market as do wallets imprinted with the singer's face. Posters from the Rock King's movies can sell for $50, and cards from the chewing gum series can run $30 apiece. Perhaps one of the most expensive collectors' items is the Emene Elvis guitar that can cost a fan from $500 to $700, regardless of musical condition.

When successful playwright Jean Kerr once checked into a hospital, the receptionist asked her occupation and was told, "Writer." The receptionist said, "I'll just put down 'housewife.'" Similarly, when a British official asked W. H. Auden, the late award-winning poet and essayist, what he did for a living, Auden replied, "I'm a writer." The official jotted down "no occupation."

Cumberland College, for example, set the record back in 1916 for the biggest loss in college ball, having allowed Georgia Tech to run up 63 points in the first quarter and ultimately succumbing to them with a final score of 222 to nothing. In pro ball, the Washington Redskins are the biggest losers, going down in defeat 73 to zero to the Chicago Bears in 1940. The award for the longest losing streak, however, goes to Northwestern University's team, who in 1981 managed to lose 29 consecutive games. During that year, morale was so low that one disgruntled fan passing a local highway sign that read "Interstate 94" couldn't resist adding "Northwestern 0."

D. Write a focused topic sentence for five of the following subjects:

1. job interviews
2. friends
3. airplanes
4. money
5. selecting a major
6. clothes
7. space exploration
8. dreams
9. dentists
10. childhood

ASSIGNMENT

Review the thesis statements with essay maps you wrote for the practice exercise on page 39. Choose two, and from each thesis create at least three topic sentences for possible body paragraphs.

APPLYING WHAT YOU'VE LEARNED TO *YOUR* WRITING

If you currently have a working thesis statement you have written in response to an assignment in your composition class, try sketching out an outline or plan for the major ideas you wish to include. After you write your first draft, underline the topic sentences in your body paragraphs. Do your topic sentences directly support your thesis? If you find that they do not clearly support your thesis, you must decide if you need to revise your draft's organization or whether you have, in fact, discovered a new, and possibly better, subject to write about. If the latter is true, you'll need to redraft your essay so that your readers will not be confused by a paper that announces one subject but discusses another. (See Chapter 5 for more information on revising your drafts.)

PARAGRAPH DEVELOPMENT

Possibly the most serious—and most common—weakness of all essays by novice writers is *the lack of adequately developed body paragraphs.* The information in each paragraph must effectively explain, exemplify, persuade, define, or in some other way support your topic sentence. In the first place, you must include enough information in each paragraph to make your readers understand your topic sentence. Secondly, you must make the information in the paragraph clear and specific enough for the readers to accept your ideas.

The next paragraph is *underdeveloped*. Although the topic sentence promises a discussion of Jesse James as a Robin Hood figure, the paragraph does not provide enough specific examples to explain this unusual view of the gunfighter.

> Although he was an outlaw, Jesse James was considered a Robin Hood figure in my hometown in Missouri. He used to be generous to the poor, and he did many good deeds like giving away money. People in my hometown still talk about how lots of the things James did weren't all bad.

Rewritten, the paragraph might read as follows:

> Although he was an outlaw, Jesse James was considered a Robin Hood figure in my hometown in Missouri. Jesse and his gang chose my hometown as a hiding place, and they set out immediately to make friends with the local people. Every Christmas for four years, the legend goes, he dumped bags of toys on the doorsteps of poor children. The parents knew the toys had been bought with money stolen from richer people, but they were grateful anyway. On three occasions, Jesse gave groceries to the dozen neediest families—he seemed to know when times were toughest— and once he supposedly held up a stage to pay for an old man's operation. In my hometown, some people still sing the praises of Jesse James, the outlaw who wasn't all bad.

The topic sentence promises a discussion of James's generosity and delivers just that by citing specific examples of his gifts to children, the poor, and the sick. The paragraph is, therefore, better developed.

Similarly, this paragraph offers supporting reasons but no specific examples or details to support those reasons:

> Living with my ex-roommate was unbearable. First, she thought everything she owned was the best. Secondly, she possessed numerous filthy habits. Finally, she constantly exhibited immature behavior.

The writer might flesh out the paragraph this way:

> Living with my ex-roommate was unbearable. First, she thought everything she owned, from clothes to cosmetics, was the best. If someone complimented my pants, she'd point out that her designer jeans looked better and would last longer because they were made of better material.

If she borrowed my shampoo, she'd let me know that it didn't get her hair as clean and shiny as hers did. My hand cream wasn't as smooth; my suntan lotion wasn't as protective; not even my wire clothes hangers were as good as her padded ones! But despite her pickiness about products, she had numerous filthy habits. Her dirty dishes remained in the sink for ages before she got the incentive to wash them. Piles of the "best" brand of tissues were regularly discarded from her upper bunk and strewn about the floor. Her desk and closets overflowed with heaps of dirty clothes, books, cosmetics, and whatever else she owned, and she rarely brushed her teeth (when she did brush, she left oozes of toothpaste on the sink). Finally, she constantly acted immaturely by throwing tantrums when things didn't go her way. A poor grade on an exam or paper, for example, meant ashtrays, shoes, or any other small object within her reach would hit the wall flying. Living with such a person taught me some valuable lessons about how not to win friends or keep roommates.

Having a well-developed paragraph is more than a matter of adding length, however. The information in each paragraph must effectively explain or support your topic sentence. *Vague generalities or repetitious ideas are not convincing.* Look, for example, at the following paragraph in which the writer offers only generalities:

Bicycles, popular for years in Europe, are becoming popular in America. Traveling by bicycle is better and easier than traveling by car. Bicycle riding is good for you, too, and it lets you get close to nature.

The paragraph is weak because none of its general statements are explained or supported with specific details. Why is travel by bicycle "better" than travel by car? "Better" in what ways? Why "easier"? "Good for you" in what ways? And what is the importance of getting "close to nature"? The writer obviously had some ideas in mind, but these ideas are not clear to the reader because they are not adequately developed in specific terms. By adding examples and details, the writer might revise the paragraph this way:

With the price of gasoline skyrocketing every year and with parking places becoming more and more scarce, an increasing number of Americans are discovering an Old World secret: bicycling. Bicycles have long been a common sight in Europe, where gasoline has always been expensive. Now bicyclists in America are learning that bicycles not only save gasoline and costly repairs, but also provide a pleasant, even exhilarating, way to exercise flabby muscles and clear clogged respiratory systems. In addition, cyclists are happily discovering a whole new way of looking at the world around them. Instead of spending their time and energy battling traffic jams and fighting for nonexistent parking spaces, they quickly sail along to their destinations, calm and relaxed, closer to the trees, flowers, and birds than any car has allowed them to be.

The reader now knows that bicycling is "better" because it improves mental and physical health and because it saves money and time.

After examining the two paragraphs below, decide which explains its point more effectively.

#1

Competing in an Ironman triathlon is one of the most demanding feats known to amateur athletes. First, they have to swim many miles and that takes a lot of endurance. Then they ride a bicycle a long way, which is also hard on their bodies. Last, they run a marathon, which can be difficult in itself but is especially hard after the first two events. Competing in the triathlon is really tough on the participants.

#2

Competing in an Ironman triathlon is one of the most demanding feats known to amateur athletes. During the first stage of the triathlon, the competitors must swim 2.4 miles in the open ocean. They have to battle the constantly choppy ocean, the strong currents, and the frequent swells. The wind is often an adversary, and stinging jellyfish are a constant threat. Once they have completed the ocean swim, the triathletes must ride 112 miles on a bicycle. In addition to the strength needed to pedal that far, the bicyclists must use a variety of hand grips to assure the continued circulation in their fingers and hands as well as to ease the strain on the neck and shoulder muscles. Moreover, the concentration necessary to steady the bicycle as well as the attention to the inclines on the course and the consequent shifting of gears causes mental fatigue for the athletes. After completing these two grueling segments, the triathletes must then run 26.2 miles, the length of a regular marathon. Dehydration is a constant concern as is the prospect of cramping. Even the pain and swelling of a friction blister can be enough to eliminate a contestant at this late stage of the event. Finally, disorientation and fatigue can set in and distort the athlete's judgment. Competing in an Ironman triathlon takes incredible physical and mental endurance.

The first paragraph contains, for the most part, repetitious generalities; it repeats the same idea (the triathlon is hard work) and gives few specific details to illustrate the point presented in the topic sentence. The second paragraph, on the other hand, does offer many specific examples and details—the exact

mileage figures, the currents, jellyfish, inclines, grips, blisters, and so forth—
that help the reader understand why the event is so demanding.

Joseph Conrad, the famous British novelist, once remarked that a
writer's purpose was to use "the power of the written word to make you hear,
to make you feel . . . before all, to make you *see*. That—and no more, and it
is everything." By using specific details instead of vague, general statements,
you can write an interesting, convincing essay. Ask yourself as you revise your
paragraphs, "Have I provided enough clear, precise details to make my readers *see* what I want them to?" In other words, a well-developed paragraph
effectively presents its point with *an appropriate amount of specific supporting
detail*. (Remember that a handwritten paragraph in your rough draft will look
much shorter when it is typed. Therefore, if you can't think of much to say
about a particular idea, you should gather more information or consider dropping it as a major point in your essay.)

PARAGRAPH LENGTH

"How long is a good paragraph?" is a question novice writers often ask. Like a
teacher's lecture or a preacher's sermon, paragraphs should be long enough to
accomplish their purpose and short enough to be interesting. In truth, there
is no set length, no prescribed number of lines or sentences, for any of your
paragraphs. In a body paragraph, your topic sentence presents the main point,
and the rest of the paragraph must give enough supporting evidence to
convince the reader. While too much unnecessary or repetitious detail is boring, too little discussion will leave the reader uninformed, unconvinced, or
confused.

Although paragraph length varies, beginning writers should try to avoid
the one- or two-sentence paragraph frequently seen in newspapers or magazine articles. (Journalists have their own rules to follow; paragraphs are
shorter in newspapers, for one reason, because large masses of print in narrow
columns are hard to read quickly.) Essay writers do occasionally use the one-
sentence paragraph, most often to produce some special effect, when the
statement is especially dramatic or significant and needs to call attention to
itself. For now, however, you may wish to practice working on paragraphs of at
least five sentences.

One more note on paragraph length: sometimes you may discover that a
particular point in your essay is so complex that your paragraph is growing far
too long—well over a typed page, for instance. If this problem occurs, look for
a logical place to divide your information and start a new paragraph. For example, you might see a convenient dividing point between a series of actions you're
describing or a break in the chronology of a narrative or between explanations
of arguments or examples. Just make sure you begin your second paragraph
with some sort of transition phrase or key words to let the reader know you are

still discussing the same point as before ("Still another problem caused by the computer's faulty memory circuit is . . .").

PRACTICING WHAT YOU'VE LEARNED

Analyze the following paragraphs. Explain how you might improve the development of each one.

1. Professor Wilson is the best teacher I've ever had. His lectures are interesting, and he's very concerned about his students. He makes the class challenging but not too hard. On tests he doesn't expect more than one can give. I think he's a great teacher.

2. Newspaper advice columns are pretty silly. The problems are generally stupid or unrealistic, and the advice is out of touch with today's world. Too often the columnist just uses the letter to make a smart remark about some pet peeve. The columns could be put to some good uses, but no one tries very hard.

3. Driving tests do not adequately examine a person's driving ability. Usually the person being tested does not have to drive very far. The test does not require the skills that are used in everyday driving situations. Supervisors of driving tests tend to be very lenient.

4. Old-age homes are sad places. They are usually located in ugly old houses unfit for anyone. The people there are lonely and bored. What's more, they're often treated badly by the people who run the homes. It's a shame something better can't be done for the elderly.

5. There is a big difference between acquaintances and friends. Acquaintances are just people you know slightly, but friends give you some important qualities. For example, they can help you gain self-esteem and confidence just by being close to you. By sharing intimate things, they also help you feel happy about being alive.

ASSIGNMENT

A. Select two of the paragraphs from above and rewrite them, adding enough specific details to make well-developed paragraphs.

B. Write a paragraph composed of generalities and vague statements. Exchange this paragraph with a classmate's, and turn each other's faulty paragraph into a clearly developed one.

C. Find at least two well-developed paragraphs in an essay or book; explain why you think the two paragraphs are successfully developed.

APPLYING WHAT YOU'VE LEARNED TO *YOUR* WRITING

If you are currently drafting an essay, look closely at your body paragraphs. Find the topic sentence in each paragraph and circle the key words that most clearly communicate the main idea of the paragraph. Then ask yourself if the information in each paragraph effectively supports, explains, or illustrates the main idea of the paragraph's topic sentence. Is there enough information? If you're not sure, try numbering your supporting details. Are there too few to be persuasive? Does the paragraph present clear, specific supporting material or does it contain too many vague generalities to be convincing? Where could you add more details to help the reader understand your ideas better and to make each paragraph more interesting? (For more help revising your paragraphs, see Chapter 5.)

PARAGRAPH UNITY

Every sentence in a body paragraph should directly relate to the main idea presented by the topic sentence. A paragraph must stick to its announced subject; it must not drift away into another discussion. In other words, a good paragraph has *unity*.

Examine the unified paragraph below; note that the topic sentence clearly states the paragraph's main point and that each sentence thereafter supports the topic sentence.

> [1]Frank Lloyd Wright, America's leading architect of the first half of the twentieth century, believed that his houses should blend naturally with their building sites. [2]Consequently, he designed several "prairie houses," whose long, low lines echoed the flat earth plan. [3]Built of brick, stone, and natural wood, the houses shared a similar texture with their backgrounds; [4]large windows were often used to blend the interior and exterior of the homes. [5]Wright also punctuated the lines and spaces of the houses with greenery in planters to further make the buildings look part of nature.

The first sentence states the main idea, that Wright thought houses should blend with their location; the other sentences support this assertion:

Topic sentence: Wright's houses blend with their natural locations
2. long, low lines echo flat prairie
3. brick, stone, wood provide same texture as location
4. windows blend inside with outside
5. greenery in planters imitates the natural surroundings

Now look at the next paragraph in which the writer strays from his original purpose:

(1)Cigarette smoke is unhealthy even for people who don't have the nicotine habit themselves. (2)Secondhand smoke can cause asthmatics and sufferers of sinusitis serious problems; (3)doctors regularly advise heart patients to avoid confined smoky areas because coronary attacks might be triggered by the lack of clean air. (4)Moreover, having the smell of smoke in one's hair and clothes is a real nuisance. (5)Even if a person is without any health problems, exhaled smoke doubles the amount of carbon monoxide in the air, a condition that may cause lung problems in the future.

Sentence 4 refers to smoke as a nuisance and therefore does not belong in a paragraph that discusses smoking as a health hazard to nonsmokers.

Sometimes a large portion of a paragraph will drift into another topic. In the paragraph below, did the writer wish to focus on her messiness or on the beneficial effects of her engagement?

I have always been a very messy person. As a child, I was a pack rat, saving every little piece of insignificant paper that I thought might be important when I grew up. As a teenager, my pockets bulged with remnants of basketball games, candy bars, gum wrappers, and other important articles from my high school education. As a college student, I became a boxer—not a fighter, but the kind who cannot throw anything away and therefore it winds up in a box in my closet. But my engagement has changed everything. I'm really pleased with the new stage of my life, and I owe it all to my fiancé. My overall outlook on life has changed because of his influences on me. I'm much much more cheerful, and I'm even getting places on time like I never did before. It's truly amazing what love can do.

Note shift from the topic of messiness

This writer may wish to discuss the changes her fiancé has inspired and then use her former messiness, tardiness, and other bad habits as examples illustrating those changes; however, as presented here, the paragraph is not unified around a central idea. On the contrary, it first seems to promise a discussion of her messiness but then wanders into comments on "what love can do."

Also beware a tendency to end your paragraph with a new idea. A new point calls for an entirely new paragraph. For example, the paragraph below focuses on the origins of Muzak; the last sentence, on Muzak's effects on workers, should be omitted or moved to a following paragraph on Muzak's uses in the workplace.

Muzak, the ever-present sound of music that pervades elevators, office buildings, and reception rooms, was created over 50 years ago by George Owen Squier, an army general. A graduate of West Point, Squier was also an inventor and scientist. During World War I he headed the Signal Corps where he began experimenting with the notion of transmitting simultaneous messages over power lines. When he retired from the army in 1922, he founded Wired

Radio, Inc., and later in 1934 the first Muzak medley was heard in Cleveland, Ohio, for homeowners willing to pay the great sum of $1.50 a month. That year he struck upon the now-famous name, which combined the idea of music with the brand name of the most popular camera of the day, Kodak. *Recent experiments show that workers get more done if they listen to Muzak.*

Breaks Unity

In general, think of paragraph unity in terms of the diagram below:

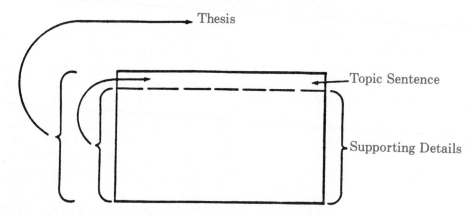

The sentences in the paragraph support the paragraph's topic sentence; the paragraph, in turn, supports the thesis statement.

PRACTICING WHAT YOU'VE LEARNED

In each of the following examples, delete or rewrite any information that interferes with the unity of the paragraph:

In the Great Depression of the 1930s, American painters suffered severely because few people had the money to spend on the luxury of owning art. To keep our artists from starving, the government ultimately set up the Federal Art Project, which paid then little-known painters such as Jackson Pollock, Arshile Gorky, and Willem de Kooning to paint murals in post offices, train stations, schools, housing projects, and other public places. During this period, songwriters were also affected by the depression, and they produced such memorable songs as "Buddy, Can You Spare a Dime?" The government-sponsored murals, usually depicting familiar American scenes and historical events, gave our young artists an opportunity to develop their skills and new techniques; in return, our country obtained thousands of elaborate works of art in over one thousand American cities. Sadly, many of these art works were destroyed in later years, as public buildings were torn down or remodeled.

After complaining in vain about the quality of food in the campus restaurant, University of Colorado students are having their revenge after all. The student body recently voted to rename the grill after Alferd Packer, the only American ever convicted of cannibalism. Packer was a Utah prospector trapped with an expedition of explorers in the southwest Colorado mountains during the winter of 1874; the sole survivor of the trip, he was later tried by a jury and sentenced to hang for dining on at least five of his companions. Colorado students are now holding an annual "Alferd Packer Day" and have installed a mural relating the prospector's story on the main wall of the restaurant. Some local wits have also suggested a new motto for the bar and grill: "Serving our fellow man since 1874." Another incident of cannibalism occurred in the winter of 1846, when the Donner party, a wagon train of eighty-seven California-bound immigrants, became trapped by ice and snow in the mountains south of the Great Salt Lake.

Inventors of food products often name their new creations after real people. In 1896 Leo Hirschfield hand-rolled a chewy candy and named it after his daughter Tootsie. In 1920 Otto Schnering gave the world the Baby Ruth candy bar, named after the daughter of former President Grover Cleveland. To publicize his new product, Schnering once dropped the candy tied to tiny parachutes from an airplane flying over Pittsburgh. And one of our most popular soft drinks was named by a young suitor who sought to please his sweetheart's physician father, none other than old Dr. Pepper. Despite the honor, the girl's father never approved of the match and the young man, Wade Morrison, married someone else.

States out West have often led the way in recognizing women's roles in politics. Wyoming, for example, was the first state to give women the right to vote and hold office, back in 1869 while the state was still a territory. Wyoming was also the first state to elect a woman as governor, Nellie Tayloe Ross, in 1924. Montana elected Jeanette Rankin as the nation's first Congresswoman. U.S. Representative from Colorado, Patricia Schroeder, claims to be the first person to take the Congressional oath of office while clutching a handbag full of diapers. Ms. Schroeder later received the National Motherhood Award.

Living in a college dorm is a good way to meet people. There are activities every weekend such as dances and parties where one can get acquainted with all kinds of students. Even just sitting by someone in the cafeteria during a meal can start a friendship. Making new friends from foreign countries can teach students more about international relations. A girl on my dorm floor, for example, is from Peru, and I've learned a lot about the customs and culture in her country. She's also helping me with my study of Spanish.

APPLYING WHAT YOU'VE LEARNED TO *YOUR* WRITING

If you have written a draft of an essay, underline the topic sentence in each body paragraph and circle the key words. For example, if in an essay on America's growing health consciousness, one of your topic sentences reads "In an effort to improve their health, Americans have increased the number of vitamins they consume," you might circle "Americans," "increased," and "vitamins." Then look closely at your paragraph. All the information in that paragraph should support the idea expressed in your topic sentence; nothing should detract from the idea of showing that Americans have increased their vitamins. Now study the paragraphs in your draft, one by one. Cross out any sentences or material that interferes with the ideas in your topic sentences. If one of your paragraphs begins to drift away from its topic-sentence idea, you will need to rethink the purpose of that paragraph and rewrite so that the reader will understand what the paragraph is about. (For additional help revising your drafts, turn to Chapter 5.)

PARAGRAPH COHERENCE

In addition to unity, *coherence* is essential to a good paragraph. Coherence means that all the sentences and ideas in your paragraph flow together to make a clear, logical point about your topic. Your paragraph should not be a confusing collection of ideas set down in random order. The readers should be able to follow what you have written and see easily and quickly how each sentence grows out of, or is related to, the preceding sentence. To achieve coherence, you should have a smooth connection or transition between the sentences in your paragraphs.

There are five important means of achieving coherence in your paragraphs:

1. A natural or easily recognized order
2. Transition words and phrases
3. Repetition of key words
4. Substitution of pronouns for key nouns
5. Parallelism

These transition devices are similar to the couplings between railroad cars; they enable the controlling engine to pull the train of thought along as a unit.

A RECOGNIZABLE ORDERING OF INFORMATION

Without consciously thinking about the process, you may often organize paragraphs in easily recognized patterns that give the reader a sense of logical movement and order. Discussed below are four common patterns of ordering sentences in a paragraph:

The order of time

Some paragraphs are composed of details arranged in chronological order. You might, for example, explain the process of changing an oil filter on your car by beginning with the first step, draining the old oil, and concluding with the last step, installing the new filter. Here is a paragraph on black holes in which the writer chronologically orders her details:

> A black hole in space, from all indications, is the result of the death of a star. Scientists speculate that stars were first formed from the gases floating in the universe at the beginning of time. In the first stage in the life of a star, the hot gas is drawn by the force of gravity into a burning sphere. In the middle stage—our own sun being a middle-aged star—the burning continues at a regular rate, giving off enormous amounts of heat and light. As it grows old, however, the star eventually explodes to become what is called a nova, a superstar. But gravity soon takes over again, and the exploded star falls back in on itself with such force that all the matter in the star is compacted into a mass no larger than a few miles in diameter. At this point, no heavenly body can be seen in that area of the sky, as the tremendous pull of gravity lets nothing escape, not even light. A black hole has thus been formed.

The order of space

When your subject is a physical object, you should select some orderly means of describing it: from left to right, top to bottom, inside to outside, and so forth. For example, you might describe a sculpture as you walk around it from front to back. Below is a paragraph describing a goalie in which the writer has ordered the details of his description in a feet-to-head pattern.

> Hockey goalies must take ample time prior to a game to be sure their protective equipment is properly fitted. They start by lacing on their steel toe skates that include extra-thick tongue pads and arch guards. Then, the outside leg pads are strapped on top of an inner set of shin and knee protectors. These are clumsy and wide but absorb the bulk of the shots the goalies will deflect during a game. Loose-fitting hockey pants come next. These must allow for ample flexibility and protection of the hips. The leather gloves used both for catching and deflecting pucks are also large and flexible. They protect the wrist area as well as the hands. The upper arms, shoulders, and chest are guarded by a single unit body pad that resembles the armor knights wore generations ago; however, the pad is made of a lightweight synthetic. The throat protector is attached to the goalie's mask, a wirecage or molded piece of fiberglass. Finally, the hockey helmet holds the face mask in place while assuring total head protection.

Deductive order

A paragraph ordered deductively moves from a generalization to particular details that explain or support the general statement. Perhaps the most common pattern of all paragraphs, the deductive paragraph begins with its topic sentence and proceeds to its supporting details, as illustrated in the following example:

If 111 ninth graders in Honolulu are typical of today's teenagers, spelling and social science teachers may be in for trouble. In a recent experiment, not one of the students tested could write the Pledge of Allegiance correctly. In addition, the results showed that the students apparently had little understanding of the pledge's meaning. For example, several students described the United States as a "nation under guard" instead of "under God," and the phrase "to the Republic for which it stands" appeared in several responses as "of the richest stand" or "for Richard stand." Many students changed the word "indivisible" to the phrase "in the visible," and over nine percent of the students, all of whom are Americans from varying racial and ethnic backgrounds, misspelled the word "America."

Inductive order

An inductive paragraph begins with an examination of particular details and then concludes with a larger point or generalization about those details. Such a paragraph often ends with its topic sentence, as does the following paragraph on Little League baseball:

At almost every Little League baseball game, one or another adult creates a minor scene by yelling obscenely at an umpire or a coach. Similarly, it is fairly common to see such adults arguing loudly with each other in the stands over whose child should have caught a missed ball. Perhaps the most astounding spectacle of all, however, is an irate father or mother yanking a child off the field after a bad play for a humiliating lecture in front of the whole team. Sadly, Little League baseball today often seems intended more for childish parents than for the children who actually play it.

TRANSITION WORDS AND PHRASES

Some paragraphs may need transition words to help you move smoothly from one thought to the next so that your ideas do not appear choppy or jerky.

Here is a list of common transition words and phrases and their uses:

giving examples	for example, for instance, specifically, in particular, namely, another
comparison	similarly, not only . . . but also, in comparison
contrast	although, but, while, in contrast, however, though, on the other hand
sequence	first . . . second . . . third, and finally, moreover, also, in addition, next, then, after, furthermore
results	therefore, thus, consequently, as a result

Notice the difference the use of transition words makes in the paragraphs below:

>Working in the neighborhood grocery store as a checker was one of the worst jobs I've ever had. In the first place, I had to wear an ugly, scratchy uniform cut at least three inches too short. My schedule of working hours was another inconvenience; because my hours were changed each week, it was impossible to make plans in advance, and getting a day off was out of the question. In addition, the lack of working space bothered me. Except for a half-hour lunch break, I was restricted to three square feet of room behind the counter and consequently felt as if I were no more than a cog in the cash register.

The same paragraph rewritten without transition words sounds choppy and childish:

>Working in the neighborhood grocery store as a checker was one of the worst jobs I've ever had. I had to wear an ugly, scratchy uniform. It was cut at least three inches too short. My schedule of working hours was inconvenient. My hours changed each week. It was impossible to make plans in advance. Getting a day off was out of the question. The lack of working space bothered me. Except for a half-hour break, I was restricted to three square feet of room behind the counter. I felt like a cog in the cash register.

While transition words and phrases are useful in bridging the gaps between your ideas, don't overuse them. Not every sentence needs a transition phrase, so use one only when the relationship between your thoughts needs clarification. It's also a mistake to place the transition word in the same position in your sentence each time. Look at the paragraph below:

>It's a shame that every high school student isn't required to take a course in first aid. *For example,* you might need to treat a friend or relative for drowning during a family picnic. Or, *for instance,* someone might break a bone or receive a snakebite on a camping trip. *Also,* you should always know what to do for a common cut or burn. *Moreover,* it's important to realize when someone is in shock. *However,* very few people take the time to learn the simple rules of first aid. *Thus,* many injured or sick people suffer more than they should. *Therefore,* everyone should take a first aid course in school or at the Red Cross Center.

As you can see, a series of sentences each beginning with a transition word quickly becomes repetitious and boring. To hold your reader's attention, use transition words only when necessary to avoid choppiness, and vary their placement in your sentences.

REPETITION OF KEY WORDS

Important words or phrases (and their synonyms) may be repeated throughout a paragraph to connect the thoughts into a coherent statement:

> One of the most common, and yet most puzzling, phobias is the *fear* of *snakes*. It's only natural, of course, to be afraid of a poisonous *snake,* but many people are just as frightened of the harmless varieties. For such people, a tiny green grass *snake* is as terrifying as a cobra. Some researchers say this unreasonable *fear* of any and all *snakes* is a legacy left to us by our tree-dwelling ancestors, for whom these *reptiles* were a real and constant danger. Others maintain that the *fear* is a result of our associating the *snake* with the notion of evil, as in the Garden of Eden. Whatever the reason, the fact remains that for many otherwise normal people, the mere sight of a *snake* slithering through the countryside is enough to keep them city dwellers forever.

The repeated words "fear," "snake," and the synonym "reptile" help tie one sentence to another so that the reader may follow the ideas easily.

PRONOUNS SUBSTITUTED FOR KEY NOUNS

A pronoun is a word that stands for a noun. In your paragraph you may use a key noun in one sentence and then use a pronoun in its place in the following sentences. The pronoun "it" often replaces "shark" in the description below:

> [1]The great white shark is perhaps the best equipped of all the ocean's predators. [2]*It* can grow up to twenty-one feet and weigh three tons, with two-inch teeth that can replace themselves within twenty-four hours when damaged. [3]The shark's sense of smell is so acute *it* can detect one ounce of fish blood in a million ounces of water. [4]In addition, *it* can sense vibrations from six hundred feet away.

Sentences 2, 3, and 4 are tied to the topic sentence by the use of the pronoun "it."

PARALLELISM

Parallelism in a paragraph means using the same grammatical structures in several sentences to establish coherence. The repeated use of similar phrasing helps tie the ideas and sentences together. Next, for example, is a paragraph predominantly unified by its use of grammatically parallel sentences:

> The weather of Texas offers something for everyone. If you are the kind who likes to see snow drifting onto mountain peaks, a visit to the

Big Bend area will satisfy your eye. If, on the other hand, you demand a bright sun to bake your skin a golden brown, stop in the southern part of the state. And for hardier souls, who ask from nature a show of force, the skies of the Panhandle regularly release ferocious springtime tornadoes. Finally, if you are the fickle type, by all means come to central Texas, where the sun at any time may shine unashamed throughout the most torrential rainstorm.

The parallel structures of sentences 2, 3, and 5 ("if you" + verb) keep the paragraph flowing smoothly from one idea to the next.

USING A VARIETY OF TRANSITION DEVICES

Most writers use a combination of transition devices in their paragraphs. In the following example, three kinds of transition devices are circled. See if you can identify each one.

Transitions are the glue that holds a paragraph together.

These devices lead the reader from sentence to sentence, smoothing

over the gaps between by indicating the relationship between the

sentences. If this glue is missing, the paragraph will almost

inevitably sound choppy or childish, even if every sentence in it

responds to a single topic commitment. However, transitions are

not substitutes for topic unity: like most glue, they are most

effective when joining similar objects, or, in this case, similar

ideas. For example, in a paragraph describing a chicken egg, no

transition could bridge the gap created by the inclusion of a

sentence concerned with naval losses in the Civil War. In other

words, transitions can call attention to the topic relationships

between sentences, but they cannot create those relationships.

transition words	repetition of pronouns	repetition of key words

PRACTICING WHAT YOU'VE LEARNED

A. Identify each of the following paragraphs as ordered by time, space, or parallelism:

My apartment is so small that it will no longer hold all my possessions. Every day when I come in the door, I am shocked by the clutter. The wall to my immediate left is completely obscured by art and movie posters that have become so numerous they often overlap, hiding even each other. Along the adjoining wall is my stereo equipment: albums and tapes are stacked several feet high on two long, low tables. The big couch that runs across the back of the room is always piled so high with schoolbooks and magazines that a guest usually ends up sitting on the floor. To my right is a large sliding glass door that opens onto a balcony—or at least it used to, before it was permanently blocked by my tennis gear, golf clubs, and ten-speed bike. Even the tiny closet next to the front door is bursting with clothes, both clean and dirty. I think the time has come for me to move.

Once-common acts of greeting may be finding renewed popularity after three centuries. According to one historian, kissing was at the height of its popularity as a greeting in seventeenth-century England, when ladies and gentlemen of the court often saluted each other in this affectionate manner. Then the country was visited by a strange plague, whose cause was unknown. Because no one knew how the plague was spread, people tried to avoid physical contact with others as much as possible. Both kissing and the handshake went out of fashion and were replaced by the bow and curtsy, so people could greet others without having to touch them. The bow and curtsy remained in vogue for over a hundred years, until the handshake—for men only—returned to popularity in the nineteenth century. Today, both men and women may shake hands upon meeting others, and kissing as a greeting is making a comeback—especially among the jet-setters and Hollywood stars.

Students have diverse ways of preparing for final exams. Some stay up the night before, trying to cram into their brains what they avoided all term. Others pace themselves, spending a little time each night going over the notes they took in class that day. Still others cross their fingers and hope they absorbed enough from lectures. A dishonest few pray that their fellow students will give them the answers. In the end, though, everyone hopes the tests are easy.

B. Circle and identify the transition devices in the following paragraphs:

Each year I follow a system when preparing firewood to use in my stove. First, I hike about a mile from my house with my bow saw in hand. I then select three good size oak trees and mark them with orange ties. Next, I saw through the base of each tree about two feet from the ground. After I fell the trees, not only do I trim away the branches, but I also sort the scrap from the usable limbs. I find cutting the trees into manageable length logs is too much for one day; however, I roll them off the ground so they will not begin to rot. The next day I cut the trees into eight-foot lengths, which allows me to handle them more easily. Once they are cut, I roll them along the fire lane to the edge of the road where I stack them neatly but not too high. The next day I borrow my uncle's van, drive to the pile of logs, and load as many logs as I can, thus reducing the number of trips. When I finally have all the logs in my backyard, I begin sawing them into eighteen-inch lengths. I create large piles that consequently have to be split and finally stacked. The logs will age and dry until winter when I will make daily trips to the woodpile.

Fans of professional baseball and football argue continually over which is America's favorite spectator sport. Though the figures on attendance for each vary with every new season, certain arguments remain the same, spelling out both the enduring appeals of each game and something about the people who love to watch. Football, for instance, is a quicker, more physical sport, and football fans enjoy the emotional involvement they feel while watching. Baseball, on the other hand, seems more mental, like chess, and attracts those fans who prefer a quieter, more complicated game. In addition, professional football teams usually play no more than fourteen games a year, providing fans with a whole week between games to work themselves up to a pitch of excitement and expectation. Baseball teams, however, play almost every day for six months, so that the typical baseball fan is not so crushed by missing a game, knowing there will be many other chances to attend. Finally, football fans seem to love the half-time pageantry, the marching bands, and the pretty cheerleaders, whereas baseball fans are more content to concentrate on the game's finer details and spend the breaks between innings filling out their own private scorecards.

C. These paragraphs lack common transition devices. Fill in each blank with the appropriate transition word or key word.

#1

Scientists continue to debate the cause of the dinosaurs' disappearance. One group claims the _____ vanished after a comet smashed into the Earth; dust and smoke _____ blocked the sun for a long time. _____ of no direct sunlight, the Earth underwent a lengthy "winter," far too cold for the huge _____ to survive. A University of Berkeley paleontologist, _____ , disputes this claim. He argues that _____ we generally think of _____ living in swampy land, fossils found in Alaska show that _____ could live in cold climates _____ warm ones. _____ group claims that the _____ became extinct following an intense period of global volcanic activity. _____ to killing the _____ themselves, these scientists _____ believe the volcanic activity killed much of the plant life that the _____ ate and, _____ , many of the great _____ who survived the volcanic eruptions starved to death. Still _____ groups of _____ claim the _____ were destroyed by acid rain, _____ by a passing "death star," _____ even by visitors from outer space.

#2

A recent study by the National Center for Health Statistics has revealed some fascinating information for those of us interested in living longer lives. The _____ shows, for _____ , that people live longest in Hawaii, where the average _____ is 77.02 years. _____ , in Washington, D.C., the expected span is the lowest: only 69.2 years. _____ to Hawaii, states that boast long expectancies include Minnesota, Iowa, and Utah, _____ residents of Louisiana, South Carolina, Mississippi are on the lower end of the scale. _____ , according to the _____ research, women can expect to live almost seven years longer than men. Congratulations to those Hawaiian women who will see us well into the twenty-first century!

D. The sentences in each of the following exercises are out of order. By noting the various transition devices, you should be able to arrange each group of sentences into a coherent paragraph.

Paragraph One: How To Purchase a New Car

- If you're happy with the car's performance, find out about available financing arrangements.
- Later, at home, study your notes carefully to help you decide which car fits your needs.
- After you have discussed various loans and interest rates, you can negotiate the final price with the salesperson.
- A visit to the showroom also allows you to test-drive the car.
- Once you have agreed on the car's price, feel confident you have made a well-chosen purchase.
- Next, a visit to a nearby showroom should help you select the color, options, and style of the car of your choice.
- First, take a trip to the library to read the current auto magazines.
- As you read, take notes on models and prices.

Paragraph Two: Henry VIII and the Problems of Succession

- After Jane, Henry took three more wives, but all these marriages were childless.

7 • Jane did produce a son, Edward VI, but he died at age fifteen.

2 • The problem of succession was therefore an important issue during the reign of Henry VIII.

6 • Still hoping for a son, Henry beheaded Anne and married Jane Seymour.

9 • Thus, despite his six marriages, Henry failed in his attempts to secure the succession.

1 • In sixteenth-century England it was considered essential for a son to assume the throne.

3 • Henry's first wife, Catherine of Aragon, had only one child, the Princess Mary.

5 • But Anne also produced a daughter, the future Queen Elizabeth I.

4 • Consequently, he divorced Catherine and married Anne Boleyn.

PARAGRAPH SEQUENCE

The order in which you present your paragraphs is another decision you must make. In some essays, the subject matter itself will suggest its own order.* For instance, in an essay designed to instruct a beginning jogger, you might want to discuss the necessary equipment—good jogging shoes, loose-fitting clothing, sweatband—before moving to a discussion of where to jog and how to jog. Other essays, however, may not suggest a natural order, in which case you yourself must decide which order will most effectively reach and hold the attention of your audience. Frequently, writers withhold their strongest point until last. (Lawyers often use this technique; they first present the jury with the weakest arguments, then pull out the most damning evidence—the "smoking pistol." Thus the jury members retire with the strongest argument freshest in their minds.) Sometimes, however, you'll find it necessary to present one particular point first, so that the other points make good sense. Study your own major points and decide which order will be the most logical, successful way of persuading your reader to accept your thesis.

TRANSITIONS BETWEEN PARAGRAPHS

As you already know, each paragraph usually signals a new major point in your discussion. These paragraphs should not appear as isolated blocks of thought, but rather as parts of a unified, step-by-step progression. To avoid a choppy essay, link each paragraph to the one before it with *transition devices*. Just as the sentences in your paragraphs are connected, so are the paragraphs themselves; therefore, you can use the same transition devices suggested on pages 64–67.

---

* For more information on easily recognized patterns of order, see pp. 62–64.

The first sentence of most body paragraphs frequently contains the transition device. To illustrate this point, here are some topic sentences lifted from the body paragraphs of a student essay criticizing a popular sports car, renamed the 'Gator to protect the guilty and to prevent lawsuits. The transition devices are italicized.

Thesis: The 'Gator is one of the worst cars on the market.

- When you buy a *'Gator,* you buy physical inconvenience. [repetition of key word from thesis]
- *Another* reason the *'Gator* is a bad buy is the cost of insurance. [transition word, key word]
- You might overlook the *inconvenient* size and exorbitant *insurance* rates if the *'Gator* were a strong, reliable car, *but* this automobile constantly needs repair. [key words from preceding paragraphs, transition word]
- When you decide to sell this *car,* you face *still another* unpleasant surprise: the extremely low resale value. [key word, transition phrase]
- *But* perhaps the most serious drawback is the *'Gator's* safety record. [transition word, key word]

Sometimes, instead of using transition words or repetition of key words or their synonyms, you can use an *idea hook.* The last idea of one paragraph may lead you smoothly into your next paragraph. Instead of repeating a key word from the previous discussion, find a phrase that refers to the entire idea just expressed. If, for example, the previous paragraph discussed the highly complimentary advertising campaign for the 'Gator, the next paragraph might begin, "This view of the 'Gator as an economy car is ridiculous to anyone who's pumped a week's salary into this gas guzzler." The phrase "this view" connects the idea of the first paragraph with the one that follows. Idea hooks also work well with transition words: "This view, however, is ridiculous . . ."

If you do use transition words, don't allow them to make your essay sound mechanical. For example, a long series of paragraphs beginning "first . . . second . . . third . . ." quickly becomes boring. Vary the type and position of your transition devices so that your essay has a subtle but logical movement from point to point.

APPLYING WHAT YOU'VE
LEARNED TO *YOUR* WRITING

If you are currently working on a draft of an essay, check each body paragraph for coherence, the smooth connection of ideas and sentences in a logical, easy-to-follow order. You might try placing brackets around key words, pronouns, and transition words that carry the reader's attention from thought to thought and from sentence to sentence. Decide whether you have enough ordering devices, placed in appropriate places, or whether you need to add (or delete) others. (For additional help in revising your draft, turn to Chapter 5.)

CHAPTER 3 SUMMARY

Here is a brief restatement of what you should know about the paragraphs in the body of your essay:

1. Each body paragraph usually contains one major point in the discussion promised by the thesis statement.
2. Each major point is presented in the topic sentence of a paragraph.
3. Each paragraph should be adequately developed with clear supporting detail.
4. Every sentence in the paragraph should support the topic sentence. (Unity)
5. There should be an orderly, logical flow from sentence to sentence, thought to thought. (Coherence)
6. The sequence of your essay's paragraphs should be logical and effective.
7. There should be a smooth flow from paragraph to paragraph.
8. The body paragraphs should successfully persuade your reader that the opinion expressed in your thesis is valid.

4

Beginnings and Endings

To complete your rough draft, you should think of an essay as a coherent, unified whole composed of three main parts: the introduction (lead-in, thesis, and essay map), the body (paragraphs with supporting evidence), and the conclusion (final address to the reader). These three parts should flow smoothly into one another, presenting the reader with an organized, logical discussion. The following pages will suggest ways to begin, end, and name your essay effectively.

HOW TO WRITE A GOOD LEAD-IN

The first few sentences of your essay are particularly important; first impressions, as you know, are often lasting ones. The beginning of your essay, then, must catch the readers' attention and make them want to keep reading. Recall the way you read a magazine: if you are like most people, you probably skim the magazine, reading a paragraph or two of each article that looks promising. If the first few paragraphs hold your interest, you read on. When you write your own introductory paragraph, assume that you have only a few sentences to attract your reader. Consequently, you must pay particular attention to making those first lines especially interesting and well-written.

In some essays, your thesis statement alone may be controversial or striking enough to capture the readers.* At other times, however, you will want to use the introductory device called a *lead-in*. The lead-in (1) catches the readers'

---

* Do note that for some writing assignments, such as certain kinds of technical reports, attention-grabbing lead-ins are not appropriate. Frequently, these reports are directed toward particular professional audiences and have their own designated format; they often begin, for example, with a statement of the problem under study or with a review of pertinent information or research.

attention, (2) announces the subject matter and tone of your essay (humorous, satiric, serious, etc.), and (3) sets up, or leads into, the presentation of your thesis and essay map.

Here are some suggestions and examples of lead-ins:

1. A paradoxical or intriguing statement

"Eat two chocolate bars and call me in the morning," says the psychiatrist to his patient. Such advice sounds like a sugar fanatic's dream, but recent studies have indeed confirmed that chocolate positively affects depression and anxiety.

2. An arresting statistic or shocking statement

One of every seven women living in Smith County will be raped this year, according to a recent report prepared by the Country Rape Information and Counseling Services.

3. A question

It is three times the number of people who belong to the Southern Baptist Convention, nine times the number who serve in the U.S. armed forces, and more than twice the number who voted for Barry Goldwater for President in 1964. What is it? It's the number of people in the U.S. who admit to having smoked marijuana: a massive 62 million.

4. A quotation or literary allusion

"I think onstage nudity is disgusting, shameful, and damaging to all things American," says actress Shelley Winters. "But if I were twenty-two with a great body, it would be artistic, tasteful, patriotic, and a progressive religious experience."

5. A relevant story, joke, or anecdote

A group of young women were questioning Saturday afternoon shoppers about their views on the 1982 defeat of the Equal Rights Amendment. One old man in overalls answered, "ERA? Well, I like it just fine. But you know, I can't pick it up on my darned old radio after dark." That was the problem—too few people knew what the ERA really stood for.

6. A description, often used for emotional appeal

With one eye blackened, one arm in a cast, and third-degree burns on both her legs, the pretty, blond two-year-old seeks corners of rooms, refuses to speak, and shakes violently at the sound of loud noises. Tammy is not the victim of a war or a natural disaster; rather, she is the helpless victim of her parents, one of the thousands of children who suffer daily from America's hidden crime, child abuse.

7. A factual statement or a summary who-what-where-when-and-why lead-in

Texas's first execution of a woman in 22 years is scheduled for September 17 at the Huntsville Unit of the state's Department of Correction, despite the protests of various human rights groups around the country.

8. An analogy or contrast

The Romans kept geese on their Capitol Hill to cackle alarm in the event of attack by night. Modern Americans, despite their technology, have hardly improved on that old system of protection. According to the latest Safety Council report, almost any door with standard locks can be opened easily with a common plastic credit card.

9. A personal experience

I realized times were changing for women when I overheard my six-year-old nephew speaking to my sister, a prominent New York lawyer. As we left her elaborate, luxurious office one evening, Tommy looked up at his mother and queried, "Mommy, can little boys grow up to be lawyers, too?"

10. A catalogue of relevant examples

A two-hundred-pound teenager quit school because no desk would hold her. A three-hundred-pound chef who could no longer stand on his feet was fired. A three-hundred-fifty-pound truck driver broke furniture in his friends' houses. All these people are now living better, happier, and thinner lives, thanks to the remarkable intestinal bypass surgery first developed in 1967.

11. Statement of a problem or a popular misconception

Some people believe that poetry is written only by aging beatniks or solemn, mournful men and women with suicidal tendencies. The Poetry in the Schools Program is working hard to correct that erroneous point of view.

Thinking of a good lead-in is often difficult when you sit down to begin your essay. Many writers, in fact, skip the lead-in until the first draft is written. They compose their working thesis first and then write the body of the essay, saving the lead-in and conclusion for last. As you write the middle of your essay, you may discover an especially interesting piece of information you might want to save to use as your lead-in.

AVOIDING ERRORS IN LEAD-INS

In addition to the previous suggestions, here is some advice to help you avoid common lead-in errors:

Make sure your lead-in introduces your thesis. A frequent weakness in introductory paragraphs is an interesting lead-in but no smooth or clear transition to the thesis statement. To avoid a gap or awkward jump in thought in your introductory paragraph, you may need to add a connecting sentence or phrase between your lead-in and thesis. Study the paragraph below, which uses a comparison as its lead-in. The italicized transition sentence takes the reader from a general comment on all disabled Americans to information about those in Smallville, smoothly preparing the reader for the thesis that follows.

lead-in	In the 1950s black Americans demanded and won the right to sit anywhere they pleased on public buses. Today, another large group of Americans—the disabled confined to wheelchairs—is fighting for the simple right to board those same buses.
transition sentence	*Here in Smallville, as well as in other cities, the lack of proper boarding facilities often denies disabled citizens basic transportation to jobs, grocery stores, and medical centers.*
thesis	In order to give persons confined to wheelchairs the same opportunities as those given to other residents, the Smallville City Council should vote the funds necessary to convert the public transportation system so that it may be used by disabled citizens.

Make your lead-in brief. Long lead-ins in short essays often give the appearance of a tail wagging the dog. Use a brief, attention-catching hook to set up your thesis; don't make your introduction the biggest part of your essay.

Don't begin with an apology or complaint. Statements such as "I don't know much about coin collecting, but . . ." and "This assignment is difficult, but . . ." do nothing to entice your reader.

Don't assume your audience already knows your subject matter. Identify the pertinent facts even though you know your teacher knows the assignment. ("The biggest flaw in this experiment occurred in the last step." What experiment?) If you are writing about a particular piece of literature, identify the title of the work and its author, using the writer's full name in the first reference.

Stay clear of overused lead-ins. If composition teachers had a nickel for every essay that began with a dictionary definition, they could all retire to Bermuda. Leave *Webster's* alone and find a livelier way to begin. Using a question for your lead-in is becoming overused, too, so use it only when it is obviously the best choice for your opener.

PRACTICING WHAT YOU'VE LEARNED

Find three good lead-ins from essays, magazine articles, or newspaper feature stories. Identify the kinds of lead-ins you found, and tell why you think each effectively catches the reader's attention and sets up the thesis.

HOW TO WRITE A GOOD CONCLUDING PARAGRAPH

Like a good story, a good essay should not stop in the middle. It should have a satisfying conclusion, one that gives the reader a sense of completion on the subject. Don't allow your essay to drop off or fade out at the end—instead, use the concluding paragraph to emphasize the validity of your argument. Remember that the concluding paragraph is your last chance to convince the reader. (As one cynical but realistic student pointed out, the conclusion is the last part of your essay the teacher reads before putting a grade on your paper.) Therefore, make your conclusion count.

Here are some suggestions for ending your essays and some samples:

1. A restatement of both the thesis and the essay's major points (for long essays only)

> As much as we may dislike the notion, it's time to reinstate the military draft. With the armed services' failure to meet its recruitment goals, the rising costs of defense, and the racism and sexism inherent in our volunteer system, we have no other choice if we wish a protected future.

2. An evaluation of the importance of the essay's subject

> These amazing, controversial photographs of the comet will continue to be the subject of debate because, according to some scientists, they yield the most important clues yet revealed about the origins of our universe.

3. A statement of the essay's broader implications

> Because these studies of feline leukemia may someday play a crucial role in the discovery of a cure for AIDS in human beings, the experiments, as expensive as they are, must continue.

4. A call to action

> The fate of Raoul Wallenberg is still unknown. While Congress has awarded him honorary citizenship, such a tribute is not enough. We must

write our Congressional representatives today to voice our demand that the Soviets either release him or cite proof of his death. No hero deserves less.

5. A prophecy or warning based on the essay's thesis

Understanding the politics that led up to Hiroshima is essential for all Americans—indeed, for all the world's peoples. Without such knowledge, the frightful possibility exists that somewhere, sometime, someone may drop the bomb again.

6. A witticism that emphasizes or sums up the point of the essay

No one said dieting was easy. But for some of us who have struggled long, the cliché "Half a loaf is better than none" has taken on new meaning!

7. A quotation, story, or joke that emphasizes or sums up the point of the essay

Bette Davis's role on and off the screen as the catty, wisecracking woman of steel helped make her an enduring star. After all, no audience, past or present, could ever resist a dame who drags on a cigarette and then mutters about a passing starlet, "There goes a good time that was had by all."

8. An image or description that lends finality to the essay

As the last of the Big Screen's giant ants are incinerated by the army scientist, one can almost hear the movie audiences of the 1950s breathing a collective sigh of relief, secure in the knowledge that once again the threat of nuclear radiation had been vanquished by the efforts of the U.S. military.

(For another brief image that captures the essence of an essay, see also the "open house" scene that concludes "To Bid the World Farewell," p. 168.)

9. A rhetorical question that makes the readers think about the essay's main point

No one wants to see hostages put in danger. But what nation can afford to let terrorists know they can get away with murder?

10. An emphatic summary of the essay's thesis, stated in fresh terms

Soap operas are popular not because they're mindless drivel formulated to distract us from our daily chores, but because they present life as many of us want it to be: fast-paced, glamorous, and full of exciting characters.

AVOIDING ERRORS IN CONCLUSIONS

Try to omit the following common errors in your concluding paragraphs:

Avoid a mechanical ending. One of the most frequent weaknesses in student essays is the conclusion that merely restates the thesis, word-for-word. A short essay of 500–750 words rarely requires a summary point-by-point conclusion—in fact, such an ending often insults the readers' intelligence by implying that their attention spans are extremely short. Only after reading long essays do most readers need a precise recap of the writer's main ideas. Instead of recopying your thesis and essay map, try finding an original, emphatic way to conclude your essay—or, as a well-known newspaper columnist recently described it, a good ending should snap with grace and authority, like the close of an expensive sports car door.

Don't introduce new points. Treat the major points of your essay in separate body paragraphs rather than in your exit.

Don't tack on a conclusion. There should be a smooth flow from your last body paragraph into your concluding statements.

Don't change your stance. Sometimes writers who have been critical of something throughout their essays will soften their stance or offer apologies in their last paragraph. For instance, someone complaining about the poor quality of a particular college course might abruptly conclude with statements that declare the class wasn't so bad after all, maybe he or she should have worked harder, or maybe he or she really did learn something after all. Such reneging may seem polite, but in actuality it undercuts the thesis and confuses the reader who has taken the writer's criticisms seriously. Instead of contradicting themselves, writers should stand their ground, forget about puffy clichés or "niceties," and find an emphatic way to conclude that is consistent with their thesis.

Avoid trite expressions. Don't begin your conclusions by declaring, "in conclusion," "in summary," or "as you can see, this essay proves my thesis that. . . ." End your essay so that the reader clearly senses completion; don't merely announce that you're finished.

PRACTICING WHAT YOU'VE LEARNED

Find three good concluding paragraphs. Identify each kind of conclusion and tell why you think it is an effective ending for the essay or article.

HOW TO WRITE A GOOD TITLE

As in the case of lead-ins, your title may be written at any time, but many writers prefer to finish their essays before naming them. A good title is similar to a good newspaper headline in that it attracts the readers' interest and makes them want to investigate the essay. Like the lead-in, the title also helps announce the tone of the essay. An informal or humorous essay, for instance, might have a catchy, funny title. Some titles show the writer's wit and love of wordplay; a survey of recent magazines revealed these titles: "Bittersweet News about Saccharin," "Coffee: New Grounds for Concern," and "The Scoop on the Best Ice Cream."

On the other hand, a serious, informative essay should have a more formal title that suggests its content as clearly and specifically as possible. Let's suppose, for example, that you are doing research on the meaning of color in dreams, and you run across an essay listed in the library's *Readers' Guide* titled merely "Dreams." You don't know whether you should read it. To avoid such confusion in your own essay and to encourage readers' interest, always use a specific title: "Animal Imagery in Dreams," "Dream Research in Dogs," and so forth. Moreover, if your subject matter is controversial, let the reader know which side you're on (e.g., "The Advantages of Solar Power"). Never substitute a mere label, such as "Football Games" or "Euthanasia," for a meaningful title. And never, never label your essays "theme one" or "comparison and contrast essay." In all your writing, including the title, use your creativity to attract the readers' attention and to invite their interest in your ideas.

If you're unsure about how to present your title, here are two basic rules:

1. Your own title should *not* be underlined or put in quotation marks. It should be written at the top of page one of your essay or on an appropriate cover sheet with no special marks of punctuation.

2. Only the first word and the important words of your title should be capitalized. Generally, we do not capitalize words such as "an," "and," "a," or "the," or prepositions, unless they appear as the first word of the title.

ASSIGNMENT

Select any three of the student or professional essays in this text; give the first one a better title; the second, a more interesting lead-in; the third, a more emphatic or smoother conclusion. Why are your choices as effective or even better than those of the original writers?

APPLYING WHAT YOU'VE LEARNED TO *YOUR* WRITING

Look at the draft of the essay you are currently working on and ask yourself these questions:

- Does the opening of my essay make my reader want to continue reading? Does the lead-in smoothly set up my thesis or do I need to add some sort of transition to help move the reader to my main idea? Is the lead-in appropriate in terms of the tone and length of my essay?

- Does the conclusion of my essay offer an emphatic ending, one that is consistent with my essay's purpose? Have I avoided a mechanical, trite, or tacked-on closing paragraph? Have I refrained from adding a new point in my conclusion that belongs in the body of my essay or in another essay?

- Does my title interest my reader? Is its content and tone appropriate for this particular essay?

If you have answered "no" to any of the above questions, you should continue revising your essay. (For more help revising your prose, turn to Chapter 5.)

CHAPTER 4 SUMMARY

Here is a brief restatement of what you should remember about writing introductions, conclusions, and titles:

1. Many essays will profit from a lead-in, the first sentences of the introductory paragraph that attract the reader's attention and smoothly set up the thesis statement.
2. Essays should end convincingly, without being repetitious or trite, with thoughts that emphasize the writer's main purpose.
3. Titles should invite the reader's interest by indicating the general nature of essay's content and its tone.

5

Revising
Your Writing

"There is no good writing, only rewriting"—James Thurber

"When I say writing, O, believe me, it is rewriting that I have chiefly in mind"—Robert Louis Stevenson

The absolute necessity of revision cannot be overemphasized. All good writers rethink, rearrange, and rewrite large portions of their prose. The French novelist Colette, for instance, wrote everything over and over. In fact, she often spent an entire morning working on a single page. Hemingway, to cite another example, rewrote the ending to *A Farewell to Arms* thirty-nine times. While no one expects you to make thirty-nine drafts of each essay, the point is clear: revision is an essential part of good writing. It is part of your commitment to your reader. Therefore, plan to spend at least a third to a half of your overall writing time revising and polishing your essay.

Try not to think of revision as an activity that is begun only after you've finished your last rough draft. Nor is revision merely proofreading for errors before you hand in your paper. Revision is a *thinking process* that can occur anytime: while you are writing a draft, or in between drafts, or at the end of a draft. In other words, you can revise a word, sentence, or paragraph as soon as you've written it or you can revise an entire essay; most writers, in fact, do both. But whenever you revise, remember that you are not merely editing for style or correcting surface errors—rather, you are making important decisions about the best ways to organize, develop, and clarify your information.

While each of us has an individual approach to revising, here are some suggestions for composing and rethinking your drafts that you may find helpful.

PREPARING THE FIRST DRAFT

1. Once you have a focused topic, a working thesis, and perhaps an essay map or rough outline to guide you, begin your first draft. One of the most important points to remember now is that no part of your rough draft is sacred or permanent. No matter what you have written, *you can always change it.* After all, one of the main purposes of the first draft is to discover what you really think about your subject. As you write, you may find that new ideas are surfacing that are better than those you first anticipated, and you may want to follow them. That's fine — the act of writing is a discovery process as well as the recording or recollecting of ideas.

2. Always write on one side of your paper only, in case you want to cut and tape together portions of your first and/or subsequent drafts rather than recopying the entire essay over and over. Leave big margins on all sides of your rough drafts so you can add information or jot down minor corrections. If you are typing, double or triple space for the same reason.

3. As you write, you may find yourself deciding to delete a sentence or an entire passage here and there. If so, mark a single "X" or line through the material; don't scratch it out completely—you might decide later you want to reinsert the material or use it elsewhere.

4. If you cannot think of a word you want, put down a word close to the one you want, circle it, and go on. Keep writing; don't agonize over every word. Similarly, put a check in the margin by sentences that don't quite hit the mark. The important point now is to keep going, to keep the ideas flowing.

5. If you experience Writer's Block, read the suggestions on pages 89–91 of this chapter.

REVISING THE FIRST DRAFT

1. Two thousand years ago, the Roman author Horace advised a young writer, "Put all your manuscript away and keep it for nine years. You can always destroy what you have not published; there is no art to unsay what you have once let go of." Of course, you won't often have the time to follow this wise advice, but it is still a good idea, after you've written the first draft, to go away for several hours—overnight, if possible. All writers become tired, and if you push yourself too hard, the fatigue will show in your prose. You're also much more aware of the weak spots in your essay when you have had some distance from your prose than when it's still hot from the pen.

2. *Important:* When you do return to your draft, *don't try to look at all the parts of your paper, from ideas to organization to word choice to mechanics, at the same time.* Doing so is impossible and will only overload and frustrate you.

At this point, reread your paper for *purpose* and *audience* only, thinking over such questions as

- Has your essay fulfilled the purpose of your assignment? (For example, if you were asked to analyze a book's character, did you or did you merely summarize plot?)
- Did you follow directions carefully? (If you were given a three-part assignment, did you treat all the parts as requested?)
- If you were asked to address a particular audience, did you do so or did you begin writing to someone else (or to yourself)?
- Did your discussion contain the information pertinent for your particular readers? (For other questions regarding audience, see pp. 16–18.)

3. Once you're satisfied with your commitment to your essay's purpose and audience, look closely at your essay's *focus* and *organization*. Ask yourself such questions as

- Is your thesis sufficiently focused and expressed in clear, specific terms? (Remember that writers often try to take on subjects that are too large or too vaguely expressed; pinning yourself down to exactly the idea you want to talk about will help you organize and develop the rest of your paper.)
- Do your major points in your body paragraphs support your thesis? (If you discover that after you've written your first draft, your body paragraphs do not support the thesis, don't despair. See if the thesis can be rewritten to fit the essay; you may have had a slightly different thesis in mind all along, or a better one may have evolved as you organized your thoughts in writing.)
- Have you included all the points you wanted to cover?
- Are your paragraphs arranged in a logical order or a pattern that's easy to follow?
- Are your ideas within each paragraph ordered sensibly?
- Is any part of your paper out of proportion? Too long or short?
- Does your paper begin or end abruptly?

If you are like most writers, you will almost certainly need to prepare a second draft to untangle some of the organizational snags.

REVISING THE SECOND DRAFT

Once you are happy with the organization of the paper, look closely at the *development* of your ideas. You might think of work on development in terms of the hourglass pictured on the following page.

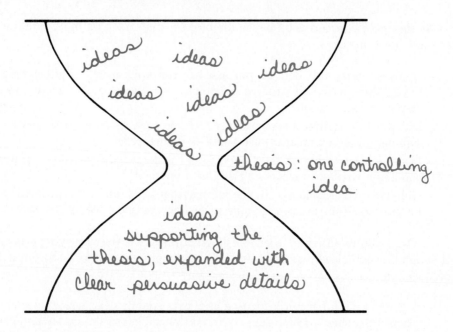

When you begin thinking about a subject, your ideas may be scattered about, random and unfocused, going off in many different directions. Then as you pre-write and find a controlling idea, your focus narrows into the presentation of one main idea or thesis. As you draft the supporting body paragraphs, your ideas must expand again, so that your readers will find enough information to convince them of the validity of your claims.

To help you revise your development, ask yourself these questions:

- Do you have enough supporting evidence to make your points clear and convincing?
- Is each of your ideas explained through use of specific details rather than fuzzy generalities?
- Which ideas need additional information or details to make them completely clear to your readers?
- Which ideas or comments should be deleted because they're off the subject or merely padding?
- Are any ideas repetitious? Any that should be combined?

Remember that for many beginning writers, underdeveloped or overly general ideas are often the biggest problems, so spend as much time as you can revising your prose to ensure that, first, you have provided enough information and, second, that the information has been expressed in enough specific detail (for more help with development, see pp. 52–56).

REVISING THE THIRD DRAFT

Revision at this point should focus on *clarity, conciseness,* and *vividness.*

1. Read each sentence carefully. Is each one as clear and precise as possible? Are there any that run on for too long or any that contain misplaced words or phrases that might cause confusion? Are your words and their connotations accurate and appropriate?

2. Almost every writer has a wordiness problem. Scrutinize your writing for ways to cut excess words. Search out and destroy deadwood phrases, circumlocutions, "to be" and other space-wasting verb-and-noun combinations (review pp. 102–105 for some specific phrases to guard against). Combine choppy or repetitive sentences wherever possible. (To help you decide if you need to combine sentences, you might try this experiment. Select a body paragraph and count the number of words it contains. Then count the number of sentences; divide the number of words by the number of sentences to discover the average number of words per sentence. If your score is less than 15-18, you may need to combine some sentences.)

3. After pruning your essay to the essentials, work on making your writing as vivid and pleasing as possible. Replace bland or passive verbs with active, vigorous ones; change blah surface descriptions into more fascinating ones by adding specific details. Delete unnecessary jargon or "officialese," and substitute original, arresting words for clichés and predictable phrases. Try to put yourself in the reader's place by thinking of the Johnny Carson Show. Carson: "The lake was so beautiful today." Audience: "How beautiful was it?" Help the reader, your audience, see how "it" was by selecting the best words to describe it.

For advice on both sentence construction and word choice, review Chapters 6 and 7.

THE FINAL TOUCHES

1. Review your essay for errors in spelling, grammar, and punctuation. Part Three, the handbook section of this text, may help you resolve any questions you have about mechanics; the section on spelling on pp. 334–336 may be helpful too. If punctuation is a major problem for you, keep a list of the mistakes you make in each essay. Read your rough draft for one of these errors at a time: once for fragments, once for comma splices, once for run-ons, and so on. In addition, while you are looking for grammar and punctuation errors, you may find it helpful to read your essay one sentence at a time—starting at the *end* of the essay and working toward the beginning. This way you are less likely to begin thinking about the content of your essay and wander off the job of looking for errors in mechanics. (Review, too, the hints in Chapter 6 on constructing clear, correct sentences.)

2. Go over the checklist on page 91–92. Revise (yes, again!) any part of your essay that seems weak.

3. Try to type your final draft. Not only will your essay look better, but you will also be able to catch more errors yourself before you hand in the paper. Misspelled words and underdeveloped paragraphs, for example, are much more obvious to a writer once the essay is typed. Avoid typing paper that smears easily or that is too slick to receive comments written with a ballpoint pen—leave onionskin to onions.

4. Proofread your final draft at least twice, preferably several hours after you have typed it. Remember that typing errors can change the meaning of an entire thought, not to mention the unintended humor they can cause (imagine, for instance, the response of new restaurant owners whose lease instructed them to "Please sing the terms stated above." Was the contract presented a cappella or in chorus?)

5. Make a copy of your final draft—or at least save your rough drafts—in case your essay is accidentally lost. If you are asked to rewrite parts of your essay, referring to the early drafts may suggest some worthwhile options.

A SPECIAL NOTE FOR WRITERS WITH WORD PROCESSORS

If you have access to a computer and any of the many word-processing programs available today, you have probably already discovered how helpful this technology can be to writers in all stages of the writing process. You can, for example, store your prewriting activities, journal entries, notes, or good ideas in various files until you need to recall certain information, and you can easily produce extra copies of your drafts or finished essay without having to search out a copy machine and correct change. Spelling checkers or dictionaries may identify many of your common errors and typos.

But the most important use of the computer to a writer may be what it can do as you draft and revise your prose. At your command, a word-processing program enables you to add, delete, or change words; it allows you to move words, sentences, even paragraphs or larger chunks of your essay. On any computer, for example, you can play "What if" by dropping the cursor below what you have written and try phrasing your idea another way. Then delete the less effective passage. With some programs, you can even compare drafts side-by-side or with special "windows" that help you to see your rhetorical choices more clearly. In other words, computers can help us as writers do the kind of *deep-structure revision* that is necessary to produce our best, most effective prose—the kind of major changes that, in the past, we may have been hesitant to make because of the time involved in recopying or retyping major portions of our rough drafts.

Whether the program you are using at home or at school is a series of simple commands or an elaborate instructional system that can ask questions or provide a sophisticated analysis of your writing, make a point of getting to know how to use the computer in the most effective ways. Study the manual that accompanies your word-processing program (or one of the many self-help manuals now on the market), and don't be afraid to ask your instructor or computer-lab monitor for assistance. The more you practice using your programs to help you organize, develop, and revise your prose, the better your writing will be. (One important piece of advice: to avoid the "agony of delete," always remember to save what you have written every ten minutes or so, and do print out a copy of each major draft or set of revisions in case your system crashes or you accidently hit the wrong keys!)

SOME LAST ADVICE: HOW TO PLAY WITH YOUR MENTAL BLOCKS

Every writer, sooner or later, suffers from some form of Writer's Block, the inability to think of and/or organize ideas. Symptoms may include sweaty palms, pencil chewing, and a pronounced tendency to sit in corners and weep. While not every "cure" works for everyone, here are a few suggestions to help minimize your misery:

Try to give yourself as much time as possible to write your essay. Don't try to write the entire paper in one sitting. By doing so, you may place yourself under too much pressure. Writer's Block often accompanies the "up against the wall" feeling that strikes at two A.M. the morning your essay is due at nine. Rome wasn't constructed in a day, and neither are most good essays.

Since most of you have had more experience talking than writing, try verbalizing your ideas. Sometimes it's helpful to discuss your ideas with a friend or classmate. Their questions and comments (not to mention their sympathy for your temporary block) will often trigger the thoughts you need to begin writing again. Or you might want to talk into a tape recorder so you can hear what you want to say.

When an irresistible force meets an immovable object, something's gotta give. Conquer the task: break the paper into manageable bits. Instead of drooping with despair over the thought of a twenty-five-page research paper, think of it as a series of small parts (explanation of the problem, review of current research, possible solutions, or whatever). Then tackle one part at a time and reward yourself when that section's done.

Get the juices flowing and the pen moving. Try writing the easiest or shortest part of your essay first. A feeling of accomplishment may give you the boost of confidence you need to undertake the other, more difficult sections.

If no part looks easy or inviting, try more prewriting exercises, like the ones described on pages 6–15, until you feel prepared to begin the essay itself.

Play "Let's Make a Deal" with yourself. Sometimes we just can't face the failure that we are predicting for ourselves. Strike a bargain with yourself: promise yourself that you are only going to work on your paper for fifteen minutes—absolutely, positively fifteen minutes, not a second more, no sir, no way. If in fifteen minutes, you're on to something good, ignore your promise to yourself and keep going. If you're not, then leave and come back for another fifteen-minute session later (if you started early enough, you can do this without increasing your anxiety).

Give yourself permission to write garbage. Take the pressure off yourself by agreeing in advance to tear up the first page or two of whatever you write. You can always change your mind if the "trash" turns out to be treasure; if it isn't, so what? You said you were going to tear it up anyway.

Imagine that your brain is a water faucet. If you're like most folks, you've probably lived in a house or apartment that contained a faucet that needed to run a few minutes before the hot water started to come out. Think of your brain in the same way, and do some other, easier writing task to warm up. Write a letter, make a grocery list, copy notes, whatever, to get your brain running. When you turn to your paper, your thoughts may be hotter than you thought.

Remove the threat by addressing a friendly face. Sometimes we can't write because we are too worried about what someone else will think about us or maybe we can't write because we can't figure out who would want to read this stuff anyway? Instead of writing into a void or to an audience that seems threatening, try writing to a friend. Imagine what that friend's responses might be and try to elaborate or clarify wherever necessary. If it helps, write the first draft as a letter ("Dear Clyde, I want to tell you what happened to me last week . . ."), and then redraft your ideas as an essay when you've found your purpose and focus, making whatever changes in tone or development are necessary to fit your real audience.

If Writer's Block does hit, remember that it is a temporary bog-down, not a permanent one. Other writers have had it—and survived to write again. Try leaving your papers and taking a walk outdoors or at least into another room. Think about your readers—what should they know or feel at this point in your essay? As you walk, try to complete the sentence "What I am trying to say is . . . ." Keep repeating this phrase and your responses aloud until you find the answer you want.

Sometimes while you're blocked at one point, a bright idea for another part of your essay will pop into your head. If possible, skip the section that's got you stuck and start working on the new part. (At least jot down the new idea somewhere so it won't be lost when you need it later.)

Change partners and dance. If you're thoroughly overcome by the vast white wasteland on the desk before you, get up and do something else for a while. Exercise, do the dishes, put on music and dance. Give your mind a break and refresh your spirit. When you come back to the paper, you may be surprised to discover that your subconscious writer has been working while the rest of you played.

Here's the single most important piece of advice to remember: relax. No one—not even the very best professional writer—produces perfect prose every time pen hits paper. If you're blocked, you may be trying too hard; if your expectations of your first draft are too high, you may not be able to write at all for fear of failure. You just might be holding yourself back by being a perfectionist at this point. You can always revise and polish your prose in another draft—the first important step is jotting down your ideas. Remember that once the first word or phrase appears on your blank page, a major battle has been won.

A CHECKLIST FOR YOUR ESSAY

If you have written an effective essay, you should be able to answer "yes" to the following questions:

1. Do I feel I have something important to say to my reader?
2. Am I sincerely committed to communicating with my reader and not just with myself?
3. Have I considered my audience's needs? (See Chapter 1.)
4. Do my title and lead-in attract the reader's attention and help set up my thesis? (See Chapter 4.)
5. Does my thesis statement assert one clearly focused idea? (See Chapter 2.)
6. Does my thesis and/or essay map give the reader an indication of what points the essay will cover? (See Chapter 2.)
7. Does each of my body paragraphs contain a main point in the essay's discussion, and is that point expressed in a clear topic sentence? (See Chapter 3.)
8. Does each body paragraph have unity, coherence, and adequate development? (See Chapter 3.)
9. Does each body paragraph have sufficient specific details to prove or explain my essay's main points? (See Chapter 3.)
10. Are all the paragraphs in my essay smoothly linked in an effective order? (See Chapter 3.)
11. Does my concluding paragraph provide a suitable ending for the essay? (See Chapter 4.)

12. Are all my sentences clear, concise, and coherent? (See Chapter 6.)

13. Are my words accurate, necessary, and meaningful? (See Chapter 7.)

14. Have I proofread for errors in grammar, punctuation, spelling, or typing? (See Part Three.)

And most important:

15. Has my essay been effectively revised so that I am proud of this piece of writing?

PRACTICING WHAT YOU'VE LEARNED

Applying what you know about effective writing, identify the strengths and weaknesses of the following two student essays. Use the checklist above to help you evaluate parts of the essays. What changes would you recommend to improve the quality of these essays?

Dorm Life

Dorm life is not at all what I had expected it to be. I had anticipated meeting friendly people, quiet hours for studying, eating decent food, and having wild parties on weekends. My dreams, I soon found out, were simply illusions, erroneous perceptions of reality.

My roommate, Kathy, and I live in Holland Hall on the third floor. The people on our dorm floor are about as unfriendly as they can possibly be. I wonder whether or not they're just shy and afraid or if they are simply snobs. Some girls, for example, ignore my roommate and me when we say "hello." Occasionally, they stare straight ahead and act like we aren't even there. Other girls respond, but it's as if they do it out of a sense of duty rather than being just friendly. The guys seem nice, but some are just as afraid or snobby as the girls.

I remember signing up for "quiet hours" when I put in my application for a dorm room last December. Unfortunately, I was assigned to a floor that doesn't have any quiet hours at all. I am a person who requires peace and quiet when studying or reading. The girls in all the rooms around us love to stay up until early in the morning and yell and turn up their stereos full blast. They turn their stereos on at about eight o'clock at night and turn them off early in the morning. There is always at least one girl who has a record playing at maximum volume. Now, I am very appreciative of music, but listening to "acid rock" until three in the morning isn't really my idea of what music is. The girls right across from us usually play Neil Diamond or Simon and Garfunkel and I enjoy that. On the other hand, though, the girls on either side of our room love to listen to Z.Z. Top or Bachman-Turner Overdrive into the wee hours of the morning. It is these girls who run up and down the hall, yell at each other, laugh obnoxiously, and try to attract attention. All this continuous racket makes it nearly impossible to study, read, or get any sleep. Kathy and I usually end up going to the library or student cafeteria to study. As far as sleep goes, it doesn't matter what time we go to bed, but rather it depends on how noisy it is, and how late the stereos are on. Sometimes the noise gets so loud and rambles on for so long that even when it stops, my ears are ringing and my stomach keeps churning. It is on nights like this that I never go to sleep. I wish the people here were a little more considerate of the people around them.

Parties, on weekends, are supposedly the most important part of dorm life. Parties provide the opportunity to meet others and have a good time. Holland Hall has had two parties that are even worth mentioning. One of them was a Fifties dance held in the courtyard approximately three weeks ago. Unfortunately, all the other dormitories, the fraternities, and the sororities heard about it, and by eight o'clock at night there were masses of people. It was so packed that it was hard to move around. The other party, much to my dismay, turned out to be a luau party. I do not really care for roast pig, and my stomach turned from the scent of it when I entered the room. Our floor never has parties. Everyone leaves their doors open, turns up the stereo, yells back and forth. I suppose that there will be more dorm parties once everyone becomes adjusted to this life and begins to socialize.

Dorm food is what I anticipated it would be, terrible, and I was right, it is awful. Breakfast is probably the hardest meal to digest. The bacon and sausage are cold, slightly uncooked, and very greasy. Sometimes, it's as though I am eating pure grease. The eggs look and taste like nothing I ever had before. They look like plastic and they are never hot. I had eggs once and I vowed I would never have another one as long as I lived in Holland Hall. The most enjoyable part of breakfast is the orange juice. It's always cold and it seems to be fresh. No one can say dorm food is totally boring because the cooks break up the monotony of the same food by serving "mystery meat" at least once every two weeks. This puts a little excitement in the student's day because everyone cracks jokes and wonders just what's in this "mystery meat." I think a lot of students are afraid to ask, fearful of the answer, and simply make snide remarks and shovel it in.

All in all, I believe dorm life isn't too great, even though there are some good times. Even though I complain about dorm food, the people, the parties, and everything else, I am glad I am here. I am happy because I have learned a lot about other people, responsibilities, consideration, and I've even learned a lot about myself.

Maybe You Shouldn't Go Away to College

Going away to college is not for everyone. There are good reasons why a student might choose to live at home and attend a local school. Money, finding stability while changes are occurring, and accepting responsibility are three to consider.

Money is likely to be most important. Not only is tuition more expensive, but extra money is needed for room and board. Whether room and board is a dorm or an apartment, the expense is great.

Most students never stop to consider that the money that could be saved from room and board may be better spent in future years on graduate school, which is likely to be more important in their careers.

Going to school is a time of many changes anyway, without adding the pressure of a new city or even a new state. Finding stability will be hard enough, without going from home to a dorm. Starting college could be an emotional time for some, and the security of their home and family might make everything easier.

When students decide to go away to school, sometimes because their friends are going away, or maybe because the school is their parents' alma mater, something that all need to decide is whether or not they can accept the responsibility of a completely new way of life.

Everyone feels as if they are ready for total independence when they decide to go away to college, but is breaking away when they are just beginning to set their futures a good idea?

Going away to school may be the right road for some, but those who feel that they are not ready might start looking to a future that is just around the corner.

ASSIGNMENT

Select a paragraph from one of the preceding student essays and rewrite it, making any changes in organization, development, sentence construction, word choice, or anything else you feel is necessary. Feel free to elaborate on, eliminate, or change the content in order to improve the paragraph's organization and development.

CHAPTER 5 SUMMARY

Here is a brief summary of what you should remember about revising your writing:

1. Revision is an activity that occurs in all stages of the writing process.
2. All good writers revise their prose extensively.
3. Revision is not merely proofreading; it involves important decisions about the writer's ideas and the organization, development, and editing of the writer's prose.
4. To revise effectively, beginning writers might try to review their drafts in stages, to avoid the frustration that can come with the attempt to fix everything at once.
5. All writers experience Writer's Block at some time but live through it to write again.

6

Effective Sentences

An insurance agent was shocked to open his mail one morning and read the following note from one of his clients: "In accordance with your instructions, I have given birth to twins in the enclosed envelope." However, he may not have been more surprised than the congregation who read this announcement in their church bulletin: "There will be a discussion tomorrow on the problem of adultery in the minister's office." Or the patrons of a health club who learned that "guest passes will not be given to members until the manager has punched each of them first."

Certainly, there were no babies born in an envelope, nor was there adultery in the minister's office, and one doubts that the club manager was planning to assault the membership. But the implications (and the unintended humor) are nevertheless present—solely because of the faulty ways in which the sentences were constructed.

To improve your own writing, you must express your thoughts in clear, coherent sentences that produce precisely the reader response you want. Effective sentences are similar to the threads in a piece of knitting or weaving: each thread helps form the larger design; if any one thread becomes tangled or lost, the pattern becomes muddled. In an essay, the same is true: if any sentence is fuzzy or obscure, the reader may lose the point of your discussion and in some cases never bother to regain it. Therefore, to retain your reader, you must concentrate on writing informative, effective sentences that consistently clarify the purpose of your essay.

Many problems in sentence clarity involve errors in grammar, usage, and word choice; the most common of these errors are discussed in Chapter 7 and Part Three of this text. In this chapter, however, you'll find some general suggestions for writing clear, concise, engaging sentences. However, *don't try to apply all the rules at one time to the first draft of your essay.* Trying to do so will probably result in panic or writer's block. Work first on your essay's content and general organization; then, in a later draft, rework your sentences so that each one is informative and persuasive. Your reader reads only the words on the page, not those in your mind—so it's up to you to make sure the sentences in your essay approximate the thoughts in your head as closely and vividly as possible.

Remember:
All good writers revise their sentences.

DEVELOP A CLEAR STYLE

When you are ready to revise the sentences in your rough draft for clarity, try to follow the next five rules:

GIVE YOUR SENTENCES CONTENT

Fuzzy sentences are often the result of fuzzy thinking. When you examine your sentences, ask yourself, "Do I know what I'm talking about here? Or are my sentences vague or confusing because I'm really not sure what my point is or where it's going?" Look at this list of content-poor sentences taken from student essays; how could you reword and put more information into each one?

> If you were to view a karate class, you would become familiar with all the aspects that make it up.
> The meaning of the poem isn't very clear the first time you read it, but after several readings, the poet's meaning comes through.
> One important factor that is the basis for determining a true friend is the ability that person has for being a real human being.
> Listening is important because we all need to be able to sit and hear all that is said to us.

Don't pad your paragraphs with sentences that run in circles, leading nowhere; rethink your ideas and revise your writing so that every sentence—like each brick in a wall—contributes to the construction of a solid discussion. In other words, commit yourself to a position and make each sentence contain information pertinent to your point; leave the job of padding to mattress manufacturers.

Sometimes, however, you may have a definite idea in mind but still continue to write "empty sentences"—statements that alone do not contain enough information to make a specific point in your discussion. Frequently, an "empty sentence" may be revised by combining it with the sentence that follows, as shown in the examples below. The "empty" or overly general sentences are underlined.

Poor   There are many kinds of beautiful tropical fish. The kind most popular with aquarium owners is the angelfish.

Better   Of the many kinds of beautiful tropical fish, none is more popular with aquarium owners than the angelfish.

Poor   D. W. Griffith introduced many new cinematic techniques. Some of these techniques were contrast editing, close-ups, fade-outs, and freeze-frame shots.

Better   D. W. Griffith made movie history by introducing such new cinematic techniques as contrast editing, close-ups, fade-outs, and the freeze-frame shot.

Poor   There is a national organization called The Couch Potatoes. The group's 8,000 members are devoted television watchers.

Better   The Couch Potatoes is a national organization whose 8,000 members are devoted television watchers.

For more help on combining sentences, see pp. 115–118.

MAKE YOUR SENTENCE SPECIFIC

In addition to containing an informative, complete thought, each of your sentences should provide the readers with enough clear details for them to "see" the picture you are creating. Sentences full of vague words produce blurry, boring prose and drowsy readers. Remember your reaction the last time you asked a friend about a recent vacation? If the only response you received was something like, "Oh, it was great—a lot of fun," you probably yawned and proceeded quickly to a new topic. But if your friend had begun an exciting account of a recent wilderness rafting trip, with detailed stories about narrow escapes from freezing white water, treacherous rocks, and uncharted whirl-pools, you'd probably have stopped and listened. The same principle works in your writing—clear, specific details are the only sure way to attract and hold the reader's interest. Therefore, make each sentence contribute something new and interesting to the overall discussion.

The examples below first show sentences far too vague to sustain anyone's attention. Rewritten, these sentences contain specific details that add clarity and interest:

Vague   She went home in a bad mood. [What kind of a bad mood? How did she act or look?]

Specific She stomped home, hands jammed in her pockets, angrily kicking rocks, dogs, small children, and anything else that crossed her path.

Vague   My neighbor bought a really nice old desk. [Why nice? How old? What kind of desk?]

Specific   My neighbor bought a solid oak roll-top desk made in 1885 that contains a secret drawer triggered by a hidden spring.

Vague   He was an attractive man. [Attractive in what ways—his appearance, personality, or both? Again, do you "see" this man?]

Specific   He had Paul Newman's eyes, Robert Redford's smile, Sylvester Stallone's body, and Howard Hughes's money.

KEEP YOUR SENTENCES SIMPLE

Because our society is becoming increasingly specialized and highly technical, we tend to equate complexity with excellence and simplicity with simplemindedness. This assumption is unfortunate, because it often leads to a preference for unnecessarily complicated and even contorted writing. In a recent survey, for example, a student chose a sample of bureaucratic hogwash over several well-written paragraphs, explaining his choice by saying that it must have been better since he didn't understand it.

Our best writers have always worked hard to present their ideas simply and specifically, so that their readers could easily understand them. Mark Twain, for instance, once praised a young author this way: "I notice that you use plain simple language, short words, and brief sentences. This is the way to write English. It is the modern way and the best way. Stick to it." And when a critic asked Hemingway to define his theory of writing, he replied, "[I] put down what I see and what I feel in the best and simplest way I can tell it."

In your own writing, therefore, work for a simple, direct style. Avoid sentences that are overpacked (too many ideas or too much information at once) as in the following example on racquetball:

> John told Phil that to achieve more control over the ball, he should practice flicking or snapping his wrist, because this action is faster in the close shots and placing a shot requires only a slight change of the wrist's angle instead of an acute movement of the whole arm, which gives a player less reaction time.

To make the overpacked sentence easier to understand, try dividing the ideas into two or more sentences:

> John told Phil that to achieve more control over the ball, he should practice flicking or snapping his wrist, because this action is faster in the close shots. Placing a shot requires only a slight change of the wrist's angle instead of an acute movement of the whole arm, which gives a player less reaction time.

Don't ever run the risk of losing your reader in a sentence that says too much to comprehend in one bite. This confusing notice, for example, came from a well-known credit card company:

The Minimum Payment Due each month shall be reduced by the amounts paid in excess of the Minimum Payment Due during the previous three months which have not already been so applied in determining the Minimum Payment Due in such earlier months, unless you have exceeded your line of credit or have paid the entire New Balance shown on your billing statement.

Try too for a straightforward construction; former President Ronald Reagan's sentence below, for example, takes far too many twists and turns for anyone to understand it easily on the first reading:

My goal is an America where something or anything that is done to or for anyone is done neither because of nor in spite of any difference between them, racially, religiously or ethnic-origin-wise.

If the sentences in your rough draft are contorted, try rephrasing your meaning in short sentences and then combining thoughts where most appropriate.

PAY ATTENTION TO WORD ORDER

The correct word order is crucial for clarity. Always place a modifier near the word it modifies. The position of a modifier can completely change the meaning of your sentence; for example, each sentence below presents a different idea because of the placement of the modifier "only."

A. Eliza said she loved only me. [Eliza loves me and no one else.]

B. Only Eliza said she loves me. [No other person said she loves me.]

C. Eliza only said she loves me. [Eliza says she loves me, but said nothing other than that.]

D. Eliza said only she loves me. [Eliza says no one else loves me.]

To avoid confusion, therefore, place your modifiers close to the words or phrases they modify.

A modifier that seems to modify the wrong part of a sentence is called "misplaced." Not only can misplaced modifiers change or distort the meaning of your sentence, they can also provide unintentional humor as well, as illustrated by the following excerpt from the 1929 Marx Brothers' movie *Coconuts:*

Woman: There's a man waiting outside to see you with a black mustache.

Groucho: Tell him I've already got one.

Of course, the woman didn't mean to imply that the man outside was waiting with (that is, accompanied by) a mustache; she meant to say, "There's a man with a black mustache who is waiting outside. . . ."

A poster advertising a lecture on campus provided this opportunity for humor: "Professor Elizabeth Sewell will discuss the latest appearance of Halley's Comet in room 104." Under the announcement a local wit had scribbled, "Shall we reserve room 105 for the tail?" Or take the case of this startling headline: "Kicking Baby Considered Healthy."

Here are some other examples of misplaced modifiers:

Misplaced	The lost little girl was finally found wandering in a frozen farmer's field. [Did the writer mean to say that the farmer was that cold?]
Revised	The lost little girl was finally found wandering in a farmer's frozen field.
Misplaced	Dilapidated and almost an eyesore, Shirley bought the old house to restore it to its original beauty. [Did the writer mean that Shirley needed a beauty treatment?]
Revised	Shirley bought the old house, which was dilapidated and almost an eyesore, to restore it to its original beauty.
Misplaced	Because she is thoroughly housebroken, Sarah can take her dog almost anywhere she goes. [Did the writer mean that Sarah—or the dog—was housebroken?]
Revised	Because she is thoroughly housebroken, Sarah's dog can accompany her almost anywhere she goes.
Misplaced	Three family members were found bound and gagged by the grandmother. [Did the writer mean that the grandmother had tied up the family?]
Revised	The grandmother found the three family members who had been bound and gagged.

In each of the preceding examples the writer forgot to place the modifying phrase so that it modifies the correct subject. In most cases, a sentence with a misplaced modifier can be corrected easily by moving the word or phrase closer to the word that should be modified.

In some sentences, however, the object of the modifying phrase is missing entirely. Such a phrase is called a "dangling modifier." Most of these errors may be corrected by adding the missing subject. Here are some examples followed by their revisions:

Dangling	Waving farewell, the plane began to roll down the runway. [Did the writer mean the plane was waving farewell?]
Revised	Waving farewell, we watched as the plane began to roll down the runway.

Dangling   After taking hours to plant hundreds of strawberry plants, the gophers came back to the garden and ate every last one of them. [Did the writer mean that the gophers had a good meal after putting in such hard work?]

Revised   After Ralph took hours to plant hundreds of strawberry plants, the gophers came back to the garden and ate every last one of them.

Dangling   While telling a joke to my roommate, a cockroach walked across my soufflé. [Did the writer mean that the cockroach was telling the joke?]

Revised   While telling a joke to my roommate, I saw a cockroach walking across my soufflé.

Dangling   Having tucked the children into bed, the cat was put out for the night. [Did the writer mean that the cat tucked the children into bed?]

Revised   Having tucked the children into bed, Mother and Father put the cat out for the night.

Misplaced and dangling modifiers frequently occur when you think faster than you write; a careful reading of your rough drafts will help you weed out any confused or unintentionally humorous sentences. (For additional examples of misplaced and dangling modifiers, see pp. 304–305 in Part Three.)

AVOID MIXED CONSTRUCTIONS AND FAULTY PREDICATION

Sometimes you may begin with a sentence pattern in mind and then shift, mid-sentence, to another pattern—a change that often results in a generally confusing sentence. In many of these cases, you will find that the subject of your sentence simply doesn't fit with the predicate. Look at the following examples and note their corrections:

Faulty   Financial aid is a growing problem for many college students. [Financial aid itself isn't a problem; rather, it's the lack of aid.]

Revised   College students are finding it harder to obtain financial aid.

Faulty   Pregnant cows are required to teach a portion of two courses in Animal Science, AS100 (Breeding of Livestock) and AS200 (Problems in Reproduction of Cattle). [Obviously, the cows will not be the instructors for the classes.]

Revised   The Animal Science Department needs to purchase pregnant cows for use in two courses, AS100 (Breeding of Livestock) and AS200 (Problems in Reproduction of Cattle).

Faulty   Love is when you start rehearsing dinner-date conversation before breakfast. [A thing is never a "when" or a "where"; rewrite all "is when" or "is where" constructions.]

Revised   You're in love if you start rehearsing dinner-date conversation before breakfast.

Many mixed constructions occur because the writer is in too much of a hurry; check your rough drafts carefully to see if you have included sentences in which you started one pattern and switched to another. (For more help on faulty predications and mixed constructions, see pp. 308–309 in Part Three.)

DEVELOP A CONCISE STYLE

Almost all writing suffers from wordiness—the tendency to use more words than necessary. When useless words weigh down your prose, the meaning is often lost, confused, or hidden. Flabby prose calls for a reducing plan: put those obese sentences on a diet by cutting out unnecessary words, just as you avoid fatty foods to keep yourself trim. Mushy prose is ponderous and boring; crisp, to-the-point writing, on the other hand, is both accessible and pleasing. Beware, however, a temptation to overdiet—you don't want your prose to become so thin or brief that your meaning disappears completely. Therefore, cut out only the *unessential* words and phrases.

Wordy prose is frequently the result of using one or more of the following: (1) deadwood constructions (2) redundancies (3) pretentiousness.

AVOID DEADWOOD CONSTRUCTIONS

Always try to cut empty "deadwood" from your sentences. Having a clear, concise style does not mean limiting your writing to choppy, childish Dick-and-Jane sentences; it only means that all unnecessary words, phrases, and clauses should be deleted. Below are some sentences containing common deadwood constructions and ways they may be pruned:

Faulty   The *reason* their football team plays on artificial turf *is because* their coach doesn't want the players to graze during halftime. ["The reason . . . is because" is both wordy and ungrammatical. If you have a reason, you don't need a "reason because."]

Revised   Their football team plays on artificial turf because their coach doesn't want the players to graze during halftime.

Poor   The land settlement *was an example where* the Indians did not receive fair treatment.

Revised   The land settlement was unfair to the Indians.

Poor   Because *of the fact that* his surfboard business failed after only a month, my brother decided to leave Minnesota.

Revised   Because his surfboard business failed after only a month, my brother decided to leave Minnesota.

Other notorious deadwood construction include:

regardless of the fact that	(use "although")
due to the fact that	(use "because")
the reason is that	(omit)
as to whether or not to	(omit "as to" and "or not")
at this point in time	(use "now" or "today")
it is believed that	(use a specific subject and "believes")
concerning the matter of	(use "about")
by means of	(use "by")
these are the kinds of . . . that	(use "these" plus a specific subject)

Watch a tendency to tack on empty "fillers" that stretch one word into an awkward phrase:

Wordy   Each candidate should be evaluated *on an individual basis.*

Concise   Each candidate should be evaluated *individually.*

Wordy   Television does not portray violence *in a realistic fashion.*

Concise   Television does not portray violence *realistically.*

Wordy   The New York blackout produced a *crisis-type situation.*

Concise   The New York blackout produced a *crisis.*

To retain your reader's interest and improve the flow of your prose, trim all the fat from your sentences.

"There are," "It is." These introductory phrases are often space wasters. When possible, omit them or replace them with specific subjects, as shown in the following:

Wordy   *There are* thirty thousand students attending this university.

Revised   Thirty thousand students attend this university.

Wordy   *It is* true that the County Fair offers many fun contests, including the ever-popular map fold-off.

Revised   The County Fair offers many fun contests, including the ever-popular map fold-off.

"Who" and "which" clauses. Some "who" and "which" clauses are unnecessary and may be turned into modifiers placed before the noun:

Wordy   The getaway car, *which* was stolen, turned the corner.

Revised   The stolen getaway car turned the corner.

Wordy   The chef, *who was* depressed, ordered his noisy lobsters to simmer down.

Revised   The depressed chef ordered his noisy lobsters to simmer down.

When adjective clauses are necessary, the words "who" and "which" may sometimes be omitted:

Wordy   Ms. Quito, who is a local English teacher, was delighted to hear that she had won the drawing for the Ethan Frome Memorial Sleigh Ride.

Revised   Ms. Quito, a local English teacher, was delighted to hear that she had won the drawing for the Ethan Frome Memorial Sleigh Ride.

"To be." Most "to be's" are unnecessary and ought not to be. Delete them every time you can.

Wordy   She seems *to be* angry.

Revised   She seems angry.

Wordy   Herb's charisma-bypass operation proved to be successful.

Revised   Herb's charisma-bypass operation proved successful.

Wordy   The new mayor wanted his archenemy, the local movie critic, *to be* arrested.

Revised   The new mayor wanted his archenemy, the local movie critic, arrested.

"Of" and infinitive phrases. Many "of" and infinitive ("to" plus verb) phrases may be omitted or revised by using possessives, adjectives, and verbs, as shown below:

Wordy   At the *time of registration* students are required *to make* payment *of their library fees.*

Revised   At registration students must pay their library fees.

Wordy   The producer fired the mother *of the director of the movie.*

Revised   The producer fired the movie director's mother.

Including deadwood phrases makes your prose puffy; streamline your sentences to present a simple, direct style.

AVOID REDUNDANCY

Many flabby sentences contain *redundancies* (words that repeat the same idea or whose meanings overlap). Consider the following examples:

> In this day and time, people expect to live at least seventy years. ["Day" and "time" present a similar idea.]
>
> He repeated the winning bingo number over again. ["Repeated" means "to say again," so there is no need for "over again."]
>
> The group consensus was that the pizza crust tasted like cardboard. ["Consensus" means "general agreement," so it's unnecessary to add "group."]

Some other common redundancies include:

reverted back	new innovation
reflected back	red in color
retreated back	burned down up
fell down	pair of twins/two twins
climb up	resulting effect (or just "result")
a true fact	final outcome

CAREFULLY CONSIDER YOUR PASSIVE VERBS

When the subject of the sentence performs the action, the verb is *active;* when the subject of the sentence is acted upon, the verb is *passive.* You can often recognize sentences with passive verbs because they contain the word *by,* telling who performed the action.

Passive   The Indians *were considered* uncivilized by the early settlers.

Active   The early settlers *considered* the Indians uncivilized.

Passive   The wedding date *was announced* by the young couple.

Active   The young couple *announced* their wedding date.

Passive   His letter of resignation *was accepted by* the Board of Trustees.

Active   The Board of Trustees *accepted* his letter of resignation.

In addition to being wordy and weak, passive sentences often disguise the performer of the action in question. You might have heard a politician, for example, say something similar to this: "It was decided this year to give all congressmen an increase in salary." The question of *who* decided to raise salaries remains foggy—perhaps purposefully so. But in your own prose, you should strive for clarity and directness; therefore, use active verbs as often as you can except when you wish to stress the person or thing that receives the action, as shown in the following samples:

The baby was born September 30, 1980.

The elderly man was struck by a drunk driver.

Special note: Authorities in some professional and technical fields still prefer the passive construction because they wish to put emphasis on the experiment or process rather than on the people performing the action. If the passive voice is preferred in your field, you should abide by that convention when you are writing reports or papers for your professional colleagues.

AVOID PRETENTIOUSNESS

Another enemy of clear, concise prose is *pretentiousness.* Pompous, inflated language surrounds us, and because it often sounds learned or official, we may be tempted to use it when we want to impress others with our writing. But as George Orwell, author of *1984,* noted, an inflated style is like "a cuttlefish squirting out ink." If you want your prose easily understood, write as clearly and plainly as possible.

To illustrate how confusing pretentious writing can be, here is a copy of a government memo announcing a blackout order, issued in 1942 during World War II:

> Such preparations shall be made as will completely obscure all Federal buildings and non-Federal buildings occupied by the Federal government during an air raid for any period of time from visibility by reason of internal or external illumination.

President Franklin Roosevelt intervened and rewrote the order in plain English, clarifying its message and reducing the number of words by half:

> Tell them that in buildings where they have to keep the work going to put something across the windows.

By translating the obscure original memo into easily understandable language, Roosevelt demonstrated that a natural prose style can get necessary information to the reader more quickly and efficiently than bureaucratic jargon. (For more advice on ridding your prose of jargon, see pp. 131–132.)

In other—shorter—words, to attract and hold your readers' attention, to communicate clearly and quickly, make your sentences as informative, straightforward, specific, and concise as possible.

PRACTICING WHAT YOU'VE LEARNED

A. Some of the following sentences are vague, "empty," overpacked, or contorted. Rewrite each one so that it is clear and specific, combining or dividing sentences as necessary.

1. Roger was a pretty neat guy who was important to his company.
2. There's a new detective show on television. It stars Phil Noir and is set in the 1940s.
3. Sarah's room was always a huge disaster.
4. The book *Biofeedback: How To Stop It* is a good one because of all the writer put into it.
5. Some people think capital punishment should be allowed to exist because it acts as a deterrent to people about to commit crimes or who are even considering them, but other people hold the view that they shouldn't have to pay for feeding and housing them for years after crimes are committed, so they should be executed instead.
6. My junk mail is incredible.
7. I've signed up for a course at my local college. The class is "Cultivating the Mold in Your Refrigerator for Fun and Profit."
8. Reading your horoscope is a fun way to get information about your life, but it's not really the real stuff.
9. I'm not sure but I think that Lois is the author of *The Underachiever's Guide to Very Small Business Opportunities* or is she the writer of *Whine Your Way to Success* because I know she's written several books since she's having an autograph party at the campus bookstore either this afternoon or tomorrow.
10. I can't help but wonder whether or not he isn't unwelcome.

B. The sentences below contain misplaced words and phrases as well as other faulty constructions. Revise them so that each sentence is clear.

1. If you are accosted in the subway at night, you should learn to escape harm from the police.
2. Desperation is when you try to lose weight through Pyramid Power.
3. Almost dead for five years now, I miss my dog so much.
4. The father fed the apple pie to the twins he earlier had dropped in the trash compactor.
5. The reason I stopped the exorcism was because my dandruff wasn't disappearing.

6. We gave our waterbed to friends we didn't want anymore.

7. The story of Rip Van Winkle is one of the dangers endured by those who oversleep.

8. The owner of the bar faced financial ruin when he was put on trial for allowing a bar patron found dead in his car to drive drunk.

9. People who are allergic to chocolate and children under 6 should not be given the new vaccine.

10. At 7 A.M. Brenda starts preparing for another busy day as an executive in her luxurious bathroom.

C. The sentences below are filled with deadwood, redundancies, and passive constructions. Rewrite each one so that it is concise and direct.

1. In point of fact, the main reason he lost the editing job was primarily because of his careless and sloppy proofreading work.

2. It was revealed today that there are some professors in the Prehistoric History department who are incompetent.

3. My brother, who happens to be a loudmouth, can't drive to work this week due to the fact that he was in a wreck in his car at 2 A.M. Saturday morning.

4. In this modern world of today, we often criticize or disapprove of advertising that is thought to be damaging to women by representing them in an unfair way.

5. When the prosecution tried to introduce the old antique gun, this was objected to by the attorney defending the two twin brothers.

6. What the poet is trying to get across to the reader in the fourth stanza is her feeling of disgust with the telephone company.

7. We very often felt that although we expressed our deepest concerns to our boss, she often just sat there and gave us the real impression that she was taking what we said in a very serious manner although, in our opinion, she did not really and truly care about our concerns.

8. It is a true fact that certainly bears repeating over and over again that learning word processing can help you perform in a more efficient way at work and also can save you lots of time too.

9. Personally, I believe that there are too many people who go to eat out in restaurants who always feel they must continually assert their superior natures by acting in a rude, nasty fashion to the people who are employed to wait on their tables.

10. In order to enhance my opportunities for advancement in the workplace at this point in time, I arrived at the decision to seek the hand of my employer's daughter in the state of matrimony.

ASSIGNMENT

Write a paragraph of at least five sentences as clearly and concisely as you can. Then rewrite this paragraph, filling it with as many vague words, redundancies, and deadwood constructions as possible. Exchange this rewritten paragraph for a similarly faulty one written by a classmate; give yourselves fifteen minutes to "translate" each other's sentences into effective prose. Compare the "translations" to the original paragraphs. Which version is clearer? Why?

DEVELOP A LIVELY STYLE

Good writing demands clarity and conciseness—but that's not all. Good prose must also be lively, forceful, and interesting. It should excite, intrigue, and charm; each line should seduce the reader into the next. Consider, for example, one of the duller textbooks you've read lately. It probably was written clearly, but it may have failed to inform because of its insufferably bland tone; by the time you finished your assignment, most likely your brain was asleep.

You can prevent your readers from succumbing to a similar case of the blahs by developing a vigorous prose style that continually surprises and pleases them. As one writer has pointed out, all subjects—with the possible exceptions of sex and money—are dull until somebody makes them interesting. As you revise your rough drafts, remember: bored readers are not born but made. Therefore, here are some practical suggestions to help you transform ho-hum prose into lively sentences and paragraphs:

Use specific, descriptive verbs. Avoid bland verbs that must be supplemented by modifiers.

Bland   His fist *broke* the window *into many little pieces.*

Better   His fist *shattered* the window.

Bland   Dr. Love *asked* his congregation *about* donating money to his "love mission" *over and over again.*

Better   Dr. Love *hounded* his congregation into donating money to his "love mission."

Bland   The exhausted runner *walked* up the last hill *very slowly.*

Better   The exhausted runner *staggered* up the last hill.

To cut wordiness that weighs down your prose, try to use active verbs instead of nouns and colorless verbs such as "to be," "to have," "to get," "to do," and "to make":

Wordy   By sunrise the rebels had *made their way* to the capital city.

Better   By sunrise the rebels had *battled* to the capital city.

Wordy   At first the players and managers *had an argument* over the money, but finally they *came to an agreement* and *got* the contract dispute settled.

Better   At first the players and managers *argued* over the money, but finally they *agreed* and *settled* the contract dispute.

Wordy   The executives *made the decision* to *have* another meeting on Tuesday.

Better   The executives *decided* to *meet* again on Tuesday.

Use specific, precise modifiers that help the reader see, hear, or feel what you are describing. Adjectives such as "good," "bad," "many," "more," "great," "a lot," "important," and "interesting" are too vague to paint the reader a clear picture. Similarly, the adverbs "very," "really," "too," and "quite" are overused and add little to sentence clarity. The following are examples of weak sentences and their revisions:

Imprecise   The potion changed the scientist into a *really old* man.

Better   The potion changed the scientist into a *one hundred-year-old* man.

Imprecise   Marcia is a *very interesting* person.

Better   Marcia is *witty, intelligent,* and *talented.*

Imprecise   The vegetables tasted *funny.*

Better   The vegetables tasted *like lichen mixed with Krazy Glue.*

(For more advice on using specific, colorful words, see also pp. 128–129 in Chapter 7.)

Emphasize people when possible. Try to focus on persons rather than abstractions whenever you can. Next to our fascinating selves, we most enjoy hearing about other people. Although all the sentences in the first paragraph following are correct, the second one, revised by a class of composition students at Brown University, is clearer and more personal because the jargon has been eliminated and the focus changed from the tuition rules to the students.

Original   Tuition regulations currently in effect provide that payment of the annual tuition entitles an undergraduate-degree candidate to full-time enrollment, which is defined as registration for three, four, or five courses per semester. This means that at no time may an undergraduate student's official registration for courses drop below three without a dean's permission for part-time status and that at no time may the official course registration exceed five. (Brown University Course Announcement 1980-81)

Revised   If students pay their tuition, they may enroll in three, four, or five courses per semester. Fewer than three or more than five can be taken only with a dean's permission.

Here's a similar example with a bureaucratic focus rather than a personal one:

Original   The salary deflations will most seriously impact the secondary educational profession.

Revised   High school teachers will suffer the biggest salary reductions.

Obviously, the revised sentence is the more easily understood of the two because the reader knows exactly who will be affected by the pay cuts. In your own prose, wherever appropriate, try to replace vague abstractions such as "society," "culture," "administrative concerns," "programmatic expectations," and so forth, with the human beings you're thinking about. In other words, remember to talk *to* people *about* people.

Vary your sentence style. The only torture worse than listening to someone's nails scraping across a blackboard is being forced to read a paragraph full of identically constructed sentences. To illustrate this point, below are a few sentences composed in the all-too-common subject + predicate pattern:

Soccer is the most popular sport in the world. Soccer exists in almost every country. Soccer players are sometimes more famous than movie stars. Soccer teams compete every few years for the World Soccer Cup. Soccer fans often riot if their team loses. Some fans even commit suicide. Soccer is the only game in the world that makes people so crazy.

Excruciatingly painful, yes? Each of us has a tendency to repeat a particular sentence pattern (though the choppy subject + predicate is by far the most popular); you can often detect your own by reading your prose aloud. To avoid overdosing your readers with the same pattern, vary the length, arrangement, and complexity of your sentences. Of course, this doesn't mean that you should contort your sentences merely for the sake of illustrating variety; just read your rough draft aloud, listening carefully to the rhythm of your prose so you can revise any monotonous passages or disharmonious sounds. (Try, also, to avoid the hiccup syndrome, in which you begin a sentence with the same words that ends the preceding sentence: The first president to install a telephone on his desk was Herbert *Hoover. Hoover* refused to use the telephone booth outside his office.)

Avoid overuse of any one kind of construction in the same sentence. Don't, for example, pile up too many negatives, "who" or "which" clauses, prepositional or infinitive phrases in one sentence.

He *couldn't* tell whether she *didn't* want him to go or *not*.

I gave the money to my brother, *who* returned it to the bank president, *who* said the decision to prosecute was up to the sheriff, *who* was out of town.

I went to the florist *for* my father *for* a dozen roses *for* his date.

Don't change your point of view between or within sentences. If, for example, you begin your essay discussing students as "they," don't switch midway—or mid-sentence—to "we" or "you."

Inconsistent	Students pay tuition, which should entitle *them* to some voice in the university's administration. Therefore, *we* deserve one student on the Board of Regents.
Consistent	Students pay tuition, which should entitle *them* to some voice in the university's administration. Therefore, *they* deserve one student on the Board of Regents.
Inconsistent	*I* like my photography class because *we* learn how to restore *our* old photos and how to take better color portraits of *your* family.
Consistent	*I* like my photography class because *I'm* learning how to restore *my* old photos and how to take better color portraits of *my* family.

Perhaps this is a good place to dispel the myth that the pronoun "I" should never be used in an essay; on the contrary, many of our best essays have been written in the first person. Some of your former teachers may have discouraged the use of "I" for these two reasons: (1) overuse of "I" makes your essay sound like the work of an egomaniac; (2) writing in the first person often results in too many empty phrases such as "I think that" and "I believe that." Nevertheless, if the situation demands a personal point of view, feel free—if you're comfortable doing so—to use the first person, but use it in moderation; make sure that every sentence doesn't begin with "I" plus a verb.

PRACTICING WHAT YOU'VE LEARNED

A. Replace the underlined words below so that the sentences are clear and vivid. In addition, rephrase any awkward constructions or unnecessarily abstract words you find.

1. Judging from the <u>crazy</u> sound of the reactor, it isn't obvious to me that nuclear power as we know it today isn't a technology with a less than wonderful future.

2. The City Council felt <u>bad</u> because the revised tourist development activities grant fund application form letters were mailed without stamps.

3. To watch Jim Bob eat pork chops was <u>most interesting</u>.

4. The teacher said loudly that he <u>did not care for</u> the student's report on common kitchen aphrodisiacs.

5. The workshop on family relationships we're attending is <u>great</u> because you learn to control your parents through blackmail and guilt.

6. The new diet made me feel <u>awful</u>, and it <u>did many horrible things</u> to my body.

7. After reading "The Looter's Guide to Riot-Prone Cities," Eddie <u>asked to have</u> a transfer <u>really</u> soon.

8. The wild oats soup was <u>very good</u>, so we drank <u>a lot of it fast</u>.

9. When Alfred <u>hit</u> the ball to the top of the fence of the park, his teammates <u>got pretty excited</u>.

10. My brother is <u>sort of different</u>, but I never thought he'd try to <u>take over</u> my aunt's estate.

B. Fill in the blanks with colorful words. Make the paragraph as interesting, exciting, or humorous as you can. Avoid clichés—make your responses original and creative.

As midnight approached, Janet and Brad _____ toward the _____ castle to escape the _____ storm. Their _____ car had _____, _____ , and finally _____ on the road nearby. The night was _____, and Brad _____ at the shadows with _____ and _____ . As they _____ up the _____ steps to the _____ door, the _____ wind was filled with _____ and _____ sounds. Janet _____ on the door, and moments later, it opened to reveal the _____ scientist, clutching a _____ . Brad and Janet _____ at each other and then _____ (complete this sentence, ending the paragraph and the story).

ASSIGNMENT

Find a short piece of writing you think is too bland, boring, abstract, or confusing. (Possible sources: your college catalogue, a business contract or letter, your student health insurance policy, or a textbook.) In a well-written paragraph of your own, identify the sample's major problems and offer some specific suggestions for improving the writing. (If time permits, read aloud several of the samples and vote to give one the Most Lifeless Prose Award.)

DEVELOP AN EMPHATIC STYLE

Some words and phrases in your sentences are more important than others and, therefore, need more emphasis. Three ways to vary emphasis are by (1) word order, (2) coordination, and (3) subordination.

WORD ORDER

The arrangement of words in a sentence can determine which ideas receive the most emphasis. To stress a word or phrase, place it at the end of the sentence or at the beginning of the sentence. Accordingly, a word or phrase receives least emphasis when buried in the middle of the sentence. Compare the examples below, in which the word "murder" receives varying degrees of emphasis:

Least emphatic	Colonel Mustard knew *murder* was his only solution.
Emphatic	*Murder* was Colonel Mustard's only solution.
Emphatic	Colonel Mustard had only one solution: *murder.*

Another use of word order to vary emphasis is *inversion,* taking a word out of its natural or usual position in a sentence and inserting it in an unexpected place.

Usual order	The *conceited* man congratulates his mother on his birthday.
Inverted order	*Conceited* is the man who congratulates his mother on his birthday.

Not all your sentences will contain words that need special emphasis; good writing generally contains a mix of some sentences in natural order and others rearranged for special effects.

COORDINATION

When you have two closely related ideas and want to stress them equally, coordinate them.* In coordination, you join two sentences with a coordinating conjunction. To remember the coordinating conjunctions ("for," "and," "nor," "but," "or," "yet," "so"), think of the acronym FANBOYS; then always join two sentences with a comma and one of the FANBOYS. Here are two samples:

Choppy	The most popular girl's name today is Jennifer. The most popular boy's name today is Michael.
Coordinated	The most popular girl's name today is Jennifer, *and* the most popular boy's name is Michael.
Choppy	Imelda brought home a pair of ruby slippers. Ferdinand made her return them.
Coordinated	Imelda brought home a pair of ruby slippers, *but* Ferdinand made her return them.

* To remember that the term "coordination" refers to equally weighted ideas, think of other words with the prefix "co," such as "copilots," "coauthors," or "cooperation."

You can use coordination to show a relationship between ideas and to add variety to your sentence structures. Be careful, however, to select the right words while linking ideas, unlike the sentence that appeared in a church newsletter: "The ladies of the church have discarded clothing of all kinds, and they have been inspected by the minister." In other words, writers often need to slow down and make sure that their thoughts are not joined in misleading or even unintentionally humorous ways: "For those of you who have children and don't know it, we have a nursery downstairs."

Sometimes when writers are in a hurry, they join ideas that are clearly related in their own minds, but whose relationship is confusing to the reader:

Confusing	My laboratory report isn't finished, and today my sister is leaving for a visit home.
Clear	I'm still working on my laboratory report, so I won't be able to catch a ride home with my sister who's leaving today.

You should also avoid using coordinating conjunctions to string too many ideas together like linked sausages:

Poor	We went inside the famous cave and the guide turned off the lights and we saw the rocks that glowed.
Revised	After we went inside the famous cave, the guide turned off the lights so we could see the rocks that glowed.

SUBORDINATION

Some sentences contain one main statement and one or more less-emphasized elements; the less important ideas are subordinate to, or are dependent upon, the sentence's main idea.* Subordinating conjunctions introducing dependent clauses show a variety of relationships between the clauses and the main part of the sentence. Here are four examples of subordinating conjunctions and their uses:

1. To show time

Without subordination	Superman stopped changing his clothes. He realized the phone booth was made of glass.
With subordination	Superman stopped changing his clothes *when* he realized the phone booth was made of glass.

2. To show cause

Without subordination	John did not pass the army's entrance exam. John did not want to be a soldier.
With subordination	John did not pass the army's entrance exam *because* he did not want to be a soldier.

---

* To remember that the term "subordination" refers to sentences containing dependent elements, think of words such as "a subordinate" (someone who works for someone else) or a post office "substation" (a branch of the post office less important than the main branch).

3. To show condition

Without subordination Susan ought to study the art of tattooing. She will work with colorful people.

With subordination *If* Susan studies the art of tattooing, she will work with colorful people.

4. To show place

Without subordination Bulldozers are smashing the old movie theater. That's the place I first saw Roy Rogers and Dale Evans ride into the sunset.

With subordination Bulldozers are smashing the old movie theater *where* I first saw Roy Rogers and Dale Evans ride into the sunset.

Subordination is especially useful in ridding your prose of choppy Dick-and-Jane sentences and those "empty sentences" discussed on pp. 96–97. Below are some examples of choppy, weak sentences and their revisions, which contain subordinate clauses:

Choppy Lew makes bagels on Tuesday. Lines in front of his store are a block long.

Revised When Lew makes bagels on Tuesday, lines in front of his store are a block long.

Choppy I have fond memories of Zilker Park. My husband and I met there.

Revised I have fond memories of Zilker Park because my husband and I met there.

A correctly subordinated sentence is one of the marks of a sophisticated writer, because it presents adequate information in one smooth flow instead of in monotonous drips. Subordination, like coordination, also adds variety to your sentence construction.

Generally, when you subordinate one idea, you emphasize another, so to avoid the tail-wagging-the-dog problem, put your important idea in the main clause. Also, don't let your most important idea become buried under an avalanche of subordinate clauses, as in the sentence that follows:

> *When* he was told by his boss, *who* had always treated him fairly, that he was being fired from a job *that* he had held for twenty years at a factory *where* he enjoyed working *because* the pay was good, Henry felt angry and frustrated.

Practice combining choppy sentences by studying the sentence-combining exercise below. In this exercise a description of a popular movie or book has been chopped into simple sentences and then combined into one complex sentence.

1. *Psycho* (1960)
Norman Bates manages a motel.
It is remote.

It is dangerous.
Norman has a mother.
She seems overly fond of knives.
He tries to protect his mom.

In a remote—and dangerous—motel, manager Norman Bates tries to protect his mother, who seems overly fond of knives.

2. *King Kong* (1933)
A showman goes to the jungle.
He captures an ape.
The ape is a giant.
The ape is taken to New York City.
He escapes.
He dies fighting for a girl.
He loves her.
She is beautiful.

A giant ape, captured in the jungle by a showman, is taken to New York City, where he escapes and dies fighting for the beautiful girl he loves.

3. *Casablanca* (1942)
Rick is an American.
He is cynical.
He owns a cafe.
He lives in Casablanca.
He meets an old flame.
She is married.
He is a French resistance leader.
Rick helps the couple.
He regains self-respect.

When Rick, a cynical American cafe-owner in Casablanca, helps his old flame and her husband, a French resistance leader, he regains his self-respect.

Please note that the sentences in these exercises may be combined effectively in a number of ways. For instance, the description of *King Kong* might be rewritten this way: "After a showman captures him in the jungle, a giant ape escapes in New York City but dies in a fight for the love of a beautiful girl." How might you rewrite the other two sample sentences?

PRACTICING WHAT YOU'VE LEARNED

A. Revise the sentences that follow so that the underlined words receive more emphasis.

1. It is said that <u>W. C. Fields</u> once filled a child-actor's baby bottle with gin to show his dislike for the little boy.

2. According to recent polls, <u>television</u> is where most Americans get their news.

3. Of all the world's problems, it is <u>hunger</u> that is most urgent.

4. I enjoyed visiting many foreign countries last year, with <u>Greece</u> being my favorite of all of them.

5. The annoying habit of <u>knuckle-cracking</u> is something I can't stand.

B. Combine the pairs of sentences below using coordination or subordination.

1. Elbert wanted to win the skateboard championship. He broke his leg the day before the contest.

2. Dr. Acula recently opened a new office. He specializes in acupuncture in the neck.

3. The earthquake shook the city. Louise was practicing primal-scream therapy at the time.

4. The police had only a few clues. They suspected Jean and David had strangled each other in a desperate struggle over control of the thermostat.

5. Bubba is thirty-five. He still lives with his mother.

6. Harold couldn't tune in "The Battle of the Butlers of the Rich and Famous." The television was broken.

7. Juanita lost some old friends when she won the lottery. She made lots of new ones.

8. Jim Bob quit drinking beer last month. Our aluminum recycling plant closed a week later.

9. Frances hit her professor with her shoe. He decided to reevaluate her essay.

10. The postman quit because the mailbag was too heavy. He also quit because he could not remember all the zip codes.

C. Combine the simple sentences below into one complex sentence. See if you can guess the name of the books or movies described in the sentences. (Answers appear on p. 120.)

1. A boy runs away from home.
   His companion is a runaway slave.
   He lives on a raft.
   The raft is on the Mississippi River.
   He has many adventures.
   The boy learns many lessons.
   Some lessons are about human kindness.
   Some lessons are about friendship.

2. A young man returns from prison.
   He returns to his family.

His family lives in the Dust Bowl.
The family decides to move.
The family expects to find jobs in California.
The family finds intolerance.
They also find dishonest employers.

3. A scientist is obsessed.
He wants to re-create life.
He creates a monster.
The monster rebels against the scientist.
The monster kills his creator.
The villagers revolt.
The villagers storm the castle.

ASSIGNMENT

A. Make up your own sentence-combining exercise by finding or writing one-sentence descriptions of popular or recent movies, books, or television episodes. Divide the complex sentences into simple sentences and exchange papers with a classmate. Give yourselves ten minutes to combine sentences and guess the titles or shows.

B. The two paragraphs below are poorly written because of their choppy, wordy, and monotonous sentences. Rewrite each passage so that it is clear, lively, and emphatic.

There is a new invention on the market. It is called a "dieter's conscience." It is a small box to be installed in one's refrigerator. When the door of the refrigerator is opened by you, a tape recorder begins to start. A really loud voice yells, "You eating again? No wonder you're getting fat." Then the very loud voice says, "Close the door; it's getting warm." Then the voice laughs a lot in an insane and crazy fashion. The idea is one that is designed to mock people into a habit of stopping eating.

In this modern world of today, man has come up with another new invention. This invention is called the "Talking Tombstone." It is made by the "Gone-But-Not-Forgotten" Company, which is located in Burbank, California. This company makes a tombstone that has a device in it that makes the tombstone appear to be talking aloud in a realistic fashion when people go close by it. The reason is that the device is really a recording machine that is turned on due to the simple fact of the heat of the bodies of the people who go by. The closer the people get, the louder the sound the tombstone makes. It is this device that individual persons who want to leave messages after death may utilize. A hypochondriac, to cite one example, might leave a recording of a message that says over and over again in a really loud voice, "See, I told you I was sick!" it may be assumed by one and all that this new invention will be a serious aspect of the whole death situation in the foreseeable future.

APPLYING WHAT YOU'VE
LEARNED TO *YOUR* WRITING

If you have drafted a piece of writing and you are satisfied with your ideas and the development of those thoughts, as well as the essay's organization, you may want to begin revising your sentences for clarity, conciseness, and emphasis. As you move through your draft, think about your readers. Ask yourself, "Are any of my sentences too vague, overpacked, or confused for my readers to understand? Can I clarify any of my ideas by using simpler, more specific language or by using different, less-confusing sentence constructions? Am I boring my readers with repetition of bland Dick-and-Jane sentences?"

Remember that it's not enough for you, the writer, to understand what your sentences mean—your readers must be able to follow your ideas too. When in doubt, always revise your writing so that it is, without a question, clear, concise, and inviting. (For more help, turn to Chapter 5 on Revision.)

CHAPTER 6 SUMMARY

Here is a brief summary of what you should remember about writing effective sentences:

1. All good writers revise their sentences.
2. You can help clarify your ideas for your readers by writing sentences that are informative, straightforward, and precise.
3. You can communicate your ideas more easily to your readers if you cut out deadwood, redundancies, confusing passives, and pretentious language.
4. You can maintain your readers' interest in your ideas if you cultivate a style that is specific, varied, and emphatic.

Answers to sentence-combining exercise:
1. *Huckleberry Finn*
2. *The Grapes of Wrath*
3. *Frankenstein* (or almost any late-night horror movie)

7

Word Logic

The English language contains over a half million words—quite a selection for you as a writer to choose from. But such a wide choice may make you feel like a starving person confronting a six-page, fancy French menu: which choice is best? how do I choose? is the choice so important?

Word choice can make an enormous difference in the quality of your writing for at least one obvious reason: if you substitute an incorrect or vague word for the right one, you take the risk of being totally misunderstood. Ages ago Confucius made the same point: "If language is incorrect, then what is said is not meant. If what is said is not meant, then what ought to be done remains undone." It isn't enough that *you* know what you mean; you must transfer your ideas onto paper in the proper words so that others understand your exact meaning.

To help you avoid possible paralysis from indecision over word choice, this chapter offers some practical suggestions on selecting words that are not only accurate and appropriate but also memorable and persuasive.

SELECTING THE CORRECT WORDS

ACCURACY: CONFUSED WORDS

Unless I get a bank loan soon, I will be forced to lead an *immortal* life.
Dobermans make good pets if you train them with enough *patients*.
He dreamed of eating *desert* after *desert*.
She had dieted for so long that she had become *emancipated*.
The young man was completely in *ah* of the starlette's beauty.

The preceding sentences share a common problem: each one contains an error in word choice. In each sentence, the *underlined* word is incorrect, causing

121

the sentence to be nonsensical or silly. To avoid such problems in word choice, make sure you check words for *accuracy*. Use only those words whose precise meaning, usage, and spelling you know; look in your dictionary to double-check any words whose definitions (or spellings) are fuzzy to you. As Mark Twain noted, the difference between the right word and the wrong one is the difference between lightning and the lightning bug.

Here is a list of words that are often confused in writing. Use your dictionary to determine the meanings or usage of any word unfamiliar to you.

affect/effect	lead/led	choose/chose
to/too/two	cite/sight/site	accept/except
there/their/they're	its/it's	council/counsel
your/you're	good/well	where/wear
complement/compliment	who's/whose	lose/loose
stationary/stationery	lay/lie	precede/proceed
capitol/capital	than/then	illusion/allusion
principal/principle		

ACCURACY: IDIOMATIC PHRASES

Occasionally you may have an essay returned to you with words marked "awkward" or "idiom." In English, as in all languages, we have word groupings that seem governed by no particular logic except the ever-popular "that's-the-way-we-say-it" rule. Many of these idiomatic expressions involve prepositions beginning writers sometimes confuse or misuse. Below are some common idiomatic errors and their corrected forms:

regardless ~~of~~ of	different t~~ha~~n ~~from~~ from	relate w~~ith~~ to
insight ~~of~~ into	must ~~of~~ have known	capable t~~o~~ of
similar w~~ith~~ to	superior th~~an~~ to	aptitude to~~ward~~ for
comply ~~to~~ with	t~~o~~ in my opinion	prior th~~an~~ to
contrast ag~~ainst~~ to	meet ~~to~~ her standards	

To avoid idiomatic errors, consult your dictionary and read your essay aloud; often your ears will catch mistakes in usage that your eyes have overlooked.*

___

* You may not immediately recognize what's wrong with words your teacher has labeled "awk" or "idiom," as these marks often cover many sins. If you're uncertain about an error, don't hesitate to ask your teacher for clarification; after all, if you don't know what's wrong with your sentence, you can't very well avoid making the same mistake again. To illustrate this point, here's a true story: A bright young woman was having trouble with prepositional phrases in her essays, and although her professor repeatedly marked her incorrect expressions with the marginal note "idiom," she never improved. Finally, one day near the end of the term, she approached her teacher in tears and wailed, "Professor Jones, I know I'm not a very good writer, but must you write 'idiot,' 'idiot,' 'idiot' all over my papers?" The moral of this story is simple: it's easy to misunderstand a correction or misread your teacher's writing; since you can't improve until you know what's wrong, always ask when you're in doubt.

LEVELS OF LANGUAGE

In addition to choosing the correct word, you should also select words whose status is suited to your purpose. For convenience here, language has been classified into three categories or levels of usage: (1) colloquial, (2) informal, (3) formal.

Colloquial language is the kind of speech you use most often in conversation with your friends, classmates, and family. It may not always be grammatically correct ("it's me"); it may include fragments of speech, contractions, some slang, words identified as nonstandard by the dictionary (such as "yuck" or "lousy"), and shortened or abbreviated words ("grad school," "photos," "TV"). Colloquial speech is everyday language, and while you may use it in some writing (personal letters, journals, memos, and so forth), you should think carefully about using colloquial language in most college essays or in professional letters, reports, or papers, because such a choice implies a casual relationship between writer and reader.

Informal language is called for in most college and professional assignments. The tone is more formal than in colloquial writing or speech; no slang or nonstandard words are permissible. Informal writing consistently uses correct grammar; fragments are used for special effect or not at all. Authorities disagree on the use of contractions in informal writing: some say avoid them entirely; others say they're permissible; still others advocate using them only to avoid stilted phrases ("let's go," for example, is preferable to "let us go"). Most, if not all, of your essays in English classes will be written in informal language.

Formal language is found in important documents and in serious, often ceremonial, speeches. Characteristics include an elevated—but not pretentious—tone, no contractions, and correct grammar. Formal writing often uses inverted word order and balanced sentence structure. John F. Kennedy's 1960 Inaugural Address, for example, was written in a formal style ("Ask not what your country can do for you; ask what you can do for your country"). Most people rarely, if ever, need to write formally; if you are called upon to do so, however, be careful to avoid formal diction that sounds pretentious, pompous, or phony.

Tone

Tone is a general word that describes writers' attitudes toward their subject matter and audience. There are as many different kinds of tones as there are emotions. Depending on how the writer feels, an essay may sound humorous, ironic, indignant, or solemn, to name but a few of the possible choices. In addition to presenting a specific attitude, a good writer gains credibility by maintaining a tone that is generally calm, reasonable, and sincere.

While it is impossible to analyze all the various kinds of tones one finds in essays, it is nevertheless beneficial to discuss some of those that repeatedly give students trouble. Listed below are some tones that should be used carefully or avoided altogether:

Invective

Invective is unrestrained anger, usually expressed in the form of violent accusation or denunciation. Let's suppose, for example, you hear a friend argue that "anyone who votes for Joe Smith is a Fascist pig"; if you are considering Smith, you are probably offended by your friend's abusive tone. Raging emotion, after all, does not sway the opinions of intelligent people; they need to hear the facts presented in a calm, clear discussion. Therefore, in your own writing, aim for a reasonable tone. You want your readers to think, "Now here is someone with a good understanding of the situation, who has evaluated it with a calm, analytical mind." Keeping a controlled tone doesn't mean you shouldn't feel strongly about your subject—on the contrary, you certainly should—but you should realize that a hysterical or outraged tone defeats your purpose by causing you to sound irrational and therefore untrustworthy. For this reason, you should probably avoid using profanity in your essays; the shock value of an obscenity may not be worth what you might lose in credibility (and besides, is anyone other than your Aunt Fanny really amazed by profanity these days?). The most effective way to get your point across is persuade, not offend, your reader.

Sarcasm

In most of your writing you'll discover that a little sarcasm—bitter, derisive remarks—goes a long way. Like invective, too much sarcasm can damage the reasonable tone your essay should present. Instead of saying, "You can recognize the supporters of the new tax law by the points on the tops of their heads," give your readers some reasons why you believe the tax bill is flawed. Sarcasm can be effective, but realize that it often backfires by causing the writer to sound like a childish name-caller rather than a judicious commentator.

Irony

Irony is a figure of speech whereby the writer or speaker says the opposite of what is meant; for the irony to be successful, however, the audience must understand the writer's true intent. For example, if you have slopped to school in a rainstorm and your drenched teacher enters the classroom saying, "Ah, nothing like this beautiful sunny weather," you know that your teacher is being ironic. Perhaps one of the most famous cases of irony occurred in 1938, when Sigmund Freud, the famous Viennese psychiatrist, was arrested by the Nazis. After being harassed by the Gestapo, he was released on the condition that he sign a statement swearing he had been treated well by the secret police. Freud signed it, but he added a few words after his signature: "I can heartily recommend the Gestapo to anyone." Looking back, we easily recognize Freud's jab at his captors; the Gestapo, however, apparently overlooked the irony and let him go.

While irony is often an effective device, it can also cause great confusion, especially when it is written rather than spoken. Unless your readers thoroughly understand your position in the first place, they may become confused by what appears to be a sudden contradiction. Irony that is too subtle, too private, or simply out of context merely complicates the issue. Therefore, you must make certain that your reader has no trouble realizing when your tongue is firmly embedded in your cheek. And unless you are assigned to write an ironic essay (in the same vein, for instance, as Swift's "A Modest Proposal"), don't overuse irony. Like any rhetorical device, its effectiveness is reduced with overkill.

Flippancy or Cuteness

If you sound too flip or bored in your essay ("I hate this assignment, but since it's two A.M., I might as well being . . ."), your readers will not take you seriously and, consequently, will disregard whatever you have to say. Writers suffering from cuteness will also antagonize their readers. For example, let's assume you're assigned the topic "Which Person Has Done the Most to Arouse the Laboring Class in Twentieth-Century England?" and you begin your essay with a discussion of the man who invented the alarm clock. While that joke might be funny in an appropriate situation, it's not likely to impress your professor, who's looking for serious commentary. How much cuteness is too much is often a matter of taste, but if you have any doubts about the quality of your humor, leave it out. Also, omit personal messages or comic asides to your teacher (such as "Ha, ha, just kidding, teach!" or "I knew you'd love this part"). Humor is often effective, but remember that the point of any essay is to persuade an audience to accept your thesis, not merely to entertain with freestanding jokes. In other words, if you use humor, make sure it is appropriate to your subject matter and that it works to help you make your point.

Sentimentality

Sentimentality is the excessive show of cheap emotions—"cheap" because they are not deeply felt but evoked by clichés and stock, tear-jerking situations. In the nineteenth century, for example, a typical melodrama played on the sentimentality of the audience by presenting a black-hatted, cold-hearted, mustache-twirling villain tying a golden-haired, pure-hearted "Little Nell" to the railroad tracks after driving her ancient, sickly mother out into a snowdrift. Today, politicians (among others) often appeal to our sentimentality by conjuring up vague images they feel will move us emotionally rather than rationally to take their side: "My friends," says Senator Stereotype, "this fine nation of ours was founded by men like myself, dedicated to the principles of family, flag, and freedom. Vote for me, and let's get back to those precious basics that make life in America so grand." Such gush is hardly convincing; good writers and speakers use logic and reason to persuade their audience. For example, don't allow yourself to become too carried away with emotion as did this student: "My dog, Cuddles, is the sweetest, cutest, most precious little puppy dog in the whole wide world, and she will always be my best friend." In addition to sending the reader into sugar shock, this passage fails to present any sound reasons why anyone should appreciate Cuddles. In other words, be sincere in your writing, but don't lost so much control of your emotions that you become mushy or maudlin.

Preachiness

Even if you are so convinced of the rightness of your position that a burning bush couldn't change your mind, try not to sound smug about it. No one likes to be lectured by someone perched atop the mountain of morality. Instead of preaching, adopt a tone that says, "I believe my position is correct, and I am glad to have this opportunity to explain why." Then give your reasons and meet objections in a positive but not holier-than-thou manner.

Pomposity

The "voice" of your essay should sound as natural as possible; don't strain to sound scholarly, scientific, or sophisticated. If you write "My summer sojourn through the western states of this grand country was immensely pleasurable" instead of "My vacation last summer in the Rockies was fun," you sound merely phony, not dignified and learned. Select only words you know and can use easily. Never write anything you wouldn't say in an ordinary conversation. (For more information on correcting pretentious writing, see p. 106 and pp. 130–132.)

> To achieve the appropriate tone, be as sincere, forthright, and reasonable as you can. Let the tone of your essay establish a basis of mutual respect between you and your reader.

CONNOTATION AND DENOTATION

A word's *denotation* refers to its literal meaning, the meaning defined by the dictionary; a word's *connotation* refers to the emotional associations surrounding its meaning. For example, "home" and "residence" both may be defined as the place where one lives, but "home" carries connotations of warmth, security, and family that "residence" lacks. Similarly, "old" and "antique" have identical denotative meanings, but "antique" has the more positive connotation because it suggests something that also has value. Reporters and journalists do the same job, but the latter name somehow seems to indicate someone more sophisticated and professional. Because many words with similar denotative meanings do carry different connotations, good writers must be careful with their word choice. *Select only words whose connotations fit your purpose.* If, for example, you want to describe your grandmother in a positive way as someone who stands up for herself, you might refer to her as "assertive" or "feisty"; if you want to present her negatively, you might call her "aggressive" or "pushy."

In addition to selecting words with the appropriate connotations for your purpose, be careful to avoid offending your audience with particular connotations. For instance, if you were trying to persuade a group of politically conservative doctors to accept your stand on Medicare, you would not want to refer to your opposition as "right-wingers" or "reactionaries," extremist terms that have negative connotations. Remember, you want to inform and persuade your audience, not antagonize them.

You should also be alert to the use of words with emotionally charged connotations, especially in advertising and propaganda of various kinds. Car manufacturers, for example, often use names of swift, bold, or graceful animals (Jaguar, Cougar, Impala) to sway prospective buyers; cosmetic manufacturers in recent years have taken advantage of the trend toward lighter makeup by associating words such as "nature," "natural," "organic," and "healthy glow" with their products. Politicians, too, are heavy users of connotation; they often drop in emotionally positive, but practically meaningless, words and phrases such as "defender of the American Way" and "friend of the common man" to describe themselves, while describing their opponents with such negative, emotionally charged labels as "radical" and "elitist." Of course, intelligent readers, like intelligent voters and consumers, want more than emotion-laden words; they want facts and logical argument. Therefore, as a good writer, you should use connotation as only one of many persuasive devices to enhance your presentation of evidence; never depend solely on an emotional appeal to convince your audience that your position—or thesis—is correct.

PRACTICING WHAT YOU'VE LEARNED

A. Some of the underlined words below are used incorrectly; some are correct. Substitute the accurate word wherever necessary.

1. The finances of the chicken ranch are in <u>fowl</u> shape because the hens are <u>lying</u> down on the job.
2. The professor, <u>whose</u> famous for his <u>photogenic</u> memory, graciously <u>excepted</u> a large <u>amount</u> of <u>complements</u>.
3. <u>Its to</u> bad you don't like <u>they're</u> new Popsicle sculpture since <u>their</u> giving it <u>to</u> you for Christmas.
4. Vacations of <u>to</u> weeks with <u>to</u> friends are always <u>to</u> short, and while <u>you're to</u> tired <u>to</u> return <u>to</u> work, <u>your to</u> broke not <u>to</u>.
5. Sara June felt she deserved an "A" in math, <u>irregardless</u> of her 59 average in the <u>coarse</u>.
6. "I am impressed by the <u>continuity</u> of his physical presence"—Howard Cosell.
7. Did the high school <u>principal</u> <u>loose</u> <u>you're</u> heavy <u>medal</u> record and <u>it's</u> album jacket <u>too</u>?
8. The new city <u>counsel</u> parade ordinance will <u>effect</u> everyone in the <u>capitol</u> city <u>except</u> members of the Lawn Chair Marching Band.

B. The sentences below contain words and phrases that interfere with the sincere, reasonable tone good writers try to create. Rewrite each sentence replacing sarcasm, sentimentality, cuteness, invective, and pretentiousness with more appropriate language.

1. The last dying rays of day were quickly ebbing in the West as if to signal the feline to begin its lonely vigil.
2. Only a jerk would support the President's Mideast peace plan.
3. I was desirous of acquiring knowledge about members of our lower income brackets.
4. If the bill to legalize marijuana is passed, we can safely assume that the whole country will soon be going to pot (heh, heh!).
5. I just love to look at those teensie little white mice with their cute, itty-bitty red eyes.

C. In each group of words listed below, identify the words with the most pleasing and most negative connotations.

1. teacher/instructor/educator/professor/lecturer
2. slender/slim/skinny/thin/slight/anorexic
3. famous/notorious/well-known/infamous
4. wealthy/opulent/rich/affluent/privileged
5. dull/drab/quiet/boring/colorless

D. Replace the underlined words in the sentences below with words arousing more positive feelings:

1. The <u>stench</u> from Jean's kitchen meant dinner was ready and was about to be served.
2. My neighbor was a <u>fat spinster lady</u>.
3. The coach had <u>rigid</u> rules for all his players.
4. His <u>obsession</u> with his yard pleased the city's beautification committee.
5. The <u>slick</u> car salesman made a <u>pitch</u> to the <u>old geezer</u> who walked in the door.
6. Textbook writers admit to having a few <u>bizarre</u> habits.
7. Carol was a <u>mediocre</u> student.
8. His <u>odd</u> clothes made Mary think he was a <u>bum</u>.
9. The High Priest explained his tribe's <u>superstitions</u>.
10. Many of the Board members were amazed to see how Algernon <u>dominated</u> the meeting.

SELECTING THE BEST WORDS

In addition to selecting the correct word and appropriate tone, good writers also choose words that firmly implant their ideas in the minds of their readers. The best prose not only makes cogent points but also states these points memorably. To help you select the best words to express your ideas, the following is a list of do's and don't's covering the most common diction (word choice) problems in students' writing today:

Do make your words as precise as possible. Always choose vigorous, active verbs and colorful, specific nouns and modifiers. "The big tree was hit by lightning," for example, is not as informative or interesting as "Lightning splintered the neighbors' thirty-foot oak." *Don't* use words whose meanings are unclear:

Vague Verbs

Unclear   She is *involved in* a lawsuit. [How?]

Clear   She is suing her dentist for filling the wrong tooth.

Unclear   Tom can *relate to* Jennifer. [What's the relationship?]

Clear   Tom understands Jennifer's family problems.

Unclear   He won't *deal* with his ex-wife. [In what way?]

Clear   He refuses to speak to his ex-wife.

Unclear   Clyde *participated* in an off-Broadway play. [How?]

Clear   Clyde held the cue cards for the actors.

Vague Nouns

Unclear   The burglar took several valuable *things* from our house.* [What items?]

Clear   The burglar took a *color TV, a stereo, and a microwave oven from our house.*

Unclear   When I have my car serviced, there is always *trouble.* [What kind?]

Clear   When I have my car serviced, *the mechanics always find additional repairs and never have the car ready when it is promised.*

Unclear   When I have *problems,* I always call my friends for advice. [What problems?]

Clear   *If my girlfriend breaks up with me, my roof needs repairing, or my heart needs surgery,* I always call my friends for advice.

Unclear   I like to have *fun* while I'm on vacation. [What sort of activities?]

Clear   I like to *eat in fancy restaurants, fly stunt kites, and walk along the beach when I'm on vacation.*

Vague Modifiers

Unclear   His *terrible* explanation left me *very* confused. [Why "terrible"? How confused?]

---

* One specific piece of advice: banish the word "thing" from your writing. In nine out of ten cases, it is a lazy substitute for some other word. Unless you mean "an inanimate object," replace "thing" with the specific word it stands for.

Clear	His disorganized explanation left me too confused to begin the project.
Unclear	The boxer hit the punching bag *really* hard. [How hard?]
Clear	The boxer hit the punching bag so hard it split open.
Unclear	*Casablanca* is a *good* movie *with something for everyone*. [Why "good" and for everyone?]
Clear	*Casablanca* is a witty, sentimental movie that successfully combines an adventure story and a romance.

Do make your word choices as fresh and original as possible. Instead of saying, "My hometown is very quiet," you might say, "My hometown's definition of an orgy is a light burning after midnight." In other words, if you can make your readers admire and remember your prose, you have a better chance of persuading them to accept your ideas.

Conversely, to avoid ho-hum prose, *don't* fill your sentences with clichés and platitudes—overworked phrases that cause your writing to sound lifeless and trite. Although we use clichés in everyday conversation, good writers avoid them in writing because (1) they are often vague or imprecise (just how pretty is "pretty as a picture?"), (2) they are used so frequently that they rob your prose style of personality and uniqueness ("it was raining cats and dogs"—does that phrase help your reader "see" the particular rainstorm you're trying to describe?).

Novice writers often include trite expressions because they do not recognize them as chichés; therefore, below is a partial list (there are literally thousands more) of phrases to avoid. Instead of using cliché, try substituting an original phrase to describe what you see or feel. Never try do disguise a cliché by putting it in quotation marks—a baboon in dark glasses and a wig is still a baboon.

crack of dawn	needle in a haystack
a crying shame	bed of roses
white as a sheet	soft as silk
depths of despair	hard as nails
dead of night	white as snow
shadow of a doubt	almighty dollar
hear a pin drop	naked truth
blessed event	after all is said and done
first and foremost	to make a long story short

It would be impossible, of course, to memorize all the clichés and trite expressions in our language, but do check your prose for recognizable overworked phrases so that your words will not be predictable and, consequently, dull. If you aren't sure if a phrase is a cliché—but you've heard it used frequently—your prose will probably be stronger if you substitute an original phrase for the suspected one.

Don't use trendy expressions or slang in your essays. Slang generally consists of commonly used words made up by special groups to communicate among themselves. Slang has many origins, from sports to space travel; for example, surfing gave us the expression "to wipe out" (to fail), the military lent "snafu" (from the first letters of "situation normal—all fouled up"), the astronauts provided "A-OK" (all systems working).

While slang often gives our speech color and vigor, it is unacceptable in many formal writing assignments for several reasons. First, slang is often part of a private language understood only by members of a particular professional, social, or age group. Secondly, slang often presents a vague picture or one that changes meanings from person to person or from context to context. More than likely, each person has a unique definition for a particular slang expression, and while these definitions may overlap, they are not precisely the same. Consequently, your reader could interpret your words one way while you mean them in another, a dilemma that might result in total miscommunication. Too often beginning writers rely on vague, popular clichés ("His behavior really grossed me out") instead of thinking of specific words to express specific ideas. Moreover, slang becomes dated quickly, and almost nothing sounds worse than yesterday's "in" expressions. (In his movie *Annie Hall,* Woody Allen pointed out the silliness of some of our psychological slang; when he was told to "mellow out," he replied, "When I get mellow, I ripen and then I rot.")

Try to write so that your prose will be as fresh and pleasing ten years from now as today. Don't allow slang to give your writing a flippant tone that detracts from a serious discussion. Therefore, to communicate clearly with your reader, avoid including slang in your essays. Putting slang in quotation marks isn't the solution—omit the slang and use precise words instead.

Do select simple, direct words your readers can easily understand. Don't use pompous or pseudosophisticated language in place of plain speech. Wherever possible, avoid *jargon*—that is, words and phrases that are unnecessarily technical, pretentious, or abstract.

Technical jargon—terms specific to one area of study or specialization— should be omitted or clearly defined in essays directed to a general audience because such language is often inaccessible to anyone outside the writer's particular field. By now most of us are familiar with bureaucratese, journalese, and psychobabble, in addition to gobbledy-gook from business, politics, advertising, and education. If, for example, you worry that "a self-actualized person such as yourself cannot transcend either your hostile environment or your passive-aggressive behavior to make a commitment to a viable lifestyle and meaningful interpersonal relationships," then you are indulging in psychological or sociological jargon; if you "review existing mechanisms of consumer input, thruput, and output via the consumer communications channel module," you are speaking business jargon. While most professions do have their own terms, you should limit your use of specialized language to writing aimed solely at your professional colleagues; always try to avoid technical jargon in prose directed at a general audience.

Today the term "jargon" also refers to prose containing an abundance of abstract, pretentious, multi-syllable words. The use of this kind of jargon often betrays a writer's attempt to sound sophisticated and intellectual; actually, it only confuses meaning and delays communication. Here, for instance, is an excerpt of incomprehensible jargon from a college president who obviously prefers twenty-five-cent words to simple, straightforward nickel ones: "We will divert the force of this fiscal stress into leverage energy and pry important budgetary considerations and control out of our fiscal and administrative procedures." Or look at the thirty-eight-word definition of "exit" written by an Occupational Safety and Health Administration bureaucrat: "That portion of a means of egress which is separated from all spaces of the building or structure by construction or equipment as required in this subpart to provide a protected way of travel to the exit discharge." Such language is not only pretentious and confusing but almost comic in its wordiness.

Jargon is so pervasive these days that even some English teachers are succumbing to its use. A group of high school teachers, for instance, was asked to indicate a preference for one of the following sentences:

> His expression of ideas that are in disagreement with those of others will often result in his rejection by them and his isolation from the life around him.

> If he expresses ideas that others disagree with, he will often be rejected by them and isolated from the life around him.

Surprisingly, only nineteen percent chose the more direct second sentence. The others saw the wordy, pompous first statement as "mature" and "educated," revealing that some teachers themselves may be both the victims and perpetrators of doublespeak.

To avoid such verbal litter in your own writing, follow these rules:

1. Always select the plainest, most direct words you know.

Jargon   I want to interface with the author because I discovered an error on the page that terminates the volume.

Revised   I want to talk to the author because I found an error on the last page of the book.

2. Replace nominalizations (nouns that are made from verbs and adjectives, usually by adding endings such as *-tion, -ism, -ness,* or *-al*) with simpler verbs and nouns.

Jargon   The departmental head has come to the recognition that the utilization of verbose verbalization renders informational content inaccessible.

Revised   The department head recognizes that wordiness confuses meaning.

3. Avoid adding *-ize* or *-wise* to verbs and adverbs.

Jargon   *Weatherwise*, it looked like a good day to *finalize* her report on wind tunnels.

Revised   The day's clear weather would help her finish her report on wind tunnels.

4. Drop out meaningless tack-on words such as "factor," "aspect," and "situation."

Jargon   The convenience factor of the neighborhood grocery store is one aspect of its success.

Revised   The convenience of the neighborhood grocery store contributes to its success.

Remember that good writing is clear and direct, never wordy, cloudy, or ostentatious. (For more hints on developing a clear style, see pp. 96–106.)

Do call things by their proper names. Don't sugarcoat your terms by substituting euphemisms—words that sound nice or pretty applied to subjects some people find distasteful. For example, you've probably heard someone say, "she passed away" instead of "she died," or "he was under the influence of alcohol" instead of "he was drunk," or "she was a lady of the night" instead of "she was a prostitute." Often euphemisms are used to soften names of jobs: "sanitary engineer" for garbage collector, "field representative" for salesperson, "information processor" for typist, "vehicle appearance specialist" for car washer, and so forth.

Some euphemisms are dated and now seem plain silly; in Victorian times, for example, the word "leg" was considered unmentionable in polite company, so people spoke of "piano limbs" and asked for the "first joint" of a chicken. The phrases "white meat" and "dark meat" were euphemisms some people used to avoid asking for a piece of chicken breast or thigh.

Today, euphemisms still abound. Though our generation is perhaps more direct about sex and death, many current euphemisms gloss over unpleasant or unpopular business, military, and political practices. Some stockbrokers, for example, once referred to an October market crash as "a fourth quarter equity retreat," and General Motors didn't really shut down one of its plants—the closing was merely a "volume-related production schedule adjustment." In a similar move, Chrysler didn't lay off 5,000 workers; it simply "initiated a career alternative enhancement program." Nuclear power plants no longer have dumps; they have "containment facilities" with radiation "migration" rather than leaks. Simple products are now complex technology: clocks are "analog temporal displacement monitors," toothbrushes are "home plaque removal instruments," sinks are part of the "hygienic hand-washing media," and pencils are "portable hand-held communications inscribers."

Euphemisms thrive in governments as officials try to hide the truth from the public. For example, during the trial of Lt. Colonel Oliver North, in trouble for his role in the sale of arms to Iran, "official lies" became "plausible deniability." Earlier, the United States did not withdraw troops from Lebanon; we merely "backloaded our augmentation personnel." A 1984 handbook for Nicaraguan rebels written and published by the CIA offered helpful advice about "neutralization" of government officials. Euphemisms also thrive in other government agencies. A former budget director gave us "revenue enhancements" instead of new taxes, and a Secretary of Health, Education, and Welfare once tried to camouflage cuts in social services by calling them "advance downward adjustments." In the same vein we learn that government programs no longer simply fail; they are "rendered inoperative."

In some jails a difficult prisoner, who once would have been sent to solitary confinement, is now placed in the "meditation room" or in the "adjustment center." In some hospitals, sick people do not die—they experience "negative patient care outcome." The military, too, has added its share of euphemisms to the language; these range from the comic transformation of the lowly shovel into a "combat emplacement evacuator" to the deadly serious use of the words "liberation" and "pacification" to mean the invasion and destruction of other countries.

Because euphemisms can be used unscrupulously to manipulate people by sugarcoating the truth, you should always avoid them in your own prose and be suspicious of them in the writing of others. As Aldous Huxley, author of *Brave New World,* noted, "An education for freedom is, among other things, an education in the proper uses of language."

In addition to weakening the credibility of one's ideas, euphemisms can make prose unnecessarily abstract, wordy, pretentious, or even silly. For a clear and natural prose style, use terms that are straightforward and simple. In other words, call a spade a spade, not "an implement for use in horticultural environments."

Avoid sexist language. Most people will agree that language helps shape thought. Consequently, writers should avoid using any language that promotes demeaning stereotypes. Sexist language, in particular, often subtly suggests that women are less rational, intelligent, or capable of handling certain tasks or jobs. In order to make your writing as accurate and unbiased as possible, here are a half-dozen simple suggestions for ways to write nonsexist prose:

1. Try using plural nouns to eliminate the need for the singular pronouns "he" and "she":

Original   Today's *doctor* knows *he* must carry extra malpractice insurance.

Revision   Today's *doctors* know *they* must carry extra malpractice insurance.

2. Try substituting nonsexist occupational titles for those ending in "man" or "woman":

Original   The *fireman* and the *saleslady* watched the *policeman* arrest the *mailman.*

Revision   The *firefighter* and the *sales clerk* watched the *police officer* arrest the *mail carrier.*

3. Don't contribute to stereotyping by assigning particular roles solely to men or women:

Original   *Mothers* concerned about the possibility of Reyes Syndrome should avoid giving their sick children aspirin.

Revision   *Parents* concerned about the possibility of Reyes Syndrome should avoid giving their sick children aspirin.

4. Try substituting nonsexist words such as "people," "persons," "one," "voters," "workers," "students," etc., for "man" or "woman":

Original   Any *man* who wants to become a corporation executive before thirty should buy this book.

Revision   *Anyone* who wants to become a corporation executive before thirty should buy this book.

5. Don't use inappropriate diminutives:

Original   In the annual office picture, the photographer asked the men to stand behind the *girls.*

Revision   In the annual office picture, the photographer asked the men to stand behind the *women.*

6. Be consistent in your treatment of men's and women's names, marital status, professional titles, and physical appearances:

Original   Neither Melville, the inspired novelist, nor Miss Emily Dickinson, the plain spinster poetess of Amherst, gained fame or fortune in their lifetimes.

Revision   Neither Melville, the novelist, nor Dickinson, the poet, gained fame or fortune in their lifetimes.

Revising your writing to eliminate sexist references does not mean turning clear phrases into awkward or confusing jumbles of "he/she told him/her that the car was his/hers. By consistently following the suggestions above, you should be able to make your prose both clear and inoffensive to all members of your audience.

Do enliven your writing with figurative language, when appropriate. Figurative language produces pictures or images in a reader's mind, often by comparing something unfamiliar to something familiar. The two most common figurative devices are the simile and the metaphor. A *simile* is a comparison between two people, places, feelings, or things, using the word "like" or "as"; a more forceful comparison, omitting the word "like" or "as," is a *metaphor*. Below are two examples:

Simile   George eats his meals like a hog.

Metaphor   George is a hog at mealtime.

In both sentences George, whose eating habits are unfamiliar to the reader, is likened to a hog, whose sloppy manners are generally well known. By comparing George to a hog, the writer gives the reader a clear picture of George at the table. Figurative language cannot only help you present your ideas in clear, concrete, economical ways, but can also make your prose more memorable—especially if the image or picture you present is a fresh, arresting one. Below are some examples of striking images designed to catch the reader's attention and to clarify the writer's point:

- An hour away from her is like a month in the country.
- The atmosphere of the meeting room was as tense as a World Series game tied up in the ninth inning.
- If love makes the world go round, jealousy is the monkey wrench thrown into the gears.
- The banker looked at my loan application like an English teacher looks at a misspelled word.
- Dreams are the mind's rewriting of reality.
- The factory squatted on the bank of the river like a huge black toad.

Figurative language can spice up your prose, but like any spice, it can be misused, thus spoiling your soup. Therefore, *don't* overuse figurative language; not every point needs a metaphor or simile for clarity or emphasis. Too many images are confusing. Moreover, *don't* use stale images. (Clichés—discussed on p. 130—are often tired metaphors or similes: snake in the grass, hot as fire, quiet as a mouse, etc.) If you can't catch your readers' attention with a fresh picture, don't bore them with a stale one.

And finally, don't mix images—this too often results in a confusing or unintentionally comic scene. For example, a former mayor of Denver once responded to a question about city fiscal requirements this way: "I think the proper approach is to go through this Garden of Gethsemane that we're in now, give birth to a budget that will come out of it, and then start putting our ducks in order with an appeal and the backup we would need to get something done at the state level." Or take ex-president Gerald Ford's description of the difficulties involved in building his presidential library: "Two years ago, we were literally back on our own goal line and we had a long row to hoe. Now we are on the doorstep of success." Perhaps a newspaper columnist wins the prize for confusion with this triple-decker: "The Assemblymen also were miffed at their

Senate counterparts because they have refused to bite the bullet that now seems to have grown to the size of a millstone to the Assemblymen whose necks are on the line."

In summary, use figurative language sparingly and consistently to present a vivid picture to your reader.

Do vary your word choice so that your prose does not sound wordy, repetitious, or monotonous. Consider the following sentence:

> According to child psychologists, depriving a child of artistic stimulation in the earliest stages of childhood can cause the child brain damage.

Reworded, the sentence below eliminates the tiresome, unnecessary repetition of the word "child":

> According to child psychologists, depriving infants of artistic stimulation can cause brain damage.

By omitting or changing repeated words, you can add variety and crispness to your prose. Of course, don't ever change your words or sentence structure to achieve variety at the expense of clarity or precision; at all times your goal is making your prose clear to your readers.

Do remember that wordiness is a major problem for all writers, even the professionals. State your thoughts directly and specifically in as few words as are necessary to communicate your meaning clearly. In addition to the advice given here on avoiding wordy, vague jargon, euphemisms, clichés, and so forth, you should review the sections on simplicity and conciseness in Chapter 6.

The most important key to effective word choice is revision.

As you write your first draft, don't fret about selecting the best words to communicate your ideas; in later drafts one of your main tasks will be replacing the inaccurate or imprecise words with better ones (Dorothy Parker, famous for her witty essays, once lamented, "I can't write five words but that I change seven"). All good writers rewrite, so revise your prose to make each word count.

PRACTICING WHAT YOU'VE LEARNED

A. Underline the vague nouns, verbs, and modifiers in the sentences below. Then rewrite each one so the sentence says something clear and specific.

1. The experiment had very bad results.
2. The speaker came up with some odd items.
3. The house was big, old, and ugly.
4. The man was a nice guy with a good personality.
5. I felt that the whole ordeal was quite an experience.
6. The machine we got was missing a few things.
7. The woman was really something special.
8. The classroom material wasn't interesting.
9. The child made a lot of very loud noises.
10. The cost of the unusual meal was amazing.

B. Rewrite the following sentences, eliminating all the clichés, sexist language, and euphemisms you find.

1. When my mother didn't return from the little girl's room, we decided she was as slow as molasses.
2. According to former-president Jimmy Carter, the aborted rescue of the hostages in Iran was an incomplete success.
3. On election day, all of us over the ripe old age of eighteen should exercise our most sacred democratic privilege.
4. After all is said and done, the range technicians and the agricultural producers will still be the new disadvantaged class.
5. Each officer in the Armed Forces realizes the someday he may be called upon to use the peacekeepers to depopulate an emerging nation in a lethal intervention.
6. Although he once regarded her as sweet and innocent, he realized then and there that she was really a wolf in sheep's clothing.
7. Any good cook will be green with envy when she tastes her neighbor's apple pie.
8. The City Councilman was stewing in his juices when he learned that his son had been arrested for fooling around with the ballot box.
9. After the policemen detained the rebels, some of the newspapermen who had been watching the riot experienced unlawful deprivation of life.
10. The successful Congressman knows when to say, "That information is classified for reasons of national security."

C. Rewrite the following sentences, replacing the jargon, slang, and vague language with clear, precise words and phrases.

1. To maintain a state of high-level wellness, one should use a wooden interdental stimulator at least once a day.

2. According to the military, one should not attempt a predawn ventical insertion without a aerodynamic personnel decelerator because it could lead to sudden deceleration trauma upon landing.

3. American Airlines' passengers can now arrive and depart planes on customer conveyance mobile lounges.

4. If you are in the armed services, you should avoid receiving a ballistically induced aperture in the subcutaneous environment that might lead to your being terminated with extreme prejudice.

5. The U.S Embassy in Budapest warned its employees: "It must be assumed that available casual indigenous female companions work for or cooperate with the Hungarian government security establishment."

6. "I thought the evening would be totally rad but my blind date turned out to be a double bagger, so I left to chill out downtown," said Arthur, who was somewhat of a geek himself.

7. The employee was outplaced for a lack of interpersonal skills and for failing to optimize productivity.

8. My institute of higher learning announced today that its academic evaluation program had been delayed and in all probability indefinitely postponed due to circumstances relating to financial insolvency.

9. All of us could relate to Mabel's essay on the significant educational factors involved in the revenue enhancement tax-base erosion control program.

10. "We were not micromanaging Grenada intelligencewise until about that time frame," said Admiral Wesley L. McDonald, when asked what was happening on the island just prior to the United States' 1983 rescue mission.

ASSIGNMENT

A. The recipe below pokes fun at bureaucractic jargon. See if you can translate the bureaucratese into clear, simple instructions. Then look at your own writing to make certain that you are not guilty of using similar gobbledygook in your own prose.

Input to output, 35 minutes

For government employees and bureaucrats who have problems with standard recipes, here's one that should make the grade—a classic version of the chocolate-chip cookie translated for easy reading.

Total Lead Time: 35 minutes.

Inputs:
    1 cup packed brown sugar
    ½ cup granulated sugar
    ½ cup softened butter
    ½ cup shortening
    2 eggs
    1½ teaspoons vanilla
    2½ cups all-purpose flour
    1 teaspoon baking soda
    ½ teaspoon salt
    12-ounce package semi-sweet chocolate pieces
    1 cup chopped walnuts or pecans

Guidance:
    After procurement actions, decontainerize inputs. Perform measurement tasks on a case-by-case basis. In a mixing type bowl, impact heavily on brown sugar, granulated sugar, softened butter and shortening. Coordinate the interface of eggs and vanilla, avoiding an overrun scenario to the best of your skills and abilities.
    At this point in time, leverage flour, baking soda and salt into a bowl and aggregate. Equalize with prior mixture and develop intense and continuous liaison among inputs until well-coordinated. Associate key chocolate and nut subsystems and execute stirring operations.
    Within this time frame, take action to prepare the heating environment for throughput by manually setting the oven baking unit by hand to temperature of 375 degrees Fahrenheit (190 Celsius). Drop mixture in an ongoing fashion from a teaspoon implement onto an ungreased cookie sheet at intervals sufficient enough apart to permit total and permanent separation of throughputs to the maximum extent practicable under operating conditions.
    Position cookie sheet in a bake situation and surveil for 8 to 10 minutes or until cooking action terminates. Initiate coordination of outputs within the cooling rack function. Containerize, wrap in red tape and disseminate to authorized staff personnel on a timely and expeditious basis.

Output:
    Six dozen official government chocolate-chip cookie units.

© 1982, *The Washington Post*

B. Write two of the following paragraphs and then exchange them with those written by a classmate. Translate faulty prose into crisp, clear sentences.

- a paragraph of clichés and vague language arguing the value of having a particular major in college

- a paragraph of jargon and euphemisms by a politician explaining why he/she accepted money from an undercover agent
- a paragraph of vague language and clichés persuading your banker to advance you funds to invest in a get-rich-quick scheme
- a paragraph of slang, clichés, and sexist language advising your friends on their approaching marriage
- a paragraph of jargon and vague language praising a product you've invented and are trying to market

APPLYING WHAT YOU'VE LEARNED TO *YOUR* WRITING

If you have drafted a piece of writing and you are satisfied with your development and organization of your ideas, you may want to begin revising your word choice. First, read your draft for accuracy: are your words used correctly? Then focus your attention on your draft's tone, on the "voice" that your words are creating. Have you selected the right words for your purpose and for your audience? Last, change any words that you feel are vague, bland, sexist, or confusing; substitute clear prose for jargon, slang, clichés, or euphemisms. Make each word count; allow your words to clarify, not muddy, your meaning.

CHAPTER 7 SUMMARY

Here is a brief restatement of what you should remember about word choice:

1. Consult a dictionary if you are in doubt about the meaning or usage of a particular word.
2. Choose words that are appropriate for your purpose and audience.
3. Choose words that are clear, specific, and fresh rather than vague, bland, or clichéd.
4. Avoid language that is sexist, trendy, or that tries to hide truth behind jargon or euphemisms.
5. Work for prose that is concise rather than wordy, precise rather than foggy.

THE BASICS OF THE SHORT ESSAY: PART ONE SUMMARY

Here are ten rules to keep in mind while you are writing the rough drafts of your essay:

1. Be confident that you have something important and interesting to say.
2. Identify your particular audience and become determined to communicate effectively with them.
3. Use prewriting techniques to help you focus on one main idea that will become the thesis of your essay.
4. Organize your essay's points logically, in a persuasive and coherent order.
5. Develop each of your ideas with enough specific details.
6. Cut out any irrelevant material that disrupts the smooth flow from idea to idea.
7. Compose sentences that are clear, concise, and informative.
8. Select accurate, vivid words.
9. Revise your prose.
10. Revise your prose.

PART
TWO

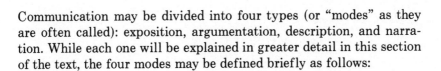

Modes and
Strategies

Communication may be divided into four types (or "modes" as they are often called): exposition, argumentation, description, and narration. While each one will be explained in greater detail in this section of the text, the four modes may be defined briefly as follows:

exposition   the writer intends to explain or inform

argumentation   the writer intends to convince or persuade

description   the writer intends to create in words a picture of a person, place, object, or feeling

narration   the writer intends to tell a story or recount an event

While we commonly refer to exposition, argumentation, description, and narration as the basic types of prose, in reality it is difficult to find any one mode in a pure form. In fact, almost all essays are combinations of two or more modes; it would be virtually impossible, for instance, to write a story—narration—without including description or to argue without also giving some information. Nevertheless, by determining a writer's *main* purpose, we can usually identify an essay or prose piece as primarily exposition, argumentation, description, or narration. In other words, an article may include a brief description of a new mousetrap, but if the writer's main intention is to explain how the trap works, then we may designate the essay as exposition. In most cases, the primary mode of any essay will be readily apparent to the reader.

In Part Two of this text, you will study each of the four modes in detail and learn some of the patterns of development, called *strategies,* that will enable you to write the kind of prose most frequently demanded in college and professional work. Mastering the most common prose patterns in their simplest forms now will help you successfully assess and organize any kind of complex writing assignment you may face in the future.

8

Exposition

Exposition refers to prose whose primary purpose is giving information. Some familiar examples of expository writing include encyclopedias, dictionaries, news magazines, and textbooks. In addition, much of your own college work may be classified as exposition: book reports, political analyses, lesson plans, laboratory and business reports, and most essay exams, to cite only a few of the possibilities.

But while all expository writing does present information, a good expository essay is more than a collection of facts, figures, and details. First, each essay should contain a thesis statement announcing the writer's purpose and position. Then the essay should be organized so that the body paragraphs explain and support that thesis. In an expository essay the writer says, in effect, here are the facts *as I see them;* therefore, the writer's main purpose is not only to inform the readers but also to convince them that this essay explains the subject matter in the clearest, most truthful way.

THE STRATEGIES OF EXPOSITION

There are a variety of ways to organize an expository essay, depending upon your purpose. The most common strategies, or patterns, of organization include development by *example, process analysis, comparison and contrast, definition, classification, and causal analysis.* However, an essay is rarely developed completely by a single strategy (an essay developed by comparison and contrast, for instance, may also contain examples; a classification essay may contain definitions, and so forth); therefore, as in the case of the four modes, we identify the kind of expository essay by its *primary* strategy of development. To help you understand every expository strategy thoroughly before going on to the next, each is presented here separately. Each discussion section follows a similar pattern, which includes the definition of the strategy, some familiar examples, tips on developing your essay, warnings about common problems, a list of essay topics, a revision worksheet, and two sample essays—one written by a student and the other by a professional writer.

STRATEGY ONE:
DEVELOPMENT BY EXAMPLE

Perhaps you've heard a friend complain lately about a roommate. "Tina is an inconsiderate boor, impossible to live with," she cries. Your natural response might be to question your friend's rather broad accusation: "What makes her so terrible? What does she do that's so bad?" Your friend might then respond with specific examples of Tina's insensitivity: she never washes her dishes, she ties up the telephone for hours, and she plays her stereo until three every morning. By citing several examples, your friend clarifies and supports her general criticism of Tina, thus persuading you to accept her point of view.

Examples in an essay work precisely the same way as in the hypothetical story above: they *support, clarify, interest,* and *persuade.*

In your writing assignments, you might want to assert that dorm food is cruel and inhuman punishment, that recycling is a profitable hobby, or that the cost of housing is rising dramatically. But without some carefully chosen examples to show the truth of your statements, these remain unsupported generalities or mere opinions. Your task, then, is to provide enough specific examples to support your general statements, to make them both clear and convincing. Below is a statement offering the reader only hazy generalities:

> Our locally supported TV channel presents a variety of excellent educational shows. The shows are informative on lots of different subjects for both children and adults. The information they offer makes channel 19 well worth the public funds that support it.

Rewritten below, the same paragraph explains its point clearly through the use of specific examples:

> Our locally supported TV channel presents a variety of excellent educational shows. For example, young children can learn their alphabet and numbers from *Sesame Street;* imaginative older children can be encouraged to create by watching *Kids' Writes,* a show on which four hosts read and act out stories written and sent in by youngsters from eight to fourteen. Adults may enjoy learning about antiques and collectibles from a program called *The Collector;* each week the show features an in-depth look at buying, selling, trading, and displaying collectible items, from Depression glass to teddy bears to Shaker furniture. Those folks wishing to become handy around the home can use information on repairs from plumbing to wiring on *This Old House,* while the nonmusical can learn the difference between

skat singing and arias on such programs as *Jazz!* and *Opera Today.* And the money-minded can profit from the tips dropped by stockbrokers who appear on *Wall Street Week.* The information offered makes these and other educational shows on channel 19 well worth the public funds that support the station.

Although the preceding example is based on real shows, you may also use personal experiences, hypothetical situations, anecdotes, research material, facts, testimony, or any combination thereof, to explain or support the points in your essays.

In some cases you may find that a series of short examples fits your purpose, illustrating clearly the idea you are presenting to your reader:

> In the earlier years of Hollywood, actors aspiring to become movie stars often adopted new names that they believed sounded more attractive to the public. Frances Ethel Gumm, for instance, decided to change her name to Judy Garland long before she flew over any rainbows, and Alexander Archibald Leach became Cary Grant on his way from England to America. Alexandra Cymboliak and Merle Johnson, Jr. might not have set teenage hearts throbbing in the early 1960s, but Sandra Dee and Troy Donahue certainly did. And while some names were changed to achieve a smoother flow, Frederic Austerlitz to Fred Astaire, for example, some may have also been changed to ensure a good fit on movie theater marquees as well as a place in their audience's memory: the little Turner girl, Julia Jean Mildred Frances, for instance, became just Lana.

Or you may decide that two or three examples, explained in some detail, is the best choice for your topic rather than a series of short examples. In the paragraph that follows the writer chose to develop two examples to illustrate her point about her unusual dog:

> Our family dog Sparky always let us know when he wasn't getting enough attention. For instance, if he thought we were away from home too much, he'd perform his record trick. While we were out, Sparky would push an album out of the record rack and then tap the album cover in just such a way that the record would roll out. Then he would chomp the record! We'd return to find our favorite LP (somehow, always our current favorite) chewed into tiny bits of black vinyl scattered about the room. Another popular Sparky trick was the cat-sit. If the family was peacefully settled on the porch, not playing with him, Sparky would grab the family cat by the ear and drag her over to the steps, whereupon he would sit on top of her until someone paid attention to him. He never hurt the cat; he simply sat on her as one would sit on a fine cushion, with her head poking out under his tail, and a silly grin on his face that said, "See, if you'd play with me, I wouldn't get into such mischief."

You may also find that in some cases, one long, detailed example (called an *extended example*) is more useful than several shorter ones. If you were writing a paragraph urging the traffic department to install a stop sign at a particularly dangerous corner, you probably should cite numerous examples of accidents there. On the other hand, if you were praising a certain kind of local architecture, you might select one representative house and discuss it in detail. In the paragraph below, for instance, the writer might have supported his main point by citing a number of cases in which lives had been saved by seat belts; he chose instead to offer one detailed example, in the form of a personal experience:

> Wearing seat belts can protect people from injury, even in serious accidents. I know because seat belts saved me and my Dad two years ago when we were driving to see my grandparents who live in California. Because of the distance, we had to travel late on a rainy, foggy Saturday night. My Dad was driving, but what he didn't know was that there was a car a short way behind us driven by a drunk who was following our car's tail lights in order to keep himself on the road. About midnight, my Dad decided to check the map to make sure we were headed in the right direction, so he signaled, pulled over to the shoulder, and began to come to a stop. Unfortunately for us, the drunk didn't see the signal and moved his car over to the shoulder thinking that the main road must have curved slightly since our car had gone that way. As Dad slowed our car, the other car plowed into us at a speed estimated later by the police as over eighty miles an hour. The car hit us like Babe Ruth's bat hitting a slow pitch; the force of the speeding car slammed us hard into the dashboard, but not through the windshield and out onto the rocky shoulder, because, lucky for us, we were wearing our seat belts. The Highway Patrolmen, who arrived quickly on the scene, testified later at the other driver's trial that without question my Dad and I would have been seriously injured, if not killed, had it not been for our seat belts restraining us in the front seat.

The story of the accident illustrates the writer's claim that seat belts can save lives; without such an example, the writer's statement would be only an unsupported generalization.

In addition to making general statements specific and thus more convincing, good examples can explain and clarify unfamiliar, abstract, or difficult concepts for the reader. For instance, Newton's law of gravity might be more easily understood once it is explained through the simple, familiar example of an apple falling from a tree.

Moreover, clear examples can add to your prose vivid details that hold the reader's attention while you explain your points. A general statement decrying animal abuse, for instance, may be more effective accompanied by several examples detailing the brutal treatment of one particular laboratory's research animals.

The use of good examples is not, however, limited only to essays primarily developed by example. In actuality, you will probably use examples in every essay you write. You couldn't, for instance, write an essay classifying kinds of popular movies without including examples to help identify your categories. Similarly, you couldn't write essays defining the characteristics of a good teacher or a comparison between two kinds of cars without ample use of specific examples. To illustrate the importance of examples in all patterns of essay development, here are two excerpts from student essays reprinted in other parts of this text. The first excerpt comes from an essay classifying the Indian eras at Mesa Verde National Park, (pp. 196–197). In his discussion of a particular time period, the writer uses a dwelling called Balcony House as an example to illustrate his claims about the Indians' new skills in building construction.

> The third period lasted until A.D. 1300 and saw the innovation of pueblos, or groups of dwellings, instead of single-family units. Nearly eight hundred dwellings show the large number of people who inhabited the complex, tunneled houses, shops, storage rooms, courtyards, and community centers whose masonry walls, often elaborately decorated, were three and four stories high. At the spacious Balcony House pueblo, for example, an adobe court lies beneath another vaulted roof; on three sides stand two-story houses with balconies that lead from one room to the next. In back of the court is a spring, and along the front side is a low wall that kept the children from falling down the seven-hundred-foot cliff to the canyon floor below. Balcony House also contains two *kivas*, circular subterranean ceremonial chambers that show the importance of fellowship and religion to the Indians of this era.

Another student uses a personal example to help her support a point in her essay that contrasts a local co-op to a big chain grocery store (pp. 176–177). By using her friend's experience as an example, the writer shows the reader how a co-op may assist local producers in the community:

> Direct selling offers two advantages for producers: they get a better price for their wares than by selling them through a middleman, and at the same time they establish an independent reputation for their business, which can be immensely valuable to their success later on. In Fort Collins, for example, Luna tofu (bean curd) stands out as an excellent illustration of this kind of mutual support. Several years ago my friend Carol Jones began making tofu in small batches to sell to the co-op as a way to earn a part-time income as well as to contribute to the co-op. Her enterprise has now grown so well that last year her husband quit his job to go into business with her full time. She currently sells to distributors and independent stores from here to Denver; even Lane Grocer, who earlier would not consider selling her tofu even on a trial basis, is now thinking about changing its policy.

Learning to support, explain, or clarify your assertions by clear, thoughtful examples will help you develop virtually every piece of writing you are assigned, both in school and on the job. Development by example is the most widely used of all the expository strategies and by far the most important.

DEVELOPING YOUR ESSAY

An essay developed by example is one of the easiest to organize. In most cases, your first paragraph will present your thesis; each body paragraph will contain a topic sentence and as many effectively arranged examples as necessary to explain or support each major point; your last paragraph will conclude your essay in some appropriate way. Although the general organization is fairly simple, you should doublecheck the examples in your rough draft by asking these questions:

Are all my examples relevant? Each specific example should support, clarify, or explain the general statement it illustrates; each example should provide readers with additional insight into the subject under discussion. Keep the purpose of your paragraphs in mind: don't wander off into an analysis of the causes of crime if you are only supposed to show examples of it in your neighborhood. Keep your audience in mind too: which examples will provide the kinds of information that your particular readers need to understand your point?

Are my examples well chosen? To persuade your readers to accept your opinion, you should select those examples that are the strongest and most convincing. Let's say you were writing a research paper exposing a government agency's wastefulness. To illustrate your claim, you would pick out those cases that most obviously show gross or ridiculous expenditures, rather than asking your readers to consider some unnecessary but minor expenses. And you would try to select cases that represent recent or current examples of wastefulness rather than discussing expenditures too dated to be persuasive. In other words, when you have a number of examples to choose from, evaluate them and then select the best ones to support your point.

Are there enough examples to make each point clear and persuasive? Put yourself in your reader's place: would you be convinced with three brief examples? Five? One extended example? Two? Use your own judgment, but be careful to support or explain your major points adequately. It's better to risk overexplaining than to leave your reader confused or unconvinced.

PROBLEMS TO AVOID

The most common weakness in essays developed by example is a lack of specific detail. Too often novice writers present a sufficient number of relevant, well-chosen examples, but the illustrations themselves are too general, vague, or brief to be helpful. Examples should be clear, specific, and adequately detailed so that the reader receives the full persuasive impact of each one. For instance, in an essay claiming that college football has become too violent, don't merely say: "Too many players got hurt last year." Such a statement only hints; it lacks enough development to be fully effective. Go into more detail by giving actual examples of jammed fingers, wrenched backs, bruised legs, broken knee-caps, and busted dreams. Present these examples in specific, vivid language; once your readers begin to "see" that field covered with blood and broken bodies, you'll have less trouble convincing them that your point of view is accurate.

The second biggest problem in example essays is the lack of coherence. The reader should never sense an interruption in the flow of thought from one example to the next in paragraphs containing more than one example. Each body paragraph of this kind should be more than a topic sentence and a choppy list of examples. You should first arrange the examples in an order that best explains the major point presented by your topic sentence; then carefully check to make sure each example is smoothly connected in thought to the statements preceding and following it. You can avoid a listing effect by using transition devices where necessary to ensure easy movement from example to example and from point to point. A few common transition words often found in essays of example include "for instance," "for example," "to illustrate," "another," and "in addition." (For a list of other transition words and additional help on writing coherent paragraphs, review pp. 62–67.)

ESSAY TOPICS

Use the statements below to lead you to your essay topic. Be sure to narrow these suggestions as you focus your thesis.

1. Heroes today are merely media creations rather than truly admirable people.
2. First impressions are often the best/worst means of judging people.
3. Failure is a better teacher than success.
4. My fear of flying (or whatever) prevents me from living a normal life.
5. The willingness to undertake adventure is a necessary part of a happy life.
6. Doing good deeds can backfire.
7. Complaining can produce unforeseen results.
8. Travel can be the best medicine.
9. Consumers are often at the mercy of unscrupulous companies.
10. Visits to the doctor/dentist/vet often prove more traumatic than the illness.

11. Failure to keep my mouth shut (or some other bad habit) gets me into trouble.

12. Success involves sacrifice.

13. Modern technology often produces more inconvenience than convenience.

14. Job hunting today is a difficult process.

15. Science fiction writers often accurately predict the future.

16. Television is designed for people with room-temperature I.Q.s.

17. Many required courses are/are not relevant to a student's education.

18. My high school did/did not adequately prepare me for college.

19. The most popular political attitude among students today is "I'm apathetic, and I don't care."

20. Fad diets can have harmful results.

Sample Student Essay

Study the use of specific examples in the brief student essay that follows. See if you can identify the transition devices that help move the reader from point to point and from example to example.

River Rafting Teaches Worthwhile Lessons

Introduction:
A description

Thesis

Essay map

Topic sentence one:
Trip teaches
respect for
environment

Two examples
of respect:
1. cleaning up trash

Sun-warmed water slaps you in the face, the blazing sun beats down on your shoulders, and canyon walls speed by as you race down rolling waves of water. No experience can equal that of river rafting. Along with being fun and exciting, rafting has many educational advantages as well, especially for those involved in school-sponsored rafting trips. River trips teach students how to prevent some of the environmental destruction that concerns the park officials and, in addition, river trips also teach students to work together in a way few other experiences can.

The most important lesson a rafting trip teaches students is respect for the environment. When students are exposed to the outdoors, they can better learn to appreciate its beauty and feel the need to preserve it. For example, I went on a rafting trip three summers ago with the biology department at my high school. Our trip lasted seven days down the Green River through the isolated Desolation Canyon in Utah. After the first day of rafting, I found myself surrounded by steep canyon walls and saw virtually no evidence of human life. The starkly beautiful, unspoiled atmosphere soon became a major influence on us during the trip. By the second day I saw classmates, whom I had previously seen fill an entire room with candy wrappers and

2. foregoing suds in
river

empty soda cans, voluntarily inspecting our campsite for trash. And when twenty-four high school students sacrifice washing their hair for the sake of a sudless and thus healthier river, some new, better attitudes about the environment have definitely been established.

Topic sentence
two: The trip
teaches cooperation

In addition to the respect for nature a rafting trip encourages, it also teaches the importance of group cooperation. Since school-associated trips put students in command of the raft, the students find that in order to stay in control each member must be reliable, able to do his or her own part, and alert to the actions of others. These skills are quickly learned when students see the consequences of noncooperation. Usually this occurs the first day, when the left side of the raft paddles in one direction, and the right the other way, and half the crew ends up seasick from going in circles. An even better illustration is another experience I had on my river trip. Because an upcoming rapid was usually not too rough, our instructor said a few of us could jump out and swim in it. Instead of deciding as a group who should go, though, five eager swimmers bailed out. This left me, an angry instructor, and another student to steer the raft. As it turned out, the rapid was fairly rough, and we soon found ourselves heading straight for a huge hole (a hole is formed from swirling funnel-like currents and can pull a raft under). The combined effort of the three of us was not enough to get the raft completely clear of the hole, and the raft tipped up vertically on its side, spilling us into the river. Luckily, no one was hurt, and the raft did not topple over, but the near loss of our food rations for the next five days, not to mention the raft itself, was enough to make us all more willing to work as a group in the future.

Two examples of
noncooperation:
1. difficulties in
paddling raft
2. a near accident

Conclusion:
Importance of
lessons

Despite the obvious benefits rafting offers, the number of river permits issued to school groups continues to decline because of financial cutbacks. It is a shame that those in charge of these cutbacks do not realize that in addition to having fun and learning about themselves, students are learning valuable lessons through rafting trips—lessons that may help preserve the rivers for future rafters.

Professional Essay

So What's So Bad about Being So-So?

Lisa Wilson Strick

Lisa Wilson Strick is a freelance writer who publishes in a variety of women's magazines, frequently on the subjects of family and education. This essay first appeared in Woman's Day in 1984.

1   The other afternoon I was playing the piano when my seven-year-old walked in. He stopped and listened awhile, then said: "Gee, Mom, you don't play that thing very well, do you?"

2   No, I don't. I am a piano lesson dropout. The fine points of fingering totally escape me. I play everything at half-speed, with many errant notes. My performance would make any serious music student wince, but I don't care. I've enjoyed playing the piano badly for years.

3   I also enjoy singing badly and drawing badly. (I used to enjoy sewing badly, but I've been doing that so long that I finally got pretty good at it.) I'm not ashamed of my incompetence in these areas. I do one or two other things well and that should be enough for anybody. But it gets boring doing the same things over and over. Every now and then it's fun to try something new.

4   Unfortunately, doing things badly has gone out of style. It used to be a mark of class if a lady or a gentleman sang a little, painted a little, played the violin a little. You didn't have to be *good* at it; the point was to be fortunate enough to have the leisure time for such pursuits. But in today's competitive world we have to be "experts"—even in our hobbies. You can't tone up your body by pulling on your sneakers and slogging around the block a couple of times anymore. Why? Because you'll be laughed off the street by the "serious" runners—the ones who log twenty-plus miles a week in their headbands, sixty-dollar running suits and fancy shoes. The shoes are really a big deal. If you say you're thinking about taking up almost any sport, the first thing the aficionados will ask is what you plan to do about shoes. Leather or canvas? What type of soles? Which brand? This is not the time to mention that the gym shoes you wore in high school are still in pretty good shape. As far as sports enthusiasts are concerned, if you don't have the latest shoes you are hopelessly committed to mediocrity.

5   The runners aren't nearly so snobbish as the dance freaks, however. In case you didn't know, "going dancing" no longer means putting on a pretty dress and doing a few turns around the ballroom with your favorite man on Saturday night. "Dancing" means squeezing into tights and a leotard and leg warmers, then sweating through six hours of warm-ups and five hours of ballet and four hours of jazz classes. Every week. Never tell anyone that you "like to

dance" unless this is the sort of activity you enjoy. (At least the costume isn't so costly, as dancers seem to be cultivating a riches-to-rags look lately.)

6   We used to do these things for fun or simply to relax. Now the competition you face in your hobbies is likely to be worse than anything you run into on the job. "Oh, you've taken up knitting," a friend recently said to me. "Let me show you the adorable cable-knit, popcorn-stitched cardigan with twelve tiny reindeer prancing across the yoke that I made for my daughter. I dyed the yarn myself." Now why did she have to go and do that? I was getting a kick out of watching my yellow stockinette muffler grow a couple of inches a week up till then. And all I wanted was something to keep my hands busy while I watched television anyway.

7   Have you noticed what this is doing to our children? "We don't want that dodo on our soccer team," I overheard a ten-year-old sneer the other day. "He doesn't know a goal kick from a head shot." As it happens, the boy was talking about my son, who did not—like some of his friends—start soccer instruction at age three (along with preschool diving, creative writing and Suzuki clarinet). I'm sorry, Son, I guess I blew it. In *my* day when we played softball on the corner lot, we expected to give a little instruction to the younger kids who didn't know how. It didn't matter if they were terrible; we weren't out to slaughter the other team. Sometimes we didn't even keep score. To us, sports were just a way of having a *good time.* Of course we didn't have some of the nifty things kids have today— such as matching uniforms and professional coaches. All we had was a bunch of kids of various ages who enjoyed each other's company.

8   I don't think kids have as much fun as they used to. Competition keeps getting in the way. The daughter of a neighbor is a nervous wreck worrying about getting into the *best* gymnastics school. "I was a late starter," she told me, "and I only get to practice five or six hours a week, so my technique may not be up to their standards." The child is nine. She doesn't want to *be* a gymnast when she grows up; she wants to be a nurse. I asked what she likes to do for fun in her free time. She seemed to think it was an odd question. "Well, I don't actually *have* a lot of free time," she said. "I mean homework and gymnastics and flute lessons kind of eat it all up. I have flute lessons three times a week now, so I have a good shot at getting into the all-state orchestra."

9   Ambition, drive and the desire to excel are all admirable within limits, but I don't know where the limits are anymore. I know a woman who has always wanted to learn a foreign language. For years she has complained that she hasn't the time to study one. I've pointed out that an evening course in French or Italian would take only a couple of hours a week, but she keeps putting it off. I suspect that what she hasn't got the time for is to become completely fluent within the year—and that any lesser level of accomplishment would embarrass her. Instead she spends her evenings watching reruns on television and tidying up her closets—occupations at which no particular expertise is expected.

10   I know others who are avoiding activities they might enjoy because they lack the time or the energy to tackle them "seriously." It strikes me as so silly. We are talking about *recreation.* I have nothing against self-improvement. But when I hear a teenager muttering "practice makes perfect" as he grimly makes his four-hundred-and-twenty-seventh try at hooking the basketball into the

net left-handed, I wonder if some of us aren't improving ourselves right into the loony bin.

11   I think it's time we put a stop to all this. For sanity's sake, each of us should vow to take up something new this week—and to make sure we never master it completely. Sing along with grand opera. Make peculiar-looking objects out of clay. I can tell you from experience that fallen soufflés still taste pretty good. The point is to enjoy being a beginner again; to rediscover the joy of creative fooling around. If you find it difficult, ask any two-year-old to teach you. Two-year-olds have a gift for tackling the impossible with zest; repeated failure hardly discourages them at all.

12   As for me, I'm getting a little out of shape so I'm looking into tennis. A lot of people I know enjoy it, and it doesn't look too hard. Given a couple of lessons I should be stumbling gracelessly around the court and playing badly in no time at all.

QUESTIONS ON CONTENT, STRUCTURE, AND STYLE

1. Why does Strick begin her essay with the comment from her son and the list of activities she does badly?
2. What is Strick's thesis? Is it specifically stated or clearly implied?
3. What examples does Strick offer to illustrate her belief that we no longer take up hobbies for fun? Are there enough well-chosen examples to make her position clear?
4. What is the effect, according to Strick, of too much competition on kids? In what ways does she show this effect?
5. What does Strick gain by using dialogue in some of her examples?
6. Why does Strick include the example of the woman who wants to learn a foreign language?
7. Does Strick use enough details in her examples to make them clear, vivid, and persuasive? Point out some of her details to support your answer.
8. What solution to the problem does Strick offer? How does she clarify her suggestion?
9. Characterize the tone of Strick's essay. Is it appropriate for her purpose and for her intended audience? Why/why not?
10. Evaluate Strick's conclusion. Does it effectively wrap up the essay?

VOCABULARY

errant (2)	excel (9)
incompetence (3)	fluent (9)
aficionados (4)	zest (11)
mediocrity (4)	

A REVISION WORKSHEET FOR YOUR EXAMPLE ESSAY

As you write your rough drafts, consult Chapter 5 for guidance through the revision process. In addition, here are a few questions to ask yourself as you revise your example essay:

1. Is the essay's thesis clear to the reader?
2. Do the topic sentences support the thesis?
3. Do the examples in each paragraph effectively illustrate the claim of the topic sentence?
4. Are there enough well-chosen examples to make each point clear and convincing?
5. Is each example developed in enough specific detail? Where could more details be added?
6. If a paragraph contains multiple examples, are they arranged in the most effective order, with smooth transition from one to another?
7. If a paragraph contains an extended example, does the action flow logically and with coherence?

After you've revised your essay extensively, you might exchange rough drafts with a classmate and answer these questions for each other, making specific suggestions for improvement wherever appropriate.

STRATEGY TWO: DEVELOPMENT BY PROCESS ANALYSIS

Process analysis identifies and explains what steps must be taken to complete an operation or procedure. There are two kinds of process analysis essays: directional and informative.

A *directional process* tells the reader how to do or make something; in other words, it gives directions. You are more familiar with directional process than you might think; when you open a telephone book, for example, you see the pages in the front explaining how to make a long-distance call. When you tell friends how to find your house, you're asking them to follow a directional process. The most widely read books in American libraries fall into the how-to-do-it (or how-to-fix-it) category: how to wire a house, how to repair a car, how to play winning poker, how to become a millionaire overnight, and so forth. And almost every home contains at least one cookbook full of recipes providing step-by-step directions for preparing various dishes. (Even Part One of this text is, in detailed fashion, a directional process telling how to write a short essay, with steps beginning with the selection of a topic and concluding with advice on revision.)

An *informative process* tells the reader how something is or was made or done, or how something works. Informative process differs from directional process in that it is not designed primarily to tell people how to do it; instead, it describes the steps by which someone other than the reader does or makes something (or how something was made or done in the past). For example, an informative process essay might describe how a television show is produced, how scientists discovered polio vaccine, how you chose your major in college, how the Huns sacked Rome, or how an engine propels a tank. In other words, this type of essay gives information on processes that are not intended to be—or cannot be—duplicated by the individual reader.

DEVELOPING YOUR ESSAY

Of all the expository essays, students usually agree that the process paper is the easiest to organize, mainly because it is presented in simple, chronological steps. To prepare a well-written process essay, however, you should remember the following advice:

Select an appropriate subject. First, make sure you know your subject thoroughly; one fuzzy step could wreck your entire process. Second, choose a process that is simple and short enough to describe in detail. In a 500–800 word essay, for instance, it's better to describe how to fold a paper boat for a child's toy than to try telling how to construct a life-size replica of Noah's Ark. On the other hand, don't choose a process so simple-minded, mundane, or mechanical that it insults your readers' intelligence. (Ten years ago at a major state university it was popular to assign a process essay on "How To Sharpen a Pencil"; with the assignment of such stirring, creative topics, it's a wonder that English department produced any majors at all that year.)

Describe any necessary equipment and define special terms. In some process essays, you will need to indicate what equipment, ingredients, or tools are required. Such information is often provided in a paragraph following the thesis, before the process itself is described; in other cases, explanation of proper equipment is presented as the need arises in each step of the process. As the writer, you must decide which method is best for your subject. The same is true for any terms that need defining. Don't lose your reader by using terms only you, the specialist, can comprehend. Always remember that you're trying to tell people about a process they don't understand.

State your steps in a logical, chronological order. Obviously, if someone wanted to know how to bake bread, you wouldn't begin with "Put the prepared dough in the oven." Start at the beginning and carefully follow through, step by step, until the process is completed. Don't omit any steps or directions, no matter how seemingly insignificant. Without complete instructions, for example, the would-be baker might end up with a gob of dough rather than a loaf of bread—simply because the directions didn't say to preheat the oven.

Explain each step clearly, sufficiently, and accurately. If you've ever tried to assemble a child's toy or a piece of furniture, you probably already know how frustrating—and infuriating—it is to work from vague, inadequate directions. Save your readers from tears and tantrums by describing each step in your process as clearly as possible. Use enough specific details to distinguish one step from another. As the readers finish each step, they should know how the subject matter is supposed to look, feel, smell, taste, or sound at that stage of the process. You might also explain why each step is necessary ("Cutting back the young avocado stem is necessary to prevent a spindly plant." "Senator Snort then had to win over the chairman of the Arms Committee to be sure his bill would go to the Senate floor for a vote."). In some cases, especially in directional processes, it's helpful to give warnings ("When you begin tightrope walking, the condition of your shoes is critical; be careful the soles are not slick.") or descriptions of errors and how to rectify them ("If you pass a white church, you've gone a block too far; turn right at the church and circle back on Candle Lane." "If the sauce appears gray and thick, add one teaspoon more of cornstarch until the gravy is white and bubbly.").

Organize your steps effectively. If you have a few big steps in your process, you probably will devote a paragraph to each one. On the other hand, if you have several small steps, you should organize them into a few manageable units. For example, in an essay on "How to Prepare Fresh Fish" the list of small steps on the left has been grouped into three larger units, each of which becomes a body paragraph:

1. scaling	I. Cleaning
2. beheading	A. scaling
3. gutting	B. beheading
4. washing	C. gutting
5. seasoning	II. Cooking
6 breading	A. washing
7. frying	B. seasoning
8. draining	C. breading
9. portioning	D. frying
10. garnishing	III. Serving
	A. draining
	B. portioning
	C. garnishing

In addition, don't forget to use enough transition devices between steps to avoid the effect of a mechanical list. Some frequently used linking words in process essays include the following:

next	first, second, third, etc.
then	at this point
now	following
to begin	when
finally	at last
before	afterward

Vary your transition words sufficiently so that your steps are not linked by a monotonous repetition of "and then" or "next."

Problems to Avoid

Don't forget to include a thesis. You already know, of course, that every essay needs a thesis, but the advice bears repeating here because for some reason some writers often omit the statement in their process essays. Your thesis might be (a) your reason for presenting this process—why you feel it's important or necessary for the readers to know ("Because rescue squads often arrive too late, every adult should know how to give artificial respiration to accident victims") or (b) an assertion about the nature of the process itself ("Needlepoint is a simple, restful, fun hobby for both men and women"). Here are some other subjects and sample theses:

- Donating blood is not the painful process one might suspect.
- The raid on Pearl Harbor wasn't altogether unexpected.
- Returning to school as an older-than-average student isn't as difficult as it may look.
- Sponsoring a five-mile run can be a fun way for your club or student organization to raise money for local charities.
- Challenging a speeding ticket is a time-consuming, energy-draining, but financially rewarding endeavor.
- The series of public protests that led to the return of the traditional Coca-Cola was an unparalleled success in the history of American consumerism.

Presenting a thesis and referring to it in each step gives your essay unity and coherence, as well as ensuring against a monotonous list of steps.

Pay special attention to your conclusion. Don't allow your essay to grind to an abrupt halt after the final step. You might conclude the essay by telling the significance of the completed process or by explaining other uses it may have. Or, if it is appropriate, finish your essay with an amusing story or comment. However you conclude, leave the reader with a feeling of satisfaction, with a sense of having completed an interesting procedure. (For more information on writing good conclusions, see pp. 78–80.)

ESSAY TOPICS

Below are suggested topics for both directional and informative process essays. Some of the topics may also be used in humorous essays such as "How to Flunk a Test," "How to Remain a Bench Warmer," or "How to Say Nothing in Eight-Hundred Words."

1. how to stop smoking (or break some other habit)
2. how a company defrauds consumers
3. how to begin a collection or hobby
4. how to buy a computer or CD player
5. how a popular product or fad originated or grew
6. how to meet the person of your dreams (or escape the nightmare when it's over)
7. how something in nature works or was formed
8. how a company makes or sells a product
9. how a piece of equipment or a machine works
10. how to cure a cold or hangover
11. how to lose or gain weight
12. how you arrived at a major decision or solved an important problem
13. how to select a car (new or used), house, apartment, roommate
14. how to vacation on five dollars a day
15. how a famous invention or discovery occurred
16. how to get rid of roaches or other pests (human or otherwise)
17. how to succeed or fail in a job interview (or in some other important endeavor)
18. how to repair some small item
19. how to plan the perfect party, wedding, funeral, birthday, etc.
20. how a historial event occurred

Sample Student Essay

The essay below is a directional process telling readers how to put on a successful garage sale. To make the instructions clear and enjoyable, the writer adopted a chronological order and used many specific examples, details, and warnings.

Catching Garage Sale Fever

Introduction: A series of questions to hook the reader

Ever need some easy money fast? To repay those incredible overdue library fines you ran up writing your last research paper? Or to raise money for that much-needed vacation to old Mexico you put on credit cards last Spring Break? Or maybe you feel you simply have to clear out some junk before the piles block the remaining sunlight from your windows? Whether the problem is cash flow or trash flow, you can solve it easily by holding what is fast becoming an all-American sport: the weekend garage sale. As a veteran of some half-dozen successful ventures, I can testify that garage sales are the easiest way to make quick money, with a minimum of physical labor and the maximum of fun.

Thesis

Step One: Taking inventory

Most garage sale "experts" start getting ready at least two weeks before the sale by taking inventory. Look through your closets and junk drawers to see if you actually have enough items to make a sale worthwhile. If all you have is a mass of miscellaneous small items, think about waiting or joining a friend's sale, because you do need at least a couple of larger items (furniture is always a big seller) to draw customers initially. Also, consider whether the season is appropriate for your items: sun dresses and shorts, for example, sell better in the spring and summer; coats and boots in the fall. As you collect your items, don't underestimate the "sale-ability" of some of your junk—the hideous purple china bulldog Aunt Clara gave you for Christmas five years ago may be perfect for someone's Ugly Mutt Collection.

Step Two: Deciding when and where

As you sort through your junk closets, begin thinking about the time and place of your sale. First, decide if you want a one- or two-day sale. If you opt for only one day, Saturdays are generally best because most people are free that day. Plan to start early—by 8 A.M. if possible—because the experienced buyers get up and get going so they can hit more sales that way. Unless you have nothing else to do that day, plan to end your sale by mid-afternoon; most people have run out of buying energy (or money) by 3 P.M. Deciding on the location of your sale depends, of course, on your housing situation, but you still might need to make some choices. For instance, do you want to put your items out in a driveway, a backyard, or actually in the garage (weather might affect this decision)? Or perhaps a side yard gets more passers-by? Wherever you decide, be sure that there are plenty of places for customers to park close by without blocking your neighbors' driveways.

Step Three: Advertising the sale

Unless you live in a very small town or on a very busy street, you'll probably want to place an inexpensive ad in the "garage sale" column of your local newspaper that is scheduled to run a day or two before, and the day of, your sale. Your ad should tell the times and place of the sale (give brief directions or mention landmarks if the location is hard to find) as well as a brief list of some of your items. Few people will turn out for "household goods" alone; some popular items include bookcases, antiques, books, fans, jewelry, toys, baby equipment, and name-brand clothes. One other piece of advice about the ad copy: it should include the phrase "no early sales" unless you want to be awakened at 6:30 A.M., as I was one Saturday, by a bunch of semi-pro garage sale buyers milling restlessly around in your yard, looking like zombies out of a George Romero horror movie. In addition to your newspaper ad, you may also wish to put up posters in places frequented by lots of people;

A warning

laundromats and grocery stores often have bulletin boards for such announcements. You can also put up signs on nearby well-traveled streets, but one warning: in some towns it's illegal to post anything on utility poles or traffic signs, so be sure to check your local ordinances first.

Another warning

Step Four: Pricing the merchandise

Tagging your items with their prices is the least fun, and it can take a day or a week depending on how many items you have and how much time each day you can devote to the project. You can buy sheets of little white stickers or use pieces of masking tape to stick on the prices, but if you want to save time, consider grouping some items and selling them all for the same price—all shirts, for example, are 50¢. Be realistic about your prices; the hand-crafted rug from Greece may have been expensive and important to you, but to others, it's a worn doormat. Some experts suggest pricing your articles at about one-fourth their original value, unless you have special reasons not to (an antique or popular collectors' item, for instance, may be more valuable now than when you bought it). Remember that you can always come down on your prices if someone is interested in a particular item.

Step Five: Setting up your sale

A note on equipment

By the day before your sale you should have all your items clean and tagged. One of the beauties of a garage sale is that there's very little equipment to collect. You'll need tables, benches, or boards supported by bricks to display your goods; a rope tied from side to side of your garage can double as a clothes rack. Try to spread out your merchandise rather than dumping articles in deep boxes; no customer wants to feel like a baglady rummaging through a trash barrel. Most importantly, you'll need a chair and a table to hold some sort of money box, preferably one with a lock. The afternoon before the sale, take a trip to the bank if you need to, to make sure you have enough one-dollar bills and coins to make plenty of change. The evening before the sale, set up your items on your display benches in the garage or indoors near the site of your sale so that you can quickly set things out in the morning. Get a good night's sleep so you can get up to open on time: the early bird does get the sales in this business.

Step Six: Running the sale

The sale itself is, of course, the real fun. Half the enjoyment is haggling with the customers, so be prepared to joke and visit with the shoppers. Watching the different kinds of people who show up is also a kick—you can get a crosssection from college students on a tight budget to harried mothers toting four kids to real eccentrics in fancy cars who will argue about the price of a 75¢ item (if you're a creative writer, don't forget to take notes for your next novel!). If the action slows in the afternoon, you can resort to a half-price or two-for-one sale by posting a large sign to that effect; many shoppers can't resist a sale at a sale!

Step Seven: Closing up

By late afternoon you should be richer and junk-free, at least to some extent. If you do have items left after the half-price sale, decide whether you want to box them up for the next sale or drop them by a charitable organization such as Goodwill (some organizations will even pick up your donations; others have convenient drop boxes). After you've taken your articles inside, don't forget to take down any signs you've posted in the neighborhood; old withered garage sale signs fluttering in the breeze are an eyesore. Last, sit down and count your profits, so you can go out in the evening to celebrate a successful business venture.

Conclusion: A
summary of the
benefits and a
humorous warning

The money you make is, of course, the biggest incentive for having one or two sales a year. But the combination of money, clean closets, and memories of the characters you met can be irresistible. Garage sales can rapidly get in your blood; once you hold a successful one, you're tempted to have another as soon as the junk starts to mount up. And having sales somehow leads to attending them too, as it becomes fun to see what other folks are selling at bargain prices. So be forewarned: you too can be transformed into a garage sale junkie, complete with a now-popular car bumper sticker that proudly proclaims to the world: "Caution! I brake for garage sales"!

Professional Essay _____

TO BID THE WORLD FAREWELL

Jessica Mitford

Jessica Mitford has written many articles and books, including Daughters and Rebels *(1960),* The Trial of Doctor Spock *(1969), and* Kind and Unusual Punishment *(1973), a critical study of the American penal system. This essay is an excerpt from her best-selling book* The American Way of Death *(1963).*

1   Embalming is indeed a most extraordinary procedure, and one must wonder at the docility of Americans who each year pay hundreds of millions of dollars for its perpetuation, blissfully ignorant of what it is all about, what is done, how it is done. Not one in ten thousand has any idea of what actually takes place. Books on the subject are extremely hard to come by. They are not to be found in most libraries or bookshops.

2   In an era when huge television audiences watch surgical operations in the comfort of their living rooms, when, thanks to the animated cartoon, the geography of the digestive system has become familiar territory even to the nursery school set, and in land where the satisfaction of curiosity about almost all matters is a national pastime, the secrecy surrounding embalming can, surely, hardly be attributed to the inherent gruesomeness of the subject. Custom in this regard has within this century suffered a complete reversal. In the early

days of American embalming, when it was performed in the home of the deceased, it was almost mandatory for some relative to stay by the embalmer's side and witness the procedure. Today, family members who might wish to be in attendance would certainly be dissuaded by the funeral director. All others, except apprentices, are excluded by law from the preparation room.

3   A close look at what does actually take place may explain in large measure the undertaker's intractable reticence concerning a procedure that has become his major *raison d'être*. Is it possible he fears that public information about embalming might lead patrons to wonder if they really want this service? If the funeral men are loath to discuss the subject outside the trade, the reader may, understandably, be equally loath to go on reading at this point. For those who have the stomach for it, let us part the formaldehyde curtain. . . .

4   The body is first laid out in the undertaker's morgue—or rather, Mr. Jones is reposing in the preparation room—to be readied to bid the world farewell.

5   The preparation room in any of the better funeral establishments has the tiled and sterile look of a surgery, and indeed the embalmer-restorative artist who does his chores there is beginning to adopt the term "dermasurgeon" (appropriately corrupted by some mortician-writers as "demisurgeon") to describe his calling. His equipment, consisting of scalpels, scissors, augers, forceps, clamps, needles, pumps, tubes, bowls and basins, is crudely imitative of the surgeon's as is his technique, acquired in a nine- or twelve-month post-high-school course in an embalming school. He is supplied by an advanced chemical industry with a bewildering array of fluids, sprays, pastes, oils, powders, creams, to fix or soften tissue, shrink or distend it as needed, dry it here, restore the moisture there. There are cosmetics, waxes and paints to fill and cover features, even plaster of Paris to replace entire limbs. There are ingenious aids to prop and stabilize the cadaver: a Vari-Pose Head Rest, the Edwards Arm and Hand Positioner, the Repose Block (to support the shoulders during the embalming), and the Throop Foot Positioner, which resembles an old-fashioned stocks.

6   Mr. John H. Eckels, president of the Eckels College of Mortuary Science, thus describes the first part of the embalming procedure: "In the hands of a skilled practitioner, this work may be done in a comparatively short time and without mutilating the body other than by slight incision—so slight that it scarcely would cause serious inconvenience if made upon a living person. It is necessary to remove the blood, and doing this not only helps in the disinfecting, but removes the principal cause of disfigurement due to discoloration."

7   Another textbook discusses the all-important time element: "The earlier this is done, the better, for every hour that elapses between death and embalming will add to the problems and complications encountered. . . ." Just how soon should one get going on the embalming? The author tells us, "On the basis of such scanty information made available to this profession through its rudimentary and haphazard system of technical research, we must conclude that the best results are to be obtained if the subject is embalmed before life is completely extinct—that is, before cellular death has occurred. In the average case, this would mean within an hour after somatic death." For those who feel that there is

something a little rudimentary, not to say haphazard, about this advice, a comforting thought is offered by another writer. Speaking of fears entertained in early days of premature burial, he points out, "One of the effects of embalming by chemical injection, however, has been to dispel fears of live burial." How true; once the blood is removed, chances of live burial are indeed remote.

8   To return to Mr. Jones, the blood is drained out through the veins and replaced by embalming fluid pumped in through the arteries. As noted in *The Principles and Practices of Embalming,* "every operator has a favorite injection and drainage point—a fact which becomes a handicap only if he fails or refuses to forsake his favorites when conditions demand it." Typical favorites are the carotid artery, femoral artery, jugular vein, subclavian vein. There are various choices of embalming fluid. If Flextone is used, it will produce a "mild flexible rigidity. The skin retains a velvety softness, the tissues are rubbery and pliable. Ideal for women and children." It may be blended with B. and G. Products Company's Lyf-Lyk tint, which is guaranteed to reproduce "nature's own skin texture . . . the velvety appearance of living tissue." Suntone comes in three separate tints: Suntan; Special Cosmetic Tint, a pink shade "especially indicated for young female subjects"; and Regular Cosmetic Tint, moderately pink.

9   About three to six gallons of a dyed and perfumed solution of formaldehyde, glycerin, borax, phenol, alcohol and water is soon circulating through Mr. Jones, whose mouth has been sewn together with a "needle directed upward between the upper lip and gum and brought out through the left nostril," with the corners raised slightly "for a more pleasant expression." If he should be bucktoothed, his teeth are cleaned with Bon Ami and coated with colorless nail polish. His eyes, meanwhile, are closed with flesh-tinted eye caps and eye cement.

10   The next step is to have at Mr. Jones with a thing called a trocar. This is a long, hollow needle attached to a tube. It is jabbed into the abdomen, poked around the entrails and chest cavity, the contents of which are pumped out and replaced with "cavity fluid." This done, and the hole in the abdomen sewn up, Mr. Jones' face is heavily creamed (to protect the skin from burns which may be caused by leakage of the chemicals), and he is covered with a sheet and left unmolested for a while. But not for long—there is more, much more, in store for him. He has been embalmed, but not yet restored, and the best time to start the restorative work is eight to ten hours after embalming, when the tissues have become firm and dry.

11   The object of all this attention to the corpse, it must be remembered, is to make it presentable for viewing in an attitude of healthy repose. "Our customs require the presentation of our dead in the semblance of normality . . . unmarred by the ravages of illness, disease or mutilation," says Mr. J. Sheridan Mayer in his *Restorative Art.* This is rather a large order since few people die in the full bloom of health, unravaged by illness and unmarked by some disfigurement. The funeral industry is equal to the challenge: "In some cases the gruesome appearance of a mutilated or disease-ridden subject may be quite discouraging. The task of restoration may seem impossible and shake the confidence of the embalmer. This is the time for intestinal fortitude and determination. Once the formative work is

begun and affected tissues are cleaned or removed, all doubts of success vanish. It is surprising and gratifying to discover the results which may be obtained."

12   The embalmer, having allowed an appropriate interval to elapse, returns to the attack, but now he brings into play the skill and equipment of sculptor and cosmetician. Is a hand missing? Casting one in plaster of Paris is a simple matter. "For replacement purposes, only a cast of the back of the hand is necessary; this is within the ability of the average operator and is quite adequate." If a lip or two, a nose or an ear should be missing, the embalmer has at hand a variety of restorative waxes with which to model replacements. Pores and skin texture are simulated by stippling with a little brush, and over this cosmetics are laid on. Head off? Decapitation cases are rather routinely handled. Ragged edges are trimmed, and head joined to torso with a series of splints, wires and sutures. It is a good idea to have a little something at the neck—a scarf or high collar—when time for viewing comes. Swollen mouth? Cut out tissue as needed from inside the lips. If too much is removed, the surface contour can easily be restored by padding with cotton. Swollen necks and cheeks are reduced by removing tissue through vertical incisions made down each side of the neck. "When the deceased is casketed, the pillow will hide the suture incisions . . . as an extra precaution against leakage, the suture may be painted with liquid sealer."

13   The opposite condition is more likely to present itself—that of emaciation. His hypodermic syringe now loaded with massage cream, the embalmer seeks out and fills the hollowed and sunken areas by injection. In this procedure the backs of the hands and fingers and the under-chin area should not be neglected.

14   Positioning the lips is a problem that recurrently challenges the ingenuity of the embalmer. Closed too tightly, they tend to give a stern, even disapproving expression. Ideally, embalmers feel, the lips should give the impression of being ever so slightly parted, the upper lip protruding slightly for a more youthful appearance. This takes some engineering, however, as the lips tend to drift apart. Lip drift can sometimes be remedied by pushing one or two straight pins through the inner margin of the lower lip and then inserting them between the two front teeth. If Mr. Jones happens to have no teeth, the pins can just as easily be anchored in his Armstrong Face Former and Denture Replacer. Another method to maintain lip closure is to dislocate the lower jaw, which is then held in its new position by a wire run through holes which have been drilled through the upper and lower jaws at the midline. As the French are fond of saying, *il faut souffrir pour être belle.**

15   If Mr. Jones has died of jaundice, the embalming fluid will very likely turn him green. Does this deter the embalmer? Not if he has intestinal fortitude. Masking pastes and cosmetics are heavily laid on, burial garments and casket interiors are color-correlated with particular care, and Jones is displayed beneath rose-colored lights. Friends will say, "How *well* he looks." Death by carbon monoxide, on the other hand, can be rather a good thing from the embalmer's viewpoint: "One advantage is the fact that this type of discoloration is

* "One must suffer in order to be beautiful."

an exaggerated form of a natural pink coloration." This is nice because the healthy glow is already present and needs but little attention.

16   The patching and filling completed, Mr. Jones is now shaved, washed and dressed. Cream-based cosmetic, available in pink, flesh, suntan, brunette and blond, is applied to his hands and face, his hair is shampooed and combed (and, in the case of Mrs. Jones, set), his hands manicured. For the horny-handed son of toil special care must be taken; cream should be applied to remove ingrained grime, and the nails cleaned. "If he were not in the habit of having them manicured in life, trimming and shaping is advised for better appearance—never questioned by kin."

17   Jones is now ready for casketing (this is the present participle of the verb "to casket"). In this operation his right shoulder should be depressed slightly "to turn the body a bit to the right and soften the appearance of lying flat on the back." Positioning the hands is a matter of importance, and special rubber positioning blocks may be used. The hands should be cupped slightly for a more lifelike, relaxed appearance. Proper placement of the body requires a delicate sense of balance. It should lie as high as possible in the casket, yet not so high that the lid, when lowered, will hit the nose. On the other hand, we are cautioned, placing the body too low "creates the impression that the body is in a box."

18   Jones is next wheeled into the appointed slumber room where a few last touches may be added—his favorite pipe placed in his hand or, if he was a great reader, a book propped into position. (In the case of little Master Jones a Teddy bear may be clutched.) Here he will hold open house for a few days, visiting hours 10 A.M. to 9 P.M.

QUESTIONS ON CONTENT, STRUCTURE, AND STYLE

1. By studying the first three paragraphs, summarize both Mitford's reason for explaining the embalming process and her attitude toward undertakers who wish to keep their patrons uninformed about this procedure.
2. Identify this process as either directional or informative.
3. Does this process flow smoothly from step to step? Identify the transition devices connecting the paragraphs.
4. Does Mitford use enough specific details to help you visualize each step as it occurs? Point out examples of details that create vivid descriptions by appealing to your sense of sight, smell, or touch.
5. How does the technique of using the hypothetical "Mr. Jones" make the explanation of the process more effective? Why didn't Mitford simply refer to "the corpse" or "a body" throughout her essay?
6. What is Mitford's general attitude toward this procedure? The overall tone of the essay? Study Mitford's choice of words and then identify the tone in each of the following passages:

"The next step is to have at Mr. Jones with a thing called a trocar." (10)*

"The embalmer, having allowed an appropriate interval to elapse, returns to the attack. . . ." (12)

"Friends will say, 'How *well* he looks.'" (15)

"On the other hand, we are cautioned, placing the body too low 'creates the impression that the body is in a box.'" (17)

"Here he will hold open house for a few days, visiting hours 10 A.M. to 9 P.M." (18)

What other words and passages reveal Mitford's attitude and tone?

7. Why does Mitford repeatedly quote various undertakers and textbooks on the embalming and restorative process ("'needle directed upward between the upper lip and gum and brought out through the left nostril'")? Why is the quote in paragraph 7 that begins, "'On the basis of such scanty information made available to this profession through its rudimentary and haphazard system of technical research'" particularly effective in emphasizing Mitford's attitude toward the funeral industry?

8. What does Mitford gain by quoting euphemisms used by the funeral business, such as "dermasurgeon," "Repose Block," and "slumber room"? What are the connotations of the words "poked," "jabbed," and "left unmolested" in paragraph 10? What effect is Mitford trying to produce with the series of questions (such as "Head off?") in paragraph 12?

9. Evaluate Mitford's last sentence. Does it successfully sum up the author's attitude and conclude the essay?

10. By supplying information about the embalming process, did Mitford change your attitude toward this procedure or toward the funeral industry? Should we subject our dead to this process? Are there advantages Mitford fails to mention? How would you prepare an essay to defend your position?

VOCABULARY

docility (1)	*raison d'être* (3)
perpetuation (1)	ingenious (5)
inherent (2)	cadaver (5)
mandatory (2)	somatic (7)
intractable (3)	rudimentary (7)
reticence (3)	dispel (7)

* Numbers in parentheses following questions and vocabulary terms refer to paragraphs in the essay.

pliable (8)   stippling (12)

semblance (11)   amemaciation (13)

ravages (11)

A REVISION WORKSHEET FOR YOUR PROCESS ESSAY

As you write your rough drafts, consult Chapter 5 for guidance through the revision process. In addition, here are a few questions to ask yourself as you revise your process essay:

1. Is the essay's purpose clear to the reader?
2. Has the need for any special equipment been noted and explained adequately? Are all terms unfamiliar to the reader defined clearly?
3. Does the essay include all the steps (and warnings, if appropriate) necessary to understanding the process?
4. Is each step described in enough detail to make it understandable to all readers? Where could more detail be effectively added?
5. Are all the steps in the process presented in an easy-to-follow chronological order, with smooth transitions between steps or stages?
6. Have any series of small steps been organized into paragraphs describing a logical stage in the process?
7. Does the essay have a pleasing conclusion?

After you've revised your essay extensively, you might exchange rough drafts with a classmate and answer these questions for each other, making specific suggestions for improvement wherever appropriate.

STRATEGY THREE: DEVELOPMENT BY COMPARISON AND CONTRAST

Every day you exercise the mental process of comparison and contrast. When you get up in the morning, for instance, you may contrast two choices of clothing —a short-sleeved shirt versus a long-sleeved one—and then make your decision after hearing the weather forecast. Or you may contrast and choose between Sugar-Coated Plastic Pops and Organic Mullet Kernels for breakfast, between the health advantages of walking to campus and the speed afforded by your car or bicycle. Once on campus, preparing to register, you may first compare both professors and courses; similarly, you probably compared the school you attend now to others before you made your choice. In short, you frequently use the process of comparison and contrast to come to a decision or make a judgment about two or more objects, persons, ideas, or feelings.

When you write a comparison or contrast essay, your judgment about the two elements* in question becomes your thesis statement; the body of the paper then shows why you arrived at that judgment. For example, if your thesis states that Mom's Kum-On-Back Hamburger Haven is preferable to McPhony's Mystery Burger Stand, your body paragraphs might contrast the two restaurants in terms of food, service, and atmosphere, revealing the superiority of Mom's on all three counts.

DEVELOPING YOUR ESSAY

There are two principal patterns of organization for comparison or contrast essays. For most short papers you should choose one of the patterns and stick with it throughout the essay. Later, if you are assigned a longer essay, you may want to mix the patterns for variety as many professional writers do, but do so only if you can maintain clarity and logical organization.

Pattern One: Point by Point

This method of organization calls for body paragraphs that compare or contrast the two subjects first on point one, then on point two, then point three, and so on. Study the example outlined below:

Thesis: Mom's Hamburger Haven is a much better restaurant than McPhony's because of its superior food, service, and atmosphere.

Point 1: Food
  A. Mom's
  B. McPhony's
Point 2: Service
  A. Mom's
  B. McPhony's
Point 3: Atmosphere
  A. Mom's
  B. McPhony's
Conclusion

If you select this pattern of organization, you must make a smooth transition from subject "A" to subject "B" in each discussion to avoid a choppy seesaw effect. Be consistent: present the same subject first in each discussion of a major point; above, for instance, Mom's is always introduced before McPhony's.

* It is, of course, possible to compare or contrast more than two elements. But until you feel confident about the organizational patterns for this kind of essay, you should probably stay with the simpler format.

Pattern Two: The Block

This method of organization presents body paragraphs in which the writer first discusses subject "A" on points one, two, three, etc., then discusses subject "B" on the same points. The model below illustrates this block pattern:

Thesis: Mom's Hamburger Haven is a better restaurant than McPhony's because of its superior food, service, and atmosphere.

    A. Mom's
        1. Food
        2. Service
        3. Atmosphere
    B. McPhony's
        1. Food
        2. Service
        3. Atmosphere

Conclusion

If you use the block pattern, you should discuss the three points—food, service, atmosphere—in the same order for each subject. In addition, you must include in your discussion of subject "B" specific references to the points you made earlier about subject "A" (see outline). In other words, because your statements about Mom's superior food may be several pages away by the time your comments on McPhony's food appear, the readers may not remember precisely what you said. Gently, unobtrusively, remind them with a specific reference to the earlier discussion. For instance, you might begin your paragraph on McPhony's service like this: "Unlike the friendly, attentive help at Mom's, service at McPhony's features grouchy persons who wait on you as if they consider your presence an intrusion on their privacy." The discussion of atmosphere might begin, "McPhony's atmosphere is as cold, sterile, and plastic as its decor, in contrast to the warm, homey feeling that pervades Mom's." Without such connecting phrases, what should be one unified essay will look more like two distinct mini-essays, forcing readers to do the job of comparing or contrasting for you.

PROBLEMS TO AVOID

The single most serious error is the "so-what" thesis. Writers of comparison and/or contrast essays often wish to convince their readers that something—a restaurant, a teacher, a product—is better (or worse) than something else: "Mom's Haven is a better place to eat than McPhony's." But not all comparison/contrast essays must assert the absolute superiority or inferiority of their subjects. Sometimes writers simply want to point out the similarities or differences in two or more people, places, objects, and that's fine, too—*as long as the writer avoids the "so-what" thesis problem.*

Too often novice writers will present thesis statements such as "My youngest sister and I are very different" or "Having a blended family with two stepbrothers and stepsisters has its advantages and disadvantages." To such theses, the readers can only respond, "So what? Who cares?" There are many similarities and differences (or advantages and disadvantages) between countless numbers of things—but why should your readers care about those described in your essay? Comparing or contrasting for no apparent reason is a waste of the readers' valuable time; instead, find a purpose that will draw in your audience. You may indeed wish to write an essay contrasting the pros and cons of your blended family, but do it in a way that has a universal appeal or application. For instance, you might revise your thesis to say something like "Although a blended family often does experience petty jealousies and juvenile bickering, the benefits of having stepsiblings as live-in friends far outweigh the problems," and then use your family to show the advantages and disadvantages. In this way, your readers realize they will learn something about the blended family, a common phenomenon today, as well as learning some information about you and your particular family.

Another way to avoid the "so-what" problem is to direct your thesis to a particular audience. For instance, you might say that "While Stella's Sweatateria and the Fitness Fanatics Gym are similar in their low student membership prices and excellent instructors, Stella's is the place to go for those seeking a variety of exercise classes rather than hardcore bodybuilding machines." Or your thesis may wish to show a particular relationship between two subjects. Instead of writing "There are many similarities between the movie *Riot of the Killer Snails* and Mary Sheeley's novel *Salt on the Sidewalk,*" write "The many similarities in character and plot—the monster, the scientist, and vegetable garden scene—clearly suggest that the movie director was greatly influenced by—if not actually guilty of stealing—parts of Mary Sheeley's novel."

In other words, tell your readers your point and then use comparison or contrast to support that idea; don't just compare or contrast items in a vacuum. Ask yourself, "What is the significant point I want my readers to learn or understand from reading this comparison/contrast essay? Why do they need to know this?"

Describe your subjects clearly and distinctly. To comprehend a difference or a similarity between two things, the reader must first be able to "see" them as you do. Consequently, you should use as many vivid examples and details as possible to describe both your subjects. Beware a tendency to overelaborate on one subject and then grossly skimp on the other, an especially easy trap to fall into in an essay that asserts "X" is preferable to "Y." By giving each side a reasonable treatment, you will do a better job of convincing your reader that you know both sides and have made a valid judgment.

Avoid a choppy essay. Whether you organize your essay by the point-by-point pattern or the block pattern, you need to use enough transition devices to ensure a smooth flow from one subject to another and from one point to the next. Without transitions, your essay may assume the distracting movement of a Ping-Pong game, as you switch back and forth between discussions of your two subjects. Listed below are some appropriate words to link your points:

COMPARISON	CONTRAST
also	however
similarly	on the contrary
too	on the other hand
both	in contrast
like	although
no only . . . but also	unlike
have in common	though
share the same	instead of
in the same manner	but

(For a review of other transition devices, see pp. 64–67.)

ESSAY TOPICS

Following are some topics that may be compared or contrasted. Remember to narrow your subject, formulate a thesis that presents a clear point, and follow one of the two organizational patterns discussed on pp. 171–172.

1. An expectation and its reality
2. A first impression and a later point of view
3. Two views on a current controversial issue (campus, local, national, or international)
4. Two conflicting theories you are studying in another college course
5. A memory of a person or place and a more recent encounter with that person or place
6. Coverage of the same story by two newspapers or magazines (the *National Enquirer* and the *Dallas Morning News,* for example, or *Time* and *Newsweek*)
7. A hero today and yesterday
8. Two commercials for a similar product
9. Two pieces of technology you've owned or operated
10. A public or private myth and its reality
11. Two solutions to a problem in your professional field

12. One of today's popular entertainments and one from an earlier era (board or card games, for instance)
13. Two places you've lived
14. Two politicians or public figures from today or from the past
15. Two books or a book and its movie or a movie and its sequel
16. Two jobs or employers (or your current job and the job of your dreams)
17. Two places that are special for you in different ways
18. An opinion you held before coming to college that has changed now that you are in college
19. Two sports or athletes or pieces of sports equipment
20. Your attitude toward a social custom or political belief and your parents' (or grandparents') attitude toward that belief or custom

Sample Student Essay

Note that this writer takes a definite stand—that local food co-ops are superior to chain stores—and then contrasts two local stores, Lane Grocer and the Fort Collins Co-op, to prove her thesis. She selected the point-by-point pattern to organize her essay, contrasting prices, atmosphere, and benefits to local producers. See if you can identify her transition devices as well as some of her uses of detail that make the essay more interesting and convincing.

Bringing Back the Joy of Market Day

Thesis

Essay map

Point one: Prices

Now that the old family-run corner grocery is almost extinct, many people are banding together to form their own neighborhood stores as food cooperatives. Locally owned by their members, food co-ops such as the one here in Fort Collins are welcome alternatives to the impersonal chain-store markets such as Lane Grocer. In exchange for volunteering a few hours each month, co-op members share savings and a friendly experience while they shop; local producers gain loyal, local support from the members as well as better prices for their goods in return for providing the freshest, purest food possible.

Perhaps the most crucial distinction between the two kinds of stores is that while supermarkets are set up to generate profit for their corporations, co-ops are nonprofit groups whose main purpose is to provide their members and the community with good, inexpensive food and basic household needs. At first glance, supermarkets such as Lane Grocer may appear to be cheaper because they offer so many specials, which they emphasize heavily through ads and in store promotions. These special deals, known as "loss-leaders" in the retail industry, are more than made up for by the extremely high markups on other products. For example, around Thanksgiving Lane Grocer might have a sale on flour and shortening and then set up the displays with utmost care so that as customers reach for the flour they will be drawn to colorful bottles of pie spices, fancy jars of mincemeat, or maybe an inviting bin of fresh-roasted holiday nuts, all of which may be marked up 100% or more—way above what is being lost on the flour and shortening.

The Fort Collins Co-op rarely bothers with such pricing gimmicks; instead, it tries to have a consistent markup—just enough to meet overhead expenses. The flour at the co-op may cost an extra few cents, but that same fancy spice bottle that costs over $1.00 from the supermarket display can be refilled at the co-op for less than 25¢. The nuts, considered by regular groceries as a seasonal "gourmet" item, are sold at the co-op for about two-thirds the price. Great savings like these are achieved by buying in bulk and having customers bag their own groceries. Recycled containers are used as much as possible, cutting down substantially on overhead. Buying in bulk may seem awkward at first, but the extra time spent bagging and weighing their own food results in welcome savings for co-op members.

Once people have gotten accustomed to bringing their own containers and taking part in the work at the co-ops, they often find that it's actually more fun to shop in the friendly, relaxed atmosphere of the co-ops. At Lane Grocer, for example, I often find shopping a battle of tangled metal carts wielded by bored customers who are frequently trying to manage one or more cranky children. The long aisles harshly lit by rows of cold fluorescent lights and the bland commercial music don't make the chore of shopping any easier either. On the other hand, the Fort Collins Co-op may not be as expertly planned, but at least the chaos is carried on in a friendly way. Parents especially appreciate that they can safely let their children loose while they shop because in the small, open-spaced co-op even toddlers don't become lost as they do in the aisles of towering supermarket shelves. Moreover, most members are willing to look after the children of other members if necessary. And while they shop, members can choose to listen to the FM radio or simply to enjoy each other's company in relative quiet.

As well as benefiting member consumers, co-ops also help small local producers by providing a direct market for their goods. Large chain stores may require minimum wholesale quantities far beyond the capacity of an individual producer, and mass markets like Lane Grocer often feel they are "too big" to negotiate with small local producers. But because of their small, independent nature co-ops welcome the chance to buy direct from the grower or producer. Direct selling offers two advantages for producers: they get a better price for their wares than by selling them through a middleman, and at the same time they establish an independent reputation for their business, which can be immensely valuable to their success later on. In Fort Collins, for example, Luna tofu (bean

Examples of Lane Grocer's prices contrasted to examples of co-op prices

Point two: Atmosphere

Description of Lane Grocer's atmosphere contrasted to description of the co-op's atmosphere

Point three: Benefits to local producers

No benefits at Lane Grocer contrasted to two benefits at the co-op

curd) stands out as an excellent illustration of this kind of mutual support. Several years ago my friend Carol Jones began making tofu in small batches to sell to the co-op as a way to earn a part-time income as well as to contribute to the co-op. Her enterprise has now grown so well that last year her husband quit his job to go into business with her full time. She currently sells to distributors and independent stores from here to Denver; even Lane Grocer, who earlier would not consider selling her tofu even on a trial basis, is now thinking about changing its policy.

Conclusion: Summarizing the advantages of co-ops over chain stores

Of course, not all co-ops are like the one here in Fort Collins, but that is one of their best features. Each one reflects the personalities of its members, unlike the supermarket chain stores that vary only slightly. Most important, though, while each has a distinctive character, co-ops share common goals of providing members with high-quality, low-cost food in a friendly, cooperative spirit.

Professional Essay _____

GRANT AND LEE: A STUDY IN CONTRASTS

Bruce Catton

Bruce Catton, an authority on the Civil War, won both the Pulitzer Prize for historical work and the National Book Award in 1955. He wrote numerous books, including Mr. Lincoln's Army *(1951),* A Stillness of Appomattox *(1953),* Never Call Retreat *(1966), and* Gettysburg: The Final Fury *(1974). This essay is a chapter of* The American Story *(1956), a collection of essays by noted historians.*

1   When Ulysses S. Grant and Robert E. Lee met in the parlor of a modest house at Appomattox Court House, Virginia, on April 9, 1865, to work out the terms for the surrender of Lee's Army of Northern Virginia, a great chapter in American life came to a close, and a great new chapter began.

2   These men were bringing the Civil War to its virtual finish. To be sure, other armies had yet to surrender, and for a few days the fugitive Confederate government would struggle desperately and vainly, trying to find some way to go on living now that its chief support was gone. But in effect it was all over when Grant and Lee signed the papers. And the little room where they wrote out the terms was the scene of one of the poignant, dramatic contrasts in American history.

3   They were two strong men, these oddly different generals, and they represented the strengths of two conflicting currents that, through them, had come
into final collision.

4   Back of Robert E. Lee was the notion that the old aristocratic concept
might somehow survive and be dominant in American life.

5   Lee was tidewater Virginia, and in his background were family, culture, and
tradition . . . the age of chivalry transplanted to a New World which was making
its own legends and its own myths. He embodied a way of life that had come down
through the age of knighthood and the English country squire. America was a
land that was beginning all over again, dedicated to nothing much more complicated than the rather hazy belief that all men had equal rights, and should have
an equal chance in the world. In such a land Lee stood for the feeling that it was
somehow of advantage to human society to have a pronounced inequality in the
social structure. There should be a leisure class, backed by ownership of land; in
turn, society itself should be keyed to the land as the chief source of wealth and
influence. It would bring forth (according to this ideal) a class of men with a
strong sense of obligation to the community; men who lived not to gain advantage
for themselves, but to meet the solemn obligations which had been laid on them by
the very fact that they were privileged. From them the country would get its leadership; to them it could look for the higher values—of thought, of conduct, of
personal deportment—to give it strength and virtue.

6   Lee embodied the noblest elements of this aristocratic ideal. Through him,
the landed nobility justified itself. For four years, the Southern states had
fought a desperate war to uphold the ideals for which Lee stood. In the end, it
almost seemed as if the Confederacy fought for Lee; as if he himself was the
Confederacy . . . the best thing that the way of life for which the Confederacy
stood could ever have to offer. He had passed into legend before Appomattox.
Thousands of tired, underfed, poorly clothed Confederate soldiers, long-since
past the simple enthusiasm of the early days of the struggle, somehow considered Lee the symbol of everything for which they had been willing to die. But
they could not quite put this feeling into words. If the Lost Cause, sanctified by
so much heroism and so many deaths, had a living justification, its justification
was General Lee.

7   Grant, the son of a tanner on the Western frontier, was everything Lee was
not. He had come up the hard way, and embodied nothing in particular except the
eternal toughness and sinewy fiber of the men who grew up beyond the mountains. He was one of a body of men who owed reverence and obeisance to no one,
who were self-reliant to a fault, who cared hardly anything for the past but who
had a sharp eye for the future.

8   These frontier men were the precise opposites of the tidewater aristocrats.
Back of them, in the great surge that had taken people over the Alleghenies and
into the opening Western country, there was a deep, implicit dissatisfaction
with a past that had settled into grooves. They stood for democracy, not from
any reasoned conclusion about the proper ordering of human society, but simply
because they had grown up in the middle of democracy and knew how it

worked. Their society might have privileges, but they would be privileges each man had won for himself. Forms and patterns meant nothing. No man was born to anything, except perhaps to a chance to show how far he could rise. Life was competition.

9   Yet along with this feeling had come a deep sense of belonging to a national community. The Westerner who developed a farm, opened a shop, or set up in business as a trader could hope to prosper only as his own community prospered—and his community ran from the Atlantic to the Pacific and from Canada down to Mexico. If the land was settled, with towns and highways and accessible markets, he could better himself. He saw his fate in terms of the nation's own destiny. As its horizons expanded, so did his. He had, in other words, an acute dollars-and-cents stake in the continued growth and development of his country.

10   And that, perhaps, is where the contrast between Grant and Lee becomes most striking. The Virginia aristocrat, inevitably, saw himself in relation to his own region. He lived in a static society which could endure almost anything except change. Instinctively, his first loyalty would go to the locality in which that society existed. He would fight to the limit of endurance to defend it, because in defending it he was defending everything that gave his own life its deepest meaning.

11   The Westerner, on the other hand, would fight with an equal tenacity for the broader concept of society. He fought so because everything he lived by was tied to growth, expansion, and a constantly widening horizon. What he lived by would survive or fall with the nation itself. He could not possibly stand by unmoved in the face of an attempt to destroy the Union. He would combat it with everything he had, because he could only see it as an effort to cut the ground out from under his feet.

12   So Grant and Lee were in complete contrast, representing two diametrically opposed elements in American life. Grant was the modern man emerging; beyond him, ready to come on the stage, was the great age of steel and machinery, of crowded cities and a restless, burgeoning vitality. Lee might have ridden down from the old age of chivalry, lance in hand, silken banner fluttering over his head. Each man was the perfect champion of his cause, drawing both his strengths and his weaknesses from the people he led.

13   Yet it was not all contrast, after all. Different as they were—in background, in personality, in underlying aspiration—these two great soldiers had much in common. Under everything else, they were marvelous fighters. Furthermore, their fighting qualities were really very much alike.

14   Each man had, to begin with, the great virtue of utter tenacity and fidelity. Grant fought his way down the Mississippi Valley in spite of acute personal discouragement and profound military handicaps. Lee hung on in the trenches at Petersburg after hope itself had died. In each man there was an indomitable quality . . . the born fighter's refusal to give up as long as he can still remain on his feet and lift his two fists.

15   Daring and resourcefulness they had, too; the ability to think faster and move faster than the enemy. These were the qualities which gave Lee the dazzling

campaigns of Second Manassas and Chancellorsville and won Vicksburg for Grant.

16   Lastly, and perhaps greatest of all, there was the ability, at the end, to turn quickly from war to peace once the fighting was over. Out of the way these two men behaved at Appomattox came the possibility of a peace of reconciliation. It was a possibility not wholly realized, in the years to come, but which did, in the end, help the two sections to become one nation again . . . after a war whose bitterness might have seemed to make such a reunion wholly impossible. No part of either man's life became him more than the part he played in their brief meeting in the McLean house at Appomattox. Their behavior there put all succeeding generations of Americans in their debt. Two great Americans, Grant and Lee—very different, yet under everything very much alike. Their encounter at Appomattox was one of the great moments of American history.

QUESTIONS ON CONTENT, STYLE, AND STRUCTURE

1. What is Catton's thesis?
2. According to Catton, how did Lee view society? Summarize the aristocratic ideal that Lee symbolized.
3. Who did Grant represent? How did they view the country's social structure?
4. After carefully studying paragraphs four through sixteen, describe the pattern of organization Catton uses to present his discussion.
5. What new means of development begins in paragraph thirteen?
6. How does Catton avoid the choppy seesaw effect as he compares and contrasts his subjects? Point out ways in which Catton makes a smooth transition from point to point.
7. Evaluate Catton's ability to write unified, coherent paragraphs with clearly stated topic sentences. Are his paragraphs adequately developed with enough specific detail? Cite evidence to support your answer.
8. What is the advantage or disadvantage of having only one sentence in paragraph three? In paragraph four?
9. What is Catton's opinion of these men? Select words and passages to support your answer. How does Catton's attitude affect the tone of this essay? Is his tone appropriate? Why or why not?
10. Instead of including a separate paragraph, Catton presents his concluding remarks in paragraph sixteen, in which he discusses his last major point about Grant and Lee. Many essays lacking concluding paragraphs end too abruptly or merely trail off; how does Catton avoid these weaknesses?

VOCABULARY

chivalry (5)	diametrically (12)
deportment (5)	burgeoning (12)
embodied (6)	indomitable (14)
tenacity (11)	reconciliation (16)

A REVISION WORKSHEET FOR YOUR COMPARISON AND CONTRAST ESSAY

As you write your rough drafts, consult Chapter 5 for guidance through the revision process. In addition, here are a few questions to ask yourself as you revise your comparison/contrast essay:

1. Does the essay contain a thesis that makes a significant point instead of a "so-what" thesis?
2. Is the material organized into the best pattern for the subject matter?
3. If the essay is developed by the point-by-point pattern, are there enough transition words used to avoid the see-saw effect?
4. If the essay is developed by the block pattern, are there enough transition devices and references connecting the two subjects to avoid the split-essay problem?
5. Are the points of comparison/contrast presented in a logical, consistent order that the reader can follow easily?
6. Are both subjects given a reasonably balanced treatment?
7. Are both subjects developed in enough specific detail so that the reader clearly understands the comparison or contrast? Where might more detail be added?

After you've revised your essay extensively, you might exchange rough drafts with a classmate and answer these questions for each other, making specific suggestions for improvement wherever appropriate.

STRATEGY FOUR: DEVELOPMENT BY DEFINITION

Frequently in conversation we must stop to ask, "What do you mean by that?" because in some cases our failure to comprehend just one particular term may lead to total misunderstanding. Suppose, for example, in a discussion with a friend, you refer to a new law as a piece of "liberal legislation"; if you and your friend do not share the same definition of "liberal," your remark may be completely misinterpreted. Take another example: you tell your parents that the Punk era is over; if they don't know what Punk is, they miss the point entirely. In other words, definition of terms or ideas is often essential to meaningful communication.

Sometimes a dictionary definition or a one- or two-sentence explanation is all a term needs (Hemingway, for example, once defined courage as "grace under pressure"). And sometimes a brief, humorous definition can cut right to the heart of the matter (comedian Robin Williams, for instance, once defined "cocaine" as "God's way of saying you're making too much money").*

Occasionally, however, you will find it necessary to provide an *extended definition*—that is, a longer, more detailed explanation that thoroughly defines the subject. Essays of extended definitions are quite common; think, for instance, of the articles you've seen lately on "mercy killing" that try to define death, or the arguments on abortion that define "life" in a variety of ways. Other recent essays have grappled with such complex concepts as poverty, palimony, animal rights, pornography, discrimination, and "reverse" discrimination. The controversial verdict in the trial of John Hinckley, accused of the attempted assassination of President Ronald Reagan in 1981, produced many articles and editorials debating the meaning of criminal "insanity." The 1985 New York subway incident in which Bernard Goetz shot several young men who had accosted him caused much debate over the notion of "self-defense." And during the 1988 presidential election campaign, the "preppie" lifestyle of George Bush was constantly contrasted to the "liberal" beliefs of Michael Dukakis, with "yuppies" and "DINKS" (double income, no kids) casting many of the deciding votes. Today we continue to be bombarded with new and controversial terms that need often clarification before we can make intelligent choices or take appropriate action.

WHY DO WE DEFINE?

Essays of extended definition are usually written for one or more of the following reasons:

1. to provide an interpretation of a vague, controversial, or misunderstood term (such as "pro-choice," "pornoviolence," or "euthanasia")
2. to explain an abstract term or concept (such as "heroic," "success," or "jealousy")
3. to define a new or unusual term, often found in slang, dialect, or the jargon of a particular field of study or industry (such as "nerdy," "objective correlative," or "computer virus")

---

* Even graffiti employs definition. One bathroom wall favorite: "Death is Nature's way of telling you to slow down." Another, obviously written by an English major: "A double negative is a no-no."

4. to offer an objective definition of an unfamiliar term for use by a particular audience ("electron microscope," "tie beam," or "soft contact lenses")

5. to entertain by presenting the interesting history, uses, effects, or examples of a common word or expression ("cajun," "slasher flick," or "science fiction")

DEVELOPING YOUR ESSAY

Here are four suggestions to help you prepare your essay of extended definition:

Know your purpose. Sometimes we need to define a term as clearly and objectively as possible; as a laboratory assistant, for instance, you might need to explain a technical measuring instrument to a group of new students. At other times, however, we may wish to persuade as well as inform our readers. People's interpretations of words, especially abstract or controversial terms, can, and often do, differ greatly depending on their point of view. After all, one person's "protest march" can be another person's street riot. Consequently, before you begin writing, decide on your purpose. If your readers need objective information only, make your definition as unbiased as you can; if your goal is to convince them that your point of view is the right or best one, you may adopt a variety of persuasive techniques as well as subjective language. For example, readers of a paper on the new 24-hour emergency-care offices springing up around the country entitled "Doc in the Box" should quickly realize that they are not getting an objective treatment.

Give your readers a reason to read. One way to introduce your subject is to explain the previous use, misuse, or misunderstanding of the term; then present your new or different interpretation of the term or concept. An introduction and thesis defining a slang word, for instance, might state: "Despite the visions of cornbread dressing and cranberries it conjures up for most Americans, the word 'turkey' does not always refer to the Thanksgiving bird. Today, 'turkey' is also a common slang expression designed primarily to tease or even insult someone." Or take this introduction and thesis aimed at a word the writer feels is unclear to many readers: "When the credits roll at the end of a movie, much of the audience may be perplexed to see the job of 'best boy' listed. No, the 'best boy' doesn't stand up with the groom at a wedding of children—he (or she) is, in fact, the key electrician's first assistant, who helps rig the lights for the movie's director of photography."

Keep your audience in mind to anticipate and avoid problems of clarity. Because you are trying to present a new or improved definition, you must strive above all for clarity. Ask yourself, "Who is my intended audience? What terms or parts of my definition are strange to them?" You don't help your audience, for example, by defining one campus slang expression in terms of other bits of unfamiliar slang. If, in other words, you defined "space cadet" as an "air head," you're probably confusing your readers more than you are informing them. If your assignment doesn't specify a specific audience, you may find it useful to imagine one. You might pretend, for instance, that you're defining a campus or slang expression to your parents or that you're explaining an ambiguous term to a foreign visitor. After all, your definition is effective only if your explanation is clear not just to you but to those unfamiliar with the term or concept under discussion.

Use as many strategies as necessary to clarify your definition. Depending on your subject, you may use any number of the following methods in your essay to define your term:

1. state some examples
2. describe the parts
3. compare and contrast to similar terms
4. explain an operation or process
5. give some familiar synonyms
6. define by negation (i.e., tell what the term doesn't mean)
7. present the history
8. discuss causes or effects

To illustrate some of the methods suggested above, let's suppose you wanted to write an extended definition of modern country music. You might choose one or more of these methods:

- describe the parts: music, lyrics, and typical subject matter
- compare or contrast to other kinds of music, such as bluegrass and western swing
- give some examples of famous country songs
- trace its historical development from traditional country music to its present state

In the paper on country music or in any definition essay, you should, of course, use only those methods that will best define your term. Never include methods purely for the sake of exhibiting a variety of techniques. You, the writer, must decide which method or methods work best, which should receive the most emphasis, and in which order the chosen methods of definition should appear.

PROBLEMS TO AVOID

Here is a list of "don'ts" for the writer of extended definition essays:

Don't present an incomplete definition. An inadequate definition is often the result of choosing a subject too broad or complex for your essay. You

supposed to decide which of four objects each blot most resembled. The choices might be a cloud, a steam engine, a caterpillar and a sofa.

3   When I finished the test, I was shocked to find that I was barely masculine at all. On a scale of 1 to 10, I was about 1.2. Me, the horse wrangler? (And not just wrangler, either. That summer, I had to skin a couple of horses that died—the camp owner wanted the hides.)

4   The results of that test were so terrifying to me that for the first time in my life I did a piece of original analysis. Having unlimited time on the train, I looked at the "masculine" answers over and over, trying to find what it was that distinguished real men from people like me—and eventually I discovered two very simple patterns. It was "masculine" to think the blots looked like man-made objects, and "feminine" to think they looked like natural objects. It was masculine to think they looked like things capable of causing harm, and feminine to think of innocent things.

5   Even at 16, I had the sense to see that the compilers of the test were using rather limited criteria—maleness and femaleness are both more complicated than *that*—and I breathed a huge sigh of relief. I wasn't necessarily a wimp, after all.

6   That the test did reveal something other than the superficiality of its makers I realized only many years later. What it revealed was that there is a large class of men and women both, to which I belong, who are essentially androgynous. That doesn't mean we're gay, or low in the appropriate hormones, or uncomfortable performing the jobs traditionally assigned our sexes. (A few years after that summer, I was leading troops in combat and, unfashionable as it now is to admit this, having a very good time. War is exciting. What a pity the 20th century went and spoiled it with high-tech weapons.)

7   What it does mean to be spiritually androgynous is a kind of freedom. Men who are all-male, or he-man, or 100 percent red-blooded Americans, have a little biological set that causes them to be attracted to physical power, and probably also to dominance. Maybe even to watching football. I don't say this to criticize them. Completely masculine men are quite often wonderful people: good husbands, good (though sometimes overwhelming) fathers, good members of society. Furthermore, they are often so unself-consciously at ease in the world that other men seek to imitate them. They just aren't as free as us androgynes. They pretty nearly have to be what they are; we have a range of choices open.

8   The sad part is that many of us never discover that. Men who are not 100 percent red-blooded Americans—say, those who are only 75 percent red-blooded —often fail to notice their freedom. They are too busy trying to copy the he-men ever to realize that men, like women, come in a wide variety of acceptable types. Why this frantic imitation? My answer is mere speculation, but not casual. I have speculated on this for a long time.

9   Partly they're just envious of the he-man's unconscious ease. Mostly they're terrified of finding that there may be something wrong with them deep down, some weakness at the heart. To avoid discovering that, they spend their lives acting out the role that the he-man naturally lives. Sad.

10   One thing that men owe to the women's movement is that this kind of failure is less common than it used to be. In releasing themselves from the single ideal of the dependent woman, women have more or less incidentally released a lot of men from the single ideal of the dominant male. The one mistake the feminists have made, I think, is in supposing that *all* men need this release, or that the world would be a better place if all men achieved it. It would just be duller.

11   So far I have been pretty vague about just what the freedom of the androgynous man is. Obviously it varies with the case. In the case I know best, my own, I can be quite specific. It has freed me most as a parent. I am, among other things, a fairly good natural mother. I like the nurturing role. It makes me feel good to see a child eat—and it turns me to mush to see a 4-year-old holding a glass with both small hands, in order to drink. I even enjoyed sewing patches on the knees of my daughter Amy's Dr. Dentons when she was at the crawling stage. All that pleasure I would have lost if I had made myself stick to the notion of the paternal role that I started with.

12   Or take a smaller and rather ridiculous example. I feel free to kiss cats. Until recently it never occurred to me that I would want to, though my daughters have been doing it all their lives. But my elder daughter is now 22, and in London. Of course, I get to look after her cat while she is gone. He's a big, handsome farm cat named Petrushka, very unsentimental, though used from kittenhood to being kissed on the top of the head by Elizabeth. I've gotten very fond of him (he's the adventurous kind of cat who likes to climb hills with you), and one night I simply felt like kissing him on the top of the head, and did. Why did no one tell me sooner how silky cat fur is?

13   Then there's my relation to cars. I am completely unembarrassed by my inability to diagnose even minor problems in whatever object I happen to be driving, and don't have to make some insider's remark to mechanics to try to establish that I, too, am a "Man With His Machine."

14   The same ease extends to household maintenance. I do it, of course. Service people are expensive. But for the last decade my house has functioned better than it used to because I've had the aid of a volume called "Home Repairs Any Woman Can Do," which is pitched just right for people at my technical level. As a youth, I'd as soon have touched such a book as I would have become a transvestite. Even though common sense says there is really nothing sexual whatsoever about fixing sinks.

15   Or take public emotion. All my life I have easily been moved by certain kinds of voices. The actress Siobhan McKenna's, to take a notable case. Give her an emotional scene in a play, and within 10 words my eyes are full of tears. In boyhood, my great dread was that someone might notice. I struggled manfully, you might say, to suppress this weakness. Now, of course, I don't see it as a weakness at all, but as a kind of fulfillment. I even suspect that the true he-men feel the same way, or one kind of them does, at least, and it's only the poor imitators who have to struggle to repress themselves.

16   Let me come back to the inkblots, with their assumption that masculine equates with machinery and science, and feminine with art and nature. I have no idea whether the right pronoun for God is He, She or It. But this I'm pretty sure of. If God could somehow be induced to take that test, God would not come out macho, and not feminismo, either, but right in the middle. Fellow androgynes, it's a nice thought.

QUESTIONS ON CONTENT, STRUCTURE, AND STYLE

1. What method does Perrin use to introduce his essay? How does his lead-in set up his thesis?

2. What is Perrin defining in his essay? Is his definition subjective or objective?

3. Discuss some of the methods Perrin uses to define what it means to be "spiritually androgynous." Which methods are the most effective, and why?

4. How does Perrin view "he-men"? Why does he mention them in this essay?

5. According to Perrin, the women's movement has helped men in what ways? What mistake, says Perrin, have feminists made in their attitude toward men? Do you agree with Perrin?

6. In paragraph 11 Perrin admits that he has been "pretty vague" and then goes on to develop his definition with what sort of support?

7. Throughout his essay, Perrin primarily uses himself as an example of someone who has benefitted from the freedom of androgyny. Is this an effective decision? What other examples can you think of that Perrin might have introduced to offer support for his claims?

8. Characterize Perrin's "voice" in this essay. How is his tone achieved? Is it appropriate and effective? Why/why not?

9. How does Perrin conclude his essay? Does his last image effectively end the essay?

10. What would you suggest is the purpose of Perrin's essay? What effect did he want to have on his readers? Do you think he was successful? Why or why not?

VOCABULARY

androgynous (title)
superficiality (6)
feminist (10)

paternal (11)
transvestite (14)
suppress (15)

A Revision Worksheet for Your
Extended Definition Essay

As you write your rough drafts, consult Chapter 5 for guidance through the revision process. In addition, here are a few questions to ask yourself as you revise your extended definition essay:

1. Is the subject narrowed to manageable size, and is the purpose of the definition clear to the readers?
2. If the definition is objective, is the language as neutral as possible?
3. If the definition is subjective, is the point of view obvious to the readers?
4. Are all the words and parts of the definition itself clear to the essay's particular audience?
5. Are there enough explanatory methods (examples, descriptions, history, causes, effects, etc.) used to make the definition clear and convincing?
6. Have the various methods been organized and ordered in an effective way?
7. Does the essay contain enough specific details to make the definition clear and distinct rather than vague or circular? Where could additional details be added?

After you've revised your essay extensively, you might exchange rough drafts with a classmate and answer these questions for each other, making specific suggestions for improvement wherever appropriate.

STRATEGY FIVE: DEVELOPMENT BY
DIVISION AND CLASSIFICATION

To make large or complex subjects easier to comprehend, we frequently apply the principles of *division* or *classification*.

DIVISION

Division is the act of separating something into its component parts so that it may be better understood or used by the reader. For example, consider a complex subject such as the national budget. Perhaps you have seen a picture on television or in the newspaper of the budget represented by a circle or a pie that has been divided into parts and labeled: a certain percentage or "slice" of the budget for military spending, a certain amount designated for social services, another for education, and so on. By studying the budget after it has been divided into its parts, taxpayers may have a better sense of how their money is being spent.

As a student, you see division in action in many of your college courses. A literature teacher, for instance, might approach a particular drama by dividing its plot into stages such as exposition, rising action, climax, falling action, or dénouement. Or your chemistry lab-instructor may ask you to break down a substance into its components to learn how the parts interact to form the chemical. Even this textbook is divided into chapters to make it easier for you to use. When you think of *division,* then, think of dividing or separating one subject (often a large or complex or unfamiliar one) into its parts to help people understand it more easily.

CLASSIFICATION

While the principle of division calls for separating one thing into its parts, *classification* systematically groups a number of things into categories to make the information easier to grasp. Without some sort of imposed system of order, a body of information can be a jumble of facts and figures. For example, at some point you've probably turned to the classified ads in the newspaper; if the ads were not classified into categories such as "houses to rent," "cars for sale," and "help wanted," you would have to search through countless ads to find the service or item you needed.

Classification occurs everywhere around you. As a student, you may be classified as a freshman, sophomore, junior, or senior; you may also be classified by your major. If you vote, you may be categorized as a Democrat, Republican, Socialist, or something else; if you attend religious services, you may be classified as Baptist, Methodist, Catholic, Jewish, and so on. The books you buy may be grouped and shelved by the bookstore into "mysteries," "westerns," "biographies," "adventure stories," and other categories; the movies you see have already been typed as "G," "PG," "PG-13," "R," or "X." Professionals classify almost every kind of knowledge: ornithologists classify birds; etymologists classify words by origins; botanists classify plants; zoologists classify animals. Remember that *classification* differs from division in that it sorts and organizes *many* things into appropriate groups, types, kinds, or categories. *Division* begins with *one* thing and separates it into its parts.

DEVELOPING YOUR ESSAY

A classification or division paper is generally easy to develop. Each part or category is identified and described in a major part of the body of the essay. Frequently, one body paragraph will be devoted to each category. Here are three additional hints for writing your essay:

Select one principle of classification or division and stick to it. If you are classifying students by major, for instance, don't suddenly switch to classification by college: French, economics, psychology, *arts and sciences,* math, and chemistry. A similar error occurs in this classification of dogs by breeds because it includes a physical characteristic: spaniels, terriers, *long-haired,* hounds, and retrievers. Decide on what basis of division you will classify or divide your subject and then be consistent throughout your essay.

Make the purpose of your division or classification clear to your audience. Don't just announce that "There are four kinds of 'X'" or that "'Z' has three important parts." Why does your particular audience need this information? Consider these sample thesis statements:

> By recognizing the three kinds of poisonous snakes in this area, campers and backpackers may be able to take the proper medical steps if they are bitten.
>
> Knowing the four types of spinning reels will enable novice fishermen to purchase the equipment best suited to their needs.
>
> While karate has become a popular form of exercise as well as of self-defense, few people know what the six levels of achievement—or "belts" as they are called—actually stand for.

Organize your material for a particular purpose and then explain to your readers what that purpose is.

Account for all the parts in your division or classification. Don't, for instance, claim to classify all the evergreen trees native to your hometown and then leave out one or more species. For a short essay, narrow your ruling principle rather than omit categories. You couldn't, for instance, classify all the architectural styles in America in a short paper, but you could discuss the *major* styles on your campus. In the same manner, the enormous task of classifying all types of mental illness could be narrowed to the most common forms of schizophrenia. However you narrow your topic, remember that in a formal classification, all the parts must be accounted for.

Like most rules, the one above has an exception. If your instructor permits, you can also write a satirical or humorous classification. In this sort of essay, you make up your own categories as well as your thesis. One writer, for example, recently wrote about the kinds of moviegoers who spoil the show for everyone else, such as "the babbling idiot," "the laughing hyena," and "the wandering dawdler." Another female student described blind dates to avoid, including "Mr. Neanderthal," "Timothy Timid," "Red, the Raging Rebel," and "Frat-Rat Freddie," among others. Still another student classified the various kinds of people who frequent the school library at two A.M. In this kind of informal essay, the thesis rule still holds true: though you start by making a humorous or satirical point about your subject, your classification must be more than mere silliness. Effective humor should ultimately make good sense, not nonsense.

PROBLEMS TO AVOID

Avoid underdeveloped categories. A classification or division essay is not a mechanical list; each category should contain enough specific details to make it clearly recognizable and interesting. To present each category or part, you may draw upon the methods of development you already know, such as example, comparison and contrast, and definition. Try to use the same techniques in each category so that no one category or part of your essay seems underdeveloped or unclear.

Avoid indistinct categories. Each category should be a separate unit; there should be no overlap among categories. For example, in a classification of shirts by fabric, the inclusion of flannel with silk, nylon, and cotton is an overlap because flannel is a kind of cotton. Similarly, in a classification of soft drinks by flavor, to include sugar-free with cola, root beer, orange, grape, and so on, is misleading because sugar-free drinks come in many different flavors. In other words, make each category unique.

Avoid too few or too many categories. A classification essay should have at least three categories, avoiding the either-or dichotomy. On the other hand, too many categories give a short essay the appearance of a list rather than a discussion. Whatever the number, don't forget to use transition devices for an easy movement from category to category.

ESSAY TOPICS

Narrow your subject by selecting an appropriate principle of division or classification. Some of the suggestions are intended for humorous essays.

1. friends or relatives
2. teachers
3. TV game shows
4. doctors or dentists
5. methods of advertising for a particular product, such as cigarettes or perfume
6. bad dates
7. a piece of technology in your field of interest
8. approaches to studying a subject
9. roommates
10. salesclerks/waiters/waitresses
11. sports fans or amateur athletes
12. chronic moochers or borrowers
13. people who accost you on campus or in airports

14. ways of accomplishing a task (such as three ways to conduct an experiment, four ways to introduce a bill into Congress, etc.)
15. people who play video games or board games
16. kinds of tools or equipment for a particular task in your field of study
17. theories explaining "X" (the disappearance of the dinosaurs, for example)
18. diets or exercise programs
19. reasons people jog (or participate in some other activity)
20. vegetarians or Breatharians (or some other special-interest group)

Sample Student Essay

In the essay below, the student writer divided the Mesa Verde Indian Era into three time periods that correspond to changes in the people's domestic skills, crafts, and housing. Note the writer's use of description and examples to help the reader see the advances from one time period to another.

The Indian Era at Mesa Verde

Introduction:
Establishing a
reason for knowing
the classification

Principle of
division of the
Indian Era

Time period one:
The beginnings

Visiting Mesa Verde National Park is a trip back in time to two-and-a-half centuries before Columbus. The Park, located in southwestern Colorado, is the setting of a silent stone city, ten ruins built into protective seven-hundred-foot cliffs that housed hundreds of Indians from the pre-Columbian era to the end of the thirteenth century. If you visit the Park, you'll enjoy its architecture and history more if you know a little about the various people who lived there. The Indian Era may be divided into three time periods that show growing sophistication in such activities as crafts, hunting, trade, and housing: Basket Maker (A.D. 1–450), Modified Basket Maker (A.D. 450–750), and Pueblo (A.D. 750–1300).*

The earliest Mesa Verdeans, the Basket Makers, whose forefathers had been nomads, sought shelter from the dry plains in the cliff caves and became farmers. During growing seasons they climbed up toe-holds cut in the cliffs and grew beans and squash on the green mesa above. Settling down also meant more time for crafts. They didn't make pottery yet but instead wove intricate baskets that held water. Instead of depending on raw meats and vegetables, they could now cook food in these baskets by dropping heated rocks into the water. Because the Basket

---

* Last summer I worked at Mesa Verde as a guide for the Parks Service; the information in this paper is based on the tour I gave three times a week to hundreds of visitors to the Park. [Student writer's note]

Makers hadn't invented the bow and arrow yet, they had to rely on the inaccurate spear, which meant little fresh meat and few animal skins. Consequently, they wore little clothing but liked bone, seed, and stone ornaments.

Time period two: Advances in skills, trade, and housing

The second period, A.D. 450–750, saw the invention of pottery, the bow and arrow, and houses. Pottery was apparently learned from other tribes. From crude clay baked in the sun, the Indians advanced to clay mixed with straw and sand and baked in kilns. Paints were concocted from plants and minerals, and the Indians produced a variety of beautifully decorated mugs, bowls, jars, pitchers, and canteens. Such pots meant that water could be stored for longer periods, and perhaps a water supply encouraged more trade with neighboring tribes. These Mesa Verdeans also acquired the bow and arrow, a weapon that improved their hunting skills, and enlarged their wardrobes to include animal skins and feather blankets. Their individual living quarters, called pithouses, consisted of twenty-foot-wide holes in the ground with log, grasses, and earthen framework over them.

Time period three: More advances in community living, trade, and skills

The third period lasted until A.D. 1300 and saw the innovation of pueblos, or groups of dwellings, instead of single-family units. Nearly eight hundred dwellings show the large number of people who inhabited the complex, tunneled houses, shops, storage rooms, courtyards, and community centers whose masonry walls, often elaborately decorated, were three and four stories high. At the spacious Balcony House pueblo, for example, an adobe court lies beneath another vaulted roof: on three sides stand two-story houses with balconies that lead from one room to the next. In back of the court is a spring, and along the front side is a low wall that kept the children from falling down the seven-hundred-foot cliff to the canyon floor below. Balcony House also contains two *kivas,* circular subterranean ceremonial chambers that show the importance of fellowship and religion to the Indians of this era. During this period the Indians were still farmers and potters, but cotton cloth and other non-native products found at the ruins suggest a healthy trade with the south. But despite the trade goods, sophisticated pottery, and such innovations in clothing as the "disposable" juniper-bark diapers of babies, life was still primitive; the Indians had no system of writing, no wheel, and no metal.

Conclusion: Decline of the Indian Era

Near the end of the thirteenth century, the cliff dwellings became ghost towns. Archaeologists don't know for certain why the Indians left their elaborate homes, but they speculate that a drought that lasted some twenty years may have driven them south into New Mexico and Arizona, where strikingly similar crafts and tools have been found. Regardless of their reason for leaving, the Indians left an amazing architectural and cultural legacy. Learning about the people who lived in Mesa Verde centuries ago provides an even deeper appreciation of the cliff palaces that awe thousands of National Park visitors every year.

Professional Essay

THE SOUND OF MUSIC:
ENOUGH ALREADY

Fran Lebowitz

Fran Lebowitz writes satirical essays on the trends and fashions of urban life in America. She was the author of "The Lebowitz Report," a regular feature of Mademoiselle *magazine from 1977–79, and she contributes book and film reviews to* Changes *magazine. Her collections of essays include* Social Studies *(1981) and* Metropolitan Life *(1978), from which this selection was taken.*

1   First off, I want to say that as far as I am concerned, in instances where I have not personally and deliberately sought it out, the only difference between music and Muzak is the spelling. Pablo Casals practicing across the hall with the door open—being trapped in an elevator, the ceiling of which is broadcasting "Parsley, Sage, Rosemary, and Thyme"—it's all the same to me. Harsh words? Perhaps. But then again these are not gentle times we live in. And they are being made no more gentle by this incessant melody that was once real life.

2   There was a time when music knew its place. No longer. Possibly this is not music's fault. It may be that music fell in with a bad crowd and lost its sense of common decency. I am willing to consider this. I am willing even to try and help. I would like to do my bit to set music straight in order that it might shape up and leave the mainstream of society. The first thing that music must understand is that there are two kinds of music—good music and bad music. Good music is music that I want to hear. Bad music is music that I don't want to hear.

3   So that music might more clearly see the error of its ways I offer the following. If you are music and you recognize yourself on this list, you are bad music.

1. Music in Other People's Clock Radios

4   There are times when I find myself spending the night in the home of another. Frequently the other is in a more reasonable line of work than I and must arise at a specific hour. Ofttimes the other, unbeknownst to me, manipulates an appliance in such a way that I am awakened by Stevie Wonder. On such occasions I announce that if I wished to be awakened by Stevie Wonder I would sleep with Stevie Wonder. I do not, however, wish to be awakened by Stevie Wonder and that is why God invented alarm clocks. Sometimes the other realizes that I am right. Sometimes the other does not. And that is why God invented *many* others.

2. Music Residing in the Hold Buttons of Other People's Business Telephones

5   I do not under any circumstances enjoy hold buttons. But I am a woman of reason. I can accept reality. I can face the facts. What I cannot face is the music. Just as there are two kinds of music—good and bad—so there are two kinds of hold buttons—good and bad. Good hold buttons are hold buttons that hold one silently. Bad hold buttons are hold buttons that hold one musically. When I hold I want to hold silently. That is the way it was meant to be, for that is what God was talking about when he said, "Forever hold your peace." He would have added, "and quiet," but he thought you were smarter.

3. Music in the Streets

6   The past few years have seen a steady increase in the number of people playing music in the streets. The past few years have also seen a steady increase in the number of malignant diseases. Are these two facts related? One wonders. But even if they are not—and, as I have pointed out, one cannot be sure—music in the streets has definitely taken its toll. For it is at the very least disorienting. When one is walking down Fifth Avenue, one does not expect to hear a string quartet playing a Strauss waltz. What one expects to hear while walking down Fifth Avenue is traffic. When one does indeed hear a string quartet playing a Strauss waltz while one is walking down Fifth Avenue, one is apt to become confused and imagine that one is not walking down Fifth Avenue at all but rather that one has somehow wound up in Old Vienna. Should one imagine that one is in Old Vienna one is likely to become quite upset when one realizes that in Old Vienna there is no sale at Charles Jourdan. And that is why when I walk down Fifth Avenue I want to hear traffic.

4. Music in the Movies

7   I'm not talking about musicals. Musicals are movies that warn you by saying, "Lots of music here. Take it or leave it." I'm talking about regular movies that extend no such courtesy but allow unsuspecting people to come to see them and then assault them with a barrage of unasked-for tunes. There are two major offenders in this category: black movies and movies set in the fifties. Both types of movies are afflicted with the same misconception. They don't know that movies are supposed to be movies. They think that movies are supposed to be records with pictures. They have failed to understand that if God had wanted records to have pictures, he would not have invented television.

5. Music in Public Places Such as Restaurants, Supermarkets, Hotel Lobbies, Airports, Etc.

8   When I am in any of the above-mentioned places I am not there to hear music. I am there for whatever reason is appropriate to the respective place. I am

no more interested in hearing "Mack the Knife" while waiting for the shuttle to Boston than someone sitting ringside at the Sands Hotel is interested in being forced to choose between sixteen varieties of cottage cheese. If God had meant for everything to happen at once, he would not have invented desk calendars.

Epilogue

9   Some people talk to themselves. Some people sing to themselves. Is one group better than the other? Did not God create all people equal? Yes, God created all people equal. Only to some he gave the ability to make up their own words.

QUESTIONS ON CONTENT, STRUCTURE AND STYLE

1. How does Lebowitz signal to her readers, from the title through the first two paragraphs, that her essay is not intended to be taken entirely seriously?
2. What is Lebowitz's announced purpose in writing this essay? To whom does Lebowitz say she is addressing her comments?
3. Lebowitz first divides music into what two types? How does this initial division set up the classification that follows?
4. What are Lebowitz's five categories of bad music? Do these categories share certain characteristics?
5. How does Lebowitz make her categories clear? Cite some examples that she uses to clarify each kind of music and her reaction to it.
6. Characterize Lebowitz's tone or "voice" in this essay. How does her choice of words and level of diction contribute to this tone? Cite some examples to support your answer.
7. Throughout the essay Lebowitz repeatedly refers to God's plan for music. Why? What does this technique add to her essay?
8. What simple transition device does Lebowitz use to move from one category to another? Is this device effective in this essay?
9. Although Lebowitz's essay is humorous, what serious points is she trying to make about modern music? Does she succeed or not?
10. Evaluate Lebowitz's conclusion. Does it provide an effective ending to her essay? Why or why not?

VOCABULARY

incessant (1)

ofttimes (4)

unbeknownst (4)

malignant (6)

epilogue (9)

A REVISION WORKSHEET FOR YOUR CLASSIFICATION ESSAY

As you write your rough drafts, consult Chapter 5 for guidance through the revision process. In addition, here are a few questions to ask yourself as you revise your classification essay:

1. Is the purpose of the division or classification clear to the reader?
2. Is the principle of division maintained consistently throughout the essay?
3. If the essay presents a formal division or classification, has the subject been narrowed so that all the parts of the subject are accounted for?
4. If the essay presents an informal or humorous division or classification, does the paper nevertheless make a significant or entertaining point?
5. Is each category developed with enough specific detail? Where might more details be effectively added?
6. Is each class distinct, with no overlap among categories?
7. Is the essay organized logically and coherently with smooth transitions between the discussions of the categories?

After you've revised your essay extensively, you might exchange rough drafts with a classmate and answer these questions for each other, making specific suggestions for improvement wherever appropriate.

STRATEGY SIX:
DEVELOPMENT BY CAUSAL ANALYSIS

Causal analysis explains the cause-and-effect relationship between two (or more) elements. When you discuss the condition producing something, you are analyzing *cause;* when you discuss the result produced by something, you are analyzing *effect.* To find examples of causal analysis, you need only look around you. If your car stops running on the way to class, for example, you may discover the cause was an empty gas tank. On campus, in your history class, you may study the causes of the Civil War; in your economics class, the effects of teenage spending on the cosmetics market; and in your biology class, both the causes and effects of heart disease. Over dinner you may discuss the effects of some crisis in the Middle East on American foreign policy, and, as you drift to sleep, you may ponder the effects of your studying—or *not* studying—for your chemistry test tomorrow.

To express it most simply, *cause* asks:

—why did "X" happen?
or, why does "X" happen?
or, why will "X" happen?

Effect, on the other hand, asks:

—what did "Y" produce?
or, what does "Y" produce?
or, what will "Y" produce?

Some essays of causal analysis focus on the cause(s) of something; others analyze only the effect(s); still others discuss both causes and effects. If, for example, you wanted to concentrate on the major causes of the Wall Street crash of 1929, you might begin by briefly describing the effects of the crash on the economy, then devote your thesis and the rest of your essay to analyzing the major causes, perhaps allotting one major section (or one paragraph, depending on the complexity of the reasons) to each cause. Conversely, an effect paper might briefly describe the causes of the crash and then detail the most important effects. An essay covering both the causes and effects of something usually demands a longer paper so that each part will be clear. (If you can select your own essay topic, ask your teacher which kind of causal analysis essay you should write.)

DEVELOPING YOUR ESSAY

Whether you are writing an essay that primarily discusses either causes or effects, or one that focuses on both, you should follow these rules:

Present a reasonable thesis statement. If your thesis makes dogmatic, unsupportable claims ("Medicare will lead to a complete collapse of quality medical treatment") or overly broad assertions ("Peer pressure causes alcoholism among students"), you won't convince your reader. Limit or qualify your thesis whenever necessary by using such phrases as "may be," "a contributing factor," "one of the main reasons," "two important factors," and so on ("Peer pressure is *one of the major causes* of alcoholism among students").

Limit your essay to a discussion of recent, major causes or effects. In a short paper you generally don't have space to discuss minor or remote causes or effects. If, for example, you analyzed your car wreck, you might decide that the three major causes were defective brakes, a hidden yield sign, and bad weather. A minor, or remote, cause might include being tired because of too little sleep, too little sleep because of staying out late the night before, staying out late because of an out-of-town visitor, and so on—back to the womb. In some cases you may want to mention a few of the indirect causes or effects, but do be reasonable. Concentrate on the most immediate, most important factors. Often, a writer of a 500–800-word essay will discuss no more than two, three, or four major causes or effects of something; to try to cover more frequently results in an underdeveloped essay.

Organize your essay clearly. Organization of your causal analysis essay will vary, of course, depending on whether you are focusing on the causes of something or the effects, or both. To avoid becoming tangled in causes and effects, you might try sketching out a drawing of your thesis and essay map before you begin your first draft. Here, for instance, are a couple of sketches for essays you might write on your recent traffic accident:

Thesis Emphasizing the Causes:

Cause (defective brakes)
Cause (hidden yield sign)   produced ———→ Effect (my car wreck)
Cause (bad weather)

Thesis Emphasizing the Effects:

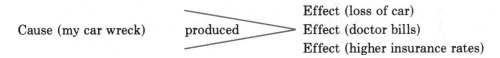

Effect (loss of car)
Cause (my car wreck)   produced ———→ Effect (doctor bills)
Effect (higher insurance rates)

Sometimes you may discover that you can't isolate "the three main causes/effects of 'X'"; some essays do in fact demand a narrative explaining a chain reaction of causes and effects. For example, a paper on the rebellion of the American colonies might show how one unjust British law or restriction after another led to the war for independence. In this kind of causal analysis essay, be careful to limit your subject so that you'll have the space necessary to show your readers how each step in the chain led to the next. Here's a sketch of a slightly different car-wreck paper presented in a narrative or chain-reaction format:

Cause ————→ 1st Effect —causes→ 2nd Effect —causes→ 3rd Effect
(bad   (wet   (car   (doctor
weather)   brakes)   wreck)   bills)

Sometimes the plan for organizing your causal analysis paper will be suggested by your subject matter; often, however, you'll have to devote some of your prewriting time to deciding, first, whether you want to emphasize causes or effects and, then, in what order you will present your analysis.

Convince your reader that a causal relationship exists by showing how the relationship works. Let's suppose you are writing an essay in which you want to discuss the three major changes you've undergone since coming to college. Don't just state the changes and describe them; your job is to show the reader how college has brought about these changes. If, for instance, your study habits have improved, then you must show the reader how the academic demands of your college courses caused you to change your habits; a simple description of your new study techniques is not enough. Remember that a causal analysis essay should stress *how* (and sometimes *why*) "X" caused "Y," rather than merely describing "Y" as it now exists.

PROBLEMS TO AVOID

Don't oversimplify by assigning one all-encompassing cause to some effect. Most complex subjects have more than one cause (or effect), so make your analysis as complete and objective as you can, especially when dealing with your own problems or beliefs. For example, was that car wreck really caused only by the bad weather—or also because of your carelessness? Did your friend do poorly in math only because the instructor didn't like her? Before judging a situation too quickly, investigate your own biases. Then provide a thoughtful, thorough analysis, effectively organized to convince your readers of the validity of your viewpoint.

Avoid the *post hoc* fallacy. This error in logic (from the Latin phrase *post hoc, ergo propter hoc,* meaning "after this, therefore because of this") results when we mistake a temporal connection for a causal relationship—or, in other words, when we assume that because one event follows another in time, the first event caused the second. Most of our superstitions are *post hoc* fallacies; we now realize that tripping after walking under a ladder is a matter of coincidence, not cause and effect. The *post hoc* fallacy provided the basis for a rather popular joke in the 1960s' debates over decriminalizing marijuana. Those against argued that marijuana led to heroin because most users of the hard drug had first smoked grass. The proponents retorted that milk, then, was the real culprit, because both marijuana and heroin users had drunk milk as babies. The point is this: in any causal analysis, you must be able to prove that one event *caused* another, not just that it preceded it in time.

Avoid circular logic. Often causal essays seem to chase their own tails when they include such circular statements as "There aren't enough parking spaces for students on campus because there are too many cars." Such a statement merely presents a second half that restates what is already implied in the first half. A revision might say, "There aren't enough parking spaces for students on campus because the parking permits are not distributed fairly." This kind of assertion can be argued specifically and effectively; the other is a dead end.

ESSAY TOPICS

The suggestions below may be developed into essays emphasizing cause, or effect, or both.

1. a pet peeve or bad habit
2. a change of mind about some important issue or belief
3. an accident
4. a family tradition or ritual
5. the popularity of some sport, hobby, fad, or style

6. ownership of a particular possession
7. a radical change in your appearance (such as losing or gaining weight, dyeing or spiking your hair)
8. a form of pollution or crime
9. cheating or dishonesty
10. an important decision or action
11. an act of heroism or sacrifice or selfishness
12. an important idea or discovery in your field of study
13. a superstition or irrational fear
14. a place that is special to you
15. a disappointment or a success
16. sexism or some other kind of discrimination or prejudice that you've witnessed or experienced
17. a friendship or influential person
18. a political action (campus, local, state, national) or a piece of legislation or a social movement
19. stress or an addiction
20. a campus problem

Sample Student Essay

In the following essay, a student explains why working in a local motel as a maid caused her to lose her self-respect, despite her attempts to do a good a job. Note that the writer uses many vivid examples and specific details to show the reader how she was treated and, consequently, how such treatment made her feel.

It's Simply Not Worth It

Introduction: Her job as a motel maid

It's hard to get a job these days, and with our town's unemployment rate reaching as high as ten percent, most people feel obligated to "take what they can get." But after working as a maid at a local motel for almost a year and a half, I decided no job is worth keeping if it causes a person to doubt his or her worth. My hard work rarely received recognition or appreciation, I was underpaid, and I was required to perform some of the most disgusting cleaning tasks imaginable. These factors caused me to devalue myself as a person and ultimately motivated me to return to school in hope of regaining my self-respect.

Thesis and map: Causes of her poor self-esteem

Cause one: Lack of appreciation

It may be obvious to say, but I believe that when a maid's hours of meticulous cleaning are met only with harsh words and complaints, she begins to lose her sense of self-esteem. I recall the care I took in making the motel's beds, imagining them as globs of clay and molding them into impeccable pieces of art. I would teeter from one side of a bed to the other, over and over again, until I smoothed out every intruding wrinkle or tuck. And the mirrors—I would vigorously massage the glass, erasing any toothpaste splotches or oil smudges that might draw my customer's disapproval. I would scrutinize the mirror first from the left side, then I'd move to the right side, once more to the left until every possible angle insured an unclouded reflection. And so my efforts went, room after room. But, without fail, each day more than one customer would approach me, not with praise for my tidy beds or spotless mirrors, but with nitpicking complaints that undermined my efforts: "Young lady, I just checked into room 143 and it only has two ashtrays. Surely for $43.95 a night you people can afford more ashtrays in the rooms."

If it wasn't a guest complaining about ashtrays, it was an impatient customer demanding extra towels or a fussy stay-over insisting his room be cleaned by the time he returned from breakfast at 8:00 A.M. "Can't you come to work early to do it?" he would urge thoughtlessly. Day after day, my spotless rooms went unnoticed, with no spoken rewards for my efforts from either guests or management. Eventually, the ruthless complaints and thankless work began wearing me down. In my mind, I became a servant undeserving of gratitude.

Cause two: Low pay

The lack of spoken rewards was compounded by the lack of financial rewards. The $3.35 appraisal of my worth was simply not enough to support my financial needs or my self-esteem. The measly $1.12 I earned for cleaning one room took a lot of rooms to add up, and by the end of the month I was barely able to pay my bills and buy some food. (My mainstay became twenty-two cent, generic macaroni and cheese dinners.) Because the flow of travelers kept the motel full for only a few months of the year, during some weeks I could only work half-time, making a mere $250.00 a month. As a result, one month I was forced to request an extension on my rent payment. Unsympathetically, my landlord threatened to evict me if I didn't pay. Embarrassed, yet desperate, I went to a friend and borrowed money. I felt uneasy and awkward and regretted having to beg a friend for money. I felt like a mooch and a bum; I felt degraded. And the constant reminder from management that there were hundreds of people standing in lines who would be more than willing to work for $3.35 an hour only aided in demeaning me further.

Cause three: Sickening duties

In addition to the thankless work and the inadequate salary, I was required to clean some of the most sickening messes. Frequently, conventions for high school clubs booked the motel. Once I opened the door of a conventioneer's room one morning and almost gagged at the odor. I immediately beheld a trail of vomit that began at the bedside and ended just short of the bathroom door. At that moment I cursed the inventor of shag carpet, for I knew it would take hours to comb this mess out of the fibers. On another day I spent thirty minutes dislodging the bed linen from the toilet where it had been stuffed. And I spent what seemed like hours removing from one of my spotless mirrors the lip-stick-drawn message that read, "Yorktown Tigers are number one." But these inconsiderate acts were relaying another message, a message I took personally: "Lady, you're not worth the consideration—you're a maid and you're not worth respecting."

Conclusion: Review of her self-esteem problem and a brief explanation of the solution she chose

I've never been afraid to work hard or do jobs that weren't particularly "fun." But the line must be drawn when a person's view of herself becomes clouded with feelings of worthlessness. The thankless efforts, the inadequate wage, and the disgusting work were just parts of a total message that degraded my character and caused me to question my worth. Therefore, I felt compelled to leave this demeaning job in search of a way to rebuilt my self-confidence. Returning to school has done just that for me. As my teachers and fellow students take time to listen to my ideas and compliment my responses, I feel once again like a vital, valued, and worthwhile person. I feel human once more.

Professional Essay

THE GREAT AMERICAN COOLING MACHINE

Frank Trippett

Frank Trippett is a journalist, author, and editor who has worked for Newsweek, Look, *and* Time, *where he is currently an associate editor. His books include* The States: United They Fell *(1967),* The First Horseman *(1974), and* Child Ellen *(1975). This essay appeared in* Time *during the energy crunch of 1979.*

1   "The greatest contribution to civilization in this century may well be air conditioning—and America leads the way." So wrote British Scholar-Politician S. F. Markham 32 years ago when a modern cooling system was still an exotic luxury. In a century that has yielded such treasures as the electric knife, spray-on deodorant and disposable diapers, anybody might question whether air conditioning is the supreme gift. There is not a whiff of doubt, however, that America is far out front in its use. As a matter of lopsided fact, the U.S. today, with a mere 5% of the population, consumes as much man-made coolness as the whole rest of the world put together.

2   Just as amazing is the speed with which this situation came to be. Air conditioning began to spread in industries as a production aid during World

War II. Yet only a generation ago a chilled sanctuary during summer's stewing heat was a happy frill that ordinary people sampled only in movie houses. Today most Americans tend to take air conditioning for granted in homes, offices, factories, stores, theaters, shops, studios, hotels and restaurants. They travel in chilled buses, trains, planes and private cars. Sporting events once associated with open sky and fresh air are increasingly boxed in and air cooled. Skiing still takes place outdoors, but such attractions as tennis, rodeos, football and, alas, even baseball are now often staged in synthetic climates like those of Houston's Astrodome and New Orleans' Superdome. A great many of the country's farming tractors are now, yup, air-conditioned.

3   It is thus no exaggeration to say that Americans have taken to mechanical cooling avidly and greedily. Many have become all but addicted, refusing to go places that are not air-conditioned. In Atlanta, shoppers in Lenox Square so resented having to endure natural heat while walking outdoors from chilled store to chilled store that the mall management enclosed and air-conditioned the whole sprawling shebang. The widespread whining about Washington's raising of thermostats to a mandatory 78° F suggests that people no longer think of interior coolness as an amenity but consider it a necessity, almost a birthright, like suffrage. The existence of such a view was proved last month when a number of federal judges, sitting too high and mighty to suffer 78°, defied and denounced the Government's energy-saving order to cut back on cooling. Significantly, there was no popular outrage at this judicial insolence; many citizens probably wished that they could be so highhanded.

4   Everybody by now is aware that the cost of the American way is enormous, that air conditioning is an energy glutton. It uses some 9% of all electricity produced. Such an extravagance merely to provide comfort is peculiarly American and strikingly at odds with all the recent rhetoric about national sacrifice in a period of menacing energy shortages. Other modern industrial nations such as Japan, Germany and France have managed all along to thrive with mere fractions of the man-made coolness used in the U.S., and precious little of that in private dwellings. Here, so profligate has its use become that the air conditioner is almost as glaring a symptom as the automobile of the national tendency to overindulge in every technical possibility, to use every convenience to such excess that the country looks downright coddled.

5   But not everybody is aware that high cost and easy comfort are merely two of the effects of the vast cooling of America. In fact, air conditioning has substantially altered the country's character and folkways. With the dog days at hand and the thermostats ostensibly up, it is a good time to begin taking stock of what air conditioning has done besides lower the indoor temperature.

6   Many of its byproducts are so conspicuous that they are scarcely noticed. To begin with, air conditioning transformed the face of urban America by making possible those glassy, boxy, sealed-in skyscrapers on which the once humane geometries of places like San Francisco, Boston and Manhattan have been impaled. It has been indispensable, no less, to the functioning of sensitive advanced computers, whose high operating temperatures require that they be constantly

cooled. Thus, in a very real way, air conditioning has made possible the ascendancy of computerized civilization. Its cooling protection has given rise not only to moon landings, space shuttles and Skylabs but to the depersonalized punch-cardification of society that regularly gets people hot under the collar even in swelter-proof environments. It has also reshaped the national economy and redistributed political power simply by encouraging the burgeoning of the sultry southerly swatch of the country, profoundly influencing major migration trends of people and industry. Sunbelt cities like Phoenix, Atlanta, Dallas and Houston (where shivering indoor frigidity became a mark of status) could never have mushroomed so prosperously without air conditioning; some communities—Las Vegas in the Nevada desert and Lake Havasu City on the Arizona-California border—would shrivel and die overnight if it were turned off.

7   It has, as well, seduced families into retreating into houses with closed doors and shut windows, reducing the commonalty of neighborhood life and all but obsoleting the front-porch society whose open casual folkways were an appealing hallmark of a sweatier America. Is it really surprising that the public's often noted withdrawal into self-pursuit and privatism has coincided with the epic spread of air conditioning? Though science has little studied how habitual air conditioning affects mind or body, some medical experts suggest that, like other technical avoidance of natural swings in climate, air conditioning may take a toll on the human capacity to adapt to stress. If so, air conditioning is only like many other greatly useful technical developments that liberate man from nature by increasing his productivity and power in some ways—while subtly weakening him in others.

8   Neither scholars nor pop sociologists have really got around to charting and diagnosing all the changes brought about by air conditioning. Professional observers have for years been preoccupied with the social implications of the automobile and television. Mere glancing analysis suggests that the car and TV, in their most decisive influences on American habits, have been powerfully aided and abetted by air conditioning. The car my have created all those shopping centers in the boondocks, but only air conditioning has made them attractive to mass clienteles. Similarly, the artificial cooling of the living room undoubtedly helped turn the typical American into a year-round TV addict. Without air conditioning, how many viewers would endure reruns (or even Johnny Carson) on one of those pestilential summer nights that used to send people out to collapse on the lawn or to sleep on the roof?

9   Many of the side effects of air conditioning are far from being fully pinned down. It is a reasonable suspicion, though, that controlled climate, by inducing Congress to stay in Washington longer than it used to during the swelter season, thus presumably passing more laws, has contributed to bloated Government. One can only speculate that the advent of the supercooled bedroom may be linked to the carnal adventurism associated with the mid-century sexual revolution. Surely it is a fact—if restaurant complaints about raised thermostats are to be believed—that air conditioning induces at least expense-account diners to eat and drink more; if so, it must be credited with adding to the national fat problem.

10   Perhaps only a sophist might be tempted to tie the spread of air conditioning to the coincidentally rising divorce rate, but every attentive realist must
have noticed that even a little window unit can instigate domestic tension and
chronic bickering between couples composed of one who likes it on all the time
and another who does not. In fact, perhaps surprisingly, not everybody likes air
conditioning. The necessarily sealed rooms or buildings make some feel claus-
trophobic, cut off from the real world. The rush, whir and clatter of cooling
units annoys others. There are even a few eccentrics who object to man-made
cool simply because they like hot weather. Still, the overwhelming majority of
Americans have taken to air conditioning like hogs to a wet wallow.

11   It might be tempting, and even fair, to chastise that vast majority for
being spoiled rotten in their cool ascendancy. It would be more just, however,
to observe that their great cooling machine carries with it a perpetual price
tag that is going to provide continued and increasing chastisement during the
energy crisis. Ultimately, the air conditioner, and the hermetic buildings it
requires, may turn out to be a more pertinent technical symbol of the American personality than the car. While the car has been a fine sign of the American impulse to dart hither and yon about the world, the mechanical cooler
more neatly suggests the maturing national compulsion to flee the natural
world in favor of a technological cocoon.

12   Already architectural designers are toiling to find ways out of the technical
trap represented by sealed buildings with immovable glass, ways that might let in
some of the naturally cool air outside. Some have lately come up with a remarkable discovery: the openable window. Presumably, that represents progress.

QUESTIONS ON CONTENT, STRUCTURE, AND STYLE

1. When Trippett begins his essay with the Markham quotation followed
by his reference to a century that has produced "such treasures as the
electric knife, spray-on deodorant and disposable diapers," what tone
is being established?

2. Why does Trippett spend several paragraphs describing America's
"addiction" to air conditioning? What is his attitude toward America's
use of this invention?

3. Where is Trippett's thesis stated? Does his essay analyze the causes
or the effects of this country's dependence on air conditioning?

4. What, in Trippett's opinion, are some of the lesser-known effects of
air conditioning?

5. What kinds of evidence does Trippett offer to support this analysis?
Cite some examples from the essay.

6. Do you think Trippett intended for his audience to take all his spec-
ulations on the effects of air conditioning entirely seriously? Why/
why not?

7. What is the effect on the reader of such words and phrases as "whiff of doubt" (paragraph 1), "yup" (2), "whole sprawling shebang" (3), "punch-cardification of society" (6), "a sweatier America" (7), and "hogs to a wet wallow" (10)? Is such language appropriate in this essay?

8. Is Trippett generally pleased or unhappy with the effects of air conditioning he describes? Support your answer with specific examples from the essay.

9. What, ultimately, may the air conditioner symbolize about modern Americans? Do you agree?

10. How does Trippett's concluding paragraph emphasize both the tone and the author's attitude toward his subject as expressed throughout the essay?

VOCABULARY

amenity (3)
suffrage (3)
profligate (4)
ostensibly (5)
conspicuous (6)

indispensable (6)
burgeoning (6)
sophist (10)
chastise (11)
hermetic (11)

A REVISION WORKSHEET FOR YOUR CAUSAL ANALYSIS ESSAY

As you write your rough drafts, consult Chapter 5 for guidance through the revision process. In addition, here are a few questions to ask yourself as you revise your causal analysis essay:

1. Is the thesis limited to a reasonable claim that can be supported in the essay?

2. Is the organization clear and consistent so that the reader can understand the purpose of the analysis?

3. Does the essay focus on the most important causes and/or effects?

4. If the essay has a narrative form, is each step in the chain reaction clearly connected to the next?

5. Does the essay convincingly show the reader how or why relationships between the causes and effects exist, instead of merely naming and describing them?

6. Does the essay provide enough evidence to show the connections between causes and effects? Where could additional details be added to make the relationships clearer?

7. Has the essay avoided the problems of oversimplification, circular logic, and the *post hoc* fallacy?

After you've revised your essay extensively, you might exchange rough drafts with a classmate and answer these questions for each other, making specific suggestions for improvement wherever appropriate.

9

Argumentation

Almost without exception, each of us, every day, argues for or against something with somebody. The discussions may be short and friendly ("Let's go to this restaurant rather than that one") or long and complex ("Mandatory seat belt laws are an intrusion on civil rights"). Because we do argue our viewpoints so often, most of us realized long ago that shifting into high whine did not always get us what we wanted; on the contrary, we've learned that we usually have a much better chance at winning a dispute or having our plan adopted or changing someone's mind if we present our side of an issue in a calm, logical fashion, giving sound reasons for our position. And this approach is just what a good argumentative essay does: it presents logical reasoning and solid evidence that will persuade your readers to accept your point of view.

Some argumentative essays declare the best solution to a problem ("Raising the drinking age will decrease traffic accidents"); others argue a certain way of looking at an issue ("Beauty pageants degrade women"); still others may urge adoption of a specific plan of action ("Voters should pass ordinance #10 to fund the new ice rink"). Whatever your exact purpose, your argument essay should be composed of a clear thesis and body paragraphs that offer enough sensible reasons and persuasive evidence to convince your readers to agree with you.

DEVELOPING YOUR ESSAY

Here are some suggestions for developing and organizing an effective argumentative essay:

Know why you hold your views. We human beings, being opinionated creatures, frequently voice beliefs that we, when pressed, can't always support effectively. Sometimes we hold an opinion simply because on the surface it seems to make good sense to us or because it fits comfortably with our other social,

213

ethical, or political beliefs. Or we may have inherited some of our beliefs from our families or friends, or perhaps we borrowed ideas from people we admired. In some cases, we may have held an opinion for so long that we can't remember why we adopted it in the first place. We may also have a purely sentimental or emotional attachment to some idea or position. Whatever the original causes of our beliefs, we need to examine the real reasons for thinking what we do before we can effectively convince others.

Once you've selected a topic for your argument essay, try writing down a list of the reasons or points that support your opinion on that subject. Then study the list—are your points logical and persuasive? Which aren't, and why not? After this bit of prewriting, you may discover that although you believe something strongly, you really don't have the kinds of factual evidence or reasoned arguments you need to support your opinion. In some cases, depending upon your topic, you may wish to talk to others who share your position or to research your subject (for help with research, see Chapter 12); in other cases, you may just need to think longer and harder about your topic and your reasons for maintaining your attitude toward it. With or without formal research, the better you know your subject, the more confident you will be about writing your argumentative essay.

Anticipate opposing views. An argument assumes that there is more than one side to an issue. To be convincing, you must be aware of your opposition's views on the subject and then organize your essay to answer or counter those views. If you don't have a good idea of the opposing arguments, you can't effectively persuade your readers to dismiss their objections and see matters your way. Therefore, before you begin your first rough draft, write down all the opposing views you can think of and an answer to each of them so that you will know your subject thoroughly. (For the sake of clarity throughout this chapter, your act of responding to those arguments against your position will be called *refuting the opposition;* "to refute" means "to prove false or wrong," and that's what you will try to do to some of the arguments of those who disagree with you.)

Know and remember your audience. While it's important to think about your readers' needs and expectations whenever you write, it is essential to consider carefully the audience of your argumentative essay both before and as you write your rough drafts. Because you are trying to persuade people to adopt some new point of view or perhaps to take some action, you need to decide what kinds of supporting evidence will be most convincing to your particular readers. Try to analyze your audience by asking yourself a series of questions, such as what do they already know about your topic? What information or terms do they need to know to understand your point of view? What biases might they already have for or against your position? What special concerns might your readers have that influence their receptiveness? To be convincing, you should consider these questions and others by carefully reviewing the discussion of audience on pp. 16–20 *before* you begin your prewriting.

Decide which points of argument to include. Once you have a good sense of your audience and of your own position and your opposition's strongest arguments, try making a Pro-and-Con Sheet to help you sort out which points you will discuss in your essay.

Let's suppose you want to write an editorial on the sale-of-class-notes controversy at your school. Should professional note-takers be allowed to sit in on a course and then sell their notes to class members? After reviewing the evidence on both sides, you have decided to argue that your school should prohibit professional note-taking services from attending classes and selling notes. To help yourself begin planning your essay, you list all the pro and con arguments you can think of concerning the controversy:

MY SIDE: AGAINST THE SALE OF CLASS NOTES	MY OPPOSITION'S SIDE: FOR THE SALE OF CLASS NOTES
1. unfair advantage for some students in some classes	1. helps students to get better test, course grades
2. note-taking is a skill students need to develop	2. helps students to learn, organize material
3. rich students can afford and poor can't	3. helps if you're sick and can't attend class
4. prevents students from learning to organize for themselves	4. shows students good models for taking notes and outlining them
5. encourages class cutting	5. other study guides are on the market, why not these?
6. missing class means no chance to ask questions, participate in discussions	6. gives starving graduate students jobs
7. notes taken by others are often inaccurate	7. no laws against sale of notes, free country
8. some professors don't like strangers in classroom	
9. students need to think for themselves	

After making your Pro-and-Con Sheet, look over the list and decide which of your strongest points you want to argue in your paper and also which of your opposition's claims you want to refute. At this point you may also see some arguments on your list that might be combined and some that might be deleted because they're irrelevant or unconvincing. (Be careful not to select more arguments or counter-arguments to discuss than the length of your writing assignment will allow. It's far better to present a persuasive analysis of a few points than it is to give an underdeveloped, shallow treatment of a host of reasons.)

Let's say you want to cover the following points in your essay:

- professional note-taking services keep students from developing own thinking and organizational skills (combination of #4 and 9)
- professional note-taking services discourage class attendance and participation (#5 and 6)
- unfair advantages to some students (#1 and 3).

Your assignment calls for a short essay of 750–1000 words, so you figure you'll only have space to refute your opposition's strongest claim, and you decide that is

- helps students to learn and organize material (#2).

The next step is to formulate a working thesis. At this stage you may find it helpful to put your working thesis in an "although-because" format so you can clearly see both your opposition's arguments and your own. An "although-because" statement for the note-taking essay might look something like this:

> *Although* some students maintain that using professional note-taking services helps them learn more, such services should be banned from our campus *because* they prevent students from developing their own thinking and organizational skills, they discourage class attendance, and they give unfair advantages to some students.

Frequently your "although-because" thesis will be too long and awkward to use in the later drafts of your essay. But for now, it can serve as a guide, allowing you to see your overall position before the writing of the first draft begins.

Organize your essay clearly. While there is no set model of organization for argumentative essays, here are some common patterns that you might use or that you might combine in some effective way.

Important Note: For the sake of simplicity, the first two outlines present two of the writer's points and two opposing ideas. Naturally, your essay may contain any number of points and refuted points, depending upon the complexity of your subject and the assigned length of your essay.

In Pattern A you devote the first few body paragraphs to arguing points on your side and then turn to refute or answer the opposition's claims.

Pattern A: Thesis

Body paragraph 1: you present your first point and its supporting evidence

Body paragraph 2: you present your second point and its supporting evidence

Body paragraph 3: you refute your opposition's first point

Body paragraph 4: you refute your opposition's second point

Conclusion

Sometimes you may wish to clear away the opposition's claims before you present the arguments for your side. To do so, you might select Pattern B:

Pattern B: Thesis

Body paragraph 1: you refute your opposition's first point

Body paragraph 2: you refute your opposition's second point

Body paragraph 3: you present your first point and its supporting evidence

Body paragraph 4: you present your second point and its supporting evidence

Conclusion

In some cases you may find that the main arguments you want to present are the very same ones that will refute or answer your opposition's primary claims. If so, try Pattern C, which allows each of your argumentative points to refute one of your opposition's claims in the same paragraph:

Pattern C: Thesis

Body paragraph 1: you present your first point and its supporting evidence, which also refutes one of your opposition's claims

Body paragraph 2: you present a second point and its supporting evidence, which also refutes a second opposition claim

Body paragraph 3: you present a third point and its supporting evidence, which also refutes a third opposition claim

Conclusion

Now you might be thinking, "What if my position on a topic as yet has no opposition?" Remember that almost all issues have more than one side, so try to anticipate objections and then answer them. For example, you might first present a thesis that calls for a new traffic signal at a dangerous intersection in your town and then address hypothetical counter-arguments, such as "The City Council may say that a stop light at Lemay and Columbia will cost too much, but the cost in lives will be much greater" or "Commuters may complain that a traffic light there will slow the continuous flow of north-south traffic, but it is precisely the uninterrupted nature of this road that encourages motorists to speed." By answering hypothetical objections, you impress your readers by showing them you've thought through your position thoroughly before you asked them to consider your point of view.

You might also be thinking, "What if my opposition actually has a valid objection, a legitimate point of criticism? Should I ignore it?" Hoping that an obviously strong opposing point will just go away is like hoping the IRS will cancel income taxes this year—a nice thought but hardly likely. Don't ignore your opposition's good point; instead, acknowledge it, but then go on quickly to show your readers why that reason, though valid, isn't compelling enough by itself to motivate people to adopt your opposition's entire position. Or you might concede that one point while simultaneously showing why your position isn't really in conflict with that criticism, but rather with other, more important, parts of your opponent's viewpoint. By admitting that you see some validity in your opposition's argument, you can again show your readers that you are both fair-minded and informed about all aspects of the controversy.

If you are feeling confident about your ability to organize an argumentative essay, you might try some combination of patterns, if your material allows such a treatment. For example, you might have a strong point to argue, another point that simultaneously answers one of your opposition's strongest claims, and another opposition point you want to refute. Your essay organization might look like this:

Combination: Thesis

Body paragraph 1: A point for your side

Body paragraph 2: One of your points, which also refutes an opposition claim

Body paragraph 3: Your refutation of another opposition claim

In other words, you can organize your essay in a variety of ways as long as your paper is logical and clear. Study your Pro-and-Con Sheet and then decide which organization best presents the arguments and counter-arguments you want to include. Try sketching out your essay following each of the patterns; look carefully to see which pattern (or variation on one of the patterns) seems to put forward your particular material most persuasively, with the least repetition or confusion. Sometimes your essay's material will clearly fall into a particular pattern of organization, so your choice will be easy; more often, however, you will have to arrange and rearrange your ideas and counter-arguments until you see the best approach. Don't be discouraged if you decide to change patterns after you've begun a rough draft; what matters is finding the most effective way to persuade the reader to your side.

If no organizational pattern seems to fit at first, ask yourself which of your points or counter-arguments is the strongest or most important. Try putting that point in one of the two most emphatic places: either first or last. Sometimes your most important discussion will lead the way into your other points and consequently should be introduced first; perhaps more often, effective writers and speakers build up to their strongest point, presenting it last as the climax of their argument. Again, the choice depends on your material itself, though it's rare that you would want to bury your strongest point in the middle of your essay.

After studying the arguments and counter-arguments you selected for the note-taking essay, let's say that you decide that your most important point concerns the development of students' learning skills. Since your opposition claims the contrary, that their service does promote learning, you see that you can make your main point as you refute theirs. But you also wish to include a couple of other points for your side. After trying several patterns, you decide to put the "thinking skills" rebuttal last for emphasis and present your other points first. Consequently, Pattern A best fits your plan. A sketchy outline might look like this:

- <u>Revised working thesis and essay map:</u> Professional note-taking services should be banned from our campus. Not only do they give some students unfair advantages and discourage class attendance, they prevent students from developing and practicing good thinking skills.
- <u>Body paragraph 1 (A first point for the writer's side):</u> services penalize some students—those who haven't enough money or take other sections or enroll in classes without notes.
- <u>Body paragraph 2 (Another point for the writer's side):</u> the service encourages class-cutting and so students miss opportunities to ask questions, participate in discussion, talk to instructor, see visual aids, etc.
- <u>Body paragraph 3 (Rebuttal of the opposition's strongest claim):</u> services claim they help students learn more, but they don't because they're doing the work students ought to be doing themselves. Students must learn to think and organize for themselves.

Once you have a general notion of where your essay is going, plan to spend some more time thinking about ways to make each of your points clear, logical, and persuasive to your particular audience. (If you wish to see how one student actually developed an essay based on the outline above, turn to the sample student paper on pp. 228–229.)

Argue your ideas logically. To convince your readers, you must provide sufficient reasons for your position. You must give more than mere opinion—you must offer logical arguments to back up your assertions. Some of the possible ways of supporting your ideas should already be familiar to you from writing expository essays; listed below are several methods and illustrations:

1. Give Examples (real or hypothetical): "Cutting class because you have access to professional notes can be harmful; for instance, you might miss seeing some slides or graphics essential to your understanding of the lecture."

2. Present a Comparison or Contrast: "In contrast to reading 'canned' notes, outlining your own notes helps you remember the material."

3. Show a Cause-and-Effect Relationship: "Dependence on professional notes may mean that some students will never learn to organize their own responses to classroom discussions."

4. Argue by Definition: "Passively reading through professional notes isn't a learning experience in which one's mind is engaged."

The well-thought out arguments you choose to support your case may be called *logical appeals* because they appeal to, and depend upon, your readers' ability to reason logically and to recognize good sense when they see it. But there is another kind of appeal often used today: the *emotional appeal*.

Emotional appeals are designed to persuade people by playing on their feelings rather than appealing to their intellect. Rather than using thoughtful, logical reasoning to support their claims, writers and speakers using *only* emotional appeals often try to accomplish their goals by misleading their audiences. Frequently, emotional appeals are characterized by language that plays on people's fears, material desires, illusions, or sympathies; such language often triggers highly favorable or unfavorable responses to a subject. For instance, emotional appeals are used constantly in advertising, where feel-good images, music, and slogans ("Come to Marlboro Country," "The Heartbeat of America is Today's Chevy Truck") are designed to sway potential customers to a product without them thinking about it too much. Some politicians also rely heavily on emotional appeals, often using scare tactics to disguise a situation or to lead people away from questioning the logic of a particular issue.

But in some cases, emotional appeals can be used for legitimate purposes. Good writers should always be aware of their audience's needs, values, and states of mind, and they may be more persuasive in some cases if they can frame their arguments in ways that appeal to both their readers' logic and their emotions. For example, when Martin Luther King, Jr., delivered his famous "I Have A Dream" speech to the crowds gathered in Washington in 1963 and described his vision of little children of different races walking hand-in-hand, being judged not "by the color of their skin but by the content of their character," he certainly spoke with passion that was aimed at the hearts of his listeners. But King was not using an emotional appeal to keep his audience from thinking about his message; on the contrary, he presented powerful emotional images that he hoped would inspire people to act on what they already thought and felt, their deepest convictions about equality and justice.

Appeals to emotions are tricky: you can use them effectively in conjunction with appeals to logic and with solid evidence, but only if you use them ethically. And too many appeals to the emotions are overwhelming; readers tire quickly from too many tugs on the heart-strings. To prevent your readers from suspecting deception, support your assertions with as many logical arguments as you can muster and only use emotional appeals when they legitimately advance your cause.

Offer evidence that effectively supports your claims. In addition to presenting thoughtful, logical reasoning, you may wish to incorporate a variety of convincing evidence to persuade your readers to your side. Your essay might profit from including, where appropriate, some of the following kinds of supporting evidence:

- personal experiences
- the experiences or testimony of others whose opinions are pertinent to the topic
- factual information you've gathered from research
- statistics from current, reliable sources
- charts, graphs, diagrams
- testimony from authorities and experts

You'll need to spend quite a bit of your prewriting time thinking about the best kinds of evidence to support your case. Remember that not all personal experiences or research materials are persuasive. For instance, the experiences we've had (or that our friends have had) may not be representative of a universal experience and consequently may lead to unconvincing generalizations. Even testimony from an authority may not be convincing if the person is not speaking on a topic from his or her field of expertise; famous football players, for instance, don't necessarily know any more about panty hose or soft drinks than anyone else. Always put yourself in the skeptical reader's place and ask, "Does this point convince me? If not, why not?" (For much more information on gathering, selecting, and incorporating research material into your essays, see Chapter 12.)

Find the appropriate tone. Sometimes when we argue, it's easy to get carried away. Remember that your goal is to persuade and perhaps change your readers, not alienate them. Instead of laying on insults or sarcasm, present your ideas in a moderate let-us-reason-together spirit. Such a tone will persuade your readers that you are sincere in your attempts to argue as truthfully and fairly as possible. If your readers do not respect you as a reasonable person, they certainly won't be swayed to your side of an issue. Don't preach or pontificate either; no one likes—or respects—a writer with a superior attitude. Write in your natural "voice"; don't adopt a pseudointellectual tone. In short, to argue effectively you should sound logical, sincere, and informed. (For additional comments on tone, review pp. 124–126.)

Consider using Rogerian techniques, if they are appropriate. In some cases, especially those involving tense or highly sensitive issues, you may wish to incorporate some of the techniques of noted psychologist Carl Rogers, who developed a procedure for presenting what he calls the nonthreatening argument. Rogers believes that people involved in a debate should strive for clear, honest communication so that the problem under discussion can be resolved. Instead of going on the defensive and trying to "win" the argument, each side should try to recognize common ground and then develop a solution that will address the needs of both parties.

A Rogerian argument uses these techniques:

a. a clear, objective statement of the problem or issue
b. a clear, objective summary of the opposition's position that shows you understand their point of view and their goals
c. a clear, objective summary of your point of view, stated in nonthreatening language
d. a discussion that emphasizes the beliefs, values, and goals that you and your opposition have in common
e. a description of any of your points that you are willing to concede or compromise
f. an explanation of a plan or proposed solution that meets the needs of both sides.

By showing your opposition that you thoroughly understand their position and that you are sincerely trying to effect a solution that is in everyone's—not just your—best interests, you may succeed in some situations that might otherwise be hopeless because of their highly emotional nature. Remember, too, that you can use some of these Rogerian techniques in any kind of argument paper you are writing, if you think they would be effective.

Problems to Avoid

Writers of argumentative essays must appear logical or their readers will reject their point of view. Here is a short list of some of the most common *logical fallacies*—that is, errors in reasoning. Check your rough drafts carefully to avoid these problems.

Incidentally, students sometimes ask, "If a logical fallacy works, why not use it? Isn't all fair in love, war, and argumentative essays?" The honest answer is "maybe." It's quite true that speakers and writers do use faulty logic and irrational emotional appeals to persuade people everyday (one needs only to look at television or a newspaper to see example after example). But the cost of the risk is high: if you do try to slide one by your readers and they see through your trick, you will lose your credibility instantly. On the whole, it's far more effective to use logical reasoning and strong evidence to convince your readers to accept your point of view.

Common Logical Fallacies

Hasty generalization: The writer bases the argument on insufficient or unrepresentative evidence. Suppose, for example, you have owned two poodles and they have both attacked you. If you declare that all poodles are vicious dogs, you are making a hasty generalization. There are, of course, thousands of poodles who have not attacked anyone. Similarly, you're in error if you interview only campus athletes and then declare, "University students favor a new stadium." What about the opinions of the students who aren't athletes? In other words, when the generalization is drawn from an unrepresentative or insufficient sample, your conclusion isn't valid.

Non sequitur ("it doesn't follow"): The writer's conclusion is not necessarily a logical result of the facts. An example of a *non sequitur* occurs when you conclude, "Professor Smith is a famous historian, so he will be a brilliant history teacher." As you may have realized by now, just that someone knows a subject well does not automatically mean that he or she can communicate the information clearly; hence, the conclusion is not necessarily valid.

Begging the question: The writer presents as truth what is supposed to be proven by the argument. For example, in the statement "All useless laws such as Reform Bill 13 should be repealed," the writer has already assumed the bill is useless without assuming responsibility for proving that accusation. Similarly, the statement "Dangerous pornography should be banned" begs the question (that is, tries like a beggar to get something for nothing from the reader) because the writer gives no evidence for what must first be argued, not merely asserted—that pornography is dangerous.

Red herring: The writer introduces an irrelevant point to divert the readers' attention from the main issue. This term originates from the old tactic, used by escaped prisoners, of dragging a smoked herring, a strong-smelling fish, across their trail to confuse tracking dogs by making them follow the wrong scent. For example, roommate A might be criticizing roommate B for his repeated failure to do the dishes when it was his turn. To escape facing the charges, roommate B brings up times in the past when the other roommate failed to repay some money he borrowed. While roommate A may indeed have a problem with remembering his debts, that discussion isn't relevant to the original argument about sharing the responsibility for the dishes. (By the way, you might have run across a newspaper photograph of a California ecology group demonstrating for more protection of dolphins, whales, and other marine life; if so, look closely to see, over in the left corner, almost hidden by the host of placards and banners, a student slyly holding up a sign that reads "Save the Red Herring!" Now, who says rhetoricians don't have a good sense of humor?)

Post hoc, ergo propter hoc: See p. 204.

Argument *ad hominem* ("to the man"): The writer attacks the opponent's character rather than the opponent's argument. The statement "Dr. Bloom can't be a competent marriage counselor because she's been divorced twice" may not be valid; Bloom's advice to her clients may be excellent regardless of her own marital status.

Faulty use of authority: See p. 221 and pp. 267–268.

Argument *ad populum* ("to the people"): The writer evades the issues by appealing to readers' emotional reactions to certain subjects. For example, instead of arguing the facts of an issue, a writer might play upon the readers' negative response to such words as "communism" and "fascism" or their positive response to words and concepts like "God," "country," and "liberty." In the statement "If you are a true American, you will vote against the referendum on busing," the writer avoids any discussion of the merits or weaknesses of the bill and merely substitutes an emotional appeal. (Advertisers, of course, play on consumers' emotions by filling their ads with pictures of babies, animals, status objects, and sexually attractive men and women.)

Circular thinking: See p. 204.

Either/or: The writer tries to convince the readers that there are only two sides to an issue—one right, one wrong. The statement "If you don't go to war against Iceland, you don't love your country" is irrational because it doesn't consider the other possibilities, such as patriotic people's right to oppose war as an expression of love for their country. A classic example of this sort of oversimplification was illustrated in the 1960s' bumper sticker that was popular during the debate over the Vietnam War: "America: Love It or Leave It." Obviously, there are other choices ("Change It or Lose It," for instance).

Hypostatization: The writer uses an abstract concept as if it were a concrete reality. Always be suspicious of a writer who uses statements beginning, "History has taught us . . . ," "Science has proven . . . ," or "Medicine has discovered. . . ." The implication in each case is that history or science or medicine has only one voice, one opinion. On the contrary, "history" is written by a multitude of historians who hold a variety of opinions; doctors and scientists also frequently disagree. Instead of generalizing about a particular field, quote a respected authority or simply qualify your statement by referring to "many" or "some" scientists, historians, or whatever.

Bandwagon appeal: The writer tries to validate a point by intimating that "everyone else believes in this." Such a tactic evades discussion of the issue itself. Advertising often uses this technique: "Everyone who demands real taste smokes Phooey cigarettes"; "Discriminating women use Smacky-Mouth lipstick." (The ultimate in "bandwagon" humor may have appeared on a recent Colorado bumper sticker: "Eat lamb—could 1000s of coyotes be wrong?")

Straw man: The writer selects the opposition's weakest or most insignificant point to argue against, to divert the readers' attention from the real issues. Instead of addressing the opposition's best arguments and defeating them, the writer "sets up a straw man"—that is, the writer picks out a trivial (or irrelevant) argument against his or her own position and easily knocks it down, just as one might easily push over a figure made of straw. Perhaps the most famous example of the "straw man" occurred in 1952 when, during his vice-presidential campaign, Richard Nixon was accused of misappropriating campaign funds for his personal use. Addressing the nation on television, Nixon described how his six-year-old daughter Tricia had received a little cocker spaniel named Checkers from a Texas supporter. Nixon went on about how much his children loved the dog and how, regardless of what anyone thought, by gosh, he was going to keep that cute dog for little Tricia. Of course, no one was asking Nixon to return the dog; they were asking about the $18,000 in missing campaign funds. But Nixon's canine gift was much easier for him to defend, and the "Checkers'" speech is now famous as one of the most notorious "straw man" diversions.

Faulty analogy: The writer uses an extended comparison as proof of a point. Look closely at all extended comparisons and metaphors to see if the two things being compared are really similar. For example, in a recent editorial a woman protested the new laws requiring parents to use car seats for small children, arguing that if the state could require the seats they could just as easily require mothers to breastfeed instead of using formula. Are the two situations alike? Car accidents are the leading cause of death of children under four; is formula dangerous? Or perhaps you've read that Politician X's plan for aid to Transylvania (or somewhere) is just like Russia's control of Poland. If the opinion isn't supported by factual evidence, then the analogy isn't persuasive. Remember that even though an analogy might suggest similarities, it alone cannot *prove* anything.

Quick fix: The writer leans too heavily on catchy phrases or empty slogans. A clever turn-of-phrase may be an attention-grabber, but it may lose its persuasiveness when scrutinized closely. For instance, a banner at a recent rally to protest a piece of anti-gun legislation read "When guns are outlawed, only outlaws will have guns." While the sentence has nice balance, it oversimplifies and thus misleads. The legislation was not trying to outlaw all guns, just the sale of the infamous Saturday Night Specials, most often used in crimes and domestic violence; the sale of guns for sport, such as hunting rifles, would remain legal. Other slogans sound good but are simply irrelevant: a particular soft drink, for example, may be "the real thing," but what drink isn't? Look closely at clever lines substituted for reasoned argument; always demand clear terms and logical explanations.*

PRACTICING WHAT YOU'VE LEARNED

Errors in reasoning can cause your reader to doubt your credibility. In the following mock essay, for example, the writer includes a variety of fallacies that undermine his argument; see if you can identify all his errors.

---

* Sometimes advertisers get more for their slogans than they bargained for. According to one news source, a popular soft drink company had to spend millions to revise its slogan after introducing its product into parts of China. Apparently the slogan "Come alive! Join the Blah-Blah-Cola Generation!" translated into some dialects as "Blah-Blah Cola Brings Your Ancestors Back from the Dead"!

BAN THOSE BOOKS!

A serious problem faces America today, a problem of such grave importance that our very existence as a nation is threatened. We must either cleanse our schools of evil-minded books, or we must reconcile ourselves to seeing our children become welfare moochers and bums.

History has shown time and time again that placement of immoral books in our schools is part of a *bona fide* Communist plot designed to weaken the moral fiber of our youth from coast to coast. In Wettuckett, Ohio, for example, the year after books by Mark Twain such as *Tom Sawyer* and *Huckleberry Finn* were introduced into the school library by liberal free-thinkers and radicals, the number of students cutting classes rose by ten percent. And in that same year the number of high school seniors going on to college dropped from thirty to twenty-two.

The reason for this could either be a natural decline in intelligence and morals or the influence of those dirty books that teach our beloved children disrespect and irresponsibility. Since there is no evidence to suggest a natural decline, the conclusion is inescapable: once our children read about Twain's characters skipping school and running away from home, they had to do likewise. If they hadn't read about such undesirable characters as Huckleberry Finn, our innocent children would never have behaved in those ways.

Now, I am a simple man, a plain old farm boy—the pseudo-intellectuals call me redneck just like they call you folks. But I can assure you that, redneck or not, I've got the guts to fight the Communist conspiracy everywhere I find it, and I urge you to do the same. For this reason I want all you good folks to come to the ban-the-books rally this Friday so we can talk it over. I can promise you all your right-thinking neighbors will be there.

ASSIGNMENT

Search for the following:

1. Two examples of advertisements that illustrate one or more of the fallacies or appeals discussed on pp. 222–225.
2. One example of illogical or fallacious reasoning in a piece of writing (you might try looking at the editorial page or letters-to-the-editor column of your local or campus newspaper).
3. One example of a logical, persuasive point in a piece of writing.

Be prepared to explain your analyses of your samples, but do not write any sort of identifying label or evaluation on the samples themselves. Bring your ads and pieces of writing to class and exchange them with those of a classmate. After ten minutes, compare notes. Do you and your classmate agree on the evaluation of each sample? Why or why not?

ESSAY TOPICS

Write a convincing argument attacking or defending one of the following statements. Narrow the topic when necessary. (Note that essays on some of the topics presented below would profit from library research material; see Chapter 12 for help.)

1. The music industry should/should not be required to rate rock 'n roll lyrics as "X," "R," "PG," and so on, as the movies do.
2. Surrogate motherhood should/should not be illegal.
3. Bilingual education in this country is beneficial/harmful.
4. Mandatory on-the-job drug tests should/should not be allowed.
5. Television advertising does/does not control the election of our presidents.
6. The advertising of alcohol should/should not be limited to the print media, as are cigarette ads.
7. Students who fail their academic courses should/should not be allowed to participate in athletic programs.
8. Throwaway bottles and cans should/should not be outlawed.
9. Televised instant replays should/should not be used to call plays in football and other sports.
10. The foreign language requirement (or any rule or requirement) at this school is worthwhile/useless.
11. Children with AIDS should/should not be prevented from attending public school.
12. High school/college competency tests in math and English should/should not be adopted across the country.
13. Students should/should not serve in a youth corps for two years before they are admitted to college.
14. Convicted murderers who committed their crime as juveniles should/should not face adult penalties.
15. Student evaluations should/should not be a major consideration in the rehiring or promotion of a teacher.
16. The CIA (or any controversial organization) should/should not be allowed to speak or recruit on campus.
17. Lie detector tests for employees should/should not be prohibited in all states.
18. Vitamin C (or herbal healing or any kind of nontraditional treatment) can/cannot help relieve illness.
19. In the event of a compulsory military draft, men and women should/should not be equally liable.

20. State lotteries (or some other form of gambling) should/should not be outlawed because they do/do not encourage crime.

Sample Student Essay

The student who wrote the essay below followed the steps for writing an argumentative paper that are discussed in this chapter. His intended audience were the readers of his school newspaper, primarily fellow students but also instructors as well. To argue his case, he chose Pattern A, presenting two of his own points and then concluding with a rebuttal of an important opposing view. Notice that this writer uses a variety of methods to convince his readers, including hypothetical examples, causal analysis, analogy, and testimony. Does the writer persuade you to his point of view? Which are his strongest and weakest arguments? What might you change to make his essay even more persuasive?

Students Take Note!

Introduction:
Presenting the
controversy

Thesis

Essay map

A point for the
writer's position:
note-taking
services are unfair
to some students

A walk across campus this week will reveal students, professors, and administrators arguing about class notes like never before. But they're not engaged in intellectual debates over chemical formulas or literary images; no, they're fighting over the taking of the notes themselves, as professional note-taking services in town are applying for permission to sit in on courses and then sell their notes to the students in those classes. Although the prospect of having "canned" notes looks inviting to many students, our administration should nevertheless ban these services from campus. Not only do such businesses give certain students unfair advantages and discourage class attendance, but they also prohibit the development of students' important learning skills, despite the services' claims to the contrary.

What is bothered for many of us about the professional-notes option is our sense of fair play. Let's face it: like it or not, school is, among other things, a place of competition, as students vie for the best academic records to send to prospective employers, graduate and professional schools, and in some cases, paying parents. In today's classes all students have an equal opportunity to come to class, take notes, study, and pass or fail on their own merits. But the expensive professional notes, already organized and outlined, may give those with plenty of money some advantages that poorer students—those on scholarships or with families, for example—just can't afford. In addition, the notes may be available only to those students who take certain sections of a course and not others, thus giving some students an extra option. The same is true for students who satisfy a requirement by taking one course that has notes available rather than another which has not. Knowing that you're doing your own work may make you feel morally superior to a classmate who isn't, but frankly, on some other level, it just plain feels irritating and unfair, sort of like watching your roommate getting away with plagiarizing his paper for a class after you spent weeks researching yours.

<aside>Another point for the writer's position: professional notes discourage students from attending and participating in class</aside>

In addition to being a potential source of conflict among students, the professional-note services aren't winning many friends among the faculty either. Several instructors have complained that the availability of notes will encourage many students, especially the weaker ones, to cut classes, assuming that they have all the material necessary to understanding the lecture, discussion, or lab. But anyone who has ever had to use borrowed notes knows something vital is not there. Someone else's interpretations of the information is often hard or impossible to follow, especially if you must understand complex relationships and problems. Moreover, skipping class may mean missed opportunities for students to ask questions or to participate in experiments or in group discussions, all of which often help clarify concepts under study. Not seeing visual aids or diagrams in person can also result in problems understanding the material. And, last, missing class can mean failure to become comfortably acquainted with the teacher, which, in turn, may discourage a student from asking for individual help when it's needed. All these possibilities are real; even Jeff Allridge, owner of the Quotable Notes service, has admitted to a campus reporter, "There *is* an incentive to skip class."

<aside>Presentation and rebuttal of the opposition's claim that students learn more using professional notes</aside>

Despite the admission that professional note-taking encourages class-cutting, the services still promote themselves by claiming that students using their notes learn more. They support this claim by arguing that their notes offer students clearly organized information and, according to one advertising brochure, "good models" for students to follow in other classes. But such arguments miss the larger point: students should be learning how to develop their own note-taking, organizing, and thinking skills rather than swallowing the material whole as neatly packaged and delivered. Memorizing class material as outlined can be important, but it's not really as valuable in the long run as learning how to think about the material and use it to solve problems or come up with new ideas later. Taking your own notes teaches you how to listen and how to spot the important concepts; organizing your own notes teaches you how to pull ideas together in a logical way, all skills students will need in other classes, on jobs, and in life in general. Having memorized the outlines but not really mastered the thinking skills won't help the medical student whose patient's symptoms vary from the textbook description or the engineer whose airplane wings suddenly fail the stress test for no apparent reason.

<aside>Conclusion: Restatement of thesis, ending on pun to emphasize the main idea</aside>

By appealing to students who believe professional notes will help them accomplish their educational goals easier and quicker, a variety of note-taking services now have franchises across the country. But our campus shouldn't allow them to move in. CSU students need to recognize that the difference between the services' definition of "learning" and the real learning experiences college can provide is of notable importance.

Professional Essays

The following professional essays present conflicting views of the proposal to adopt a uniform poll-closing time for national elections. As you read the essays, notice how each writer tries to support his own points and how each responds to those who oppose his position. Which essay do you find the most persuasive? Why? What arguments could you add to either side to make the essays stronger?

WE NEED A UNIFORM POLL-CLOSING TIME

Al Swift

Al Swift is a Democratic congressman from the state of Washington. He is currently the chairman of the House Elections Sub-committee. His essay advocating a uniform poll-closing time appeared on the editorial page of the USA Today *newspaper on April 6, 1989.*

In 1980, when the networks told us Ronald Reagan had been elected president, polls were still open in every time zone. Citizens, especially but not exclusively in the West, were outraged. After many hearings, Congress developed a solution that did not threaten the First Amendment or require any state to do anything not already done in some states.

There are two parts: The networks adopted a policy they have followed since 1986 of not using exit-poll information to predict an election until the polls in that state are closed. That policy permits the government to adjust its election schedules so that all polls close at the same time. Together, these solve this vexing problem.

The House has twice passed a bill that creates a single poll-closing time in the continental USA. Polls would close simultaneously at 9 P.M. in the Eastern time zone, 8 P.M. Central, 7 P.M. Mountain, and daylight-saving time would be extended in the Pacific time zone for an additional two weeks in presidential election years, allowing polls to close at 7 P.M. PDT.

The uniform poll-closing bill being considered by the House today was first proposed by the secretaries of state of Massachusetts and California and was recently endorsed by the National Governors Association. A similar bill is moving through the Senate. The 101st Congress has the opportunity to put a uniform poll-closing time into law before the 1992 election.

There are those who argue that there is no real problem. Yet, it is difficult to accept that argument about an issue that created a firestorm of protest in 1980 and is still drawing broad interest and new additional concern.

Others say there is no statistical basis for concern, yet studies repeatedly indicate a voter drop-off of about 2%. This is not to be sneezed at. The last two Senate races in my state were won by less than 2%.

Being told who won before you've voted erodes the public's confidence in the importance of its role in the process. Allowing that situation to continue in a democracy strikes at the very foundation of our system. Fortunately, it does not have to happen. We have a solution that will work. Congress needs to implement it.

QUESTIONS ON CONTENT, STRUCTURE, AND STYLE

1. What problem does this essay address?
2. Does the author convince you that this problem exists and deserves serious attention? Why or why not?
3. What is the author's solution to this problem? Is the solution presented clearly enough?
4. What pattern of organization does Swift use in his essay? Is it an effective choice?
5. What is Swift's strongest argument favoring the uniform closing time?
6. Where would Swift's essay benefit from more detailed development? Can you think of additional arguments to add to this essay?
7. Where in the essay does Swift address his opposition? What is his rebuttal to the opposition's claims? Is his rebuttal convincing? Why or why not?
8. Characterize the author's tone throughout the essay. Is the tone effective? Cite several lines that support your answer.
9. Evaluate Swift's conclusion. Is it an effective ending to his essay? Why or why not?
10. Overall, how effective is Swift's argument? Do you find any logical fallacies or unreasonable appeals to emotion?

VOCABULARY

vexing (2)
simultaneously (3)
endorsed (4)

erodes (7)
implement (7)

WE DON'T NEED A UNIFORM POLL-CLOSING

Robert Gillmore

Robert Gillmore is a columnist, author, and a former professor of political science at St. Anselm College in Manchester, N.H. He was invited to be a guest columnist for USA Today, *to argue against the position taken by Representative Al Swift. Gillmore's essay appeared with Swift's, on April 6, 1989.*

A uniform poll closing time is a solution without a problem.

Even opponents of network reporting of early voting returns admit that reporting reduces voter turnout by no more than 3%, and perhaps as little as 1%. In fact, some studies find absolutely no effect on turnout.

Surprised? Don't be. Many voters vote before the returns are announced or before they've listened to the news. Others do hear the returns but vote anyway—because of habit or a sense of civic duty or reasonably because they want to vote not only for president but also for or against the dozens of state, county, regional and local offices and propositions also on the ballot.

And even if reporting early returns does reduce turnout, it certainly doesn't change the election outcome. As many studies have shown, the opinions of non-voters are not significantly different from those of voters. If non-voters voted, they wouldn't change the result. They would just make the numbers larger.

So a uniform national poll-closing time would do nothing good. But it would do two bad things:

It would require either absurdly late closing times in the East or, worse, inconveniently early closing times in the West—so early that many voters would find it difficult if not impossible to vote.

It would manipulate voters like laboratory rats. It would say to them, in effect: We don't like the fact you're (allegedly) not voting because of early election returns. Therefore, we're going to monkey with the election laws to get you to do what we want.

A free government doesn't treat its citizens like that. It obeys Kant's dictum: Human beings are to be treated as ends, not means. It doesn't use them as means to an (imaginary) larger turnout. On the contrary, it gives them the freest possible choice whether to vote or not.

The question is not a "state's rights" issue. It's not about whether the folks up in Dixville Notch should be able to close their poll minutes after midnight so they can win recognition as "first in the nation" to vote.

The question is a human rights issue—the right not to be led around by the nose.

QUESTIONS ON CONTENT, STRUCTURE, AND STYLE

1. What is Gillmore's thesis? Where is it stated?

2. Evaluate Gillmore's choice of a one-sentence opening paragraph. Is this an effective beginning for this essay? Why or why not?

3. Where does Gillmore address the claims of the opposition? Is this an effective choice? Why or why not?

4. How does Gillmore counter his opposition's arguments? Is he successful or not? Explain the strengths or weaknesses that you see.

5. What points does Gillmore offer in support of his own position? Are these points sufficiently developed or could they profit from a more detailed discussion?

6. Which of Gillmore's points are the strongest? the weakest? Why? Do you find any logical fallacies or unreasonable appeals?

7. Does "Kant's dictum" strengthen Gillmore's argument? What effect is this reference intended to have on Gillmore's readers?

8. Evaluate the effectiveness of Gillmore's conclusion. Does it provide an emphatic ending? Why does Gillmore start the last two paragraphs with similar phrasing?

9. Describe Gillmore's "voice" as it appears in this essay. Contrast its effectiveness to that of Swift's in his essay.

10. After comparing and contrasting Gillmore's arguments to Swift's, which essay do you find the most persuasive? How could you revise these essays to make each one more convincing?

VOCABULARY

civic (3) manipulate (7) dictum (8)

PRO/CON ADVERTISING: "I'M THE NRA" AND "A $29 HANDGUN SHATTERED MY FAMILY'S LIFE"

The National Rifle Association published a series of ads, including the one presented on page 234, to tell people about the organization. According to the NRA, one of their purposes is to protect Second Amendment rights. However, after the attempted assassination of President Ronald Reagan and the shooting of his Press Secretary James Brady, an organization called Handgun Control, Inc., supported by Sarah Brady, countered with an ad of its own (p. 235). Study these ads and determine what sort of appeals they use to persuade readers to their side. Which appeals do you find the most persuasive and why?

REP. ALBERTO GUTMAN: Florida Legislator, Businessman, Husband, Member of the National Rifle Association.

"Being from a country that was once a democracy and turned communist, I really feel I know what the right to bear arms is all about. In Cuba, where I was born, the first thing the communist government did was take away everybody's firearms, leaving them defenseless and intimidated with fear. That's why our constitutional right to bear arms is so important to our country's survival.

"As a legislator I have to deal with reality. And the reality is that gun control does not work. It actually eliminates the rights of the law-abiding citizen, not the criminal. Criminals will always have guns, and they won't follow gun control laws anyway. I would like to see tougher laws on criminals as opposed to tougher laws on legitimate gun owners. We need to attack the problem of crime at its roots, instead of blaming crime on gun ownership and citizens who use them lawfully.

"It's a big responsibility that we face retaining the right to bear arms. That's why I joined the NRA. The NRA is instrumental in protecting these freedoms. It helps train and educate people, supporting legislation that benefits not only those who bear arms but all citizens of the United States. The NRA helps keep America free." **I'm the NRA.**

The NRA's lobbying organization, the Institute for Legislative Action, is the nation's largest and most influential protector of the constitutional right to keep and bear arms. At every level of government and through local grassroots efforts, the Institute guards against infringement upon the freedoms of law-abiding gun owners. If you would like to join the NRA or want more information about our programs and benefits, write J. Warren Cassidy, Executive Vice President, P.O. Box 37484, Dept. AG-15, Washington, D.C. 20013.

Paid for by the members of the National Rifle Association of America. Copyright 1986.

Reprinted with permission of the National Rifle Association.

−Mrs. James S. Brady−

"A $29 handgun shattered my family's life."

"Seven years ago, John Hinckley pulled a $29 revolver from his pocket and opened fire on a Washington street. He shot the President. He also shot my husband.

I'm not asking for your sympathy. I'm asking for your help.

I've learned from my own experience that, alone, there's only so much you can do to stop handgun violence. But that together, we can confront the mightiest gun lobby– the N.R.A.– and win.

I've only to look at my husband Jim to remember that awful day... the unending TV coverage of the handgun firing over and over... the nightmare panic and fear.

It's an absolute miracle nobody was killed. After all, twenty thousand Americans are killed by handguns every year. Thousands more–men, women, even children– are maimed for life.

Like me, I know you support *stronger* handgun control laws. So does the vast majority of Americans. But the National Rifle Association can spend so much in elections that Congress is afraid to pass an effective national handgun law.

It's time to change that. Before it's too late for another family like mine... a family like yours.

I joined Handgun Control, Inc. because they're willing to take on the N.R.A. Right now we're campaigning for a national waiting period and background check on handgun purchases.

If such simple, basic measures had been on the books seven years ago, John Hinckley would never have walked out of that Texas pawnshop with the handgun which came within an inch of killing Ronald Reagan. He lied on his purchase application. Given time, the police could have caught the lie and put him in jail.

Of course, John Hinckley's not the only one. Police report that thousands of known criminals buy handguns right over the counter in this country. We have to stop them.

So, please, pick up a pen. Write me to find out how you can help. And support our work with a generous contribution.

It's time we kept handguns out of the wrong hands. It's time to break the National Rifle Association's grip on Congress and start making our cities and neighborhoods safe again.

Thank you and God bless you."

"Don't let it happen to you."

Dear Sarah,
It's time to break the N.R.A.'s grip on Congress once and for all. Here's my contribution to Handgun Control, Inc., the million-strong nonprofit citizens' group you help direct:
☐ $15   ☐ $29   ☐ $35   ☐ $50   ☐ $100 or $_____ .
☐ Tell me more about how I can help.

NAME _____

ADDRESS _____

CITY _____ STATE _____ ZIP _____

HANDGUN CONTROL

1400 K Street, N.W., Washington, D.C. 20005, (202) 898-0792

Contributions to Handgun Control, Inc. are not tax deductible.

Reprinted with permission of Handgun Control, Inc.

A REVISION WORKSHEET FOR YOUR ARGUMENTATIVE ESSAY

As you write your rough drafts, consult Chapter 5 for guidance through the revision process. In addition, here are a few questions to ask yourself as you revise your argumentative essay:

1. Does this essay present a clear thesis limited to fit the assigned length of this paper?

2. Does this essay contain a number of strong, persuasive points in support of its thesis?

3. Is the essay organized in an easy-to-follow pattern that avoids repetition or confusion?

4. Does the essay present enough supporting evidence to make each of its points convincing? Where could additional examples, factual information, testimony, or other kinds of supporting material be added to make the arguments even more effective?

5. Will all the supporting evidence be clear to the essay's particular audience? Do any terms or examples need additional explanation or special definition?

6. Have the major opposing arguments been refuted?

7. Does the essay avoid any logical fallacies or problems in tone?

After you've revised your essay extensively, you might exchange rough drafts with a classmate and answer these questions for each other, making specific suggestions for improvement wherever appropriate.

10

Description

The writer of description creates a word-picture of persons, places, objects, and emotions, using a careful selection of details to make an impression on the reader. If you have already written expository or argumentative essays in your composition course, then you almost certainly have written some descriptive prose. Nearly every essay, after all, calls for some kind of description; for example, in the student comparison/contrast essay (pp. 175–177), the writer describes two kinds of stores; in the professional process essay (pp. 164–168), the writer describes the embalming procedure in great detail. To help you write better description in your other essays, however, you may want to practice writing descriptive paragraphs or a short descriptive essay.

HOW TO WRITE EFFECTIVE DESCRIPTION

Regardless of the kind of description you are writing, you should follow the three basic suggestions below:

Recognize your purpose. Description is not free-floating; it appears in your writing for a particular reason—to help you explain, persuade, create a mood, or whatever. In some essays you will want your description as *objective* as you can make it; for example, you might describe a scientific experiment or a business transaction in straight factual detail. Most of the time, however, you will want to convey a particular attitude toward your subject; this approach to description is called *subjective* or *impressionistic*. Note the differences between the following two descriptions of a tall, thin boy: the objective writer sticks to the facts by saying, "The eighteen-year-old boy was 6'1" and weighed 125 pounds," whereas the subjective writer gives an impressionistic description, "The young boy was as tall and scrawny as a birch tree in winter." Therefore, before you begin describing anything, you must first decide your purpose and then whether it calls for objective or subjective reporting.

Describe clearly, using specific details. To make any description clear to your reader, you must include a sufficient number of details that are specific rather than fuzzy or vague. If, for example, your family dog had become lost, you wouldn't call the animal shelter and ask if they'd seen a "big brown dog with a short tail"—naturally, you'd mention every distinguishing detail about your pet you could think of: size, color, breed, cut of ears, special markings, etc. Similarly, if your car was stolen, you'd give the police as clear and as complete a description of your vehicle as possible.

Look at the two paragraphs below; which more fully answers the question, "What's a vaulting horse?"?

A vaulting horse is a thing usually found in gyms that has four legs and a beam and is used by gymnasts to make jumps.

If you didn't already know what a vaulting horse was, you might have trouble picking it out in a gymnasium crowded with equipment. A description with additional details would help you locate it:

A vaulting horse is a piece of equipment used by gymnasts during competition to help propel them into the air when they perform any of a variety of leaps known as vaults. The gymnasts usually approach the vaulting horse from a running start and then place their hands on the horse for support or for a push off as they perform their vaults. The horse itself resembles a carpenter's sawhorse, but the main beam is composed of padded leather rather than wood. The rectangular beam is approximately five feet, three inches long and thirteen-and-a-half inches wide. Supported by four legs usually made of steel, the padded leather beam is approximately four feet, one-half inch above the floor in men's competitions and three feet, seven inches in women's competitions. The padded leather beam has two white lines marking off three sections on top: the croup, the saddle, and the neck. The two end sections—the croup and the neck—are each fifteen and one-half inches long. Gymnasts place their hands on the neck or croup depending on the type of vault they are attempting.

Moreover, the reader cannot imagine your subject clearly if your description is couched in vague generalities. The sentence below, for example, presents only a hazy picture:

Larry is so overweight that his clothes don't fit him right.

Revised, the picture is now sharply in focus:

Larry is so fat that his shirt constantly bulges over his belt, his trousers will not stay snapped, and his countless chins spill over his collar like dough rising out of a too-small pan.

Specific details can turn cloudy prose into crisp, clear images that can be reproduced in the mind like photographs.

Select only appropriate details. In any description the choice of details depends largely on the writer's purpose and audience. However, many descriptions—especially the more subjective ones—will present a *dominant impression;* that is, the writer selects only those details that communicate a particular mood or feeling to the reader. The dominant impression is the controlling focus of a description; for example, if you wrote a description of your grandmother to show her thoughtfulness, then you would select only those details that convey an impression of a sweet, kindly old lady. Below are two brief descriptions illustrating the concept of dominant impression. The first writer tries to create a mood of mystery:

> Down a black winding road stands the abandoned old mansion, silhouetted against the cloud-shrouded moon, creaking and moaning in the wet chill wind.

The second writer tries to present a feeling of joy and innocence.

> A dozen kites filled the spring air, and around the bright picnic tables spread with hot dogs, hamburgers, and slices of watermelon, Tom and Annie played away the warm April day.

In the description of the deserted mansion, the writer would have violated the impression of mystery had the sentence read:

> Down the black winding road stands the abandoned old mansion, surrounded by bright, multicolored tulips in early bloom.

Including the cheerful flowers as a detail in the description destroys the dominant mood of bleakness and mystery. Similarly, example two would be spoiled had the writer ended it this way:

> . . . Tom and Annie played away the warm April day until Tom got so sunburned he became ill and had to go home.

Therefore, remember to select only those details that advance your descriptive purpose. Omit any details you consider unimportant or distracting.

See if you can determine the dominant impression of each description below:

> The wind had curled up to sleep in the distant mountains. Leaves hung limp and motionless from the silent trees, while birds perched on the branches like little statues. As I sat on the edge of the clearing, holding my breath, I could hear a squirrel scampering through the underbrush. Somewhere far away a dog barked twice, and then the woods were hushed once more.

This poor thing has seen better days, but one should expect the sofa in a fraternity house den to be well worn. The large, plump, brown corduroy pillows strewn lazily on the floor and propped comfortably against the threadbare arms bear the pencil-point scars of frustrated students and foam-bleeding cuts of multiple pillow wars. No less than four pairs of rotting Nikes stand twenty-four-hour guard at the corners of its carefully mended frame. Obviously the relaxed, inviting appearance masks the permanent odors of cheap cigars and Michelob from Thursday night poker parties; at least two or three guests each weekend sift through the popcorn kernels and Doritos crumbs, sprawl facedown, and pass out for the duration. However, frequent inhabitants have learned to avoid the dark stains courtesy of the house pup and the red-punch designs of the chapter klutz. Habitually, they strategically lunge over the back of the sofa to an unsoiled area easily identifiable in flight by the large depression left by previous regulars. The quiet *hmmph* of the cushions and harmonious squeal of the exhausted springs signal a perfect landing and utter a warm greeting from an old and faithful friend.

Make your descriptions vivid. By using clear, precise words, you can improve any kind of writing. Chapters 7 (on words) and 6 (on sentences) offer a variety of tips on clarifying your prose style. In addition to the advice given there, here are two other ways to enliven your descriptions, particularly those that call for a subjective approach:

Use sensory details. If it's appropriate, try using images that appeal to your readers' five senses. If, for example, you are describing your broken leg and the ensuing stay in a hospital, tell your readers how the place smelled, how it looked, what your cast felt like, how your pills tasted, and what noises you heard. Below are some specific examples using sensory details:

Sight   The clean white corridors of the hospital resembled the set of a sci-fi movie, with everyone scurrying around in identical starched uniforms.

Hearing   At night, the only sounds I heard were the quiet squeakings of sensible white shoes as the nurses made their rounds.

Smell   The green beans on the hospital cafeteria tray smelled stale and waxy, like crayons.

Touch   The hospital bed sheet felt as rough and heavy as a feed sack.

Taste   Every four hours they gave me an enormous gray pill whose aftertaste reminded me of the castor oil my grandmother insisted on giving me when I was a kid.

By appealing to the readers' senses, you better enable them to identify with and imagine the subject you are describing. Joseph Conrad, the famous nineteenth-century novelist, agreed, believing that all art "appeals primarily to the senses, and the artistic aim when expressing itself in written words must also make its appeal through the senses, if its highest desire is to reach the secret spring of responsive emotions." In other words, to make your readers feel, first make them "see."

Use figurative language when appropriate. As you may recall from Chapter 7, figurative language produces images or pictures in the readers' minds, helping them to understand unfamiliar or abstract subjects. Here are some devices you might use to clarify or spice up your prose:

1. Simile: a comparison between two things using the words "like" or "as" (see also pp. 135–136)

Example Seeing exactly the shirt he wanted, he moved as quickly as a starving teenager finding a piece of favorite pie in a refrigerator full of leftover vegetables.

2. Metaphor: a direct comparison between two things that does not use "like" or "as" (see also pp. 135–136)

Example After the holidays her body resembled all the "before" shots in every diet ad she'd ever seen.

3. Personification: the attribution of human characteristics and emotions to inanimate objects, animals, or abstract ideas

Example The old stuffed teddy bear sat in a corner, dozing before the fireplace.

4. Hyperbole: intentional exaggeration or overstatement

Example "Bring me a steak that's still mooing," roared the cowboy.

5. Understatement: intentional representation of a subject as less important than the facts would warrant (see also irony, p. 124)

Example "The reports of my death are greatly exaggerated."—Mark Twain

6. Synecdoche: a part of something is used to represent the whole

Example A hundred tired feet hit the dance floor for one last jitterbug. (Here "feet" stand for the dancing couples themselves.)

Using figures of speech in appropriate places can make your descriptions clear, lively, and memorable.

PROBLEMS TO AVOID

Keep in mind these three bits of advice to solve problems that frequently arise in description:

Remember your audience. Sometimes the object of our description is so clear in our minds we forget that our readers haven't seen it too. Consequently, the description we write turns out to be vague, bland, or skimpy. Ask yourself about your audience: what do they need to know to see this sight as clearly as I do? Then fill in your description with ample, precise details that reveal the best picture possible. Don't forget to define or explain any terms you use that may be puzzling to your audience.

Avoid an erratic organization of details. Too often descriptions are a hodgepodge of details, jotted down randomly. When you write a lengthy description, you should select a plan that will arrange your details in an orderly fashion. Depending upon your subject matter and your purpose, you might adopt a plan calling for a description of something from top to bottom, left to right, front to back, etc. For example, a description of a woman might begin at the head and move to the feet; furniture in a room might be described as your eyes move from one side of the room to another. A second plan for arranging details presents the subject's outstanding characteristics first and then fills in the lesser information; a child's red hair, for example, might be his most striking feature and therefore would be described first. A third plan presents details in the order you see them approaching: dust, then a car, then details about the car, its occupants, and so on. Or you might describe a subject as it unfolds chronologically, as in some kind of a process or operation. Regardless of which plan of organization you choose, the reader should feel a sense of order in your description.

Avoid any sudden change in perspective. If, for example, you are describing the White House from the outside, don't suddenly include details that could be seen only from inside. Similarly, if you are describing a car from a distance, you might be able to tell the car's model, year, and color, but you could hardly describe the upholstery or reveal the mileage. It is, of course, possible for you—or your observer—to approach or move around the subject of your description, but the reader must be aware of this movement. Any shift in point of view must be presented clearly and logically, with no sudden, confusing leaps from a front to a back view, from outside to inside, and so on.

ESSAY TOPICS

Here are some suggestions for a descriptive essay or paragraph; narrow your topic to fit your assignment. Don't forget that every description, whether objective or subjective, has a purpose and that every detail should support that purpose.

1. a campus character
2. a childhood photograph of yourself
3. a piece of equipment important to your major or to a hobby or favorite sport
4. a building or place you're fond of (such as a "haunted" house in your neighborhood or even a childhood tree house)
5. one dish or foodstuff that should be forever banned
6. a family member or family pet
7. your most valuable material possession
8. the ugliest/most beautiful building on your campus or in town
9. a typical family dinner at your home
10. your first or worst car (or your dream car)
11. a place where you've worked
12. a strange-but-wonderful friend or relative
13. a computer, microscope, or some other complex machine
14. a favorite painting, sculpture, photograph, or art object
15. your most unforgettable character
16. a laboratory experiment or an event in nature
17. a doctor's or dentist's waiting room
18. your face—or your face after plastic surgery
19. a special day in your life (birthday, holiday, graduation, etc.)
20. the inside of your refrigerator or closet or some other equally loathsome place in your home

Sample Student Essay

In his descriptive essay, this student tries to capture the changes in his hometown that he saw after having been away for several years. Notice the use of metaphor that runs throughout the essay. Is it effective or overdone?

The Battle of Progress

Introduction:
Contrast of old and
new presented in
battlefield imagery

When I went home for the first time after a tour of duty in Vietnam and then a couple of years bumming around, I was struck by a scene at the city limits. On the left of the highway was a group of brand-new, look-alike houses, all mobbed together like they were plotting something secret. Directly across the highway were two falling-down farm houses, each at least eighty years old. There they were, the old and the new, enemies staring at each other across the road. As I drove between them, I felt strange, as if I were entering a battlefield that was temporarily quiet.

Elaboration of the
"battle" metaphor

My town, you see, is, like other small places, caught in the battle of progress. I see the victims everywhere, as the old falls before the new. Old wooden buildings with handcarved faces are torn down everyday to make way for impersonal, mirrored highrises. The rain-fed creeks and streams like the ones I played in as a kid are being bulldozed and replaced by sidewalks and artificial fountains that spray the same water day after day. Everywhere I look I see evidence of the struggle, and everywhere I see that the inevitable victor, progress, is winning skirmishes.

The writer moves
through the
"invaded" town.

A simile

After turning off the highway, I head for the town square; the impression of the invasion grows stronger. All along the main drag, the old hamburger joints have been replaced by fast-food restaurants with red and green flashing neon signs exploding like rockets in the air. Where once there was a group of sturdy old homes with wide white porches and big rolling yards, I now see a washateria and hear the loud grumblings of its machines. The sound reminds me of a huge stomach, and the stale smell of old detergent and dirty clothes fills the air. The intruders have taken over and devoured the block.

An extended
metaphor

Invasion imagery
continues

Personification

When I reach the square, I can see that it too has been sacked. The small brown stores—Duke and Ayres Hardware, Woolworth's, Smith's Dry Goods—all have been remodeled into modern boutiques and video-game dives, decorated in glaring victory colors of orange, blue, green. The stores' once-solemn, comfortable faces grin ridiculously at me now. I don't recognize them, and they sure don't know me. The dark little bookstore on the southeast corner, where I grew up reading men's magazines on the sly, is now a jolly ice cream parlor, decked out with fake red-and-white barber poles and a big, lighted plate-glass window filled with giant pictures of nineteen weird flavors of ice cream. I move on. The three-story, castle-like pink granite courthouse is gone too, and in its place is a functional, unfriendly red-brick office building with humming air conditioners in its small windows and a sign on its automatic door that says "no solicitors or dogs allowed." As I look around the square without recognizing a single old face, I feel like a stranger. I have gone away and come back to find my little town overrun by barbarians who've done away with all I once knew.

More war imagery
as the writer leaves
the town.

Leaving the square and heading back to the highway, I pass through the poor section on the edge of town. Here, I find, the battle rages. Half the little rundown, unpainted, grey shanties are gone, replaced by a squat tire factory, mud-colored and sooty. Where are the people who used to sit out on their tumble-down steps? The kids that played kick-the-can in the streets and grassless yards? Casualties of war. The black smoke tumbles out of the factory, smelling like gunpowder.

I drive on.

Conclusion: A
return to the
images of the
introduction

Leaving town on the main highway, I once again see the armies peering at each other in the afternoon glare as I drive between them. I shake my head a little sadly. The old will fight, but it is useless. The new always win—they are younger and stronger. I glance in my rear view mirror at the faded two-story farmhouses sitting proudly on their green acres of alfalfa, while the army of track houses across the way grows larger and stronger. Soon the highway will be no barrier. I look closely in my mirror at the farmhouses, because I know I may never see them again.

Professional Essay _____

THE DISCUS THROWER

Richard Selzer

Richard Selzer has taught surgery at Yale Medical School and has contributed both stories and essays to a number of magazines. He has published a collection of short stories, and two collections of essays, Mortal Lessons *(1978) and* Confessions of a Knife *(1987). While most of his writing is related to the medical field, it appeals to a general audience as well. This essay was published in* Harper's *in 1977.*

1   I spy on my patients. Ought not a doctor to observe his patients by any means and from any stance, that he might the more fully assemble evidence? So I stand in the doorways of hospital rooms and gaze. Oh, it is not all that furtive an act. Those in bed need only look up to discover me. But they never do.

2   From the doorway of Room 542 the man in the bed seems deeply tanned. Blue eyes and close-cropped white hair give him the appearance of vigor and good health. But I know that his skin is not brown from the sun. It is rusted, rather, in the last stage of containing the vile repose within. And the blue eyes are frosted, looking inward like the windows of a snowbound cottage. This man is blind. This man is also legless—the right leg missing from midthigh down, the left from just below the knee. It gives him the look of a bonsai, roots and branches pruned into the dwarfed facsimile of a great tree.

3   Propped on pillows, he cups his right thigh in both hands. Now and then he shakes his head as though acknowledging the intensity of his suffering. In all of this he makes no sound. Is he mute as well as blind?

4   The room in which he dwells is empty of all possessions—no get-well cards, small, private caches of food, day-old flowers, slippers, all the usual kickshaws of the sickroom. There is only the bed, a chair, a nightstand, and a tray on wheels that can be swung across his lap for meals.

5   "What time is it?" he asks.

"Three o'clock."

"Morning or afternoon?"

"Afternoon."

He is silent. There is nothing else he wants to know.

10   "How are you?" I say.

"Who is it?" he asks.

"It's the doctor. How do you feel?"

He does not answer right away.

"Feel?" he says.

15   "I hope you feel better," I say.

I press the button at the side of the bed.

"Down you go," I say.

"Yes, down," he says.

He falls back upon the bed awkwardly. His stumps, unweighted by legs and feet, rise in the air, presenting themselves. I unwrap the bandages from the stumps, and begin to cut away the black scabs and the dead, glazed fat with scissors and forceps. A shard of white bone comes loose. I pick it away. I wash the wounds with disinfectant and redress the stumps. All this while, he does not speak. What is he thinking behind those lids that do not blink? Is he remembering a time when he was whole? Does he dream of feet? Of when his body was not a rotting log?

20   He lies solid and inert. In spite of everything, he remains impressive, as though he were a sailor standing athwart a slanting deck.

"Anything more I can do for you?" I ask.

For a long moment he is silent.

"Yes," he says at last and without the least irony. "You can bring me a pair of shoes."

In the corridor, the head nurse is waiting for me.

25   "We have to do something about him," she says. "Every morning he orders scrambled eggs for breakfast, and, instead of eating them, he picks up the plate and throws it against the wall."

"Throws his plate?"

"Nasty. That's what he is. No wonder his family doesn't come to visit. They probably can't stand him any more than we can."

She is waiting for me to do something.

"Well?"

30   "We'll see," I say.

The next morning I am waiting in the corridor when the kitchen delivers his breakfast. I watch the aide place the tray on the stand and swing it across his lap. She presses the button to raise the head of the bed. Then she leaves.

In time the man reaches to find the rim of the tray, then on to find the dome of the covered dish. He lifts off the cover and places it on the stand. He fingers across the plate until he probes the eggs. He lifts the plate in both hands, sets it on the palm of his right hand, centers it, balances it. He hefts it up and down slightly, getting the feel of it. Abruptly, he draws back his right arm as far as he can.

There is the crack of the plate breaking against the wall at the foot of his bed and the small wet sound of the scrambled eggs dropping to the floor.

And then he laughs. It is a sound you have never heard. It is something new under the sun. It could cure cancer.

35 Out in the corridor, the eyes of the head nurse narrow.

"Laughed, did he?"

She writes something down on her clipboard.

A second aide arrives, brings a second breakfast tray, puts it on the nightstand, out of his reach. She looks over at me shaking her head and making her mouth go. I see that we are to be accomplices.

"I've got to feed you," she says to the man.

40 "Oh, no you don't," the man says.

"Oh, yes I do," the aide says, "after the way you just did. Nurse says so."

"Get me my shoes," the man says.

"Here's oatmeal," the aide says. "Open." And she touches the spoon to his lower lip.

"I ordered scrambled eggs," says the man.

45 "That's right," the aide says.

I step forward.

"Is there anything I can do?" I say.

"Who are you?" the man asks.

In the evening I go once more to that ward to make my rounds. The head nurse reports to me that Room 542 is deceased. She has discovered this quite by accident, she says. No, there had been no sound. Nothing. It's a blessing, she says.

50 I go into his room, a spy looking for secrets. He is still there in his bed. His face is relaxed, grave, dignified. After a while, I turn to leave. My gaze sweeps the wall at the foot of the bed, and I see the place where it has been repeatedly washed, where the wall looks very clean and very white.

QUESTIONS ON CONTENT, STRUCTURE, AND STYLE

1. This essay presents several scenes in a hospital. From whose point of view do we see these scenes? How is this point of view introduced?

2. Does this essay contain objective or subjective description, or both? Are there enough clear, specific details to make the descriptions vivid to the reader? Cite some details to support your answer.

3. What does Selzer's description of the hospital room itself suggest about the patient?

4. Why does the patient throw his eggs on the wall each day? Why does he laugh? Call for his shoes? What do these details tell you about the patient and his attitude toward his situation?

5. What is Selzer's attitude toward his patient? How do you know? What is the attitude of the head nurse?

6. What is Selzer's purpose in describing this patient and his actions? Why doesn't he "do something" about the patient, as the nurse wants?

7. Point out several examples of metaphor and simile in this essay. What do these add to the effectiveness of Selzer's descriptions?

8. Why does Selzer use dialogue in some occasions instead of describing what is taking place?

9. Why does Selzer end his essay by referring to the clean wall? Is this an effective conclusion? Why/why not?

10. Selzer's subtitle for this essay was "Do Not Go Gentle," a reference to a well-known poem by Dylan Thomas. In the poem Thomas tells his dying father "Do not go gentle" into that good night. /Rage, rage against the dying of the light." Why is Selzer's subtitle an appropriate complement to this essay?

VOCABULARY

furtive (1)	caches (4)	athwart (20)
vile (2)	kickshaws (4)	irony (23)
repose (2)	shard (19)	
facsimile (2)	inert (20)	

A REVISION WORKSHEET FOR YOUR DESCRIPTIVE ESSAY

As you write your rough drafts, consult Chapter 5 for guidance through the revision process. In addition, here are a few questions to ask yourself as you revise your description:

1. Is the descriptive essay's purpose clear to the reader?

2. Are there enough specific details in the description to make the subject matter distinct to readers who are unfamiliar with the scene, person, or object? Where might more detail be added?

3. Are the details arranged in an order that's easy to follow?

4. If the assignment called for an objective description, are the details as "neutral" as possible?

5. If the assignment called for a subjective description, does the writer's particular attitude come through clearly with a consistent use of well-chosen details or imagery?

6. Could any sensory details or figurative language be added to help the reader "see" the subject matter?

7. What is the strongest part of this essay? How could you make the rest of the essay as good as that part?

After you've revised your essay extensively, you might exchange rough drafts with a classmate and answer these questions for each other, making specific suggestions for improvement wherever appropriate.

11

Narration

When many people hear the word "narrative," they think of a made-up story. But not all stories are fiction. In this chapter we are not concerned with writing literary short stories—that's a skill you may work on in a creative writing class —but rather with nonfiction *narratives,* stories that may be used in your essays to explain or prove a point. We most often use two kinds of these stories:

1. the *extended narrative*—a long episode that by itself illustrates or supports an essay's thesis
2. the *brief narrative*—a shorter incident that is often used in a body paragraph to support or illustrate a particular point in an expository or argumentative essay.

Let's suppose, for example, you wanted to write an essay showing how confusing the registration system is at your school. To illustrate the problems vividly, you might devote your entire essay to the retelling of a friend's horrible experience signing up for classes last fall, thus making use of extended narration. Or take another example: in an argumentative essay advocating the nationwide use of automobile air-bags, you might use a brief narrative about a car wreck to support a paragraph's point about air-bags' ability to save lives. Regardless of which type of narrative you decide best fits your purpose, the telling of a story or incident can be an informative, persuasive means of swaying your readers to your point of view.

HOW TO WRITE EFFECTIVE NARRATION

Know your purpose. Because narratives in most essays are intended to support or illustrate a thesis or paragraph's point, you must be careful not to allow your story to run on until the reader wonders, "Where is this going? What is the reason for this story?" Once you have decided on your thesis or paragraph point, tailor all the events and details in your narrative to fit your purpose. On the other hand, don't let your narrative turn into a sermonette—support your thesis with a story that informs and illustrates rather than preaches.

Maintain a consistent point of view. This subject is complex, and teachers of literature courses often spend much time explaining it in detail. For your purposes, however, a brief treatment will suffice. In the first place, you should decide whether the narrative will be told by you in the first person, by a character involved in the action, or by an omniscient ("all-knowing") narrator who may reveal the thoughts, feelings, and actions of any character. The selection of a point of view is important because it determines whose thoughts or actions will be described. If, for example, one of your female characters narrates an event, she is limited to giving only the information that she can know; that is, she cannot reveal another character's thoughts or describe actions that took place across town, out of her sight. Once you have decided which point of view is best for your purpose, be consistent; don't abruptly change point of view in mid-story.

Follow a logical time sequence. Many extended narrative essays—and virtually all brief stories used in other kinds of essays—follow a chronological order, presenting events as they naturally occur in the story. Occasionally, however, a writer will use the flashback technique, which takes the readers back in time to reveal an incident that occurred before the present scene of the story. Many novelists and short story writers use a variety of techniques to alter time sequences in their fiction; Joseph Heller's famous novel *Catch-22,* for example, contains chaotic time shifts to emphasize the absurd nature of war. If you decide to use shifts in time, make certain your readers don't become confused or lost.

Use details to present the setting. Most extended narratives are set in particular times and places. If the setting plays an important role in your story, you must describe it in vivid terms so that your readers can imagine it easily. For example, let's suppose you are pointing out the necessity of life preservers on sailboats by telling the story of how you spent a horrible, stormy night in the lake, clinging to your capsized boat. To convince your readers, let them "feel" the stinging rain and the icy current trying to drag you under; let them "see" the black waves, the dark menacing sky; let them "hear" the howling wind and the gradual splitting apart of the boat. Effective narration often depends upon effective description, and effective description depends upon vivid, specific detail. (For more help on writing description, see Chapter 10.)

Make your characters believable. Again, the use of detail is crucial. Your readers should be able to visualize the people in your narrative clearly; if your characters are drawn too thinly, or if they seem phony or stereotyped, your readers will not fully grasp the intensity of your story, and thus its meaning will be lost. Show the readers a realistic picture of the major characters by commenting unobtrusively on their appearances, speech, and actions.

In addition, a successful narrative depends upon the reader's understanding of people's motives—why they act the way they do in certain situations. A narrative about your hometown's grouchiest miser who suddenly donated a large sum of money to a poor family isn't very believable unless we know the motive behind the action. In other words, let your readers know what is happening to whom by explaining or showing why.

Use dialogue realistically. If your narrative calls for dialogue, be sure the word choice and the manner of speaking are in keeping with the character's education, background, age, location, and so forth. Don't, for example, put a sophisticated philosophical treatise into the mouth of a ten-year-old boy or the latest campus slang into the speeches of an auto mechanic from Two Egg, Florida. Also, make sure that your dialogue doesn't sound "wooden" or phony. The right dialogue can help make your characters more realistic and interesting, provided that the conversations are essential to the narrative and are not merely substituted for dramatic action. (To see extensive use of dialogue in an essay, read "The Discus Thrower," pp. 245–247. For help in punctuating dialogue, see pp. 321–322 in Part Three.)

Problems to Avoid

Unconvincing, boring narratives are often the result of problems with subject matter or poor pacing; therefore, you should keep in mind the following advice:

Choose your subject carefully. Most of the best narrative essays come from personal experience, and the reason is fairly obvious; it's much more difficult to write convincingly about something you've never seen or done or read about. You probably couldn't, for instance, write a realistic account of a bullfight unless you'd seen one or at least had studied the subject in great detail. The simplest, easiest, most interesting non-fiction narrative you can write is likely to be about an event with which you are personally familiar. This doesn't mean that you can't improvise many details or occasionally create a brief hypothetical story to illustrate a point. Even so, you will probably still have better luck basing your narrative—real or hypothetical—on something or someone you know well.

Limit your scope. If you wish to use an extended narrative to illustrate a thesis, don't select an event or series of actions whose retelling will be too long or complex for your assignment. In general, it's better to select one episode and flesh it out with many specific details so that your readers may clearly see your point. For instance, you may have had many rewarding experiences during the summer you worked as a lifeguard, but you can't tell them all. Instead, you might focus on one experience that captures the essence of your attitude toward your job—say, the time you saved a child from drowning—and present the story so vividly that the readers can easily understand your point of view.

Don't let your story lag with insignificant detail. At some time you've probably listened to a storyteller who became stuck on some insignificant detail ("Was it Friday or Saturday the letter came? Let's see now. . . ." "Then Joe said to me—no, it was Sally—no, wait, it was. . . ."). And you've probably also heard bores who insist on making a short story long by including too many unimportant details or digressions. These mistakes ruin the *pacing* of their stories; in other words, the story's tempo or movement becomes bogged down until the readers are bored witless. To avoid putting your readers to sleep, dismiss all unessential details and focus your attention—and use of detail—on the important events, people, and places. Skip uneventful periods of time by using such phrases as "A week went by before Mr. Smith called. . . ." or "Later that evening, around nine o'clock. . . ." In short, keep the story moving quickly enough to hold the readers' interest. Moreover, you should use a variety of transition devices to move the readers from one action to another; don't rely continuously on the childish "and then . . . and then . . ." method.

Essay Topics

Use one of the topics below to suggest an essay that is at least partially, if not entirely, supported by narration. Remember that each essay must have a clear purpose or thesis.

1. an experience with an older person or a child
2. the worst mix-up of your life
3. your best Christmas (birthday or any holiday)
4. your worst accident or brush with death
5. an act of courage or cowardice
6. your most frightening or wonderful childhood experience
7. a memorable event governed by Nature
8. a time you gained self-confidence
9. an event that changed your thinking on a particular subject
10. challenging an authority
11. an event that influenced your choice of career (or some other important decision)
12. your first introduction to prejudice or sexism
13. giving in to or resisting peer pressure
14. a loss of something or someone important
15. a risk that paid off (or a triumph against the odds)
16. a non-academic lesson learned at school or on a job
17. a trip or special time spent by yourself
18. a bad habit that got you into (or out of) trouble
19. a family story passed down through the generations
20. an episode marking your passage from one stage of your life to another

Sample Student Essay

In this extended narrative a student uses a story about a sick but fierce dog to show how she learned a valuable lesson in her job as a veterinarian's assistant. Notice the student's good use of vivid details that makes this well-paced story both clear and interesting.

Never Underestimate the Little Things

Introduction: A misconception

When I went to work as a veterinarian's assistant for Dr. Sam Holt and Dr. Jack Gunn last summer, I was under the false impression that the hardest part of veterinary surgery would be the actual performance of an operation. The small chores demanded before this feat didn't occur to me as being of any importance.

Thesis

As it happened, I had been in the veterinary clinic only a total of four hours before I met a little animal who convinced me that the operation itself was probably the easiest part of treatment. This animal, to whom I owe thanks for so enlightening me, was a chocolate-colored chihuahua of tiny size and immense perversity named Smokey.

Description of the main character: His appearance

Now Smokey could have very easily passed for some creature from another planet. It wasn't so much his gaunt little frame and overly large head, or his bony paws with nearly saberlike claws, as it was his grossly infected eyes. Those once-shining eyes were now distorted and swollen into grotesque balls of septic, sightless flesh. The only vague similarity they had to what we'd normally think of as the organs of vision was a slightly upraised dot, all that was left of the pupil, in the center of a pink and purply marble. As if that were not enough, Smokey had a temper to match his ugly sight.

His personality

He also had surprisingly good aim, considering his largely diminished vision, toward any moving object that happened to place itself unwisely before his ever-inquisitive nose, and with sudden and wholly vicious intent he would snap and snarl at whatever blocked the little light that could filter through his swollen and ruptured blood vessels. Truly, in many respects, Smokey was a fearful dog to behold.

The difficulty of moving the dog to the surgery room

Such an appearance and personality did nothing to encourage my already flagging confidence in my capabilities as a vet's assistant. How was I supposed to get that little demon out of his cage? Jack had casually requested that I bring Smokey to the surgery room, but did he really expect me to put my hands into the mouth of the cage of that devil dog? I suppose it must have been my anxious expression that saved me, for as I turned uncertainly toward the kennel, Jack chuckled nonchalantly and accompanied me to demonstrate how professionals in his line of business dealt with professionals in Smokey's. He took a small rope about four feet long with a slipnoose at one end and began to unlatch Smokey's cage. Then cautiously he reached in and dangled the noose before the dog's snarling jaws. Since Smokey could only barely see what he was biting at, his attacks were directed haphazardly in a semicircle around his body. The tiny area of his cage led to his capture, for during one of Smokey's forward lunges, Jack dropped the noose over his head and dragged the struggling creature out onto the floor. The fight had only just begun for Smokey, however, and he braced his feet against the slippery linoleum tiling and forced us to drag him, like a little pull toy on a string, to the surgery.

In the surgery room: the difficulty of moving the dog to the table

Once in the surgery, however, the question that hung before our eyes like a veritable presence was how to get the dog from the floor to table. Simply picking him up and plopping him down was out of the question. One glance at the quivering little figure emitting ominous and throaty warnings was enough to assure us of that. Realizing that the game was over, Jack grimly handed me the rope and reached for a muzzle. It was a doomed attempt from the start; the closer Jack dangled the tiny leather cup to the dog's nose the more violent did Smokey's contortions and rage-filled cries become and the more frantic our efforts became to try to keep our feet and fingers clear of the angry jaws. Deciding that a firmer method had to be used, Jack instructed me to raise the rope up high enough so that Smokey'd have to stand on his hind legs. This greatly reduced his maneuverability but served to increase his tenacity, for at this the little dog nearly went into paroxysms of frustration and rage. In his struggles, however, Smokey caught his forepaw on his swollen eye, and the blood that had been building up pressure behind the fragile cornea burst out and dripped to the floor. In the midst of our surprise and the twinge of panic startling the three of us, Jack saw his chance and swiftly muzzled the animal and lifted him to the operating table.

The difficulty of putting the dog to sleep before the surgery

Even at that point it wasn't easy to put the now terrified dog to sleep. He fought even the local anesthesia and caused Jack to curse as he was forced to give Smokey far more of the drug than should have been necessary for such a small beast. After what seemed an eternity, Smokey lay prone on the table, breathing deeply and emitting soft snores and gentle whines. We also breathed deeply in relief, and I relaxed to watch fascinated, while Jack performed a very delicate operation quite smoothly and without mishap.

Conclusion: Restatement of thesis

Such was my harrowing induction into the life of a veterinary surgeon. But Smokey did teach me a valuable lesson that has proven its importance to me many times since, and that is that wherever animals are concerned, even the smallest detail should never be taken for granted.

SHAME

Dick Gregory

Dick Gregory is a comedian, civil-rights activist, lecturer, and author of a number of books, including The Shadow That Scares Me *(1971),* Dick Gregory's Political Primer *(1971), and* Code Name Zorro *(1977). This story is taken from* nigger: An Autobiography *(1964).*

1   I never learned hate at home, or shame. I had to go to school for that. I was about seven years old when I got my first big lesson. I was in love with a little girl named Helene Tucker, a light-complected little girl with pigtails and nice manners. She was always clean and she was smart in school. I think I went to school mostly to look at her. I brushed my hair and even got me a little old handkerchief. It was a lady's handkerchief, but I didn't want Helene to see me wipe my nose on my hand. The pipes were frozen again, there was no water in the house, but I washed my socks and shirt every night. I'd get a pot, and go over to Mr. Ben's grocery store, and stick my pot down into his soda machine. Scoop out some chopped ice. By evening the ice melted to water for washing. I got sick a lot that winter because the fire would go out at night before the clothes were dry. In the morning I'd put them on, wet or dry, because they were the only clothes I had.

2   Everybody's got a Helene Tucker, a symbol of everything you want. I loved her for her goodness, her cleanliness, her popularity. She'd walk down my street and my brothers and sisters would yell, "Here comes Helene," and I'd rub my tennis sneakers on the back of my pants and wish my hair wasn't so nappy and the white folks' shirt fit me better. I'd run out on the street. If I knew my place and didn't come too close, she'd wink at me and say hello. That was a good feeling. Sometimes I'd follow her all the way home, and shovel the snow off her walk and try to make friends with her Momma and her aunts. I'd drop money on her stoop late at night on my way back from shining shoes in the taverns. And she had a Daddy, and he had a good job. He was a paper hanger.

3   I guess I would have gotten over Helene by summertime, but something happened in that classroom that made her face hang in front of me for the next twenty-two years. When I played the drums in high school it was for Helene and when I broke track records in college it was for Helene and when I started standing behind microphones and heard applause I wished Helene could hear it,

too. It wasn't until I was twenty-nine years old and married and making money that I really got her out of my system. Helene was sitting in that classroom when I learned to be ashamed of myself.

4 It was on a Thursday. I was sitting in the back of the room, in a seat with a chalk circle drawn around it. The idiot's seat, the troublemaker's seat.

5 The teacher thought I was stupid. Couldn't spell, couldn't read, couldn't do arithmetic. Just stupid. Teachers were never interested in finding out that you couldn't concentrate because you were so hungry, because you hadn't had any breakfast. All you could think about was noontime, would it ever come? Maybe you could sneak into the cloakroom and steal a bite of some kid's lunch out of a coat pocket. A bite of something. Paste. You can't really make a meal out of paste, or put it on bread for a sandwich, but sometimes I'd scoop a few spoonfuls out of the paste jar in the back of the room. Pregnant people get strange tastes. I was pregnant with poverty. Pregnant with dirt and pregnant with smells that made people turn away, pregnant with cold and pregnant with shoes that were never bought for me, pregnant with five other people in my bed and no Daddy in the next room, and pregnant with hunger. Paste doesn't taste too bad when you're hungry.

6 The teacher thought I was a troublemaker. All she saw from the front of the room was a little black boy who squirmed in his idiot's seat and made noises and poked the kids around him. I guess she couldn't see a kid who made noises because he wanted someone to know he was there.

7 It was on a Thursday, the day before the Negro payday. The eagle always flew on Friday. The teacher was asking each student how much his father would give to the Community Chest. On Friday night, each kid would get the money from his father, and on Monday he would bring it to the school. I decided I was going to buy me a Daddy right then. I had money in my pocket from shining shoes and selling papers, and whatever Helene Tucker pledged for her Daddy I was going to top it. And I'd hand the money right in. I wasn't going to wait until Monday to buy me a Daddy.

8 I was shaking, scared to death. The teacher opened her book and started calling out names alphabetically.

9 "Helene Tucker?"

10 "My daddy said he'd give two dollars and fifty cents."

11 "That's very nice, Helene. Very, very nice indeed."

12 That made me feel pretty good. It wouldn't take too much to top that. I had almost three dollars in dimes and quarters in my pocket. I stuck my hand in my pocket and held onto the money, waiting for her to call my name. But the teacher closed her book after she called everybody else in the class.

13 I stood up and raised my hand.

14 "What is it now?"

15 "You forgot me."

16 She turned toward the blackboard. "I don't have time to be playing with you, Richard."

17 "My Daddy said he'd . . ."

18   "Sit down, Richard, you're disturbing the class."

19   "My Daddy said he'd give . . . fifteen dollars."

20   She turned and looked mad. "We are collecting this money for you and your kind, Richard Gregory. If your Daddy can give fifteen dollars you have no business being on relief."

21   "I got it right now, I got it right now, my Daddy gave it to me to turn in today, my Daddy said . . ."

22   "And furthermore," she said, looking right at me, her nostrils getting big and her lips getting thin and her eyes opening wide, "we know you don't have a Daddy."

23   Helene Tucker turned around, her eyes full of tears. She felt sorry for me. Then I couldn't see her too well because I was crying, too.

24   "Sit down, Richard."

25   And I always thought the teacher kind of liked me. She always picked me to wash the blackboard on Friday, after school. That was a big thrill, it made me feel important. If I didn't wash it, come Monday the school might not function right.

26   "Where are you going, Richard?"

27   I walked out of school that day, and for a long time I didn't go back very often. There was shame there.

28   Now there was shame everywhere. It seemed like the whole world had been inside that classroom, everyone had heard what the teacher had said, everyone had turned around and felt sorry for me. There was shame in going to the Worthy Boys Annual Christmas Dinner for you and your kind, because everybody knew what a worthy boy was. Why couldn't they just call it the Boys Annual Dinner, why'd they have to give it a name? There was shame in wearing the brown and orange and white plaid mackinaw the welfare gave to 3,000 boys. Why'd it have to be the same for everybody so when you walked down the street the people could see you were on relief? It was a nice warm mackinaw and it had a hood, and my Momma beat me and called me a little rat when she found out I stuffed it in the bottom of a pail full of garbage way over on Cottage Street. There was shame in running over to Mister Ben's at the end of the day and asking for his rotten peaches, there was shame in asking Mrs. Simmons for a spoonful of sugar, there was shame in running out to meet the relief truck. I hated that truck, full of food for you and your kind. I ran into the house and hid when it came. And then I started to sneak through alleys, to take the long way home so the people going into White's Eat Shop wouldn't see me. Yeah, the whole world heard the teacher that day, we all know you don't have a Daddy.

Questions on Content, Structure, and Style

1. What is Gregory's purpose in telling this story from his childhood? What information about himself is he trying to explain to the reader?

2. For Gregory, who was Helene Tucker, and why was it important to "buy" himself a Daddy? Why did Helene's face hang before Gregory until he was twenty-nine? How did he finally get her "out of his system"?

3. Are the events in this story told in strict chronological order? If not, where are the deviations and why are they included?

4. Does Gregory use enough vivid detail to help you visualize the people and events of his story? Support your answer by citing specific passages.

5. Which characters are most developed in this story? How does Gregory help you understand the motivations for their actions? Is there any one character more fully developed than the others? If so, why?

6. Evaluate Gregory's use of dialogue. What does it add to the story?

7. Comment on Gregory's use of parallel construction in paragraphs 5 and 28.

8. Point out examples of slang and colloquial language in this story. Why did Gregory use such language?

9. How effective is Gregory's conclusion?

10. Describe Gregory's "voice" in this narrative. Is it effective or too full of self-pity?

VOCABULARY

nappy (2)   pregnant (5)   mackinaw (28)

A REVISION WORKSHEET FOR YOUR NARRATIVE ESSAY

As you write your rough drafts, consult Chapter 5 for guidance through the revision process. In addition, here are a few questions to ask yourself as you revise your narrative:

1. Is the narrative essay's purpose clear to the reader?

2. Is the thesis plainly stated or at least clearly implied?

3. Does the narrative convincingly support or illustrate its intended point? If not, how might the story be changed?

4. Does the story maintain a consistent point of view and an understandable order of action?

5. Are the characters, actions, and settings presented in enough vivid detail to make them clear and believable? Where could more detail be effectively added?

6. Is the story coherent and well-placed or does it wander or bog down in places because of irrelevant or repetitious details? What might be condensed or cut?

7. What is the strongest part of your essay? How could you make the rest of your essay as good as that part?

After you've revised your essay extensively, you might exchange rough drafts with a classmate and answer these questions for each other, making specific suggestions for improvement wherever appropriate.

12

Writing the Research Paper

Although the words "upcoming research paper" have been known to produce anxiety equal to or worse than that caused by the sound of the dentist's drill or the news that the Huns have invaded Manhattan, you should try to relax. A research paper is similar to the kinds of expository and argumentative essays described in the earlier parts of this book, with the primary difference being the use of documented source material to support, illustrate, or expand your ideas. Research papers still call for thesis statements, logical sequences of paragraphs, well-developed supporting evidence, smooth conclusions—or in other words, all the skills you've been practicing throughout this book. By citing sources in your essays or reports, you merely show your readers that you have researched your ideas and found support for them; in addition, using sources affords your readers the opportunity to look into your subject further if they so desire, following your references as a guide to additional readings.

The process described in the next few pages should help you write a research paper that is carefully and effectively documented. This chapter also contains sample documentation forms and a sample student paper (pp. 285–289).

SEARCHING FOR YOUR TOPIC

In some cases you will be assigned your topic, and you will be able to begin your research right away. In other classes, however, you may be encouraged to select your own subject, or you may be given only a general subject ("cults," "pornography," "violence on T.V.") that you must narrow and then focus into a specific, manageable topic. If the topic is your choice, you need to do some preliminary thinking about what interests you; as in any assignment, you should make the essay a learning experience from which both you and your readers will profit. Therefore, you may want to brainstorm for a while on your general subject before you go to the library, asking yourself questions about what you already know and don't know. Some of the most interesting research papers are problem-solving essays in which writers set about to find an answer to a controversy or to find support for a solution they suspect might work. Other research papers expose or illuminate a situation or a problem for its audience. Whatever the goal of your particular research, remember that your readers want to finish your paper knowing more about a significant subject than when they started.

Once you have at least a general topic in mind, your next step is to familiarize yourself with the school or public library where you will do your research. Most libraries have handouts, maps, or librarians who will help you locate the important parts of the library; do not be shy about asking for such information *before* you start your search.

After you become comfortable in the library, you can begin to compile a *working bibliography,* that is, a list of possible sources for your topic. You may find it useful to start by investigating one or more of the following reference room tools:

THE CARD CATALOG

The card catalog is usually a series of cabinets containing alphabetized index cards; in some libraries the card catalog is divided into three parts so that you

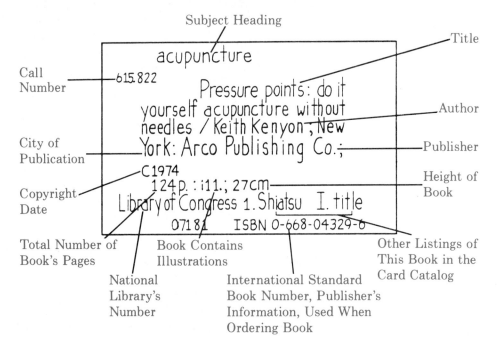

may look up information under "subject," "author," and "titles." Unless you are already familiar with authorities or their books on your subject, you will most likely begin with the "subject" catalog. If your subject is "acupuncture," you might find a typical subject card that looks like the sample on page 262. You may have to look under several headings in the subject catalog to find the one your library uses for your topic.

If your library has become computerized, as so many have in the past several years, the information you would ordinarily find in the card catalog will now be found on a computer screen. Because libraries today are often in a state of transition, you may need to consult your librarian about the system in current use at your school or public library.

PERIODICAL INDEXES

Periodical indexes list magazines and journals that may contain articles you will wish to consult. There are several kinds of periodical indexes, and your library will carry a number of them to help you with your search. If your subject is of interest to a general audience, you might begin by checking *The Reader's Guide to Periodical Literature,* an index that lists 160 magazines of general interest, such as *Time* and *Newsweek. The New York Times* index is also useful if your subject has been in the national or international news. However, if your subject is particular to a field of study, you may wish to try first those indexes that list only magazines and journals in specific areas, such as the *Business Periodicals Index,* the *Humanities Index,* the *Applied Science* and *Technology Index,* or the *Social Sciences Index.* Note too that your topic may be listed under slightly different headings from index to index (for instance, "wife abuse" in one index might be "battered wife syndrome" in another). If you can't find your subject under the headings that first come to your mind, ask your librarian for the *Library of Congress Subject Headings,* a common reference book that will suggest other names for your topic.

SPECIAL COLLECTIONS

Your library may also contain special collections that will help you research your subject. Some libraries, for example, have extensive collections of government documents or educational materials or newspapers from certain cities. Other libraries may have invested in manuscripts from famous authors or in a series of works on a particular subject, such as your state's history, a Vietnam War collection, or studies on human rights in post-World War II Latin America. Remember, too, that some libraries contain collections of early films, rare recordings, or unique photographs. Consult your librarian or the handouts describing your library's special holdings.

Looking through the card catalog and periodical indexes may take time, but seeing what's been published on your subject may help you focus on a specific topic. You may also find it useful at this point to skim a number of articles on your subject, so that eventually you reach the idea you want to research and write about. (And don't underestimate the value of browsing—sometimes the most interesting book on your subject is on the shelf next to the book you were looking for.)

Once you have a narrowed topic, you are ready to prepare a *working bibliography,* a list of the most promising sources for your paper. To compile a working bibliography, you should note on an index card the following information for each source: author's name, title of work, publisher, date and city of publication, page numbers of the material you're interested in, and library call number.

TAKING NOTES

Begin to look up the sources listed in your working bibliography and take notes on *content* cards. Most researchers recommend that you take notes on index cards rather than on notebook paper because the cards can be shuffled around more easily later when you are organizing your paper. In addition, you may find it helpful to use cards of a different color or size from the bibliography cards, just for ease of sorting.

When you find a useful book, be sure you have a bibliography card for it that contains the author's name, the book's full title, publisher, city and date of publication, and the page numbers from which your notes are taken. If your notes are from a magazine or journal, the card should contain the author's name, journal's name, article's name, volume number, issue number, date of issue, page numbers of the article within the journal, and the page numbers from which you took your notes. Plan to use several content cards for each book or article because you may wish to divide your notes into categories of ideas that will later help you organize your paragraphs. Write on one side of the content cards only, to avoid having some material out of sight and mind while you're organizing your notes for your first rough draft.

Your notes will probably be of four kinds:

1. *Direct quotations.* When you lift material word-for-word,* you must always use quotation marks and note the precise page number of the quotation. If the quoted material runs from one page onto another, always use some sort of signal to yourself such as a slash bar (child/abuse) or arrow ($\rightarrow$ p. 10) at the break so if you only use part of the quoted material in your paper, you will know on which page it appeared. If the quoted material contains odd, archaic, or incorrect spelling, punctuation marks, or grammar, insert the word [*sic*] in brackets next to the item in question; [sic] means "this is the way I

---

* Please note that all tables, graphs, and charts that you copy must also be directly attributed to their sources, though you do not enclose graphics in quotation marks.

found it in the original text," and such a symbol will remind you later that you did not miscopy the quotation. Otherwise, always double check to make sure you did copy the material accurately and completely to avoid having to come back to the source as you prepare your essay. If the material you want to quote is lengthy, you will find it easier—though not cheaper—to photocopy the material rather than transcribe it (almost all libraries have one or more photocopy machines, but be prepared to bring your own bag of correct change).

2. *Paraphrase.* You paraphrase when you put into your own words what someone else has written or said. Please note: *Paraphrased ideas are borrowed ideas, not your original thoughts, and consequently they must be attributed to their owner just as direct quotations are.*

To remind yourself that certain information on your notecards is paraphrased, always leave space in the left-hand margin for some sort of notation such as a circled (P). Quotation marks will always tell you what you borrowed directly, but sometimes when writers take notes one week and write their first draft a week or two later, it's hard to remember if a note was paraphrased or if it's original thinking. Writers occasionally plagiarize unintentionally because they believe only direct quotations and statistics must be attributed to their proper sources, so make your notes as clear as possible (for more information on avoiding plagiarism, see pp. 271–273).

3. *Summary.* You may wish to condense a piece of writing so that you may offer it as support for your own ideas. Using your own words, you should present in shorter form the writer's thesis and supporting ideas. In addition, you may find it helpful to include a few direct quotations in your summary to retain the flavor of the original work. Of course, you will tell your readers what you are summarizing and by whom it was written. Remember to make a note in the margin to indicate summarized, rather than original, material.

4. *Your own ideas.* Your note cards should also contain your personal comments (judgments, flashes of brilliance, notions of how to use something you've just read, notes to yourself about connections between sources, and so forth) that will aid you in the writing of your paper. It might be helpful to jot these down in a different colored pen or put them in brackets that you've initialed, so that you will recognize them later as your own responses when your note cards are cold.

DISTINGUISHING PARAPHRASE FROM SUMMARY

Because novice writers sometimes have a hard time telling the difference between paraphrase and summary, here is a sample of each.

First, here is a paragraph from an article suggesting a way to stop juvenile delinquency that might be pertinent in a research paper you're preparing on the current theories for controlling juvenile crime.

Another successful approach to the prevention of criminality has been to target very young children in a school setting before problems arise. The Perry Preschool Program, started 22 years ago in a low socioeconomic area of Ypsilanti, Michigan, has offered some of the most solid evidence to date that early intervention through a high-quality preschool program can significantly alter a child's life. A study released this fall tells what happened to 123 disadvantaged children from preshcool age to present. The detention and arrest rates for the 58 children who had attended the preschool program was 31 percent, compared to 51 percent for the 65 who did not. Similarly, those in the preschool program were more likely to have graduated from high school, have enrolled in postsecondary education programs and be employed, and less likely to have become pregnant as teenagers.

—from "Arresting Delinquency,"
Dan Hurley, *Psychology Today,*
March 1985, p. 66.

A *paraphrase* puts the information in the researcher's own words, but it does follow the order of the original text, and it does include the important details.

PARAPHRASE

Quality preschooling for high-risk children may help stop crime before it starts. A recent study from the twenty-two-year-old Perry Preschool Program located in a poor area of Ypsilanti, Michigan, shows that of 123 socially and economically disadvantaged children the 58 who attended preschool had an arrest rate of 31% as compared to 51% for those 65 who did not attend. The adults with preschool experience had also graduated from high school in larger numbers; in addition, more of them had attended postsecondary education programs, were employed, and had avoided teenage pregnancy (Hurley 66).

A *summary* is generally much shorter than the original; the researcher picks out the key ideas but often omits many of the supporting details.

SUMMARY

A recent study from the Perry Preschool Program in Michigan suggests that disadvantaged children who attend preschool are less likely to be arrested as adults. Those in this study with preschool experience also chose more education, had better employment records, and avoided teenage pregnancy more often than those without preschool (Hurley 66).

Remember:
   Both paraphrased and summarized ideas must be attributed to their sources, even if you did not reproduce exact words or figures.

CHOOSING YOUR SOURCES

Once you have collected and reviewed your notes, you may be ready to begin sketching out your outline and first draft. In doing so, you must decide which sources to use, where to use them, and in what form: paraphrase, summary, or direct quotation.

   To help you choose your sources, here are some questions to consider as you try to decide which facts, figures, and testimonies will best support or illustrate your ideas.

   Are your sources reliable? Newspapers are frequently faulted for basing entire stories on unnamed, so-called "reliable sources." Be sure that your sources are dependable and well-respected in the particular area under discussion. An expert in organic chemistry, for example, might know an enormous amount about his or her own field but actually very little about genetics.

   Are your sources unreasonably biased? Some authorities stand to gain economically or politically from taking a particular point of view. The president of a tobacco company, for instance, might insist that secondary smoke from the cigarettes of others will not harm non-smokers, but does he or she have an objective opinion? Try to present testimony from those authorities whose views will sway your readers.

   Is your research sensibly balanced? Your treatment of your subject—especially if it's a controversial one—should show your readers that you investigated all sides of the issue before reaching a conclusion. If your sources are drawn only from authorities well known for voicing one position, your readers will tend to become skeptical about the quality of your research. For instance, if on a paper on prayer in the schools, you refer only to the opinions of William Buckley, Phyllis Schaefly, and the president of the Eagle Forum, all well-known conservatives, you may antagonize the reader who wants a thorough analysis of all sides of the questions. Do use sources that support your position—but don't overload your argument with only obviously biased sources. (Be careful with certain publications, too; check the origins and publishers of your magazines and pamphlets. Naturally, a brochure on abortion printed by Planned Parenthood will have a different point of view from one printed by the local right-to-life organization.)

   Are your sources reporting valid research? Is your source the original researcher or is he or she reporting someone else's study? If the information is being reported secondhand, has your source been accurate and clear? Is the original source named or footnoted in some way so that the information could be checked? Look too at the way the information was obtained in the first place. Did the original researchers themselves draw the logical conclusions from their evidence? Did they run their study or experiment (or whatever) in a fair, impartial way? For example, a survey of people whose names were obtained from the rolls of the Democratic Party will hardly constitute a representative sampling of voters' opinion on an upcoming election.

Moreover, be especially careful with statistics as they can be manipulated quite easily to give a distorted picture. A recent survey, for instance, asked a large sample of people to rate a number of American cities on questions dealing with quality of life. Pittsburgh—a lovely city, to be sure—came out the winner, but only if one agrees that all the questions should be weighted equally; that is, the figures averaged out with Pittsburgh boasting the highest score only if one rates "weather" as equally important as "educational opportunities," "amount of crime," "cultural opportunities," and other factors. In short, always evaluate the quality of your sources' research and the validity of their conclusions before you decide to incorporate their findings into your own paper. (And don't forget Mark Twain's reference to "lies, damned lies, and statistics.")

Are your sources still current? While it's true that some famous experiments or studies have withstood the years, for many controversial topics you should use research as current as possible. What may have been written ten, or even five, years ago may have been disproved or surpassed since, especially in some of our rapidly expanding fields of technology. If they're appropriate, journals and other periodicals may contain more up-to-date reports than books printed several years ago. Readers usually appreciate hearing the current word on the topic under examination, though you certainly shouldn't ignore a "classic" study on your subject, especially if it is the one against which all the other studies are measured.

Are you using your sources in a clear, logical way? First, make certain that you understand your source material well enough to use it in support of your own thoughts. Once you have selected the best references to use, be as convincing as possible. Ask yourself if you're using enough evidence and if the information you're offering really does clearly support your point. As in any essay, you need to avoid oversimplification, hasty generalizations, *non sequiturs,* and other problems in logic (for a review of common logical fallacies, see pp. 222–225). Resist the temptation to add quotations, facts, or statistics that are interesting but not really relevant to your paper.

INCORPORATING YOUR SOURCE MATERIAL

Remember that a research paper is not a massive collection of quotations and paraphrased ideas glued together with a few transition phrases. It is, instead, an essay in which you offer *your* thesis and ideas based upon and supported by your research. Consequently, you will need to incorporate and blend in your reference material in a variety of smooth, persuasive ways. Here are some suggestions:

Don't overuse direct quotations. It's best to use a direct quotation *only* when it expresses a point in a far more impressive, emphatic, or concise way than you could say it yourself. Suppose, for instance, you were analyzing the films of a particular director and wanted to include a sample of critical reviews:

> As one movie critic wrote, "This film is really terrible, and people should ignore it" (Dennison 14).

(This direct quotation isn't remarkable and could be easily paraphrased.)

> As one movie critic wrote, "This film's plot is so inane that the director must have intended it for people who move their lips not only when they read but also when they watch T.V." (Dennison 14).

(You might be tempted to quote this line to show your readers an emphatically negative review of this movie.)

When you do decide to use direct quotations, don't merely drop them in next to your prose. Instead, lead into them smoothly so that they obviously support or clarify what you are saying.

Dropped in   Scientists have been studying the ill effects of nitrites on test animals since 1961. "Nitrites produced malignant tumors in 62 percent of the test animals within six months" (Smith 109).

Better   Scientists have been studying the ill effects of nitrites on test animals since 1961. According to Dr. William Smith, head of the Farrell Institute of Research, "Nitrites produced malignant tumors in 62 percent of the test animals within six months" (109).

Vary your sentence pattern when you present your quotations. Here are some sample phrases for quotations:

> In his introduction to *The Great Gatsby,* Professor William Smith points out that "Fitzgerald wrote about himself and produced a narcissistic masterpiece" (5).

> William Smith, author of *Impact,* summarized the situation this way: "Eighty-eight percent of the sales force threaten a walkout" (21).

> "Only the President controls the black box," according to the White House Press Secretary (Smith 129).

> As drama critic William Smith observed last year in *The Saturday Review,* the play was "a rousing failure" (212).

Perhaps the well-known poet William Smith expressed the idea best when he wrote, "Love is a spider waiting to entangle its victims" (14).

Congressman William Smith presented the opposing view when he claimed, "Employment figures are down ten percent from last year" (32).

In other words, don't simply repeat "William Smith said," "John Jones said," "Mary Brown said."

Punctuate your quotations correctly. The proper punctuation will help your reader understand who said what. For information on the appropriate uses of quotation marks, see pp. 321–322.

Make certain your support is in the paper, not still in your head or back in the original source. Sometimes when you've read a number of persuasive facts in an article or book, it's easy to forget that your reader doesn't know them as you do now. For instance, the writer of the paragraph below isn't as persuasive as she might be because she hides the support for her point in the reference to the article, forgetting that the reader needs to know what the article actually said:

An organ transplant from one human to another is becoming an everyday occurrence in America, an operation that is generally applauded by everyone as a life-saving effort. But people are overlooking many of the serious problems that come with the increase in transplant surgery. One of the biggest problems today is the traffic in the buying and selling of organs on the Black Market. Many studies show that the cases recorded recently have risen to an alarming number and that poor people are the most affected (Wood 35).

For the reader to be persuaded, he or she needs to know what the writer learned from the article: what studies? how many cases are there? who has recorded these? in what time period? how and why are poor people affected? Instead of offering the necessary support in the essay, the writer merely points to the article as proof. Few readers will take the time to look up the article to find the information they need to understand your point. Therefore, when you use source material, always be sure that you have remembered to put your support on the page, *in the essay* itself, for the reader to see. Don't let the essence of your case remain hidden.

Don't let reference material dominate your essay. Remember that your reader is interested in *your* thesis and *your* conclusions, not just in a string of references. Use your researched material wisely whenever your statements need clarification, support, or amplification. But don't use quotations, paraphrased, or summarized material at every turn, just to show that you've done your homework.

AVOIDING PLAGIARISM

Unfortunately, most discussions of research papers must include a brief word about plagiarism. Novice writers often unintentionally plagiarize, as noted before, because they fail to recognize the necessity to attribute paraphrased, summarized, and borrowed ideas to their original owners. And indeed it is difficult sometimes after days of research to know exactly what one has borrowed and what one originally thought. Also, there's frequently a thin line between general or common knowledge ("Henry Ford was the father of the automobile industry in America") that does not have to be documented and those ideas and statements that do ("U.S. Steel reported an operating loss of four million in its last quarter"). As a rule of thumb, ask yourself whether the majority of your readers would recognize the fact or opinion you're expressing or if it's repeatedly found in commonly used sources; if so, you may not need to document it. For example, most people would acknowledge that the Wall Street Crash of 1929 ushered in the Great Depression of the 1930s, but the exact number of bank foreclosurers in 1933 is not common knowledge and needs documenting. Similarly, a well-known quotation from the Bible or Mother Goose or even the Declaration of Independence might pass without documentation, but a line from the vice-president's latest speech needs a reference to its source. When in doubt, the best choice is to document anything that you feel may be in question.

To help you understand the difference between plagiarism and proper documentation, here is an original passage and both incorrect and correct ways to use it in a paper of your own:

Original   It is a familiar nightmare: a person suffers a heart attack, and as the ambulance fights heavy traffic, the patient dies. In fact, 350,000 American heart-attack.victims each year die without ever reaching a hospital. The killer in many cases is ventricular fibrillation, uncoordinated contraction of the heart muscle. Last week a team of Dutch physicians reported in *The New England Journal of Medicine* that these early deaths can often be prevented by administration of a common heart drug called lidocaine, injected into the patient's shoulder muscle by ambulance paramedics as soon as they arrive on the scene.

> —From "First Aid for Heart Attacks,"
> *Newsweek,* November 11, 1985,
> page 88

Plagiarized   It is a common nightmare: a person with a heart attack dies as the ambulance sits in heavy traffic, often a victim of ventricular fibrillation, uncoordinated contraction of the heart muscle. Today, however, these early deaths can often be prevented by an injection into the patient's shoulder of a common heart drug called lidocaine, which may be administered by paramedics on the scene.

This writer has changed some of the words and sentences, but the passage has obviously been borrowed and must be attributed to its source.

Also plagiarized   According to *Newsweek*, 350,000 American heart attack victims die before reaching help in hospitals ("First Aid for Heart Attacks" 88). However, a common heart drug called lidocaine, which may be injected into the patient by paramedics on the scene of the attack, may save many victims who die en route to doctors and sophisticated life-saving equipment.

This writer did attribute the statistic to its source, but the remainder of the paragraph is still borrowed and must be documented.

Properly documented   Ambulance paramedics can, and often do, play a vital life-saving role today. They are frequently the first medical assistance available, especially to those patients or accident victims far away from hospitals. Moreover, according to a recent *Newsweek* report, paramedics are now being trained to administer powerful drugs to help the sick survive until they reach doctors and medical equipment. For instance, paramedics can inject the common heart drug lidocaine into heart attack victims on the scene, an act that may save many of the 350,000 Americans who die of heart attacks before ever reaching a hospital ("First Aid for Heart Attacks" 88).

This writer used the properly documented information to support her own point about paramedics and has not tried to pass off any of the article as her own.

Although plagiarism is often unintentional, it's your job to be as honest as possible. If you're in doubt about your use of a particular idea, consult your instructor for a second opinion.

Here's a suggestion that might help you avoid plagiarizing by accident. When you are drafting your essay and come to a spot in which you want to incorporate the ideas of someone else, think of the borrowed material as if it were in a window. Always frame the window at the top with some sort of introduction that mentions the author and frame the window on the bottom with a reference to the location of the material:

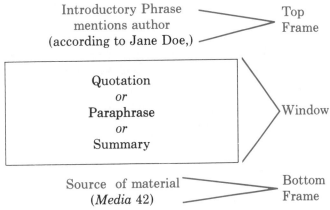

A sample might look like this:

Introductory Phrase
mentions author

As writer Mike McGrady once said of housekeeping, "Any
job that requires six hours to do and can be undone in six minutes
Window by one small child carrying a plate of crackers and a Monopoly
set—this is not a job that will long capture my interest" (13).

Source

In a later draft, you'll probably want to vary your style so that all your
borrowed material doesn't appear in exactly the same "window" format (see
pp. 268–269 for suggestions). But until you get the habit of *always* documenting
your sources, you might try using the "window" technique in your early drafts.*

PRACTICING WHAT YOU'VE LEARNED

To practice some of the skills you've learned so far, read the following passage
on Alexander II of Russia (1855–1881) and do the tasks listed below it.

> Alexander's greatest single achievement was his emancipation of some forty
> million Russian serfs, a deed which won him the title of "Tsar Liberator."
> To visit a rural Russian community in the earlier nineteenth century was
> like stepping back into the Middle Ages. Nine-tenths of the land was held
> by something less than one hundred thousand noble families. The serfs,

---

* I am indebted to Professor John Clark Pratt of Colorado State University for this useful
suggestion. Professor Pratt is the author of *Writing from Scratch: The Essay* (1987) published by
Hamilton Press, and the editor of the *Writing from Scratch* series.

attached to the soil, could be sold with the estates to new landlords, conscripted into the nobleman's household to work as domestic servants, or even sent to the factories in the towns for their master's profit. Though some nobles exercised their authority in a kindly and paternal fashion, others overworked their serfs, flogged them cruelly for slight faults, and interfered insolently in their private affairs and family relations. A serf could not marry without his master's consent, could not leave the estate without permission, and might be pursued, brought back, and punished if he sought to escape. He lived at the mercy of his master's caprice.

1. The book from which the above passage was taken contains the information listed below. Select the appropriate information and prepare a bibliography card.

A Survey of European Civilization Part Two, Since 1660
Third Edition
Houghton Mifflin Company, Publishers
Boston
First edition, 1936
853.21
1012 pages
Authors:
   Wallace K. Ferguson, The University of Western Ontario
   Geoffrey Brun, Formerly Visiting Professor of History, Cornell University
Indexes: general, list of maps
Picture Acknowledgments, xxvii
copyright 1962
p. 716
44 chapters

2. Paraphrase the passage.
3. Summarize the passage, but do not quote from it.
4. Select an important idea from the passage to quote directly and lead into the quotation with a smooth acknowledgment of its source.
5. Select an idea or a quotation from the passage and use it as support for a point of your own, being careful not to plagiarize the borrowed material.

ASSIGNMENT

In your school or local library, look up a newspaper from any city or state and find the issue published on the day of your birth. Prepare a bibliography card for the issue you chose. Then summarize the most important or "lead" article located on the front page. (Don't forget to acknowledge the source of your summary.)

CHOOSING THE DOCUMENTATION STYLE FOR YOUR ESSAY

Once you've begun to write your paper incorporating your source material, you need to know how to show your readers where your material came from. You may have already learned a system for using footnotes (or endnotes), but since today's researchers and scholars use a number of different documentation styles, it's important that you know which style is appropriate for your essay. In some cases your instructors (or the audience for whom you are writing) will designate a particular style; at other times, the choice will be yours. In this chapter, we will look at three of the most widely used systems:

1. New MLA Style
2. Traditional Footnotes/Endnotes
3. APA Style

I. New MLA Style

Many instructors of writing across the country assign the documentation form prescribed by the Modern Language Association of America (MLA). Since 1984, the MLA has recommended a new form of documentation that no longer uses traditional footnotes or endnotes to show references.* This new form calls for *parenthetical documentation,* most often consisting of the author's last name and the appropriate page number(s) in parentheses immediately following the source material in your paper. The information in the parentheses is then keyed to a "Works Cited" page at the end of your discussion, a list of the sources used in your essay (see pp. 277–281 for more explanation and samples).

MLA Citations in Your Essay

Here are some guidelines for using the MLA parenthetical reference form within your paper:

1. If you use a source by one author, place the author's name and page number right after the quoted, paraphrased, or summarized material. Note that the parentheses go *before* the end punctuation, and there is no punctuation between the author's name and page number.

---

* If you wish a more detailed description of the new MLA form, you should ask your local bookstore for the *MLA Handbook for Writers of Research Papers,* 2nd ed. (New York: MLA, 1984) by Joseph Gibaldi and Walter S. Achtert.

Example Although pop art often resembles the comic strip, it owes a debt to such painters as Magritte, Matisse, and de Kooning (Rose 184).

2. If you use a source by one author and give credit to that author by name within your paper, you need only give the page number in the parentheses.

Example According to art critic Barbara Rose, pop art owes a large debt to such painters as Magritte, Matisse, and de Kooning (184).

3. If you are directly quoting material of five or more typed lines, set off the material by five spaces on the left margin and do not use quotation marks. Note that in this case, the parentheses appears *after* the punctuation that ends the quoted material.

Example In addition to causing tragedy for others, Crane's characters who are motivated by a desire to appear heroic to their peers may also cause themselves serious trouble. Collins, in "A Mystery of Heroism," for example, almost causes his own death because of his vain desire to act bravely in front of his fellow soldiers. (Hall 16)

4. If you are citing more than one work by the same author, include a short title in the parentheses.

Example Within 50 years the Inca and Aztec civilizations were defeated and overthrown by outside invaders (Thomas, *Lost Cultures* 198).

5. If you are citing a work by more than one author, use all last names and page number.

Example Prisons today are overcrowded to the point of emergency; conditions could not be worse, and the state budget for prison reform is at an all-time low (Smith and Jones 72).

6. If you cite a work that has no author given, use the work's title and the page number.

Example Each year 350,000 Americans will die of a heart attack before reaching a hospital ("First Aid for Heart Attacks" 88).

7. If the work you are citing appears in a series, include the volume and page number with the author's name.

Example The most common view camera format is 4″ by 5″, though many sizes are available on today's market (Pursell 1:29).

If the material you are citing contains a quoted passage from another source, indicate the use of the quotation in the parentheses.

Example   According to George Orwell, "Good writing is like a window-pane" (qtd. in Murray 142).

COMPILING A WORKS CITED LIST

If you are using the MLA format, at the end of your essay you should include a *works cited list*—a formal listing of the sources you used in your essay. Arrange the entries alphabetically by the authors' last names; if no name is given, arrange your sources by the first important word of the title. Double-space each entry, and double-space after each one. If an entry takes more than one line, indent the subsequent lines five spaces. See the sample entries that follow.

SAMPLE ENTRIES: MLA STYLE

Here are some sample entries to help you prepare a Works Cited page according to the MLA guidelines. Please note that MLA style recommends shortened forms of publishers' names: Holt for Holt, Rinehart and Winston; Harper for Harper & Row; "UP" for "university press," and so forth. Also, omit business descriptions, such as "Inc.," "Co.," "Press," or "House."

Remember, too, when you type your paper, the titles of books and journals should be underlined even though you may see them printed in books or magazines in italics, and the titles of articles, essays, and chapters should be enclosed in quotation marks.

Books

• Book with one author

Tuchman, Barbara. *A Distant Mirror: The Calamitous Fourteenth Century.* New York: Knopf, 1978.

• Two books by same author

Tuchman, Barbara. *A Distant Mirror: The Calamitous Fourteenth Century.* New York: Knopf, 1978.
———. *Stillwell and the American Experience in China.* New Jersey: Macmillan, 1971.

• Book with two or three authors

Weider, Ben, and David Hapgood. *The Death of Napoleon.* New York: Congdon, 1982.

• Book with more than three authors

Guerin, Wilfred L., et al. *A Handbook of Critical Approaches to Literature.* New York: Harper, 1979.

• Book with author and editor

Chaucer, Geoffrey. *The Tales of Canterbury.* Ed. Robert Pratt. Boston: Houghton, 1974.

• Book with corporate authorship

United States Council on Fire Prevention. *Stopping Arson Before It Starts.* Washington: Edmondson, 1982.

• Book with an editor

Baugh, Albert C., ed. *A Literary History of England.* New York: Appleton, 1974.

• Selection or chapter from an anthology or collection with an editor

Chopin, Kate. "La Belle Zoraide." *Classic American Women Writers.* Ed. Cynthia Griffin Wolff. New York: Harper, 1980. 250–273.

• Work in more than one volume

Sharp, Harold. *Handbook of Pseudonyms and Personal Nicknames.* Vol. 1. New York: Scarecrow, 1972. 2 vols.

• Work in a series

Berg, Barbara L. *The Remembered Gate: Origins of American Feminism.* Urban Life in America Series. New York: Oxford UP, 1978.

• Translation

Proust, Marcel. *Remembrance of Things Past.* Trans. C. K. S. Moncrieff. New York: Random, 1970.

• Reprint

Thaxter, Celia. *Among the Isles of Shoals.* 1873. Hampton, NH: Heritage, 1978.

Magazines and Periodicals

• Signed article in magazine

Dellinger, Walter. "Another Route to the ERA." *Newsweek* 2 Aug. 1982: 8.

• Unsigned article in magazine

"Men's and Women's Trenchcoats." *Consumer Reports* Oct. 1982: 491–97.

• Signed article in periodical

Lockwood, Thomas. "Divided Attention in *Persuasion.*" *Nineteenth-Century Fiction* 33 (1978): 309–23.

- A review

Musto, Michael. Rev. of *Goddess, The Secret Lives of Marilyn Monroe,* by Anthony
Summers. *Saturday Review* Dec. 1985: 65–66.

Newspapers

- Signed article in newspaper

Branscombe, Art. "American Students Not Getting 'Basics.'" *Denver Post* 19 Sept.
1982: A17.

- Unsigned article in newspaper

"Soviet Union Buys 7.6 Million Metric Tons of Grain from Canada." *Wall Street
Journal* 14 Oct. 1982: A18.

- Unsigned editorial

"Give Life after Death." Editorial. *Coloradoan* [Ft. Collins, CO] 23 Dec. 1985: A4.

(If the newspaper's city of publication is not clear from the title, put the
location in brackets following the paper's name, as shown above.)

- A letter to the newspaper

Franklin, Charles. Letter. *Denver Post* 10 Sept. 1985: B10.

Encyclopedias, Pamphlets, Dissertations

- Signed article in an encyclopedia

Langlotz, Ernst. "Greek Art." *Encyclopedia of World Art.* 1963.

- Unsigned article in an encyclopedia

"Sailfish." *The International Wildlife Encyclopedia.* 1970 ed.

- A pamphlet

Young, Leslie. *Baby Care Essentials for the New Mother.* Austin: Hall, 1985.

- A government document

Department of Health. National Institute on Drug Abuse. *Drug Abuse Prevention.*
Washington: GPO, 1980.

- Unpublished dissertations and theses

Harmon, Gail A. "Poor Writing Skills at the College Level: A Program for Correction." Diss. U of Colorado, 1982.

Films, Television, Radio, Performances, Records

- A film

La Cage aux Folles. Dir. Edouard Molinaro. With Ugo Tognazzi and Michel Serrault.
United Artists, 1979.

If you are referring to the contribution of a particular individual, such as the director, writer, actor, or composer, begin with that person's name:

Molinaro, Edouard, dir. *La Cage aux Folles.* With Ugo Tognazzi and Michel Serrault. United Artists, 1979.

- A television or radio show

Innovation. WNET, Newark. 12 Oct. 1985.

If your reference is to a particular episode or person associated with the show, cite that name first, before the show's name:

"A Tribute to Beethoven." *Sounds Alive.* CBS. WXYZ, Dallas. 10 May 1983.

Moyers, Bill, writ. and narr. *Bill Moyers' Journal.* PBS. WABC, Denver. 30 Sept. 1980.

- Performances (plays, concerts, ballets, operas)

Julius Caesar. By William Shakespeare. With Royal Shakespeare Company. Booth Theater, New York. 13 Oct. 1982.

If you are referring to the contribution of a particular person associated with the performance, put that person's name first:

Shostakovich, Maxim, cond. New York Philharmonic Orch. Concert. Avery Fisher Hall, New York. 12 Nov. 1982.

- A record

Seger, Bob. "Night Moves." Rec. 20 May 1980. *Nine Tonight.* Capitol, 7777-12182-1, 1981.

Letters, Lectures, and Speeches

- A letter

Moore, Thomas. To Lord Byron. 28 Oct. 1821. Letter 112 in *Memoirs, Journals and Correspondence.* Ed. Lord John Russell. Vol. 3. London: Longman, 1853. 352–53. 8 vols. 1953–55.

- A lecture or speech

Give the speaker's name and the title of the talk first, before the sponsoring organization (or occasion) and location. If there is no title, substitute the appropriate label, such as "lecture" or "speech."

Dippity, Sarah N. "The Importance of Prewriting." CLAS Convention. Colorado Springs, 15 Feb. 1984.

Interviews

- A published interview

Cite the person interviewed first. Use the word "Interview" if the interview has no title:

Mailer, Norman. *Dialogue with Mailer.* With Andrew Gordon. *Berkeley Times* 15 Jan. 1969.

- A personal interview

Johns, Professor Henry. Dept. of Political Science, Colorado State University. Personal interview. 4 Sept. 1982.

Clay, Marilyn. City Council Office, Loveland, CO. Telephone interview. 13 April 1985.

II. FOOTNOTE/ENDNOTE FORM

In case your assignment calls for traditional footnotes rather than for the new MLA format, here is a brief description of that form.

Each idea you borrow and each quotation you include must be attributed to its author(s) in a footnote that appears at the bottom of the appropriate page.* Number your footnotes consecutively throughout the essay (do not start over with "1" on each new page), and place the number in the text to the right of and slightly above the end of the passage, whether it is a direction quotation, a paraphrase, or a summary. Place the corresponding number, indented (five spaces) and slightly raised, before the footnote at the bottom of the page. Double-space each entry, and double-space after each footnote if more than one appears on the same page. See below for sample footnote entries.

Once you have provided a first full reference, subsequent footnotes for that source may only include the author's last name and page number. However, some authorities still require the use of Latin abbreviations such as *ibid.* ("in the same place") and *op. cit.* ("in the work cited"); if your assignment does require these Latin abbreviations, use *ibid.* immediately after the original footnote to substitute for the author's name, the title, and the publication information; add a page number only if it differs from the one in the original footnote. Use *op. cit.* with the author's name to substitute for the title in later references.

First reference	[5]Barbara Tuchman, *A Distant Mirror: The Calamitous Fourteenth Century* (New York: Knopf, 1978), p. 77.
Next footnote	[6]*Ibid.*, p. 82.
Later reference	[12]Tuchman, *op. cit.*, p. 120.

III. APA STYLE

The American Psychological Association (APA) recommends a documentation style for research papers in the social sciences. Your instructors in psychology

---

* Some writing situations permit the use of endnotes, a list of your footnotes that appears following the essay or report. Consult your teacher or the person (or publication) for whom you are writing to see if endnotes are permissible or even preferred.

and sociology classes, for example, may prefer that you use APA form when you write essays for them.

The APA style is similar to the MLA style in that it calls for parenthetical documentation within the essay itself, although the information cited in the parentheses differs slightly from that presented according to the MLA format. For example, you will note that in APA style the date of publication follows the author's last name and precedes the page number in the parentheses. Another important difference concerns capitalization of titles: in MLA style, all important words are capitalized, but in the APA style, only the first word and any words appearing after a colon are capitalized. And instead of a "Works Cited" page, APA style uses a "References" list at the end of the essay.*

APA Citations In Your Essay

Here are some guidelines for using the APA parenthetical form within your paper:

1. If you use a source by one author, place the author's name, the date of publication, and the page number in a parentheses right after the quoted, paraphrased, or summarized material. Note that in APA style, you use commas between the items in the parentheses, and you do include the "p." abbreviation for page (these are omitted in MLA style). The entire parentheses goes before the end punctuation of your sentence.

Example   One crucial step in developing a so-called "deviant" personality may, in fact, be the experience of being caught in some act and consequently being publicly labeled as a deviant (Becker, 1963, p. 31).

2. If you use a source by one author and give credit to that author by name within your paper, you need only give the date and the page number. Note that the publication date can follow directly after the name of the author.

Example   According to Green (1988), gang members from upper-class families are rarely convicted for their crimes and almost never labeled as delinquent (p. 101).

3. If you are citing a work with more than one author, list all last names in the first reference; in subsequent references, use only the first author's last name and "*et al.*" (which means "all the rest").

---

* If you wish a more detailed description of the APA style, you might order a copy of the *Publication Manual of the American Psychological Association,* 3rd ed. (Washington: Psychological Association. 1983).

Example First reference: After divorce, men's standard of living generally rises some 75% whereas women's falls to approximately 25% of what it once was (Bird, Gordon, and Smith, 1989, p. 203).

Subsequent references: Almost half of all the poor households in America today are headed by single women, most of whom are supporting a number of children (Bird *et al.,* 1989, p. 285).

4. If you cite a work that has a corporate author, cite the group responsible for producing the work.

Example In contrast, the State Highway Research Commission (1989) argues, "The return to the sixty-five-mile-an-hour speed limit on some of our state's highways has resulted in an increase in traffic fatalities" (p. 3).

COMPILING A LIST OF REFERENCES

If you are using the APA style, at the end of your essay you should include a page of References—a formal listing of the sources you cited in your essay. Arrange the entries alphabetically by the authors' last names; if there are two or more works by one author, list them chronologically, beginning with the earliest publication date. If an author published two or more works in the same year, the first reference is designated *a,* the second *b,* and so on (Feinstein 1989a, Feinstein 1989b).

Remember that in APA style, you underline books and journals but you do not put the names of articles in quotation marks. While you do capitalize the major words in the title of magazine and periodicals, you do not capitalize any letters in the titles of books or articles except that one which begins the first word in each title and the first letter of any word following a colon. Study the form of the samples given below.

SAMPLE ENTRIES: APA STYLE

Books

- Book with one author

Baars, Bernard J. (1986). *The cognitive revolution in psychology.* New York: Guilford Press.

- Book with two or more authors

Garrison, Karl Claudins, & Force, Dewey G., Jr., (1965). *The psychology of exceptional children.* New York: Ronald Press.

• Books by one author published in the same year

Hall, Sarah L. (1980a). *Attention deficit disorder.* Denver: Bald Mountain Press.

Hall, Sarah L. (1980b). *Taming your adolescent.* Detroit: Morrison Books.

• Book with an editor

Bornstein, Marc H. (Ed.) (1980). *Comparative methods in psychology.* Hillsdale, NJ: L. Erlbaum Associates.

• Selection or chapter from collection with an editor

Newcomb, T. M. (1958). Attitude development as a function of reference groups: The Bennington study. In E. Maccoby, T. M. Newcomb, & E. L. Hartley (Eds.), *Readings in social psychology* (3rd. ed.). New York: Holt, Rinehart and Winston.

• A book with a corporate author

Population Reference Bureau. (1985). *1985 world population data.* Washington, DC: U. S. Government Printing Office.

Articles

• An article in a magazine

Langer, Ellen T. (1989, May). The mindset of health. *Psychology Today,* 48-41.

• An article in a periodical

Nyden, P. W. (1985). Democratizing organizations: A case study of a union reform movement. *American Journal of Sociology, 90,* 1119–1203.

(Note that when a volume number appears, it is also underlined.)

• An article in a newspaper

Noble, K. B. (1986, September 1). For ex-Hormel workers, no forgive and forget. *New York Times,* p. A5.

Interviews

• A published interview

Backus, Ralph. (1985). [Interview with Lorena Smith.] In Frank Reagon (Ed.). *Today's sociology studies* (pp. 32–45). Washington: Scientific Library.

• An unpublished interview

Bear, Flo. [Personal interview.] 10 June 1989.

USING SUPPLEMENTARY NOTES

Sometimes when writers of research papers wish to give their readers additional information about their topic or about a particular piece of source material, they include *supplementary notes.* If you are using the MLA or APA format, these notes should be indicated by using a raised number in your text (The study seemed incomplete at the time of its publication.[2]); the explanations appear on a page called "Notes" that follows the end of your essay. If you are using traditional footnote form, simply include the supplementary notes in your list of footnotes at the bottom of the page or in the list of endnotes following your essay's conclusion.

Supplementary notes can offer a wide variety of additional information.

Examples

[1] For a different interpretation of this imagery, see Robert Spiller, *Literary History of the United States* (New York: Macmillian, 1953), 1021.

[2] Simon and Brown have also contributed to this area of investigation. For a description of their results, see *Report on the Star Wars Project* (Chicago: Indigo, 1985), 98–102.

[3] It is important to note here that Brown's study followed Smith's by at least six months.

[4] Later in his report Carducci himself contradicts his earlier evaluation by saying, "Our experiment was contaminated from the beginning" (319).

Don't, of course, overdo supplementary notes; use them only when you think the additional information would be truly valuable to your readers. Obviously, information critical to your essay's points should go in the appropriate body paragraphs.

Sample Student Paper Using MLA Style

The "problem-solving" assignment that resulted in this paper asked students to select a current controversy in a professional or personal area of interest and research possible solutions. They were then to report on their findings: was there a feasible answer to a particular problem? If not, why not?

The student-writer of this paper is, as she indicates in her introduction, both fascinated and repelled by boxing. At first, she wanted to write a paper banning boxing entirely, but, after some thought, she decided to research the most-often suggested reforms. Firmly convinced that the thesis of her paper would call *for* the reforms, she was amazed to discover, after some weeks in the library, that her evidence was mounting *against* adopting the reforms. Consequently, she wrote a rather controversial essay to support a position only discovered after her research. As you read her essay, ask yourself how effectively she uses supporting evidence to back up her analysis. Where might she have used other sources to support her claims? Other kinds of evidence? Do you find her essay convincing or not? Why?

The Case Against Boxing Reforms

For years I've been one of the millions of people who a half-dozen times a year witness the brutality and savagery of a sport whose principal purpose is to incapacitate or maim the opponent: boxing. Although every bit of sense I have tells me I shouldn't approve of this demoralizing contest, some instinctive appeal urges me to sit through the fifteen rounds of bashing blows and paralyzing punches. Yes, I was at television's ringside in 1971 when the hammering left hook of defending heavyweight champion Joe Frazier sent the once-champ Muhammad Ali to the canvas in the fourteenth round to clinch a unanimous decision over the no-longer skipping and dancing Ali, in what the whole world referred to as "The Fight." I witnessed the bout between former champion Larry Holmes and his courageous, although inept, challenger Randall "Tex" Cobb, in what proved to be a massacre of the worst sort. And then there was the knock out (and eventual death) of twenty-three-year-old Duk Koo Kim after a thirty-nine blow bombardment from Boom Boom Mancini in the fourteenth round of his challenge for the WBA championship. Indeed, I saw all of these. I cheered. I cringed. I grieved.

Since the death of Kim many prominent people have called for the banning of professional boxing, including sports authorities such as announcer Howard Cosell and sports writer George Vecsey of *The New York Times* ("Abolish Boxing?" 1528). Such powerful organizations as the American Medical Association have called for an end to the sport (Leershen and Katz 67).[1] But cooler heads have pointed out the uselessness of demanding the extinction of one of the world's oldest and most popular sports; instead, they have offered a series of proposals to reduce the number of boxing fatalities caused by head injuries (Axthelm 60). Those proposals most often suggested include changing the weight of gloves, using protective headgear, and requiring rigorous medical tests before and after each match. But while such reforms sound beneficial, they will not, unfortunately, significantly reduce the number of boxing deaths; consequently, they would only be an unnecessary and expensive burden on the sport.

Perhaps the most widely voiced proposal calls for an increase in the padding of the gloves. Back in the early 1960s when the deaths of Benny Paret and Davey Moore, among others, raised questions about glove reform, boxers were fighting with six-ounce gloves. After many deaths occurred while fighters were using this glove, the New York State Athletic Commission set down a new rule for the use of a more heavily padded, eight-ounce glove ("Ring Safety" 16). At the time, however, many people associated with the sport agreed that the eight-ounce glove was actually more dangerous because the increase in weight made the glove a heavier weapon, and because the boxer's hands would be better protected, the fighters would be apt to strike with more force

Supporting study

Second reform:
headgear

Supporting
examples

Third reform:
medical exams
and tests

Supporting
examples

Testimony from
medical authority

Supporting fact

Writer reassesses
the problem

Supporting studies

Testimony

("Ring Safety" 18). Since then, boxers have fought with various glove weights ranging from six-ounce to fourteen-ounce, and the number of ring deaths has continued with no significant change (Goldman 100). Because fatal head injuries occur as often with light gloves as heavier ones, imposing larger gloves is not the solution for minimizing the number of unfortunate deaths.

A second proposal to reduce the number of fatal injuries calls for the use of protective headgear. But because the record shows that deadly head injuries occur despite the use of head protection, this promising solution takes its own fatal blow. To cite a few cases: in the fight that resulted in the 1960 death of Charlie Mohr, a middleweight from the University of Wisconsin, and the subsequent banning of collegiate boxing, the fighters were wearing protective headpieces (Boyle and Ames 54). In 1982 twenty-two-year-old Benjamin Davis died after a fight during which he was required to wear headgear; Charles Love died wearing headgear at the hands of Daryl Stitch that same year (Deford 70). The list goes on. There just isn't any significant correlation between the use of protective headgear and the reduction of fatal head injuries.

A third proposal, raised more recently, demands more rigorous medical exams before and after matches. A prefight exam, for instance, would include an EEG and a CAT scan in order to trace changes or abnormalities in the brain that might mean vulnerability to a blow to the head. But do these exams really help identify potential problems? Both Benny Peret and Davey Moore had taken and passed a prefight EEG examination (Boyle and Ames 55); similarly, Koo had no diagnosed medical vulnerabilities ("Abolish Boxing?" 1528). Even the Council on Scientific Affairs of the American Medical Association admits that there exists no reliable test that could identify boxers who are at risk of sudden death ("Brain Injury in Boxers" 256). In addition to the tests' lack of accuracy, one must also consider the high costs of CAT scans and full neurological exams in terms of a fighter's time and money. While the top prizewinners might be able to afford the expensive tests, could fighters just starting out afford the CAT scan that carries a $300 price tag for each use (Boyle and Ames 67)? Once again, the proposed extensive exams don't seem the answer to the problem.

Before requiring new equipment or expensive tests, perhaps one needs to take a closer look at the extent of the problem itself. Boxing does occasionally result in death, but the fatality rate is actually not as bad as in other high risk sports. In studies reported in *Sporting News* and substantiated by two other studies described in the *Journal of the American Medical Association,* popular sports such as mountaineering, sky diving, hang gliding, horse racing, and even scuba diving had higher fatality rates for a given period ("Brain Injury" 255).[2] Dr. Bennet Derby of the New York State Boxing Commission has also pointed out that while football and ice hockey also produce head injuries, they have escaped the furor directed at boxing (Leershen and Katz 67). Moreover, according to

Supporting
statistics

Ring Magazine, 439 deaths have occurred between 1918 and 1982 among amateur and professional boxers worldwide (Callahan 84).[3] This is fewer than seven deaths per year for sixty-four years. Even one death from boxing is deplorable, of course—but when one considers the hundreds of thousands of young men, participating in a sport found virtually in every country on the globe, seven deaths per year seems relatively small, especially compared to the number of annual swimming accidents, for instance.

Conclusion:
admission of
boxing as violent
sport but rejection
of current reform
proposals

Obviously, no one wants to see a sporting event result in a death. And boxing *is* violent and it *is* dangerous—that's the nature of the sport. Perhaps Sugar Ray Robinson said it best at the 1947 inquest after the death of Jimmy Doyle. When the judge asked Robinson if he knew Doyle was in trouble, Robinson replied softly, "Sir, getting people in trouble is my business" (qtd. in Callahan 84). If the critics believe a sport that demands "getting people in trouble" is immoral, they should work for its abolition on ethical grounds. But the flurry of recently proposed reforms that have followed the latest tragedy in the ring will do nothing to stop the number of fatalities. If the sport of boxing continues, perhaps we must resign ourselves to looking at the tragic deaths as the few, unfortunate accidents they really are.

Notes

[1] Interestingly, the critics themselves don't always agree on *why* boxing should be banned. Popular columnist George Will, for example, called for an end to the sport to "protect the audience from a brutalizing spectacle," rather than to save the fighters (qtd. in "Abolish Boxing?" 1528).

[2] The sporting fatalities per 1,000 participants were as follows: boxing: 0.13; mountaineering: 5.1; hang gliding: 5.6; sky diving: 12.3; horse racing: 12.8; and scuba diving: 1.1 ("Brain Injury" 255).

[3] Figures vary slightly as authorities disagree on whether some deaths were the result of the boxing matches. Deford, for example, cites 353 deaths since 1945 (70).

Works Cited

"Abolish Boxing?" *National Review* 10 Dec. 1982: 1528–29.

Axthelm, Pete. "Don't Count Boxing Out." *Newsweek* 20 Dec. 1982: 60.

Boyle, Robert and Wilmur Ames. "Too Many Punches, Too Little Concern." *Sports Illustrated* 11 April 1983: 44–67.

Callahan, Tom. "Boxing Shadows." *Time* 29 Nov. 1982: 84–86.

Council on Scientific Affairs. "Brain Injury in Boxers." *Journal of the American Medical Association* 14 Jan. 1983: 254–57.

Deford, Frank. "An Encounter to Last an Eternity." *Sports Illustrated* 11 April 1983: 70–82.

Goldman, Herbert G., ed. *The Ring, 1982 Record Book and Boxing Encyclopedia.* New York: Ring, 1982.

Leershen, Charles and Susan Katz. "The AMA Tries to KO Boxing." *Newsweek* 17 Dec. 1984: 67.

"The Search for Ring Safety." *Sports Illustrated.* 15 April 1963: 16–18.

PART
THREE

A Concise
Handbook

In this section you will learn to recognize and correct the most common errors in grammar, punctuation, and mechanics. Each error will be explained as simply as possible, with a minimum of technical language. Beside each rule you will find the mark most teachers use to indicate that error in your essays.

13

Major Errors in Grammar

ERRORS WITH VERBS

FAULTY AGREEMENT   S-V AGR

Make your verb agree in number with its subject; a singular subject takes a singular verb, and a plural subject takes a plural verb.

Incorrect *Lester Peabody,* principal of the Kung Fu School of Grammar, *don't* agree that gum chewing should be banned in the classroom.

Correct *Lester Peabody,* principal of the Kung Fu School of Grammar, *doesn't* agree that gum chewing should be banned in the classroom.

Incorrect The *actions* of the new Senator *hasn't* been consistent with his campaign promises.

Correct The *actions* of the new Senator *haven't* been consistent with his campaign promises.

A compound subject takes a plural verb, unless the subject denotes a single person or a single unit.

Examples *Bean sprouts* and *tofu are* dishes Jim Bob won't consider eating. ["Bean Sprouts" and "tofu" are two elements in a compound subject; therefore, use a plural verb.]

The *winner* and new *champion refuses* to give up the microphone at the news conference. ["Winner" and "champion" denote a single person; therefore, use a singular verb.]

Listed below are some of the most confusing subject-verb agreement problems:

1. With a collective noun: a singular noun referring to a collection of elements as a unit generally takes a singular verb.

Incorrect   During boring parts of the Transcendental Vegetation lecture, the class often *chant* dirty mantras.

Correct   During boring parts of the Transcendental Vegetation lecture, the class often *chants* dirty mantras.

Incorrect   The *army* of the new nation *want* shoes, bullets, and weekend passes.

Correct   The *army* of the new nation *wants* shoes, bullets, and weekend passes.

However, you sometimes use a plural verb when the collective noun refers to its members as parts rather than to the group as a unit.

Incorrect   After Sticky Fingers O'Hoolihan visited the Queen, a *number of the crown jewels was* missing.

Correct   After Sticky Fingers O'Hoolihan visited the Queen, a *number of the crown jewels were* missing.

Incorrect   A small *group of the actors has* forgotten their lines.

Correct   A small *group of the actors have* forgotten their lines.

2. With a relative pronoun ("that," "which," "who") used as a subject: the verb agrees with its antecedent.

Incorrect   The boss rejected a shipment of *shirts* that *was* torn.

Correct   The boss rejected a shipment of *shirts* that *were* torn.

3. With "each," "none," "everyone," "neither" as the subject: use a singular verb even when followed by a plural construction.

Incorrect   *Each* of the children *think* Mom and Dad are automatic teller machines.

Correct   *Each* of the children *thinks* Mom and Dad are automatic teller machines.

Incorrect   All the students saw the teacher pull out his hair, but *none know* why he did it.

Correct   All the students saw the teacher pull out his hair, but *none knows* why he did it.

Incorrect	*Neither have* a dime left by the second of the month.
Correct	*Neither has* a dime left by the second of the month.

4. With "either . . . or," "neither . . . nor": the verb agrees with the nearer item.

Incorrect	Neither rain nor dogs nor *gloom of night keep* the mailman from delivering bills.
Correct	Neither rain nor dogs or *gloom of night keeps* the mailman from delivering bills.
Incorrect	Either Betty or her *neighbors is* hosting a come-as-you-are break-fast.
Correct	Either Betty or her *neighbors are* hosting a come-as-you-are break-fast.

5. With "here is (are)," "there is (are)": the verb agrees with the number indicated by the subject following the verb.

Incorrect	*There is* only two good *reasons* for missing this law class: death and jury duty.
Correct	*There are* only two good *reasons* for missing this law class: death and jury duty.
Incorrect	To help you do your shopping quickly, Mr. Scrooge, *here are* a *list* of gifts under a dollar.
Correct	To help you do your shopping quickly, Mr. Scrooge, *here is* a *list* of gifts under a dollar.

6. With plural nouns intervening between subject and verb: the verb still agrees with the subject.

Incorrect	The *jungle,* with its poisonous plants, wild animals, and biting in-sects, *make* Herman long for the sidewalks of Topeka.
Correct	The *jungle,* with its poisonous plants, wild animals, and biting in-sects, *makes* Herman long for the sidewalks of Topeka.

7. With nouns plural in form but singular in meaning: a singular verb is usually correct.

Examples	*News travels* slowly if it comes through the post office.
	Charades is the exhibitionist's game of choice.
	Politics is often the rich person's hobby.

SUBJUNCTIVE   V SUB

When you make a wish or a statement that is contrary to fact, use the subjunctive verb form "were."

Incorrect   My mother always wished she *was* queen so she could levy a tax on men who cursed.

Correct   My mother always wished she *were* queen so she could levy a tax on men who cursed. [This expresses a wish.]

Incorrect   If "Fightin' Henry" *was* a foot taller and thirty pounds heavier, we would all be in trouble.

Correct   If "Fightin' Henry" *were* a foot taller and thirty pounds heavier, we would all be in trouble. [This proposes a statement contrary to fact.]

TENSE SHIFT   T

In most cases the first verb in a sentence establishes the tense of any later verb. Keep your verbs within the same time frame.

Incorrect   Big Joe *saw* the police car coming up behind, so he *turns* into the next alley.

Correct   Big Joe *saw* the police car coming up behind, so he *turned* into the next alley.

Incorrect   Horace *uses* an artificial sweetener in his coffee all day, so he *felt* a pizza and a hot-fudge sundae were fine for dinner.

Correct   Horace *uses* an artificial sweetener in his coffee all day, so he *feels* a pizza and a hot-fudge sundae are fine for dinner.

Incorrect   Rex the Wonder Horse *was* obviously very smart because he *taps* out the telephone numbers of the stars with his hoof.

Correct   Rex the Wonder Horse *was* obviously very smart because he *tapped* out the telephone numbers of the stars with his hoof.

SPLIT INFINITIVE   SP I

Many authorities insist that you never separate *to* from its verb; today, however, some grammarians allow the split infinitive except in the most formal kinds of writing. Nevertheless, because it offends some readers, it is probably best to avoid the construction unless clarity or emphasis is clearly served by its use.

Traditional   A swift kick is needed to *start* the machine properly.

Untraditional   A swift kick is needed *to* properly *start* the machine.

| Traditional | The teacher wanted Lori *to communicate* her ideas clearly. |
| Untraditional | The teacher wanted Lori *to* clearly *communicate* her ideas. |

DOUBLE NEGATIVES D NEG

Don't use a negative verb and a negative qualifier together.

Incorrect	I *can't hardly* wait until Jim Bob gets his jaw out of traction, so I can challenge him to a bubble gum blowing contest again.
Incorrect	I *can hardly* wait until Jim Bob gets his jaw out of traction, so I can challenge him to a bubble gum blowing contest again.
Incorrect	Even when he flew his helicopter upside-down over her house, she *wouldn't scarcely* look at him.
Correct	Even when he flew his helicopter upside-down over her house, she *would scarcely* look at him.

PASSIVE VOICE PASS

For the most part, your prose style will improve if you choose strong, active voice verbs over wordy or unclear passive constructions.

Wordy passive construction	It is obvious that dirty words are being written on the rest room walls by the company's junior executives.
Strong active verb	The company's junior executives write dirty words on the rest room walls.
Wordy passive construction	After the successful nose-transplant operation, the surgeon and his staff were given a round of applause by the malpractice lawyers in attendance.
Strong active verb	After the successful nose-transplant operation, the malpractice lawyers in attendance applauded the surgeon and his staff.
Unclear passive construction	Much protest is being voiced over the new Z.A.P. bomb. [Who is protesting?]
Strong active verb	Members of the Fuse Lighters Association are protesting the new Z.A.P. bomb.

(For more examples of active and passive voice verbs, see pp. 105–106.)

PRACTICING WHAT YOU'VE LEARNED

Errors with Verbs

Correct the sentences below.

1. None of the students know that both mystery writer Agatha Christie and inventor Thomas Edison was dyslexic.
2. For years Johnny Appleseed was considered a mythical figure by many scholars, but now two local historians, the authors of a well-known book, argues he was a real person named John Chapman.
3. Either the cocker spaniel or the poodle hold the honor of being the most popular breed of dog in the United States, say the American Kennel Club.
4. The team from Houston College are considering switching from basketball to volleyball because passing athletics are required for graduation.
5. Observation of Cuban land crabs show they can run faster than horses.
6. The folklore professor's articles on modern horror stories reminds me of the tale often referred to as "The Hook."
7. In the story of the hook, a couple of teenagers are parked on a lonely road, but neither realize that a crazy man with a hook instead of an arm was lurking nearby.
8. Each of us have heard how the couple decides to quickly drive away and later discover that there is a hook hanging on the car door.
9. Neither Clyde nor his brothers can hardly believe that such stories are being collected by university anthropologists, who refers to them as "urban legends."
10. Tammy wishes she was teaching the class on urban legends, so she could tell the story of the window viper.

ERRORS WITH NOUNS   N

POSSESSIVE WITH "-ING" NOUNS

When the emphasis is on the action, use the possessive pronoun plus the "-ing" noun.

Example   He hated *my* singing around the house, so I made him live in the garage. [The emphasis is on *singing.*]

When the emphasis is not on the action, you may use a noun or pronoun plus the "-ing" noun.

Example   He hated *me* singing around the house, so I made him live in the garage. [The emphasis is on the person singing—me—not the action; he might have liked someone else singing.]

MISUSE OF NOUNS AS ADJECTIVES

Some nouns may be used as adjectives modifying other nouns: "horse show," "movie star," "theater seats." But some nouns used as adjectives sound awkward or like jargon. To avoid such awkwardness, you may need to change the noun to an appropriate adjective or reword the sentence.

Awkward   The group decided to work on local *environment* problems.

Better   The group decided to work on local *environmental* problems.

Jargon   The executive began a *cost estimation comparison study* of the two products.

Better   The executive began to *study a comparison* of the two products' costs.

(For more information on ridding your prose of jargon, see pp. 131–132.)

ERRORS WITH PRONOUNS

FAULTY AGREEMENT   P AGR

A pronoun should agree in number and gender with its antecedent (that is, the word the pronoun stands for).

Incorrect   To get a temperamental *actress* to sign a contract, the director would lock *them* in their dressing room.

Correct   To get a temperamental *actress* to sign a contract, the director would lock *her* in her dressing room.

Use the singular pronoun with "everyone," "anyone," and "each."

Incorrect   When the belly dancer asked for a volunteer partner from the audience, *everyone* in the YMCA raised *their* hand.

Correct   When the belly dancer asked for a volunteer partner from the audience, *everyone* in the YMCA raised *his* hand.

Incorrect   *Each* of the new wives decided to keep *their* own name.

Correct   *Each* of the new wives decided to keep *her* own name.

In the past, writers have traditionally used the masculine pronoun "he" when the gender of the antecedent is unknown, as in the following: "If a *spy* refuses to answer questions, *he* should be forced to watch James Bond movies until *he* cracks." Today, however, many authorities prefer the nonsexist "she/he" even though the construction can be awkward when maintained over a stretch of prose. Perhaps the best solution is to use the impersonal "one" when possible or simply rewrite the sentence in the plural: "If *spies* refuse to answer questions, *they* should be forced to watch James Bond movies until *they* crack." (For more examples, see pp. 134–135.)

VAGUE REFERENCE   REF

Your pronoun references should be clear.

Vague	If the trained seal won't eat its dinner, throw *it* into the lion's cage. [What goes into the lion's cage?]
Clear	If the trained seal won't eat its dinner, throw *the food* into the lion's cage.
Vague	After the dog bit Harry, he raised such a fuss at the police station that the sergeant finally had *him* impounded. [Who was impounded?]
Clear	After being bitten, Harry raised such a fuss at the police station that the sergeant finally had the *dog* impounded.

Sometimes you must add a word or rewrite the sentence to make the pronoun reference clear:

Vague	I'm a lab instructor in the biology department and am also taking a composition course. *This* has always been difficult for me. [What is difficult?]
Clear	I'm a lab instructor in the biology department and am also taking composition, a *course* that has always been difficult for me.
Also clear	I'm a lab instructor in the biology department and am also taking a composition course. Being a teacher and a student at the same time is difficult for me.

SHIFT IN PRONOUNS   P SH

Be consistent in your use of pronouns; don't shift from one person to another.

Incorrect	One shouldn't eat pudding with your fingers.
Correct	One shouldn't eat pudding with one's fingers.
Correct	You shouldn't eat pudding with your fingers.

Incorrect   *We* left-handed people are at a disadvantage because most of the time *you* can't rent left-handed golf clubs or bowling balls.

Correct   *We* left-handed people are at a disadvantage because most of the time *we* can't rent left-handed golf clubs or bowling balls.

(For additional examples, see p. 112.)

INCORRECT CASE   Ca

The case of a pronoun is determined by its function. If the pronoun is a subject, use the nominative case: "I," "he," "she," "we," "they"; if the pronoun is an object, use the objective case: "me," "him," "her," "us," "them." To check your usage, all you need to do in most cases is isolate the pronoun in the manner shown here and see if it makes sense alone.

Incorrect   Give the treasure map to Frankie and *I*.

Isolated   Give the treasure map to *I*.

Correct   Give the treasure map to Frankie and *me*.

Incorrect   Bertram and *her* suspect that the moon is hollow.

Isolated   *Her* suspects that the moon is hollow.

Correct   Bertram and *she* suspect that the moon is hollow.

In other cases, to determine the correct pronoun, you will need to add implied but unstated sentence elements:

Examples   Mother always liked Dickie more than *me*. [Mother liked Dickie more than *she liked* me.]
             She is younger than *I* by three days. [She is younger than I *am* by three days.]

To solve the confusing *who/whom* pronoun problem, first determine the case of the pronoun in its own clause in each sentence.

1. If the pronoun is the subject of a clause, use "who" or "whoever."

Examples   I don't know *who* spread the peanut butter on my English paper. ["Who" is the subject of the verb "spread" in the clause "who spread the peanut butter on my English paper."]

             Rachel is a librarian who only likes books with pictures. ["Who" is the subject of the verb "likes" in the clause "who only likes books with pictures."]

He will sell secrets to *whoever* offers the largest sum of money. ["Whoever" is the subject of the verb "offers" in the clause "whoever offers the largest sum of money."]

2. If the pronoun is the object of a verb, use "whom" or "whomever."

Examples   *Whom* am I kicking? ["Whom" is the direct object of the verb "kicking."]

Sid is a man *whom* I distrust. ["Whom" is the direct object of the verb "distrust."]

Whomever he kicked will probably be angry.

["Whomever" is the direct object of the verb "kicked."]

3. If the pronoun occurs as the object of a preposition, use "whom," especially when the preposition immediately precedes the pronoun.

Examples   *With whom* am I speaking?

To whom does the credit belong for spreading peanut butter on my English paper?

Do not ask *for whom* the bell tolls.

PRACTICING WHAT YOU'VE LEARNED

Errors with Nouns and Pronouns

Correct the sentences below. Skip any correct sentences.

1. The executive knew she was in trouble when her salary underwent a [modification reduction] adjustment of fifty percent.
2. Of whom did Oscar Wilde once say, "He hasn't a single redeeming vice"?
3. It was a surprise to both Mary and I to learn that Switzerland didn't give women the right to vote until 1971.
4. Each of the young women in the Family Life class decided not to marry after they read that couples today have 2.3 children.
5. Jim Bob explained to Frankie that the best way for him to avoid his recurring nosebleeds was to stay out of his cousin's marital arguments.
6. Those of us who had had the flu agreed that one can always get your doctor to return your call quicker if you get in the shower.

7. The stranger gave the free movie tickets to Louise and I after he saw
   people standing in line to leave the theater.

8. The personnel director told each of the employees, most of who opposed him, to signify their "no" vote by saying, "I resign."

9. Clarence and he have an uncle who is so mean he writes the name of
   the murderer on the first page of mystery novels that are passed
   around the family.

10. The first movie to gross over one million dollars was *Tarzan of the
    Apes* (1932) starring Johnny Weismuller, a former Olympic star who
    became an actor. This didn't happen often in the movie industry at
    that time.

ERRORS WITH ADVERBS AND ADJECTIVES

INCORRECT USAGE   ADV ADJ

Incorrect use of adverbs and adjectives often occurs when you confuse the two
modifiers. Adverbs qualify the meaning of verbs, adjectives, and other adverbs;
they frequently end in "-ly," and they often answer the question "how?"

Incorrect   After Kay argued with the mechanic, her car began running *bad.*

Correct   After Kay argued with the mechanic, her car began running *badly.*

Adjectives, on the other hand, describe or qualify the meanings of nouns
only.

Example   The *angry* mechanic neglected to put oil into Kay's car.

One of the most confusing pairs of modifiers is "well" and "good." We often
use "good" as an adjective modifying a noun and "well" as an adverb modifying a
verb.

Examples   *A Sap's Fables* is a *good* book for children, although it is not *well*
organized.

Bubba was such a *good* liar his wife had to call in the children at
suppertime.

After eating the Rocky Mountain oysters, Susie did not feel *well.*

Did you do *well* on your math test?

If you cannot determine whether a word is an adverb or adjective, consult
your dictionary.

FAULTY COMPARISON   COMP

When you compare two elements to a higher or lower degree, you often add "-er" or "-r" to the adjective.

Incorrect   Of the two sisters, Sarah is the *loudest.*

Correct   Of the two sisters, Sarah is the *louder.*

When you compare more than two elements, you often add "-est" to the adjective.

Example   Sarah is the loudest of the four children in the family.

Other adjectives use the words "more," "most," "less," and "least" to indicate comparison.

Examples   Bela Lugosi is *more* handsome than Lon Chaney but *less* handsome than Vincent Price.

Boris Karloff is the *most* handsome, and Christopher Lee is the *least* handsome of all the horror film stars.

ERRORS IN MODIFYING PHRASES

DANGLING MODIFIERS   DM

A modifying—or descriptive—phrase must have a logical relationship to some specific words in the sentence. When those words are omitted, the phrase "dangles" without anything to modify. Dangling modifiers frequently occur at the beginnings of sentences and often may be corrected by adding the proper subjects to the main clauses.

Dangling   Not knowing how to swim, buying scuba gear was foolish.

Correct   Not knowing how to swim, *we* decided that buying scuba gear was foolish.

Dangling   After seeing a number of flying saucers, pinching the waitress seemed a bad idea.

Correct   After seeing a number of flying saucers, *Jim Bob* admitted that pinching the waitress had been a bad idea.

(For additional examples, see pp. 100–101.)

MISPLACED MODIFIERS   MM

When modifying words, phrases, or clauses are not placed near the word they describe, confusion or unintentional humor often results.

Misplaced   Teddy swatted the fly still dressed in his pajamas.

Correct   Still dressed in his pajamas, Teddy swatted the fly.

Misplaced   The cook prepared turkey tartu for his guests made primarily of spinach.

Correct   The cook prepared turkey tartu, made primarily of spinach, for his guests.

(For additional examples, see pp. 99–100.)

PRACTICING WHAT YOU'VE LEARNED

Errors with Adverbs, Adjectives, and Modifying Phrases

Correct the errors in the sentences below.

1. Squeezing the can, it was hard to tell if the tomatoes were ripe.
2. While liver is probably the worse food in the world, buttermilk is hardly more better.
3. After the optometrist pulled her eye tooth, Hortense didn't behave very (good/well) in the waiting room.
4. He didn't think the car would make it over the mountains, being eight years old.
5. The James brothers decided to have their cattle engraved instead of branded, since they were so rich.
6. In the Death Valley Swim Meet, Maria could use the back stroke or side stroke in the first race, whichever was best for her.
7. I didn't do (good/well) on my nature project because my bonsai sequoia tree grew real bad in its small container.
8. After boarding Hard Luck Airways, the meals we were offered convinced us to return by ship.
9. I've read that a number of modern sailors, like Thor Heyerdahl, have sailed primitive vessels across the ocean in a book from the public library.
10. We are enclosing with this letter the new telephone number for notifying the fire department of any fires that may be attached to your telephone.

ERRORS IN SENTENCES

FRAGMENTS   FRAG

A complete sentence must contain a subject and a verb. A fragment is an incomplete sentence; it is often a participial phrase or dependent clause that belongs to the preceding sentence. To check for fragments, try reading your prose, one sentence at a time, starting at the *end* of your essay. If you find a "sentence" that makes no sense alone, it's probably a fragment that should either be rewritten or connected to another sentence.

Incorrect   Bubba's parents refuse to send him to a psychiatrist. Although they both know he eats shoelaces and light bulbs.

Correct   Bubba's parents refuse to send him to a psychiatrist although they both know he eats shoelaces and light bulbs.

Incorrect   This tape recording of the symphony's latest concert is so clear you can hear every sound. Including the coughs and whispers of the audience.

Correct   This tape recording of the symphony's latest concert is so clear you can hear every sound, including the coughs and whispers of the audience.

Incorrect   At Liz's most recent wedding, the photographer used an instant camera. Because her marriages break up so fast.

Correct   At Liz's most recent wedding, the photographer used an instant camera because her marriages break up so fast.

You can also try this test to see if a group of words is a fragment: say the phrase "It is true that" in front of the words in question; a complete sentence will still make sense, but a fragment won't.

Example   At Liz's most recent wedding, the photographer used an instant camera. Because her marriages break up so fast.

Which is a fragment?

It is true that *at Liz's most recent wedding the photographer used an instant camera.* [This sentence makes sense, so there's no fragment.]

It is true that *because her marriages break up so fast.* [Yes, this is a fragment.]

COMMA SPLICE   CS

A comma splice occurs when two sentences are linked with a comma. To correct this error, you can (1) separate the two sentences with a period, (2) separate the two sentences with a semicolon, (3) insert a coordinating conjunction (such as "and," "or," "nor," "so," "yet") after the comma, (4) subordinate one clause.

Incorrect	Grover won a stuffed gila monster at the church raffle, his mother threw it away the next day while he was in school.
Correct	Grover won a stuffed gila monster at the church raffle. His mother threw it away the next day while he was in school.
Correct	Grover won a stuffed gila monster at the church raffle; his mother threw it away the next day while he was in school.
Correct	Grover won a stuffed gila monster at the church raffle, but his mother threw it away the next day while he was in school.
Correct	Although Grover won a stuffed gila monster at the church raffle, his mother threw it away the next day while he was in school.

(For more help on correcting comma splices, see p. 313; coordination and subordination are discussed in detail on pp. 115–117.)

RUN-ON SENTENCE   R-O

Don't run two sentences together without any punctuation. Use a period, a semicolon, a comma plus a coordinating conjunction (if appropriate), or subordinate one clause.

Incorrect	The indicted police chief submitted his resignation the mayor accepted it gratefully.
Correct	The indicted police chief submitted his resignation. The mayor accepted it gratefully.
Correct	The indicted police chief submitted his resignation; the mayor accepted it gratefully.
Correct	The indicted police chief submitted his resignation, and the mayor accepted it gratefully.
Correct	When the indicted police chief submitted his resignation, the mayor accepted it gratefully.

FAULTY PARALLELISM   //

Parallel thoughts should be expressed in similar constructions.

Awkward	Boa constrictors like *to lie* in the sun, *to hang* from limbs, and *swallowing* small animals.
Better	Boa constrictors like *to lie* in the sun, *to hang* from limbs, and *to swallow* small animals.

Awkward	Whether *working* on his greasy car, *fistfighting* at the hamburger joint, or in bed, my brother always kept his hair combed.
Better	Whether *working* on his greasy car, *fistfighting* at the hamburger joint, or *lounging* in bed, my brother always kept his hair combed.

FALSE PREDICATION   PRED

This error occurs when the predicate (that part of the sentence that says something about the subject) doesn't fit properly with the subject. Illogical constructions result.

Incorrect	The meaning of the sermon deals with love. [A "meaning" cannot deal with anything; the author, speaker, or work itself can, however.]
Correct	The sermon deals with love.
Incorrect	Energy is one of the world's biggest problems. ["Energy" itself is not a problem.]
Correct	The lack of fuel for energy is one of the world's biggest problems.
Incorrect	True failure is when you make an error and don't learn anything from it. [Avoid all "is when" and "is where" constructions. The subject does not denote a time, so the predicate is faulty.]
Correct	You have truly failed only when you make an error and don't learn anything from it.
Incorrect	Her first comment after winning the lottery was exciting. [Her comment wasn't exciting; her feeling was.]
Correct	Her first comment after winning the lottery expressed her excitement.

(For other examples of faulty predication, see pp. 101–102.)

MIXED STRUCTURE   MIX S

"Mixed structure" is a catchall term that applies to a variety of sentence construction errors. Usually, the term refers to a sentence in which the writer begins with one kind of structure and then shifts to another in mid-sentence. Such a shift often occurs when the writer is in a hurry, and the mind has already jumped ahead to the next thought.

Confused	By the time one litter of cats is given away seems to bring a new one.
Clear	Giving away one litter of cats seems to tell the mother cat that it's time to produce a new batch.

Confused	The bank robber realized that in his crime spree how very little fun he was having.
Clear	The bank robber realized that he was having very little fun in his crime spree.
Confused	The novel is too confusing for what the author meant.
Clear	The novel is too confused for me to understand what the author meant.
Confused	Children with messages from their parents will be stapled to the bulletin board.
Clear	Children will find messages from their parents stapled to the bulletin board.

(For other examples of mixed structure, see pp. 101–102.)

PRACTICING WHAT YOU'VE LEARNED

Errors in Sentences

Correct the following sentences; skip any that are correct.

1. Mary Lou decided not to eat the alphabet soup the letters spelled out "botulism."
2. An example of his intelligence is when he brought home a twenty-pound block of ice after ice fishing all day.
3. A friend of mine offers this definition of nasty theater critics on opening night, according to him, they're the people who can't wait to stone the first cast.
4. My father told me never to ask people where they're from because if they're from Texas they'll tell you, however, if they're not, don't embarrass them.
5. The mother of the triplets got rid of her headache by following the advice on the aspirin bottle of taking two pills and keep away from children.
6. Americans forget how large the Soviet Union is, for example, they don't realize that it encompasses eleven time zones.
7. The new baby kept the textbook author awake all night. Thus causing her to conclude that people who say they sleep like a baby don't have one in the house.
8. Is it true that Superman could leap tall buildings, run faster than a locomotive, and that bullets would bounce off his skin?

9. People always find the time to complain about how busy they are. Despite the fact that they say they are too busy to stop.

10. According to a study by the Fish and Wildlife Service, Americans' favorite animals are dogs, horses, swans, robins, and butterflies. Whereas their least favorites are cockroaches, mosquitos, rats, wasps, and rattlesnakes.

14

A Concise Guide to Punctuation

Punctuation marks do not exist, as one student recently complained, to make your life miserable. They are used to clarify your written thoughts so that the reader understands your meaning. Just as traffic signs and signals tell a driver to slow down, stop, or go faster or slower, so punctuation is intended to guide the reader through your prose. Look, for example, at the confusion in the sentences below when the necessary punctuation marks are omitted:

Confusing   Has the tiger been fed Bill? [Bill was the tiger's dinner?]

Clear   Has the tiger been fed, Bill?

Confusing   After we had finished raking the dog jumped into the pile of leaves. [Raking the dog?]

Clear   After we had finished raking, the dog jumped into the pile of leaves.

Confusing   The teacher called the students names. [Was the teacher fired for verbally abusing the students?]

Clear   The teacher called the students' names.

Because punctuation helps you communicate clearly with your reader, you should familiarize yourself with the following rules.

THE PERIOD (.)   P

1. Use a period to end a sentence.

Examples   Ralph quit school to go live with the Pygmies in Africa. He returned shortly thereafter.

311

2. Use a period after initials and many abbreviations.

Examples   W. B. Yeats, 12 A.M., Dr., etc., M.A.

3. Only one period is necessary if the sentence ends with an abbreviation.

Examples   The elephant was delivered C.O.D.

To find a good job, you should obtain a B.S. or B.A.

THE QUESTION MARK (?)   P

1. Use a question mark after every direct question.

Examples   May I borrow your galoshes?

Is the sandstorm over now?

2. No question mark is necessary after an indirect question.

Examples   Jean asked why no one makes a paper milk carton that opens without tearing.

Dave wondered how the television detective always found a parking place next to the scene of the crime.

THE EXCLAMATION POINT (!)   P

The exclamation point follows words, phrases, or sentences to show strong feelings.

Examples   Fire! Call the rescue squad!

THE COMMA (,)   P

1. Use a comma to separate two independent clauses[1] joined by a coordinating conjunction. To remember the coordinating conjunctions, think of the acronym FANBOYS: "for," "and," "nor," "but," "or," "yet," and "so." Always use one of the FANBOYS and a comma when you join two independent clauses.

---

[1] An independent clause looks like a complete sentence; it contains a subject and a verb, and it makes sense by itself.

Examples   You can bury your savings in the backyard, *but* don't expect Mother Nature to pay interest.

I'm going home tomorrow, *and* I'm never coming back.

After six weeks Louie's diet was making him feel lonely and depressed, *so* he had a bumper sticker printed that said, "Honk if you love groceries."

Do *not* join two sentences with a comma only; such an error is called a comma splice. Use a comma plus one of the coordinating conjunctions listed previously, a period, a semicolon, or subordination.

Comma splice   Beatrice washes and grooms the chickens, Samantha feeds the spiders.

Correct   Beatrice washes and grooms the chickens, and Samantha feeds the spiders.

Correct   Beatrice washes and grooms the chickens. Samantha feeds the spiders.

Correct   Beatrice washes and grooms the chickens; Samantha feeds the spiders.

Correct   When Beatrice washes and grooms the chickens, Samantha feeds the spiders.

Comma splice   Jack doesn't like double features, he won't go with us to see *Dr. Jekyll and Mr. Hyde.*

Correct   Jack doesn't like double features, so he won't go with us to see *Dr. Jekyll and Mr. Hyde.*

Correct   Jack doesn't like double features. He won't go with us to see *Dr. Jekyll and Mr. Hyde.*

Correct   Jack doesn't like double features; he won't go with us to see *Dr. Jekyll and Mr. Hyde.*

Correct   Because Jack doesn't like double features, he won't go with us to see *Dr. Jekyll and Mr. Hyde.*

(For additional help, see p. 306–307.)

2. Conjunctive adverbs, such as "however," "moreover," "thus," "consequently," and "therefore," are used to show continuity and are frequently set off by commas when they appear in mid-sentence.

Examples   She soon discovered, *however,* that he had stolen her monogrammed towels in addition to her pet avocado plant.

She felt, *consequently,* that he was not trustworthy.

When a conjunctive adverb occurs at the beginning of a sentence, it may be followed by a comma, especially if a pause is intended. If no pause is intended, you may omit the comma, but inserting the comma is never wrong.

Examples   *Thus,* she resolved never to speak to him again.
Thus she resolved never to speak to him again.

Therefore, he resolved never to speak to her again.
Therefore he resolved never to speak to her again.

Please note that "however" can never, never be used as a coordinating conjunction joining two independent clauses. Incorrect use of "however" most often results in a comma splice.

Comma splice   The police arrested the thief, *however,* they had to release him because the plant wouldn't talk.

Correct   The police arrested the thief; *however,* they had to release him because the plant wouldn't talk.

Also correct   The police arrested the thief. *However,* they had to release him because the plant wouldn't talk.

3. Set off with a comma an introductory phrase or clause.

Examples   After we had finished our laundry, we discovered one sock was missing.

According to the owner of the laundromat, customers have conflicting theories about missing laundry.

For example, one man claims his socks make a break for freedom when no one is watching the dryers.

4. Set off nonessential phrases and clauses. If the information can be omitted without changing the meaning of the main clause, then the phrase or clause is nonessential. Do *not* set off clauses or phrases that are essential to the meaning of the main clause.

Essential   He reminds me of my friend *who was always confused by a discussion of anything more complicated than a phillips screwdriver.* [The "who" clause is essential to explain which friend.]

The storm *that destroyed Mr. Peartree's outhouse* left him speechless with anger. [The "that" clause is essential to explain why the storm angered Mr. Peartree.]

The movie *showing now at the Ritz* is very obscene and very popular. [The participial phrase is essential to identify the movie.]

Nonessential Joe Medusa, *who won the jalapeno-eating contest last year,* is this year's champion cow-chip tosser. [The 'who" clause is nonessential because it only supplies additional information to the main clause.]

Black widow spiders, *which eat their spouses after mating,* are easily identifiable by the orange hour glass design on their abdomens. [The "which" clause is nonessential because it only supplies additional information.]

Bernie Patooka, *playing second base for the Dodgers,* broke his nose yesterday when he swatted a mosquito without letting go of the ball. [The participial phrase is nonessential because it only supplies additional information.]

5. Use commas to separate items in a series of words, phrases, or clauses.

Examples Julio collects coins, stamps, bottle caps, erasers, and pocket lint.

Mrs. Jones chased her husband out the window, around the ledge, down the fire escape, and into the busy street.

While journalists and some grammarians permit the omission of the last comma before the "and," many authorities believe the comma is necessary for clarity. For example, how many pints of ice cream are listed in the sentence below?

Please buy the following pints of ice cream: strawberry, peach, coffee, vanilla and chocolate swirl.

Four or five pints? Without a comma before the "and," the reader doesn't know if vanilla and chocolate swirl are (is?) one item or two. By inserting the last comma, you clarify the sentence:

Please buy the following pints of ice cream: strawberry, peach, coffee, vanilla, and chocolate swirl.

6. Use commas to separate adjectives of equal emphasis that modify the same noun. To determine if a comma should be used, see if you can insert the word "and" between the adjectives; if the phrase still makes proper sense with the substituted "and," use a comma.

Examples She finally moved out of her cold, dark apartment.
She finally moved out of her cold and dark apartment.

I have a sweet, handsome husband.
I have a sweet and handsome husband.

He called from a convenient telephone booth.
But not: He called from a convenient and telephone booth. ["Convenient" modifies the unit "telephone booth," so there is no comma.]

Hand me some of that homemade pecan pie.
But not: Hand me some of that homemade and pecan pie. ["Homemade" modifies the unit "pecan pie," so there is no comma.]

7. Set off a direct address with commas.

Examples   Gentlemen, keep your seats.

Car fifty-four, where are you?

Not now, Eleanor, I'm busy.

8. Use commas to set off items in addresses and dates.

Examples   The sheriff followed me from Austin, Texas, to question me about my uncle.

He found me on February 2, 1978, when I stopped for gas in Fairbanks, Alaska.

9. Use commas to set off a degree or title following a name.

Examples   John Dough, M.D., was audited when he reported only $5.68 in taxable income last year.

The Neanderthal Award went to Samuel Lyle, Ph.D.

10. Use commas to set off dialogue from the speaker.

Examples   Alexander announced, "I don't think I want a second helping of possum."

"Eat hearty," said Marie, "because this is the last of the food."

11. Use commas to set off "yes," "no," "well," and other weak exclamations.

Examples   Yes, I am in the cat condo business.

No, all the units with decks are sold.

Well, perhaps one with a pool will do.

12. Set off interrupters or parenthetical elements appearing in the midst of a sentence. A parenthetical element is additional information placed as explanation or comment within an already complete sentence. This element may be a word (such as "certainly" or "fortunately"), a phrase ("for example," "in

fact"), or a clause ("I believe," "you know"). The word, phrase, or clause is parenthetical if the sentence parts before and after it fit together.

Examples   Jack is, I think, still a compulsive gambler.

Harvey, my brother, sometimes has breakfast with him.

Jack cannot, for example, resist shuffling the toast or dealing the pancakes.

PRACTICING WHAT YOU'VE LEARNED

Errors with Commas, Periods, Question Marks

The sentences below contain errors that may be corrected by changing, adding, or deleting commas, periods, and question marks.

1. The father decided to recapture his youth, he took his son's car keys away.
2. Researchers in Balboa, Panama have discovered that the poisonous, yellow-belly, sea snake which descended from the cobra, is the most deadly serpent in the world.
3. Yes in fact I have often asked myself why it's always the last key on the key ring that fits the lock?
4. Lulu Belle, my cousin, spent the week of Sept 1–7, 1986 in the woods near Dimebox, Texas looking for additions to her extinct, butterfly collection, however she wasn't at all successful in her search.
5. William Faulkner, the famous writer was apparently not such a great father, for example, when his daughter Jill begged him to stop drinking he asked her who had ever heard of Shakespeare's child?
6. "Tom did you realize," said Janie. "That khaki pants first gained popularity during Queen Victoria's Afghan campaigns, unfortunately, the British soldier's traditional white uniform made too good a target"
7. Although ice cream didn't appear in America until the 1700s our country now leads the world in ice cream consumption, Australia is second I think.
8. Last summer the large friendly family that lives next door flew Discount Airlines and visited three cities on their vacation, however, their suitcases visited five.
9. According to the Georgia-Pacific Corporation which is a wood products company, the phrase "by hook or crook" originated in feudal times when all forests belonged to the local lord of the manor, peasants could gather only those sticks of wood they could cut with a pruning hook, or snare with a shepherd's crook.

10. Arthur thought that most of the movies made in Hollywood California were too silly, therefore he started a letter writing campaign urging the film producers to shoot less film and more writers.

THE SEMICOLON (;)   P

1. Use a semicolon to link two closely related independent clauses.

Examples   Jean has been cooking cajun-style for years without realizing it; her specialty is blackened toast.

Kate's mother does not have to begin a jogging program; she gets all the exercise she needs by worrying in place.

2. Use a semicolon to avoid a comma splice when connecting two independent clauses with words like "however," "moreover," "thus," "therefore," and "consequently."

Examples   Vincent Van Gogh sold only one painting in his entire life: however, in 1987 his *Sunflowers* sold for almost forty million dollars.

All Esmeralda's plants die shortly after she gets them home from the store; consequently, she has the best compost heap in town.

This town is not big enough for both of us; therefore, I suggest we expand the city limits.

3. Use a semicolon in a series between items that already contain internal punctuation.

Examples   Last year the Wildcats suffered enough injuries to keep them from winning the pennant, as Jake Pritchett, third baseman, broke his arm in a fight; Hugh Rosenbloom, starting pitcher, sprained his back on a trampoline; and Boris Baker, star outfielder, ate rotten clams and nearly died.

Her children were born a year apart: Moe, 1936; Curley, 1937; and Larry, 1938.

THE COLON (:)   P

1. Use a colon to introduce a long or formal list, but do not use one after "to be" verbs.

Correct   Please pick up these items at the store: garlic, wolfbane, mirrors, a prayer book, a hammer, and a wooden stake.

Incorrect   Jean is such a bad cook that she thinks the four basic food groups are: canned, frozen, ready-to-mix, and take-out.

Correct   Jean is such a bad cook that she thinks the four basic food groups are canned, frozen, ready-to-mix, and take-out.

Avoid needless colons.

Incorrect   At the store I couldn't find: wolfbane or a wooden stake.

Correct   At the store I couldn't find wolfbane or a wooden stake.

2. A colon may be used to introduce a quotation or definition.

Examples   The late statesman Hubert Humphrey once jokingly apologized to reporters about his having been born in a small apartment above a drugstore: "They were short on log cabins that year."

Chicago film critic Roger Ebert once offered this definition of the ever-popular movie "crash scene": "An alternative to dialogue; a substitute for Burt Reynolds' continuing growth as an actor."

In Jimmy Buffett's Margaritaville shop and cafe in Key West, a sign warns: "Shoplifters will be forced to listen to Barry Manilow."

3. Use a colon to introduce a word, phrase, or sentence that emphatically explains, summarizes, or amplifies the preceding sentence.

Examples   Harriet knew the one ingredient that would improve any diet dinner: chocolate.

Jean's explanation for avoiding exercise is simple: no pain, no pain gain.

Horace made a big mistake at the office party: he kissed his boss's wife hello and his job goodbye.

PRACTICING WHAT YOU'VE LEARNED

Errors with Semicolons and Colons

Correct the semicolon and colon errors below by adding, deleting, or substituting an appropriate mark of punctuation. Skip over any correct sentences.

1. My doctor failed in his career as a kidnapper, no one could read his ransom notes.
2. Some of the cars manufactured between 1907 and 1912 that didn't achieve the popularity of the Model T were: the Black Crow, the Swallow, the Bugmobile, and the Carnation.

3. The highest point in the United States is Mt. McKinley at 20,320 feet, in contrast, the lowest point is Death Valley at 282 feet below sea level.

4. There's only one thing that can make our yard look as good as our neighbor's; snow.

5. In a Thurmont, Maryland, cemetery can be found this epitaph "Here lies an Atheist, all dressed up, and no place to go."

6. According to an 1863 book of etiquette, the perfect hostess will see to it that the works of male and female authors are properly separated on her bookshelves, however, if the authors happen to be married, their proximity may be tolerated.

7. Some inventors who named weapons after themselves include Samuel Colt, the Colt revolver, Henry Deringer, Jr., the derringer pistol, Dr. Richard J. Gatling, the crank machine gun, Col. John T. Thompson, the submachine or "tommy" gun, and Oliver F. Winchester, the repeating rifle.

8. George Bernard Shaw, the famous playwright, claimed he wanted the following epitaph on his tombstone: "I knew if I stayed around long enough, something like this would happen."

9. As we drove down the highway we saw a sign that said "See the World's Largest Prairie Dog Turn Right at this Exit," therefore we stopped to look.

10. The next billboard read "See Live Rattlesnakes Pet Baby Pigs"; making us want to stop again.

THE APOSTROPHE (')   AP

1. Use an apostrophe to indicate a contraction.

Examples   *It's* too bad your car burned.*

           Wouldn't the insurance company believe your story?

2. Add an apostrophe plus "s" to a noun to show possession.

Examples   *Jack's* dog ate the *cat's* dinner.

           The *veterinarian's* assistant later doctored the *puppy's* wounds.

3. Add only an apostrophe to a plural noun ending in "s" to show possession.

Examples   Goldilocks invaded the *bears'* house.

           She ignored her *parents'* warning about breaking and entering.

* Don't confuse the contraction "it's" (for "it is") with the possessive pronoun "its," which never takes an apostrophe. (The car was old, but *its* coat of paint was new.)

4. In some cases you may add an apostrophe plus "s" to a singular word ending in "s," especially when the word is a proper name.

Examples   Bill Jones's car

Doris's chair

the class's project

5. To avoid confusion, you may use an apostrophe plus "s" to form the plurals of letters, figures, and words discussed as words; no apostrophe is also acceptable.

Examples   He made four *"C's"* last fall. [or *"Cs"*]

The right to resist the draft was a major issue in the *1960's.* [or *1960s*]

You use too many *"and's* in your sentence. [or *"ands"*]

QUOTATION MARKS (" " and ' ')   P

1. Use quotation marks to enclose someone's spoken or written words.

Examples   The daughter wrote, "Remember, Daddy, when you pass on you can't take your money with you."

"But I've already bought a fireproof money belt," answered her father.

2. Use quotation marks around the titles of essays,* articles, chapter headings, short stories, short poems, and songs.

Examples   "How to Paint Ceramic Ashtrays"

"The Fall of the House of Usher"

"Stopping by Woods on a Snowy Evening"

"Born in the U.S.A."

3. You may either underline or place quotation marks around a word, phrase, or letter used as the subject of discussion.

Examples   Never use "however" as a coordinating conjunction.

The "which" clause in your sentence is misplaced.

---

* Do *not*, however, put quotation marks around your own essay's title on either the title page or the first page of your paper.

Is your middle initial "X" or "Y"?

Her use of such words as "drab," "bleak," and "musty" gives the poem a somber tone.

4. Place quotation marks around uncommon nicknames and words used ironically. Do not, however, try to apologize for slang or clichés by enclosing them in quotation marks; instead, substitute specific words.

Examples   "Scat-cat" Malone takes candy from babies.

Her "friend" was an old scarecrow in an abandoned barn.

Slang   After work Chuck liked to "simple out" in front of the T.V.

Specific   After work Chuck liked to relax by watching old movies on T.V.

5. The period and the comma go inside quotation marks; the semicolon and the colon go outside. If the quoted material is a question, the question mark goes inside; if quoted material is a part of a whole sentence that is a question, the mark goes outside. The same is true for exclamation points.

Examples   According to cartoonist Matt Groening, "Love is a snowmobile racing across the tundra; suddenly it flips over, pins you underneath, and at night the ice weasels come."

"Love is a snowmobile racing across the tundra; suddenly it flips over, pins you underneath, and at night the ice weasels come," says cartoonist Matt Groening.

According to cartoonist Matt Groening, "Love is a snowmobile . . . suddenly it flips over, pins you underneath, and at night the ice weasels come"; Groening also advises that bored friends are one of the first signs that you're in love.

Did he really say, "At night the ice weasels come"?

Sally asked, "Do you think you're in love or just in a snowmobile?"

6. Use single quotation marks to enclose a quotation (or words requiring quotation marks) within a quotation.

Examples   Professor Hall then asked his class, "Do you agree with Samuel Johnson, who once said that a second marriage represents 'the triumph of hope over experience'?"

"One of my favorite songs is 'In My Life' by the Beatles," said Jane.

"I'm so proud of the 'A' on my grammar test," Sue wrote her parents.

PRACTICING WHAT YOU'VE LEARNED

Errors with Apostrophes and Quotation Marks

Correct the errors below by adding, changing, or deleting apostrophes and quotation marks; skip any correct sentences.

1. Its true that when famous wit Dorothy Parker was told that President Coolidge, also known as Silent Cal, was dead, she exclaimed, How can they tell?

2. When a woman seated next to Coolidge at a dinner party once told him she had made a bet with a friend that she could get more than two words out of him, he replied You lose.

3. Twenty-one of Elvis Presleys albums have sold over a million copies; twenty of the Beatles albums have also done so.

4. Cinderellas stepmother wasn't pleased that her daughter received an F in her creative writing class on her poem Seven Guys and a Gal, which she had plagiarized from her friend's Snow White and Dopey.

5. Wasn't it Mae West who said, When choosing between two evils, I always like to try the one I've never tried before? asked Olivia.

6. Horace said Believe me, its to everybodies' advantage to sing the popular song You Stole My Heart and Stomped That Sucker Flat, if thats what the holdup man wants.

7. A scholars research has revealed that the five most commonly used words in written English are the, of, and, a, and to.

8. The triplets mother said that while its' hard for her to choose, O. Henrys famous short story The Ransom of Red Chief is probably her favorite.

9. Despite both her lawyers advice, she used the words terrifying, hideous, and unforgettable to describe her latest flight on Golden Fleece Airways, piloted by Jack One-Eye Marcus.

10. Its clear that Bubba didnt know if the Christmas' tree thrown in the neighbors yard was ours, theirs', or your's.

PARENTHESES ( )   P

1. Use parentheses to set off statements that give additional information, explain, or qualify the main thought.

Examples To encourage sales, some automobile manufacturers name their cars after fast or sleek animals (Impala, Mustang, and Thunderbird, for example).

The Ford Motor Company once rejected the name Utopian Turtle-top for one of its new cars, choosing instead to call it the Edsel (that name obviously didn't help either).

2. The period comes inside the close parenthesis if a complete sentence is enclosed; it occurs after the close parenthesis when the enclosed matter comes at the end of the main sentence and is only a part of the main sentence.

Examples The Colorado winters of 1978 and 1979 broke records for low temperatures. (See pages 72–73 for temperature charts.)

Jean hates Colorado winters and would prefer a warmer environment (such as Alaska, the North Pole, or a meat locker in Philadelphia).

3. If you are confused trying to distinguish whether information should be set off by commas, parentheses, or dashes, here are three general guidelines:

a. Use commas to set off information closely related to the rest of the sentence.

Example When Billy Clyde married Maybelle, his brother's young widow, the family was shocked. [The information identifies Maybelle and tells why the family was shocked.]

b. Use parentheses to set off information loosely related to the rest of the sentence or material that would disturb the grammatical structure of the main sentence.

Examples Billy Clyde married Maybelle (his fourth marriage, her second) in Las Vegas on Friday. [The information is merely additional comment not closely related to the meaning of the sentence.]

Billy Clyde married Maybelle (she was previously married to his brother) in Las Vegas on Friday. [The information is an additional comment that would also disturb the grammatical structure of the main sentence were it not enclosed in parentheses.]

c. Use dashes to set off information dramatically or emphatically.

Example Billy Clyde eloped with Maybelle—only three days after her husband's funeral—without saying a word to anyone in the family.

BRACKETS [ ]   P

1. Use brackets to set off editorial explanations in quoted material.

Examples   According to the old letter, the treasure map could be found "in the library taped to the back of the portrait [of Gertrude the Great] that faces north."

The country singer ended the interview by saying, "My biggest hit so far is 'You're the Reason Our Kids are Ugly'" [original version by Lola Jean Dillon].

2. Use brackets to set off editorial corrections in quoted material. By placing the bracketed word "sic" (meaning "thus") next to an error, you indicate that the mistake appeared in the original text and that *you* are not misquoting or misspelling.

Examples   The student wrote, "I think it's unfair for teachers to count off for speling [sic]."

["Sic" in brackets indicates that the student who is quoted misspelled the word "spelling."]

The highway advertisement read as follows: "For great stakes [sic], eat at Joe's, located right behind Daisy's Glue Factory." [Here, "sic" in brackets indicates an error in word choice; the restaurant owner incorrectly advertised "stakes" instead of "steaks."]

THE DASH (—)   P

1. Use a dash to indicate a strong or sudden shift in thought.

Examples   Now, let's be reasonable—wait, put down that ice pick!

"It's not athlete's foot—it's deadly coreopsis!" cried Dr. Mitty.

2. Use dashes to set off parenthetical matter that deserves more emphasis than parentheses denote.

Examples   Wanda's newest guru—the one who practiced catatonic hedonism—taught her to rest and play at the same time.

He was amazed to learn his test score—a pitiful 43.

(To clear up any confusion over the uses of dashes, commas, and parentheses, see the guidelines on pp. 323–324.)

3. Use a dash before a statement that summarizes or amplifies the preceding thought.

Examples   Wine, food, someone else picking up the check—the dinner was perfect.

Not everyone agrees with football coach Vince Lombardi, who said, "Winning isn't everything—it's the only thing."

THE HYPHEN (-)   P

1. Use a hyphen to join words into a single adjective before a noun.

Examples   a wind-blown wig

the mud-caked sneakers

a made-for-television movie

a well-written essay

a five-year-old boy

Do not use a hyphen when the modifier ends in "ly."

Examples   a highly regarded worker

a beautifully landscaped yard

2. Some compound words use a hyphen; always check your dictionary when you're in doubt.

Examples   mother-in-law

President-elect

runner-up

good-for-nothing

twenty-one

3. Some words with prefixes use a hyphen; again, check your dictionary if necessary.

Examples   all-American

ex-wife

self-esteem

non-English

4. Use a hyphen to mark the separation of syllables when you divide a word at the end of a line. Do not divide one-syllable words; do not leave one or two letters at the end of a line. (In most dictionaries, dots are used to indicate the division of syllables. Example: va·ca·tion)

Examples In your essays you should avoid using fragment sentences.

Did your father try to help you with your homework?

ITALICS (UNDERLINING) (———) **Ital**

1. Underline or place quotation marks around a word, phrase, or letter used as the subject of discussion. Whether you underline or use quotation marks, always be consistent. (See also pp. 321–322.)

Examples No matter how I spell offered, it always looks wrong.

Is your middle initial X or Y?

Her use of such words as drab, bleak, and musty give the poem a somber tone.

2. Underline the title of books, magazines, newspapers, movies, works of art, television programs (but use quotation marks for individual episodes), airplanes, trains, and ships.

Examples Moby Dick
The Reader's Digest
Texarkana Gazette
Gone with the Wind
Mona Lisa
Sixty Minutes
Spirit of St. Louis
Queen Mary

Exceptions: Do not underline the Bible or the titles of legal documents, including the United States Constitution, or the name of your own essay when it appears on your title page. Do not underline the city in a newspaper title unless the city's name is actually part of the newspaper's title.

3. Underline foreign words that are not commonly regarded as part of the English language.

Examples   He shrugged and said, "<u>C'est la vie</u>."

Under the "For Sale" sign on the old rusty truck, the farmer had written the words "<u>caveat emptor</u>," meaning "let the buyer beware."

4. Use underlining sparingly to show emphasis.

Examples   Everyone was surprised to discover that the butler <u>didn't</u> do it.

"Do you realize that <u>your</u> son just ate a piece of a priceless Bamzant sculpture?" the husband screamed at his wife.

THE ELLIPSIS MARK (. . . or . . . .)   P

1. To show an omission in quoted material within a sentence, use three periods, with spaces before and after each one.

Example   Every time my father tells the children about having to trudge barefooted to school in the snow, the walk gets longer and the snow gets deeper.

Every time my father tells the children about having to trudge barefooted to school . . . the snow gets deeper.

2. Three periods with spaces may be used to show an incomplete or interrupted thought.

Example   My wife is an intelligent, beautiful woman who wants me to live a long time. On the other hand, Harry's wife . . .

3. If you omit any words at the end of a quotation and you are also ending your sentence, use three dots plus a fourth to indicate your period. Do not space before the first dot.

Example   Lincoln wrote, "Four score and seven years ago our fathers brought forth upon this continent, a new nation. . . ."

4. If the omission of one or more sentences occurs at the end of a quoted sentence, use four periods with no space before the first dot.

Example   "The Lord is my shepherd; I shall not want. . . . he leadeth me in the paths of righteousness for his name's sake."

PRACTICING WHAT YOU'VE LEARNED

Errors with Parentheses, Brackets, Dashes, Hyphens, Italics, and Ellipses

Correct the errors below by adding, changing, or deleting parentheses, brackets, dashes, hyphens, italics, and ellipses.

1. Many movie goers know that the ape in King Kong the original 1933 version, not the re-make was only an eighteen inch tall animated figure, but not everyone realizes that the Red Sea Moses parted in the 1923 movie of the Ten Commandments was a quivering slab of Jell O sliced down-the-middle.

2. Jean has found a way to keep the oven sparkling clean never turn it on.

3. In a person to person telephone call the twenty five year old starlet promised the hard working gossip columnist that she would "tell the truth . . . and nothing but the truth" about her highly-publicized feud with her exhusband, editor in chief of Meat Eaters' Digest.

4. While sailing across the Atlantic on board the celebrity filled yacht the Princess Diana, Dottie Mae Haskell she's the author of the popular new self help book Finding Wolves to Raise Your Children confided that until recently she thought chutzpah was an Italian side dish.

5. During their twenty four hour sit in at the melt down site, the anti nuclear protestors began to sing, "Oh, say can you see . . . "

6. Few people know that James Arness later Matt Dillon in the long running television series Gunsmoke got his start by playing the vegetable creature in the postwar monster movie The Thing 1951.

7. Similarly, well known T.V. star Michael Landon played the leading role in the 1957 classic I Was a Teenage Werewolf what a terrible movie!

8. A French chemist named Georges Claude invented the first neon sign in 1910. For additional information on his unsuccessful attempts to use seawater to generate electricity, see pp. 200-205.

9. When Lucille Ball, star of I Love Lucy, became pregnant with her first child, the network executives decided that the word expecting could be used on the air to refer to her condition, but not the word pregnant.

10. In mystery stories the detective often advises the police to cherchez la femme. Editor's note: Cherchez la femme means "look for the woman."

15

A Concise
Guide to Mechanics

CAPITALIZATION   **Cap**

1. Capitalize the first word of every sentence.

Example   The lazy horse leans against a tree all day.

    2. Capitalize the proper names of people, places, and products, and also proper adjectives.

Examples   John Doe

                 Austin, Texas

                 First National Bank

                 Chevrolets

                 Japanese cameras

                 Spanish class

    3. Always capitalize the days of the week, the names of the months, and holidays.

Examples   Saturday, December 14

                 Tuesday's meeting

                 Halloween parties

4. Capitalize titles when they are accompanied by proper names.

Examples   President Jones, Major Smith, Governor Brown, Judge Wheeler, Professor Plum, Queen Elizabeth

5. Capitalize all the principal words in titles of books, articles, stories, plays, movies, and poems. Prepositions, articles, and conjunctions are not capitalized unless they begin the title or contain more than four letters.

Examples   "The Face on the Barroom Floor"

A Short History of the War Between the States

For Whom the Bell Tolls

6. Capitalize the first word of a direct quotation.

Examples   Shocked at actor John Barrymore's use of profanity, the woman said, "Sir, I'll have you know I'm a lady!"
Barrymore replied, "Your secret is safe with me."

7. Capitalize "east," "west," "north," and "south" when they refer to particular sections of the country but not when they merely indicate direction.

Examples   The South may or may not rise again. ["South" here refers to a section of the country.]

If you travel south for ten miles, you'll see the papier-mâché replica of the world's largest hamburger. [In this case, "south" is a direction.]

8. Capitalize a title when referring to a particular person;* do not capitalize a title if a pronoun precedes it.

Examples   The President announced that anyone opposing the new peace plan would be shot.

The new car Dad bought is guaranteed for 10,000 miles or until something goes wrong.

My mother is such a bad cook that she goes to the grocery store and looks for toast.

ABBREVIATIONS   Ab

1. Abbreviate the titles "Mr.," "Mrs.," "Ms.," "St.," and "Dr." when they precede names.

* Some authorities disagree; others consider such capitalization optional.

Examples   Dr. Scott, Ms. Steinham, Mrs. White, St. Jude

2. Abbreviate titles and degrees when they follow names.

Examples   Charles Byrd, Jr.; Andrew Gordon, Ph.D.; Dudley Carpenter, D.D.S.

3. You may abbreviate the following in even the most formal writing: A.M. (*ante meridiem,* before noon), P.M. (*post meridiem,* after noon), A.D. (*anno Domini,* in the year of our Lord), B.C. (before Christ), etc. (*et cetera,* and others), i.e. (*id est,* that is), and e.g. (*exempli gratia,* for example).

4. In formal writing do *not* abbreviate the names of days, months, centuries, states, countries, or units of measure, Do *not* use an ampersand ("&") unless it is an official part of a title.

Incorrect in formal writing	Tues., Sept., 18th century, Ark., Mex., lbs.
Correct	Tuesday, September, eighteenth century, Arkansas, Mexico, pounds
Incorrect	Tony & Gus went to the store to buy ginseng root.
Correct	Tony *and* Gus went to the A & P to buy ginseng root. [The "&" in "A & P" is correct because it is part of the store's official name.]

5. Do *not* abbreviate the words for page, chapter, volume, and so forth, except in footnotes and bibliographies, which have prescribed rules of abbreviation. (For additional information on proper abbreviation, consult your dictionary.)

NUMBERS

1. Use figures for dates, street numbers, page numbers, telephone numbers, and hours with A.M. and P.M.*

Examples   April 22, 1946

710 West 14th Street

page 242

476–1423

10 A.M.

---

* 8 A.M. but *eight* o'clock.

2. Some authorities say spell out numbers that can be expressed in one or two words; others say spell out numbers under one hundred.

Examples   Ten thousand dollars or $10,000

Twenty-four hours

Thirty-nine years

Five partridges

$12.99 per pair

1,294 essays

3. When several numbers are used in a short passage, use figures.

Examples   On the punctuation test, Jennifer made 82, Juan made 91, Pete made 86, and I made 60.

The hole in the ground was 12 feet long, 10 feet wide, and 21 feet deep.

4. Never begin a sentence with a figure.

Incorrect   50 spectators turned out to watch the surfing exhibition at Niagara Falls.

Correct   Fifty spectators turned out to watch the surfing exhibition at Niagara Falls.

PRACTICING WHAT YOU'VE LEARNED

Errors with Capitalization, Abbreviations, and Numbers

Correct the errors below by adding, deleting, or changing capitals, abbreviations, and numbers. Skip any correct words, letters, or numbers you may find.

1. According to Abigail Van Buren, newspaper Columnist, in 1980 handguns killed 4 people in Australia, 8 in Canada, 18 in Sweden, 8 in England, 23 in Israel, and 11,522 in the United States.
2. My sister, who lives in the east, was amazed to read studies by Thomas Radecki, MD, showing that 12-year-olds commit 300 percent more murders than did the same age group 30 years ago.
3. In sixty-seven A.D. the roman emperor Nero entered the chariot race at the olympic games, and although he failed to finish the race, the judges unanimously declared him The Winner.

4. On p. 21 of *Famous Claims For The Future,* author Sara N. Dipity, Ph.d., reminds us that in the 1st decade of the 20th century, Grover Cleveland once declared, "sensible and responsible women do not want to vote."

5. The official chinese news agency, located in the city of xinhua, estimates that there are ten million guitar players in their country today, an amazing number considering that the instrument had been banned during the cultural revolution that lasted 10 years, from nineteen sixty-six to nineteen seventy-six.

6. 231 electoral votes were cast for James Monroe but only 1 for John Quincy Adams in the 1820 Presidential race.

7. The british soldier T. E. Lawrence, better known as "lawrence of arabia," stood less than 5 ft. 6 in. tall.

8. Drinking a glass of french wine makes me giddy before my 10 a.m. english class, held in wrigley field every other friday except on New Year's day.

9. When a political opponent once called him "two-faced," president Lincoln retorted, "if I had another face, do you think I would wear this one?"

10. In 1883, when american aviator Orville Wright was in the 6th grade, he was expelled from his Richmond, Ind., school for mischievous behavior.

SPELLING

For some folks, learning to spell correctly is harder than trying to herd cats. Entire books have been written to teach people to become better spellers, and copies of some of these are probably available at your local book store (and, no, not listed under witchcraft, either). Here, however, are a few suggestions to keep in mind that seem to work for a number of students:

1. Keep a list of the little beasties you misspell. After a few weeks you may notice that you tend to misspell the same words again and again or that the words you misspell tend to fit a pattern—that is, you can't remember when the *i* goes before the *e* or when to change the *y* to *i* before *ed.* Try to memorize the words you repeatedly misspell, or at least keep the list somewhere handy so you can refer to it when you're editing your last draft (listing the words on the inside cover of your dictionary makes sense).

2. Become aware of a few rules that govern some of our spelling in English. For example, most people know the rule in the jingle "*I* before *E* except after *C* or when sounded like *A* as in *neighbor* and *weigh.*" Not everyone, however, knows

the follow-up line that contains most of the exceptions to that jingle: "Neither the weird financier nor the foreigner seizes leisure at its height."

3. Here are some other rules, without jingles, for adding suffixes, a common plague for poor spellers:

- change final *y* to *i* if the *y* follows a consonant
    - bury = buried
    - married = marries
- but if the suffix is *-ing*, keep the *y*
    - marry + ing = marrying
    - worry + ing = worrying
- if the word ends in a single consonant after a single vowel and the accent is on the last syllable, double the consonant before adding the suffix
    - occur = occurred
    - cut = cutting
    - swim = swimmer
- if a word ends in a silent *e*, drop the *e* before adding *-able* or *-ing*
    - love + able = lovable
    - believe + able = believable

4. And here's an easy rule governing the doubling of letters with the addition of prefixes: Most of the time, you simply add all the letters you've got when you mix the word and the prefix.

mis + spell = misspell
un + natural = unnatural
re + entry = reentry

5. Teach yourself to spell the words that you miss often by making up your own silly rules or jingles. For instance:

dessert (one s or two?): I always want two helpings so I double the *s*.
separate (separete?): I'd be a *rat* to sepa*rat*e from you, darling.
recommendation (one or two m's?): *Mm,* let me think of something good to say about her.
a lot (or alot?): A cot (not acot) provides *a lot* of comfort.

And so on.

6. Don't forget to proofread your papers carefully. Anything that looks misspelled probably is, and deserves to be looked up in your dictionary. Reading your paper one sentence at a time from the end helps too, because you tend

to start thinking about your ideas when you read from the beginning of your paper. (And if you are writing on a word processor that has a Spell Program, don't forget to run it!)

While these few suggestions won't completely cure your spelling problems, they may make a dramatic improvement in the quality of your papers and give you the confidence to continue learning and practicing other rules that govern the spelling of our language. Good luck!

PART
FOUR

Additional
Readings

16

Exposition: Development by Example

CLEVER ANIMALS

Lewis Thomas

Lewis Thomas, former chancellor of Memorial Sloan-Kettering Cancer Center, was a distinguished physician, biologist, researcher, professor, writer, and winner of the National Book Award for The Lives of a Cell: Notes of a Biology Watcher *(1974). His prolific writings can also be found in two other collections of essays,* The Medusa and the Snail: More Notes of a Biology Watcher *(1979) and* Late Night Thoughts on Listening to Mahler's Ninth Symphony *(1979), from which this essay is taken.*

1   Scientists who work on animal behavior are occupationally obliged to live chancier lives than most of their colleagues, always at risk of being fooled by the animals they are studying or, worse, fooling themselves. Whether their experiments involve domesticated laboratory animals or wild creatures in the field, there is no end to the surprises that an animal can think up in the presence of an investigator. Sometimes it seems as if animals are genetically programmed to puzzle human beings, especially psychologists.

2   The risks are especially high when the scientist is engaged in training the animal to do something or other and must bank his professional reputation on the integrity of his experimental subject. The most famous case in point is that

of Clever Hans, the urn-of-the-century German horse now immortalized in the lexicon of behavioral science by the technical term, the "Clever Hans Error." The horse, owned and trained by Herr von Osten, could not only solve complex arithmetical problems, but even read the instructions on a blackboard and tap out infallibly, with one hoof, the right answer. What is more, he could perform the same computations when total strangers posed questions to him, with his trainer nowhere nearby. For several years Clever Hans was studied intensively by groups of puzzled scientists and taken seriously as a horse with something very like a human brain, quite possibly even better than human. But finally in 1911, it was discovered by Professor O. Pfungst that Hans was not really doing arithmetic at all, he was simply observing the behavior of the human experimenter. Subtle, unconscious gestures—nods of the head, the holding of breath, the cessation of nodding when the correct count was reached—were accurately read by the horse as cues to stop tapping.

3   Whenever I read about that phenomenon, usually recounted as the exposure of a sort of unconscious fraud on the part of either the experimenter or the horse or both, I wish Clever Hans would be given more credit than he generally gets. To be sure, the horse couldn't really do arithmetic, but the record shows that he was considerably better at observing human beings and interpreting their behavior than humans are at comprehending horses or, for that matter, other humans.

4   Cats are a standing rebuke to behavior scientists wanting to know how the minds of animals work. The mind of a cat is an inscrutable mystery, beyond human reach, the least human of all creatures and at the same time, as any cat owner will attest, the most intelligent. In 1979, a paper was published in *Science* by B. R. Moore and S. Stuttard entitled "Dr. Guthrie and Felis domesticus or: tripping over the cat," a wonderful account of the kind of scientific mischief native to this species. Thirty-five years ago, E. R. Guthrie and G. P. Horton described an experiment in which cats were placed in a glass-fronted puzzle box and trained to find their way out by jostling a slender vertical rod at the front of the box, thereby causing a door to open. What interested these investigators was not so much that the cats could learn to bump into the vertical rod, but that before doing so each animal performed a long ritual of highly stereotyped movements, rubbing their heads and backs against the front of the box, turning in circles, and finally touching the rod. The experiment has ranked as something of a classic in experimental psychology, even raising in some minds the notion of a ceremony of superstition on the part of cats: before the rod will open the door, it is necessary to go through a magical sequence of motions.

5   Moore and Stuttard repeated the Guthrie experiment, observed the same complex "learning" behavior, but then discovered that it occurred only when a human being was visible to the cat. If no one was in the room with the box, the cat did nothing but take naps. The sight of a human being was all that was needed to launch the animal on the series of sinuous movements, rod or no rod, door or no door. It was not a learned pattern of behavior, it was a cat greeting a person.

6   The French investigator R. Chauvin was once engaged in a field study of

the boundaries of ant colonies and enlisted the help of some enthusiastic physicists equipped with radioactive compounds and Geiger counters. The ants of one anthill were labeled and then tracked to learn whether they entered the territory of a neighboring hill. In the middle of the work the physicists suddenly began leaping like ballet dancers, terminating the experiment, while hundreds of ants from both colonies swarmed over their shoes and up inside their pants. To Chauvin's ethological eye it looked like purposeful behavior on both sides.

7   Bees are filled with astonishments, confounding anyone who studies them, producing volumes of anecdotes. A lady of our acquaintance visited her sister, who raised honeybees in northern California. They left their car on a side road, suited up in a protective gear, and walked across the fields to have a look at the hives. For reasons unknown, the bees were in a furious mood that afternoon, attacking in platoons, settling on them from all sides. Let us walk away slowly, advised the beekeeper sister, they'll give it up sooner or later. They walked until bee-free, then circled the fields and went back to the car, and found the bees there, waiting for them.

8   There is a new anecdote for everyone to wonder about. It was reported from Brazil that male bees of the plant-pollinating euglossine species are addicted to DDT. Houses that had been sprayed for mosquito control in the Amazonas region were promptly invaded by thousands of bees that gathered on the walls, collected the DDT in pouches on their hind legs, and flew off with it. Most of the houses were virtually stripped of DDT during the summer months, and the residents in the area complained bitterly of the noise. There is as yet no explanation for this behavior. They are not harmed by the substance; while a honeybee is quickly killed by as little as six micrograms of DDT, these bees can cart away two thousand micrograms without being discommoded. Possibly the euglossine bees like the taste of DDT or its smell, or maybe they are determined to protect other insect cousins. Nothing about bees, or other animals, seems beyond imagining.

WHY DON'T WE COMPLAIN?

William F. Buckley, Jr.

William F. Buckley, Jr., is editor of National Review *and host of public television's weekly show* Firing Line, *which offers debate on current controversial social and political issues. Buckley is the author of numerous books of non-fiction and fiction, including* Right Reason *(1985),* High Jinx *(1986),* Racing Through Paradise *(1987), and* Mongoose R.I.P. *(1988). This essay first appeared in* Esquire *in 1960.*

1   It was the very last coach and the only empty seat on the entire train, so there was no turning back. The problem was to breathe. Outside, the temperature was below freezing. Inside the railroad car the temperature must have been about 85 degrees. I took off my overcoat, and a few minutes later my jacket, and noticed that the car was flecked with the white shirts of the passengers. I soon found my hand moving to loosen my tie. From one end of the car to the other, as we rattled through Westchester County, we sweated; but we did not moan.

2   I watched the train conductor appear at the head of the car. "Tickets, all tickets, please!" In a more virile age, I thought, the passengers would seize the conductor and strap him down on a seat over the radiator to share the fate of his patrons. He shuffled down the aisle, picking up tickets, punching commutation cards. *No one addressed a word to him.* He approached my seat, and I drew a deep breath of resolution. "Conductor," I began with a considerable edge to my voice. . . . Instantly the doleful eyes of my seatmate turned tiredly from his newspaper to fix me with a resentful stare: what question could be so important as to justify my sibilant intrusion into his stupor? I was shaken by those eyes. I am incapable of making a discreet fuss, so I mumbled a question about what time were we due in Stamford (I didn't even ask whether it would be before or after dehydration could be expected to set in), got my reply, and went back to my newspaper and to wiping my brow.

3   The conductor had nonchalantly walked down the gauntlet of eighty sweating American freemen, and not one of them had asked him to explain why the passengers in that car had consigned to suffer. There is nothing to be done when the temperature *outdoors* is 85 degrees, and indoors the air conditioner has broken down; obviously when that happens there is nothing to do, except perhaps curse the day that one was born. But when the temperature outdoors is below freezing, it takes a positive act of will on somebody's part to set the temperature *indoors* at 85. Somewhere a valve was turned too far, a furnace overstocked, a thermostat maladjusted: something that could easily be remedied by turning off the heat and allowing the great outdoors to come indoors. All this is so obvious. What is not obvious is what has happened to the American people.

4   It isn't just the commuters, whom we have come to visualize as a supine breed who have got on to the trick of suspending their sensory faculties twice a day while they submit to the creeping dissolution of the railroad industry. It isn't just they who have given up trying to rectify irrational vexations. It is the American people everywhere.

5   A few weeks ago at a large movie theatre I turned to my wife and said, "The picture is out of focus." "Be quiet," she answered. I obeyed. But a few minutes later I raised the point again, with mounting impatience. "It will be all right in a minute," she said apprehensively. (She would rather lose her eyesight than be around when I make one of my infrequent scenes.) I waited. It was *just* out of focus—not glaringly out, but out. My vision is 20–20, and I assume that is the vision, adjusted, of most people in the movie house. So, after hectoring my wife throughout the first reel, I finally prevailed upon her to admit that it

was off, and very annoying. We then settled down, coming to rest on the presumption that: a) someone connected with the management of the theatre must soon notice the blur and make the correction; or b) that someone seated near the rear of the house would make the complaint in behalf of those of us up front; or c) that—any minute now—the entire house would explode into catcalls and foot stamping, calling dramatic attention to the irksome distortion.

6 What happened was nothing. The movie ended, as it had begun *just* out of focus, and we trooped out, we stretched our faces in a variety of contortions to accustom the eye to the shock of normal focus.

7 I think it is safe to say that everybody suffered on that occasion. And I think it is safe to assume that everyone was expecting someone else to take the initiative in going back to speak to the manager. And it is probably true even that if we had supposed the movie would run right through the blurred image, someone surely would have summoned up the purposive indignation to get up out of his seat and file his complaint.

8 But notice that no one did. And the reason no one did is because we are all increasingly anxious in America to be unobtrusive; we are reluctant to make our voices heard, hesitant about claiming our rights; we are afraid that our cause is unjust, or that if it is not unjust, that it is ambiguous; or if not even that, that it is too trivial to justify the horrors of a confrontation with Authority; we will sit in an oven or endure a racking headache before undertaking a head-on, I'm-here-to-tell-you complaint. That tendency to passive compliance, to a heedless endurance, is something to keep one's eyes on—in sharp focus.

9 I myself can occasionally summon the courage to complain, but I cannot, as I have intimated, complain softly. My own instinct is so strong to let the thing ride, to forget about it—to expect that someone will take the matter up, when the grievance is collective, in my behalf—that it is only when the provocation is at a very special key, whose vibrations touch simultaneously a complexus of nerves, allergies, and passions, that I catch fire and find the reserves of courage and assertiveness to speak up. When that happens, I get quite carried away. My blood gets hot, my brow wet, I become unbearably and unconscionably sarcastic and bellicose; I am girded for a total showdown.

10 Why should that be? Why could not I (or anyone else) on that railroad coach have said simply to the conductor, "Sir"—I take that back: that sounds sarcastic—"Conductor, would you be good enough to turn down the heat? I am extremely hot. In fact, I tend to get hot every time the temperature reaches 85 degr—" Strike that last sentence. Just end it with the simple statement that you are extremely hot, and let the conductor infer the cause.

11 Every New Year's Eve I resolve to do something about the Milquetoast in me and vow to speak up, calmly, for my rights, and for the betterment of our society, on every appropriate occasion. Entering last New Year's Eve I was fortified in my resolve because that morning at breakfast I had had to ask the waitress three times for a glass of milk. She finally brought it—after I had finished my eggs, which is when I don't want it any more. I did not have the manliness to order her to take the milk back, but settled instead for a cowardly

sulk, and ostentatiously refused to drink the milk—though I later paid for it—rather than state plainly to the hostess, as I should have, why I had not drunk it, and would not pay for it.

12 So by the time the New Year ushered out the Old, riding in on my morning's indignation and stimulated by the gastric juices of resolution that flow so faithfully on New Year's Eve, I rendered my vow. Henceforward I would conquer my shyness, my despicable disposition to supineness. I would speak out like a man against the unnecessary annoyances of our time.

13 Forty-eight hours later, I was standing in line at the ski repair store in Pico Peak, Vermont. All I needed, to get on with my skiing, was the loan, for one minute, of a small screwdriver, to tighten a loose binding. Behind the counter in the workshop were two men. One was industriously engaged in servicing the complicated requirements of a young lady at the head of the line, and obviously he would be tied up for quite a while. The other—"Jiggs," his workmate called him—was a middle-aged man, who sat in a chair puffing a pipe, exchanging small talk with his working partner. My pulse began its telltale acceleration. The minutes ticked on. I stared at the idle shopkeeper, hoping to shame him into action, but he was impervious to my telepathic reproof and continued his small talk with his friend, brazenly insensitive to the nervous demands of six good men who were raring to ski.

14 Suddenly my New Year's Eve resolution struck me. It was now or never. I broke from my place in line and marched to the counter. I was going to control myself. I dug my nails into my palms. My effort was only partially successful.

15 "If you are not too busy," I said icily, "would you mind handing me a screwdriver?"

16 Work stopped and everyone turned his eyes on me, and I experienced that mortification I always feel when I am the center of centripetal shafts of curiosity, resentment, perplexity.

17 But the worst was yet to come. "I am sorry, sir," said Jiggs deferentially, moving the pipe from his mouth. "I am not supposed to move. I have just had a heart attack." That was the signal for a great whirring noise that descended from heaven. We looked, stricken, out the window, and it appeared as though a cyclone had suddenly focused on the snowy courtyard between the shop and the ski lift. Suddenly a gigantic army helicopter materialized, and hovered down to a landing. Two men jumped out of the plane carrying a stretcher, tore into the ski shop, and lifted the shopkeeper onto the stretcher. Jiggs bade his companion goodby, was whisked out the door, into the plane, up to the heavens, down—we learned—to a near-by army hospital. I looked up manfully—into a score of maneating eyes. I put the experience down as a reversal.

18 As I write this, on an airplane, I have run out of paper and need to reach into my briefcase under my legs for more. I cannot do this until my empty lunch tray is removed from my lap. I arrested the stewardess as she passed empty-handed down the aisle on the way to the kitchen to fetch the lunch trays for the passengers up forward who haven't been served yet "Would you please take my

tray?" "Just a *moment,* sir!" she said, and marched on sternly. Shall I tell her that since she is headed for the kitchen *anyway,* it could not delay the feeding of the other passengers by more than two seconds necessary to stash away my empty tray? Or remind her that not fifteen minutes ago she spoke unctuously into the loudspeaker the words undoubtedly devised by the airline's highly paid public relations counselor: "If there is anything I or Miss French can do for you to make your trip more enjoyable, *please* let us—" I have run out of paper.

19   I think the observable reluctance of the majority of Americans to assert themselves in minor matters is related to our increased sense of helplessness in an age of technology and centralized political and economic power. For generations, Americans who were too hot, or too cold, got up and did something about it. Now we call the plumber, or the electrician, or the furnace man. The habit of looking after our own needs obviously had something to do with the assertiveness that characterized the American family familiar to readers of American literature. With the technification of life goes our direct responsibility for our material environment, and we are conditioned to adopt a position of helplessness not only as regards the broken air conditioner, but as regards the overheated train. It takes an expert to fix the former, but not the latter; yet these distinctions, as we withdraw into helplessness, tend to fade away.

20   Our notorious political apathy is a related phenomenon. Every year, whether the Republican or the Democratic Party is in office, more and more power drains away from the individual to feed vast reservoirs in far-off places; and we have less and less to say about the shape of events which shape our future. From this alienation of personal power comes the sense of resignation with which we accept the political dispensations of a powerful government whose hold upon us continues to increase.

21   An editor of a national weekly news magazine told me a few years ago that as few as a dozen letters of protest against an editorial stance of his magazine was enough to convene a plenipotentiary meeting of the board of editors to review policy. "So few people complain, or make their voices heard," he explained to me, "that we assume a dozen letters represent the inarticulated views of thousands of readers." In the past ten years, he said, the volume of mail has noticeably decreased, even though the circulation of his magazine has risen.

22   When our voices are finally mute, when we have finally suppressed the natural instinct to complain, whether the vexation is trivial or grave, we shall have become automatons, incapable of feeling. When Premier Khrushchev first came to this country late in 1959 he was primed, we are informed, to experience the bitter resentment of the American people against his tyranny, against his persecutions, against the movement which is responsible for the great number of American deaths in Korea, for billions in taxes every year, and for life everlasting on the brink of disaster; but Khrushchev was pleasantly surprised, and reported back to the Russian people that he had been met with overwhelming cordiality (read: apathy), except, to be sure, for "a few fascists who followed me around with their wretched posters, and should be horsewhipped."

23   I may be crazy, but I say there would have been lots more posters in a society where train temperatures in the dead of winter are not allowed to climb to 85 degrees without complaint.

A DYING ART: THE CLASSY EXIT LINE

Lance Morrow

Lance Morrow is a senior editor at Time Magazine *and a frequent contributor to that magazine's weekly essay column. He is also the author of* The Chief: A Memoir of Fathers and Sons *(1985) and* Fishing in the Tiber *(1988). This essay was published in* Time *in 1984.*

1   There was a time when the deathbed was a kind of proscenium, from which the personage could issue one last dramatic utterance, full of the compacted significance of his life. Last words were to sound as if all the individual's earthly time had been sharpened to that point: he could now etch the grand summation. "More light!" the great Goethe of the Enlightment is said to have cried as he expired. There is some opinion, however, that what he actually said was "Little wife, give me your little paw."

2   In any case, the genre of great last words died quite a few years ago. There are those who think the last genuinely memorable last words were spoken in 1900, when, according to one version, the dying Oscar Wilde said, "Either that wallpaper goes, or I do."

3   Others set the date in 1904, when Chekhov on his deathbed declared, "It's a long time since I drank champagne." Appropriately, his coffin then rode to burial in a freight car marked FRESH OYSTERS.

4   Only now and then does one catch a handsome exit line today. Gary Gilmore, the murderer executed in Utah in 1977, managed a moment of brisk existentialist machismo when he told the warden, "Let's do it." There was a charm, a mist of the fey overlaying the terror, in the official last words that William Saroyan telephoned to the Associated Press before he died in 1981: "Everybody has got to die, but I have always believed an exception would be made in my case. Now what?" Last fall the British Actor John Le Mesurier dictated to his wife his own death announcement, which ran in the *Times* of London. It said, "John Le Mesurier wishes it to be known that he conked out on Nov. 15. He sadly misses family and friends."

5   Last words are a matter of taste, of course, and judgments about them tend to be subjective. A strong though eccentric case might be made for the final utterance of Britain's Lord Chief Justice Gordon Hewart, who died on a spring morning in 1944 with the words "Damn it! There's that cuckoo again!" Tallulah Bankhead used a splendid economy of language at her parting in New York City's St. Luke's Hospital in 1968. "Bourbon," she said. The Irish writer Brendan Behan rose to the occasion in 1964 when he turned to the nun who had just wiped his brow and said, "Ah, bless you, Sister, may all your sons be bishops," Some sort of award for sharp terminal repartee should be bestowed (posthumously) upon an uncle of Oliver Wendell Holmes Jr., John Holmes, who lay dying in his Boston home in 1899. A nurse kept feeling his feet, and explained to someone in the room, "If his feet are warm, he is alive . . . Nobody ever died with his feet warm." Holmes rose out of his coma long enough to observe, "John Rogers* did!" Then he slipped away.

6   The great last words traditionally included in anthologies have usually been more serious than that, and often sound suspiciously perfect. *Le style, c'est l'homme.* General Robert E. Lee is said to have gone in 1870 with just the right military-metaphysical command: "Strike the tent!" The great 18th century classicist and prig Nicolas Boileau managed a sentence of wonderfully plump self-congratulation: "It is a consolation to a poet on the point of death that he has never written a line injurious to good morals."

7   While such goodbyes are usually retrospective, looking back on the life, they sometimes peer forward. Such lines derive considerable fascination from the fact that they have been spoken at a vantage that is the closest that mortals can legitimately come to a glimpse of what lies on the other side. Thomas A. Edison said as he died in 1931, "It's very beautiful over there." (It is also possible, however, that he was referring to the view outside his window.) Voltaire had a mordant premonition. The lamp next to his deathbed flared momentarily, and his last words were "What? The flames already?"

8   Last words are supposed to be a drama of truth-telling, of nothing left to hide, nothing more to lose. Why, then, do they so often have that clunk of the bogus about them? Possibly because the majority of them may have been composed by others—keepers of the flame, hagiologists, busybodies. One hears the little sound of a pious fraud. The last breath is put into service to inflate the larger cause one last time, as with a regret that one has only one life to give for one's country. There is a long-running controversy, for example, over whether the younger Pitt, when departing this life, said, "My country! How I love my country!" or "I think I could eat one of Bellamy's pork pies."

9   As Hamlet says in *his* last words, "the rest is silence." Great terminal summations are a form of theater, really. They demand an audience—someone has to hear them, after all. More than that, they have been traditionally uttered with a high solemnity. Some last words have the irony of inadvertence—as when Civil War General John Sedgwick was heard to say during the battle of

*An English Protestant divine burned at the stake for heresy in 1555 [author's note]

Spotsylvania Court House, "Why, they couldn't hit an elephant at this dist—" But premeditated last words—the deathbed equivalent of Neil Armstrong's "One small step for a man, one giant leap for mankind," the canned speech uttered when setting off for other worlds—have a Shakespearean grandiloquence about them.

10   Last words are not a congenial form of theater any more. Suitable stages no longer seem to be available for such death scenes, nor is there much inclination to witness them. People tend either to die suddenly, unexpectedly, without the necessary editorial preparation, or to expire in hospitals, under sedation and probably not during visiting hours. The sedative dusk descends hours or days before the last darkness.

11   Perhaps the demise of great last words has something to do with a decline in the 20th century of the augustness of death. The departure of a single soul was once an imposing occasion. An age of holocausts is less disposed to hear the individual goodbyes.

12   Perhaps some entrepreneur will try to revive the genre of last words by enlisting videotape, a newer form of theater. Customers could write their own final script—or choose appropriate last words from the company's handsome selection ("Pick the goodbye that is you"), and then, well before the actual end, videotape their own official death scenes. The trouble is that most people tend to be windy and predictable when asked to say a few words on an important occasion. Maybe the best way to be memorable at the end is be enigmatic. When in doubt, simply mutter, "Rosebud."

17

Exposition: Process Analysis

ORANGES

John McPhee

John McPhee has been a reporter for Time *magazine and has written many essays for the* The New Yorker. *He has taught a writing seminar at Princeton University and has published a number of books, including* A Sense of Where You Are *(1965),* Coming Into The Country *(1977), and* La Place De La Concored Suisse *(1984). This essay is an excerpt from his book called* Oranges *(1967).*

1   The enormous factories that the frozen people have built more closely resemble oil refineries than auto plants. The evaporators are tall assemblages of looping pipes, quite similar to the cat-cracking towers that turn crude oil into gasoline. When oranges arrive, in semitrailers, they are poured into giant bins, so that a plant can have a kind of reservoir to draw upon. At Minute Maid's plant in Auburndale, for example, forty bins hold four million oranges, or enough to keep the plant going for half a day. From samples analyzed by technicians who are employed by the State of Florida, the plant manager knows what the juice, sugar, and acid content is of the fruit in each bin, and blends the oranges into the assembly line accordingly, always attempting to achieve as uniform a product as possible. An individual orange obviously means nothing in

this process, and the rise of concentrate has brought about a basic change in the system by which oranges are sold.

2   Growers used to sell oranges as oranges. They now sell "pounds-solids," and modern citrus men seem to use the term in every other sentence they utter. The rise of concentrate has not only changed the landscape and the language; it has, in a sense, turned the orange inside out. Because the concentrate plants are making a product of which the preponderant ingredient is sugar, it is sugar that they buy as raw material. They pay for the number of pounds of solids that come dissolved in the juice in each truckload of oranges, and these solids are almost wholly sugars. Growers now worry more about the number of pounds of sugar they are producing per acre than the quality of the individual oranges on their trees. If the concentrate plants bought oranges by weight alone, growers could plant, say, Hamlins on Rough Lemon in light sand—a scion, rootstock, and soil combination that will produce extremely heavy yields of insipid and watery oranges.

3   As the fruit starts to move along a concentrate plant's assembly line, it is first culled. In what some citrus people remember as "the old fresh-fruit days," before the Second World War, about forty per cent of all oranges grown in Florida were eliminated at packinghouses and dumped in fields. Florida milk tasted like orangeade. Now, with the exception of the split and rotten fruit, all of Florida's orange crop is used. Moving up a conveyor belt, oranges are scrubbed with detergent before they roll on into juicing machines. There are several kinds of juicing machines, and they are something to see. One is called the Brown Seven Hundred. Seven hundred oranges a minute go into it and are split and reamed on the same kind of rosettes that are in the centers of ordinary kitchen reamers. The rinds that come pelting out the bottom are integral halves, just like the rinds of oranges squeezed in a kitchen. Another machine is the Food Machinery Corporation's FMC In-line Extractor. It has a shining row of aluminum jaws, upper and lower, with shining aluminum teeth. When an orange tumbles in, the upper jaw comes crunching down on it while at the same time the orange is penetrated from below by a perforated steel tube. As the jaws crush the outside, the juice goes through the perforations in the tube and down into the plumbing of the concentrate plant. All in a second, the juice has been removed and the rind has been crushed and shredded beyond recognition.

4   From either machine, the juice flows on into a thing called the finisher, where seeds, rag, and pulp are removed. The finisher has a big stainless steel screw that steadily drives the juice through a fine-mesh screen. From the finisher, it flows on into holding tanks. Orange juice squeezed at home should be consumed fairly soon after it is expressed, because air reacts with it and before long produces a bitter taste, and the juice has fatty constituents that can become rancid. In the extractors, the finishers, and the troughs of concentrate plants, a good bit of air gets into the juice. Bacilli and other organisms may have started growing in it. So the juice has to be pasteurized. In some plants, this occurs before it is concentrated. In others, pasteurization is part of the vacuum-evaporating process—for example, in the Minute Maid plant in

Auburndale, which uses the Thermal Accelerated Short time Evaporator (T.A.S.T.E.). A great, airy network of bright-red, looping tubes, the Short Time stands about fifty feet high. Old-style evaporators keep one load of juice within them for about an hour, gradually boiling the water out. In the Short Time, juice flows in at one end in a continuous stream and comes out the other end eight minutes later.

5   Specific gravity, figured according to a special scale for sugar solutions, is the measurement of concentrate. The special scale, worked out by a nineteenth-century German scientist named Adolf F. W. Brix, is read in "degrees Brix." Orange juice as it comes out of oranges is usually about twelve degrees Brix— that is, for every hundred pounds of water there are twelve pounds of sugar. In the Short Time, orange juice passes through seven stages. At each stage, there are sampling valves. The juice at the start is plain, straightforward orange juice but with a notable absence of pulp or juice vesicles. By the third stage, the juice is up to nineteen degrees Brix and has the viscosity and heat of fairly thick hot chocolate. The flavor is rich and the aftertaste is clean. At the fifth stage, the juice is up to forty-six degrees Brix—already thicker than the ultimate product that goes into the six-ounce can—and it has the consistency of cough syrup, with a biting aftertaste. After the seventh stage, the orange juice can be as high as seventy degrees Brix. It is a deep apricot-orange in color. It is thick enough to chew, and its taste actually suggests apricot-flavored gum. Stirred into enough water to take it back to twelve degrees Brix, it tastes like nothing much but sweetened water.

6   As a season progresses, the sugar-acid ratio of oranges improves. Pineapple oranges, at their peak, are better in this respect than Hamlins at theirs; and Valencias are the best of all. So the concentrators keep big drums of out-of-season concentrate in cold-storage rooms and blend them with in-season concentrates in order to achieve even more uniformity. Advertisements can be misleading, however, when they show four or five kinds of oranges and imply that each can of the advertiser's concentrate contains an exact blend of all of them. It would be all but impossible to achieve that. The blending phase of the process is at best only an educated stab at long-term uniformity, using whatever happens to be on hand in the cold rooms and the fresh-fruit bins. The blending is, moreover, merely a mixing of old and new concentrates, still at sixty degrees Brix and still all but tasteless if reconstituted with water.

7   The most important moment comes when the cutback is poured in, taking the super-concentrated juice down to forty-five degrees Brix, which MacDowell and his colleagues worked out as a suitable level, because three cans of tap water seemed to be enough to thaw the juice fairly quickly but not so much that the cooling effect of the cold concentrate would be lost in the reconstituted juice. Cutback is mainly fresh orange juice, but it contains additional flavor essences, peel oil, and pulp. Among the components that get boiled away in the evaporator are at least eight hydrocarbons, four esters, fifteen carbonyls, and sixteen kinds of alcohol. The chemistry of orange juice is so subtle and complicated that most identifications are tentative, and no one can guess

which components form its taste, let alone in what proportion. Some of these essences are recovered in condensation chambers in the evaporators, and they are put back into the juice. The chief flavoring element in cutback is d-limonene, which is the main ingredient of peel oil. The oil cells in the skins of all citrus fruit are ninety per cent d-limonene. It is d-limonene that burns the lips of children sucking oranges. D-limonene reddened the lips of the ladies of the seventeenth-century French court, who bit into limes for the purpose. D-limonene is what makes the leaves of all orange and grapefruit trees smell like lemons when crushed in the hand. D-limonene is what the Martini drinker rubs on the rim of his glass and then drops into his drink in a twist of lemon. The modern Martini drinker has stouter taste buds than his predecessors of the seventeenth century, when people in Europe used to spray a little peel oil on the outside of their wineglasses, in the belief that it was so strong that it would penetrate the glass and impart a restrained flavor to the wine. In the same century, peel oil was widely used in Germany in the manufacture of "preservative plague-lozenges." In the fourteenth century in Ceylon, men who dived into lakes to search the bottom for precious stones first rubbed their bodies with orange-peel oil in order to repel crocodiles and poisonous snakes. Peel oil is flammable. Peel oil is the principal flavoring essence that people put into frozen concentrated orange juice in order to attempt to recover the flavor of fresh orange juice. "We have always had the flavor of fresh oranges to come up against," MacDowell told me, "People who make things like tomato juice and pineapple juice have not had this problem." . . .

8   Plants that make "chilled juice" are set up as concentrate plants are, but without the evaporators. Instead, the juice goes into bottles and cartons and is shipped to places as distant as Nome. Tropicana, by far the biggest company in the chilled-juice business, ships twelve thousand quarts of orange juice to Nome each month. People in Los Angeles, surprisingly enough, drink two hundred and forty thousand quarts of Tropicana orange juice a month, and the company's Los Angeles sales are second only to sales in New York.

9   Tropicana used to ship orange juice by sea from Florida to New York in a glistening white tanker with seven hundred and thirty thousand gallons of juice slurping around in the hold. For guests of the company, the ship had four double staterooms and a gourmet chef. Among freeloaders, it was considered one of the seven wonders of commerce. To sailors of the merchant marine, it was the most attractive billet on the high seas. A typical week consisted of three nights in New York, two nights at sea, and two nights in Florida. There was almost no work to do. There were forty-two men in the crew, some with homes at each end. White as a yacht, the ship would glide impressively past Wall Street and under the bridges of the East River, put forth a stainless-steel tube, and quickly drain its cargo into tanks in Queens.

10   Tropicana unfortunately found that although this was a stylish way to transport orange juice, it was also uneconomical. The juice now goes by rail, already packed in bottles or cartons. The cartons are being phased out because they admit too much oxygen. Tropicana people are frank in appraisal of their

product. "It's the closest thing to freshly squeezed orange juice you can get and not have to do the work yourself," one of the company's executives told me. To maintain the cloud in the juice and keep it from settling, enzymes have to be killed by raising the temperature of the juice to nearly two hundred degrees. Even so, there is some loss of Vitamin C if the juice remains unconsumed too long, just as there is a loss of Vitamin C if concentrate is mixed in advance and allowed to stand for some time.

11   During the winter, Tropicana freezes surplus orange juice in huge floes and stores it until summer, when it is cracked up, fed into an ice crusher, melted down, and shipped. In this way, the company avoids the more usual practice of chilled-juice shippers, who sell reconstituted concentrate in the summertime, adding dry juice-sacs in order to create the illusion of freshness. The juice-sacs come from California as "barreled washed pulp."

12   Leftover rinds, rag, pulp, and seeds at chilled-juice and concentrate plants have considerable value of their own. In most years, about fourteen million dollars are returned to the citrus industry through its by-products. Orange wine tastes like a one-for-one mixture of dry vermouth and sauterne. It varies from estate-bottled types like Pool's and Vino del Sol to Florida Fruit Bowl Orange Wine, the *vin ordinaire* of Florida shopping centers, made by National Grape Products of Jacksonville, and sold for ninety-nine cents. Florida winos are said to like the price. Florida Life cordials are made from citrus fruit, as are Consul gin, Surf Side gin, Five Flag gin, Fleet Street gin, and Consul vodka.

13   Peel oil has been used to make not only paint but varnish as well. It hardens rubber, too, but is more commonly used in perfumes and as a flavor essence for anything that is supposed to taste of orange, from candy to cake-mixes and soft drinks. Carvone, a synthetic spearmint oil which is used to flavor spearmint gum, is made from citrus peel oil. The Coca-Cola Company is one of the world's largest users of peel oil, as anyone knows who happens to have noticed the lemony smell of the d-limonene that clings to the inside of an empty Coke bottle.

14   A million and a half pounds of polyunsaturated citrus-seed oil is processed and sold each year, for cooking. Hydrogenated orange-seed oil is more like butter, by-products researchers told me, than oleomargarine. Noticing a refrigerator in their laboratory, I asked if they had some on hand. They said they were sorry, but all they had was real butter. Would I care for an English muffin?

15   Looking out a window over an orange grove, one researcher remarked, "We are growing chemicals now, not oranges." Dried juice vesicles, powdered and mixed with water, produce a thick and foamy solution which is used to fight forest fires. Albedecone, a pharmaceutical which stops leaks in blood vessels, is made from hesperidin, a substance in the peels of oranges. But the main use of the leftover rinds is cattle feed, either as molasses made from the peel sugars or as dried shredded meal. Citrus pulp and chopped rinds are dried for dairy feed much in the same way that clothes are dried in a home dryer—in a drum within a drum, whirling. The exhaust vapors perform the countryside for miles around concentrate plants with a heavy aroma of oranges. The evaporators themselves are odorless. People often assume that they are smelling the making of orange

juice when they are actually smelling cattle feed. If the aroma is not as delicate as the odor of blossoms, it is nonetheless superior to the aroma of a tire and rubber plant, a Limburger cheese factory, a pea cannery, a paper mill, or an oil refinery. Actually, the orange atmospheres of the Florida concentrate towns are quite agreeable, and in my own subjective view, the only town in the United States which outdoes them in this respect is Hershey, Pennsylvania.

ATTITUDE

Garrison Keillor

Garrison Keillor is the former host of National Public Radio's long-running A Prairie Home Companion, *which presented the mythical town of Lake Woebegon, where "all the women are strong, all the men are good-looking, and all the children are above average." Keillor is the author of the bestseller* Lake Woebegon Days *(1985) and has published essays in* The New Yorker *and* The Atlantic. *His most recent collection of down-home wisdom can be found in* We Are Still Married *(1989). The following essay is from* Happy To Be Here *(1982), a collection of many of his* New Yorker *articles.*

1   Long ago I passed the point in life when major-league ballplayers begin to be younger than yourself. Now all of them are, except for a few aging trigenarians and a couple of quadros who don't get around on the fastball as well as they used to and who sit out the second games of doubleheaders. However, despite my age (thirty-nine), I am still active and have a lot of interests. One of them is slow-pitch softball, a game that lets me go through the motions of baseball without getting beaned or having to run too hard. I play on a pretty casual team, one that drinks beer on the bench and substitutes freely. If a player's wife or girlfriend wants to play, we give her a glove and send her out to right field, no questions asked, and if she lets a pop fly drop six feet in front of her, nobody agonizes over it.

2   Except me. This year. For the first time in my life, just as I am entering the dark twilight of my slow-pitch career, I find myself taking the game seriously. It isn't the bonehead play that bothers me especially—the pop fly that drops untouched, the slow roller juggled and the ball then heaved ten feet over the first baseman's head and into the next diamond, the routine singles that go through outfielders' legs for doubles and triples with gloves flung after them. No, it isn't our stone-glove fielding or pussyfoot base-running or limp-wristed hitting

that gives me fits, though these have put us on the short end of some mighty ridiculous scores this summer. It's our attitude.

3   Bottom of the ninth, down 18–3, two outs, a man on first and a woman on third, and our third baseman strikes out. *Strikes out!* In slow-pitch, not even your grandmother strikes out, but this guy does, and after his third strike—a wild swing at a ball that bounces on the plate—he topples over in the dirt and lies flat on his back, laughing. *Laughing!*

4   Same game, earlier. They have the bases loaded. A weak grounder is hit toward our second baseperson. The runners are running. She picks up the ball, and she looks at them. She looks at first, at second, at home. We yell, "Throw it! Throw it!" and she throws it, underhand, at the pitcher, who has turned and run to back up the catcher. The ball rolls across the third-base line and under the bench. Three runs score. The batter, a fatso, chugs into second. The other team hoots and hollers, and what does she do? She shrugs and smiles ("Oh, silly me"); after all, it's only a game. Like the aforementioned strikeout artist, she treats her error as a joke. They have forgiven themselves instantly, which is unforgivable. It is *we* who should forgive them, who can say, "It's all right, it's only a game." They are supposed to throw up their hands and kick the dirt and hang their heads, as if this boner, even if it is their sixteenth of the afternoon— *this* is the one that really and truly breaks their hearts.

5   That attitude sweetens the game for everyone. The sinner feels sweet remorse. The fatso feels some sense of accomplishment; this is no bunch of rum-dums he forced into an error but a team with some class. We, the sinner's teammates, feel momentary anger at her—dumb! dumb play!—but then, seeing her grief, we sympathize with her in our hearts (any one of us might have made that mistake or one worse), and we yell encouragement, including the shortstop, who, moments before, dropped an easy throw for a force at second. "That's all right! Come on! We got 'em!" we yell. "Shake it off! These turkeys can't hit!" This makes us all feel good, even though the turkeys now lead us by ten runs. We're getting clobbered, but we have a winning attitude.

6   Let me say this about attitude: Each player is responsible for his or her own attitude, and to a considerable degree you can *create* a good attitude by doing certain little things on the field. These are certain little things that ballplayers do in the Bigs, and we ought to be doing them in the Slows.

1. When going up to bat, don't step right into the batter's box as if it were an elevator. The box is your turf, your stage. Take possession of it slowly and deliberately, starting with a lot of back-bending, knee-stretching, and torso-revolving in the on-deck circle. Then, approaching the box, stop outside it and tap the dirt off your spikes with your bat. You don't have spikes, you have sneakers, of course, but the significance of the tapping is the same. Then, upon entering the box, spit on the ground. It's a way of saying, "This here is mine. This is where I get my hits."

2. Spit frequently. Spit at all crucial moments. Spit correctly. Spit should be *blown*, not ptuied weakly with the lips, which often results in dribble. Spitting

should convey forcefulness of purpose, concentration, pride. Spit down, not in the direction of others. Spit in the glove and on the fingers, especially after making a real knucklehead play; it's a way of saying, "I dropped the ball because my glove was dry."

3. At bat and in the field, pick up dirt. Rub dirt in the fingers (especially after spitting on them). Toss dirt, as if testing the wind for velocity and direction. Smooth the dirt. Be involved with dirt. If no dirt is available (e.g., in the outfield), pluck tufts of grass. Fielders should be grooming their areas constantly between plays, flicking away tiny sticks and bits of gravel.

4. Take your time. Tie your laces. Confer with your teammates about possible situations that may arise and conceivable options in dealing with them. Extend the game. Three errors on three consecutive plays can be humiliating if the plays occur within the space of a couple of minutes, but if each error is separated from the next by extensive conferences on the mound, lace-tying, glove adjustments, and arguing close calls (if any), the effect on morale is minimized.

5. Talk. Not just an occasional "Let's get a hit now" but continuous rhythmic chatter, a flow of syllables: "Hey babe hey babe c'mon babe good stick now hey babe long tater take him downtown babe . . . hey good eye good eye."

Infield chatter is harder to maintain. Since the slow-pitch pitch is required to be a soft underhand lob, infielders hesitate to say, "Smoke him babe hey low heat hey throw it on the black babe chuck it in there back him up babe no hit no hit." Say it anyway.

6. One final rule, perhaps the most important of all: When your team is up and has made the third out, the batter and the players who were left on base do not come back to the bench for their gloves. *They remain on the field, and their teammates bring their gloves out to them.* This requires some organization and discipline, but it pays off big in morale. It says, "Although we're getting our pants knocked off, still we must conserve our energy."

7   Imagine that you have bobbled two fly balls in this rout and now you have just tried to stretch a single into a double and have been easily thrown out sliding into second base, where the base runner ahead of you had stopped. It was the third out and a dumb play, and your opponents smirk at you as they run off the field. You are the goat, a lonely and tragic figure sitting in the dirt. You curse yourself, jerking your head sharply forward. You stand up and kick the base. How miserable! How degrading! You utter shame, though brief, bears silent testimony to the worthiness of your teammates, whom you have let down, and they appreciate it. They call out to you now as they take the field, and as the second baseman runs to his position he says, "Let's get 'em now," and tosses you your glove. Lowering your head, you trot slowly out to right. There you do some deep knee bends. You pick grass. You find a pebble and fling it into foul territory. As the first batter comes to the plate, you check the sun. You get set in your stance, poised to fly. Feet spread, hands on hips, you bend slightly at the waist and spit the expert spit of a veteran ballplayer—a player who has

known the agony of defeat but who always bounces back, a player who has lost a stride on the base paths but can still make the big play.

8   This is *ball*, ladies and gentlemen. This is what it's all about.

How to Write an "F" Paper:
Fresh Advice for Students of Freshman English

Joseph C. Pattison

Joseph C. Pattison taught composition and literature at California State University at Sacramento until he retired in 1977; he now lives on Cape Cod. This essay first appeared in College English, *a journal published by the National Council of Teachers of English, in 1963.*

1   Writing an "F" paper is admittedly not an easy task, but one can learn to do it by grasp of the principles to use. The thirteen below, if practiced at all diligently, should lead any student to that fortune in his writing.

Obscure the Ideas:

2   1. Select a topic that is big enough to let you wander around the main idea without ever being forced to state it precisely. If an assigned topic has been limited for you, take a detour that will allow you to amble away from it for a while.

3   2. Pad! Pad! Pad! Do not develop your ideas. Simply restate them in safe, spongy generalizations to avoid the need to find evidence to support what you say. Always point out repetition with the phrase, "As previously noted. . . ." Better yet, repeat word-for-word at least one or two of your statements.

4   3. Disorganize your discussion. For example, if you are using the time order to present your material, keep the reader alert by making a jump from the past to the present only to spring back into the past preparatory to a leap into the future preceding a return hop into the present just before the finish of the point about the past. Devise comparable stratagems to use with such other principles for organizing a discussion as space, contrast, cause-effect, and climax.

5   4. Begin a new paragraph every sentence or two.

6   By generous use of white space, make the reader aware that he is looking at a page blank of sustained thought.

7   Like this.

Mangle the Sentences:

8   5. Fill all the areas of your sentences with deadwood. Incidentally, "the area of" will deaden almost any sentence, and it is particularly flat when displayed prominently at the beginning of a sentence.

9   6. Using fragments and run-on or comma-spliced sentences. Do not use a main subject and a main verb, for the reader will get the complete thought too easily. Just toss him part of the idea at a time, as in "Using fragments. . . ." To gain sentence variety, throw in an occasional run-on sentence thus the reader will have to read slowly and carefully to get the idea.

10   7. Your sentence order invert for statement of the least important matters. That will force the reader to be attentive to understand even the simplest points you make.

11   8. You, in the introduction, body, and conclusion of your paper, to show that you can contrive ornate, graceful sentences, should use involution. Frequent separation of subject from verbs by insertion of involved phrases and clauses will prove that you know what can be done to a sentence.

Slovenize the Diction:

12   9. Add the popular "-wise" and "-ize" endings to words. Say, "Timewise, it is fastest to go by U.S. 40," rather than simply, "It is fastest to go by U.S. 40." Choose "circularize" in preference to "circulate." Practice will smartenize your style.

13   10. Use vague words in place of precise ones. From the start, establish vagueness of tone by saying, "The thing is . . ." instead of, "The issue is. . . ." Make the reader be imaginative throughout his reading of your paper.

14   11. Employ lengthy Latinate locutions wherever possible. Shun the simplicity of style that comes from apt use of short, old, familiar words, especially those of Anglo-Saxon origin. Show that you can get the *maximum* (L.), not merely the *most* (A.S.), from every word choice you make.

15   12. Inject humor into your writing by using the wrong word occasionally. Write "then" when you mean "than" or "to" when you mean "too." Every reader likes to laugh.

16   13. Find a "tried and true" phrase to use to clinch a point. It will have a comfortingly folksy sound for the reader. Best of all, since you want to end in a conversational and friendly way, sprinkle your conclusions with clichés. "Put a little frosting on the cake," as the saying goes.

17   Well, to ensconce this whole business in a nutshell, you, above all, an erudite discourse on nothing in the field of your topic should pen. Thereby gaining the reader's credence in what you say.

18   Suggestion-wise, one last thing: file-ize this list for handy reference the next time you a paper write.

18

Exposition: Comparison/Contrast

Two Ways of Viewing the River

Samuel Clemens

Samuel Clemens, whose pen name was Mark Twain, is regarded as one of America's most outstanding writers. Well known for his humorous stories and books, Twain was also a pioneer of fictional realism and local color. His most famous novel, The Adventures of Huckleberry Finn *(1884), is often hailed as a masterpiece. This selection is from the autobiographical book* Life on the Mississippi *(1883), which recounts Clemens' job as a riverboat pilot.*

1   Now when I had mastered the language of this water and had come to know every trifling feature that bordered the great river as familiarly as I knew the letters of the alphabet, I had made a valuable acquisition. But I had lost something, too. I had lost something which could never be restored to me while I lived. All the grace, the beauty, the poetry, had gone out of the majestic river! I still kept in mind a certain wonderful sunset which I witnessed when steamboating was new to me. A broad expanse of the river was turned to blood; in the middle distance the red hue brightened into gold, through which a solitary log came floating, black and conspicuous; in one place a long, slanting mark lay sparkling upon the water; in another the surface was broken by boiling, tumbling rings, that were as many-tinted as an opal; where the ruddy flush was faintest, was a smooth spot that was covered with graceful circles and radiating

lines, ever so delicately traced; the shore on our left was densely wooded and the somber shadow that fell from this forest was broken in one place by a long, ruffled trail that shone like silver; and high above the forest wall a clean-stemmed dead tree waved a single leafy bough that glowed like a flame in the unobstructed splendor that was flowing from the sun. There were graceful curves, reflected images, woody heights, soft distances, and over the whole scene, far and near, the dissolving lights drifted steadily, enriching it every passing moment with new marvels of coloring.

2   I stood like one bewitched. I drank it in, in a speechless rapture. The world was new to me and I had never seen anything like this at home. But as I have said, a day came when I began to cease from noting the glories and the charms which the moon and the sun and the twilight wrought upon the river's face; another day came when I ceased altogether to note them. Then, if that sunset scene had been repeated, I should have looked upon it without rapture, and should have commented upon it inwardly after this fashion: "This sun means that we are going to have wind to-morrow; that floating log means that the river is rising, small thanks to it; that slanting mark on the water refers to a bluff reef which is going to kill somebody's steamboat one of these nights, if it keeps on stretching out like that; those tumbling 'boils' show a dissolving bar and a changing channel there; the lines and circles in the slick water over yonder are a warning that that troublesome place is shoaling up dangerously; that silver streak in the shadow of the forest is the 'break' from a new snag and he has located himself in the very best place he could have found to fish for steam-boats; that tall dead tree, with a single living branch, is not going to last long, and then how is a body ever going to get through this blind place at night without the friendly old landmark?"

3   No, the romance and beauty were all gone from the river. All the value any feature of it had for me now was the amount of usefulness it could furnish to-ward compassing the safe piloting of a steamboat. Since those days, I have pitied doctors from my heart. What does the lovely flush in a beauty's cheek mean to a doctor but a "break" that ripples above some deadly disease? Are not all her visible charms sown thick with what are to him the signs and symbols of hidden decay? Does he ever see her beauty at all, or doesn't he simply view her profes-sionally and comment upon her unwholesome condition all to himself? And doesn't he sometimes wonder whether he has gained most or lost most by learn-ing his trade?

THAT LEAN AND HUNGRY LOOK

Suzanne Britt

Suzanne Britt taught English at North Carolina State University at Raleigh from 1976–1979. She is currently a free-lance writer whose articles have appeared in a variety of magazines and newspapers. This playful essay, originally published in the "My Turn" column of Newsweek *in 1978, became the inspiration for her book* Skinny People Are Dull and Crunchy Like Carrots *(1982).*

1   Caesar was right. Thin people need watching. I've been watching them for most of my adult life, and I don't like what I see. When these narrow fellows spring at me, I quiver to my toes. Thin people come in all personalities, most of them menacing. You've got your "together" thin person, your mechanical thin person, your condescending thin person, your tsk-tsk thin person, your efficiency-expert thin person. All of them are dangerous.

2   In the first place, thin people aren't fun. They don't know how to goof off, at least in the best, fat sense of the word. They've always got to be adoing. Give them a coffee break, and they'll jog around the block. Supply them with a quiet evening at home, and they'll fix the screen door and lick S&H green stamps. They say things like "there aren't enough hours in the day." Fat people never say that. Fat people think the day is too damn long already.

3   Thin people make me tired. They've got speedy little metabolisms that cause them to bustle briskly. They're forever rubbing their bony hands together and eyeing new problems to "tackle." I like to surround myself with sluggish, inert, easygoing fat people, the kind who believe that if you clean it up today, it'll just get dirty again tomorrow.

4   Some people say the business about the jolly fat person is a myth, that all of us chubbies are neurotic, sick, sad people. I disagree. Fat people may not be chortling all day long, but they're a hell of a lot *nicer* than the wizened and shriveled. Thin people turn surly, mean, and hard at a young age because they never learn the value of a hot-fudge sundae for easing tension. Thin people don't like gooey soft things because they themselves are neither gooey nor soft. They are crunchy and dull, like carrots. They go straight to the heart of the matter while fat people let things stay all blurry and hazy and vague, the way things actually are. Thin people want to face the truth. Fat people know there is no truth. One of my thin friends is always staring at complex, unsolvable problems and saying, "The key thing is. . . ." Fat people never say that. They know there isn't any such thing as the key thing about anything.

5   Thin people believe in logic. Fat people see all sides. The sides fat people

see are rounded blobs, usually gray, always nebulous and truly not worth worrying about. But the thin person persists. "If you consume more calories than you burn," says one of my thin friends, "you will gain weight. It's that simple." Fat people always grin when they hear statements like that. They know better.

6   Fat people realize that life is illogical and unfair. They know very well that God is not in his heaven and all is not right with the world. If God was up there, fat people could have two doughnuts and a big orange drink anytime they wanted it.

7   Thin people have a long list of logical things they are always spouting off to me. They hold up one finger at a time as they reel off these things, so I won't lose track. They speak slowly as if to a young child. The list is long and full of holes. It contains tidbits like "get a grip on yourself," "cigarettes kill," "cholesterol clogs," "fit as a fiddle," "ducks in a row," "organize," and "sound fiscal management." Phrases like that.

8   They think these 2,000-point plans lead to happiness. Fat people know happiness is elusive at best and even if they could get the kind thin people talk about, they wouldn't want it. Wisely, fat people see that such programs are too dull, too hard, too off the mark. They are never better than a whole cheesecake.

9   Fat people know all about the mystery of life. They are the ones acquainted with the night, with luck, with fate, with playing it by ear. One thin person I know once suggested that we arrange all the parts of a jigsaw puzzle into groups according to size, shape, and color. He figured this would cut the time needed to complete the puzzle by at least 50 percent. I said I wouldn't do it. One, I like to muddle through. Two, what good would it do to finish early? Three, the jigsaw puzzle isn't the important thing. The important thing is the fun of four people (one thin person included) sitting around a card table, working on a jigsaw puzzle. My thin friend had no use for my list. Instead of joining us, he went outside and mulched the boxwoods. The three remaining fat people finished the puzzle and made chocolate, double-fudged brownies to celebrate.

10   The main problem with thin people is they oppress. Their good intentions, bony torsos, tight ships, neat corners, cerebral machinations, and pat solutions loom like dark clouds over the loose, comfortable, spread-out, soft world of the fat. Long after fat people have removed their coats and shoes and put their feet up on the coffee table, thin people are still sitting on the edge of the sofa, looking neat as a pin, discussing rutabagas. Fat people are heavily into fits of laughter, slapping their thighs and whooping it up, while thin people are still politely waiting for the punch line.

11   Thin people are downers. They like math and morality and reasoned evaluation of the limitations of human beings. They have their skinny little acts together. They expound, prognose, probe, and prick.

12   Fat people are convivial. They will like you even if you're irregular and have acne. They will come up with a good reason why you never wrote the great American novel. They will cry in your beer with you. They will put your name in the pot. They will let you off the hook. Fat people will gab, giggle, guffaw, gallumph, gyrate, and gossip. They are generous, giving, and gallant. They are gluttonous

and goodly and great. What you want when you're down is soft and jiggly, not muscled and stable. Fat people know this. Fat people have plenty of room. Fat people will take you in.

THE GOOD SCYTHE
Wendell Berry

A distinguished professor of English at University of Kentucky and a farmer, Wendell Berry has published many books of essays, poetry, and fiction. His collections of essays include The Long-Legged House *(1969),* The Unsettling of America *(1977), and* Standing by the Woods *(1985). The following essay comes from* The Gift of the Good Land *(1981).*

1   When we moved to our little farm in the Kentucky River Valley in 1965, we came with a lot of assumptions that we have abandoned or changed in response to the demands of place and time. We assumed, for example, that there would be good motor-powered solutions for all of our practical problems.

2   One of the biggest problems from the beginning was that our place was mostly on a hillside and included a good deal of ground near the house and along the road that was too steep to mow with a lawn mower. Also, we were using some electric fence, which needed to be moved out once or twice a year.

3   When I saw that Sears Roebuck sold a "power scythe," it seemed the ideal solution, and I bought one. I don't remember what I paid for it, but it was expensive, considering the relatively small amount of work I needed it for. It consisted of a one-cylinder gasoline engine mounted on a frame with a handlebar, a long metal tube enclosing a flexible drive shaft, and a rotary blade. To use it, you hung it from your shoulder by a web strap, and swept the whirling blade over the ground at the desired height.

4   It did a fairly good job of mowing, cutting the grass and weeds off clean and close to the ground. An added advantage was that it readily whacked off small bushes and tree sprouts. But this solution to the mowing problem involved a whole package of new problems:

1. The power scythe was heavy.
2. It was clumsy to use, and it got clumsier as the ground got steeper and rougher. The tool that was supposed to solve the problem of steep ground worked best on level ground.

3. It was dangerous. As long as the scythe was attached to you by the shoulder strap, you weren't likely to fall onto that naked blade. But it *was* a naked blade, and it did create a constant threat of flying rock chips, pieces of glass, etc.

4. It enveloped you in noise, and in the smudge and stench of exhaust fumes.

5. In rank growth, the blade tended to choke—in which case you had to kill the engine in a hurry or it would twist the drive shaft in two.

6. Like a lot of small gas engines not regularly used, this one was temperamental and undependable. And dependence on an engine that won't run is a plague and a curse.

5   When I review my own history, I am always amazed at how slow I have been to see the obvious. I don't remember how long I used that "labor-saving" power scythe before I finally donated it to help enlighten one of my friends— but it was too long. Nor do I remember all the stages of my own enlightenment.

6   The turning point, anyhow, was the day when Harlan Hubbard showed me an old-fashioned, human-powered scythe that was clearly the best that I had ever seen. It was light, comfortable to hold and handle. The blade was very sharp, angled and curved precisely to the path of its stroke. There was an intelligence and refinement in its design that made it a pleasure to handle and look at and think about. I asked where I could get one, and Harlan gave me an address: The Marugg Company, Tracy City, Tennessee 37387.

7   I wrote for a price list and promptly received a sheet exhibiting the stock in trade of the Marugg Company: grass scythes, bush scythes, snaths, sickles, hoes, stock bells, carrying yokes, whetstones, and the hammers and anvils used in beating out the "dangle" cutting edge that is an essential feature of the grass scythes.

8   In due time I became the owner of a grass scythe, hammer and anvil, and whetstone. Learning to use the hammer and anvil properly (the Marugg Company provides a sheet of instructions) takes some effort and some considering. And so does learning to use the scythe. It is essential to hold the point so that it won't dig into the ground, for instance; and you must learn to swing so that you slice rather than hack.

9   Once these fundamentals are mastered, the Marugg grass scythe proves itself an excellent tool. It is the most satisfying hand tool that I have ever used. In tough grass it cuts a little less uniformly than the power scythe. In all other ways, in my opinion it is a better tool:

1. It is light.
2. It handles gracefully and comfortably even on steep ground.
3. It is far less dangerous than the power scythe.
4. It is quiet and makes no fumes.
5. It is much more adaptable to conditions than the power scythe: in ranker growth, narrow the cut and shorten the stroke.
6. It always starts—provided the user will start. Aside from reasonable skill and care in use, there are no maintenance problems.

7. It requires no fuel or oil. It runs on what you ate for breakfast.

8. It is at least as fast as the power scythe. Where the cutting is either light or extra heavy, it can be appreciably faster.

9. It is far cheaper than the power scythe, both to buy and to use.

10   Since I bought my power scythe, a new version has come on the market, using a short length of nylon string in place of the metal blade. It is undoubtedly safer. But I believe the other drawbacks remain. Though I have not used one of these, I have observed them in use, and they appear to me to be slower than the metal-bladed power scythe, and less effective on large-stemmed plants.

11   I have noticed two further differences between the power scythe and the Marugg scythe that are not so practical as those listed above, but which I think are just as significant. The first is that I never took the least pleasure in using the power scythe, whereas in using the Marugg scythe, whatever the weather and however difficult the cutting, I always work with the pleasure that one invariably gets from using a good tool. And because it is not motor driven and is quiet and odorless, the Marugg scythe also allows the pleasure of awareness of what is going on around you as you work.

12   The other difference is between kinds of weariness. Using the Marugg scythe causes the simple bodily weariness that comes with exertion. This is a kind of weariness that, when not extreme, can in itself be one of the pleasures of work. The power scythe, on the other hand, adds to the weariness of exertion the unpleasant and destructive weariness of strain. This is partly because, in addition to carrying and handling it, your attention is necessarily clenched to it; if you are to use it effectively and safely, you *must* not look away. And partly it is because the power scythe, like all motor-driven tools, imposes patterns of endurance that are alien to the body. As long as the motor is running there is a pressure to keep going. You don't stop to consider or rest or look around. You keep on until the motor stops or the job is finished or you have some kind of trouble. (This explains why the tractor soon evolved headlights, and farmers began to do daywork at night.)

13   These differences have come to have, for me, the force of a parable. Once you have mastered the Marugg scythe, what an absurd thing it makes of the power scythe! What possible sense can there be in carrying a heavy weight on your shoulder in order to reduce by a very little the use of your arms? Or to use quite a lot of money as a substitute for a little skill?

14   The power scythe—and it is far from being an isolated or unusual example—is *not* a labor saver or a shortcut. It is a labor maker (you have to work to pay for it as well as to use it) and a long cut. Apologists for such expensive technological solutions love to say that "you can't turn back the clock." But when it makes perfect sense to do so—as when the clock is wrong—of *course* you can!

19

Exposition: Definition

In Praise of the Humble Comma

Pico Iyer

Pico Iyer has written numerous essays for Time *magazine since 1982 and has contributed articles to various other journals, including* Smithsonian, Partisan Review, *and* Conde Nast Traveler. *He is the author of a book of essays on travel in Asia,* Video Night in Kathmandu *(1988), and is currently completing a book on Japan. This essay first appeared in* Time *in 1988.*

1   The gods, they say, give breath, and they take it away. But the same could be said—could it not?—of the humble comma. Add it to the present clause, and, of a sudden, the mind is, quite literally, given pause to think; take it out if you wish or forget it and the mind is deprived of a resting place. Yet still the comma gets no respect. It seems just a slip of a thing, a pedant's tick, a blip on the edge of our consciousness, a kind of printer's smudge almost. Small, we claim, is beautiful (especially in the age of the microchip). Yet what is so often used, and so rarely recalled, as the comma—unless it be breath itself?

2   Punctuation, one is taught, has a point: to keep up law and order. Punctuation marks are the road signs placed along the highway of our communication—to control speeds, provide directions and prevent head-on collisions. A period has the unblinking finality of a red light; the comma is a flashing yellow light that asks us only to slow down; and the semicolon is a stop sign that tells

us to ease gradually to a halt, before gradually starting up again. By establishing the relations between words, punctuation establishes the relations between the people using words. That may be one reason why schoolteachers exalt it and lovers defy it ("We love each other and belong to each other let's don't ever hurt each other Nicole let's don't ever hurt each other," wrote Gary Gilmore to his girlfriend). A comma, he must have known, "separates inseparables," in the clinching words of H.W. Fowler, King of English Usage.

3   Punctuation, then, is a civic prop, a pillar that holds society upright. (A run-on sentence, its phrases piling up without division, is as unsightly as a sink piled high with dirty dishes.) Small wonder, then, that punctuation was one of the first proprieties of the Victorian age, the age of the corset, that the modernists threw off: the sexual revolution might be said to have begun when Joyce's Molly Bloom spilled out all her private thoughts in 36 pages of unbridled, almost unperioded and officially censored prose; and another rebellion was surely marked when E.E. Cummings first felt free to commit "God" to the lower case.

4   Punctuation thus becomes the signature of cultures. The hot-blooded Spaniard seems to be revealed in the passion and urgency of his doubled exclamation points and question marks ("¡Caramba! ¿Quien sabe?"), while the impassive Chinese traditionally added to his so-called inscrutability by omitting directions from his ideograms. The anarchy and commotion of the '60s were given voice in the exploding exclamation marks, riotous capital letters and Day-Glo italics of Tom Wolfe's spray-paint prose; and in Communist societies, where the State is absolute, the dignity—and divinity—of capital letters is reserved for Ministries, Sub-Committees and Secretariats.

5   Yet punctuation is something more than a culture's birthmark; it scores the music in our minds, gets our thoughts moving to the rhythm of our hearts. Punctuation is the notation in the sheet music of our words, telling us when to rest, or when to raise our voices; it acknowledges that the meaning of our discourse, as of any symphonic composition, lies not in the units but in the pauses, the pacing and the phrasing. Punctuation is the way one bats one's eyes, lowers one's voice or blushes demurely. Punctuation adjusts the tone and color and volume till the feeling comes into perfect focus: not disgust exactly, but distaste; not lust, or like, but love.

6   Punctuation, in short, gives us the human voice, and all the meanings that lie between the words. "You aren't young, are you?" loses its innocence when it loses the question mark. Every child knows the menace of a dropped apostrophe (the parent's "Don't do that" shifting into the more slowly enunciated "Do not do that"), and every believer, the ignominy of having his faith reduced to "faith." Add an exclamation point to "To be or not to be . . ." and the gloomy Dane has all the resolve he needs; add a comma, and the noble sobriety of "God save the Queen" becomes a cry of desperation bordering on double sacrilege.

7   Sometimes, of course, our markings may be simply a matter of aesthetics. Popping in a comma can be like slipping on the necklace that gives an outfit quiet elegance, or like catching the sound of running water that complements, as it completes, the silence of a Japanese landscape. When V.S. Naipaul, in his latest

novel, writes, "He was a middle-aged man, with glasses," the first comma can seem a little precious. Yet it gives the description a spin, as well as a subtlety, that it otherwise lacks, and it shows that the glasses are not part of the middle-agedness, but something else.

8   Thus all these tiny scratches give us breadth and heft and depth. A world that has only periods is a world without inflections. It is a world without shade. It has a music without sharps and flats. It is a martial music. It has a jackboot rhythm. Words cannot bend and curve. A comma, by comparison, catches the gentle drift of the mind in thought, turning in on itself and back on itself, reversing, redoubling and returning along the course of its own sweet river music; while the semicolon brings clauses and thoughts together with all the silent discretion of a hostess arranging guests around her dinner table.

9   Punctuation, then, is a matter of care. Care for words, yes, but also, and more important, for what the words imply. Only a lover notices the small things: the way the afternoon light catches the nape of a neck, or how a strand of hair slips out from behind an ear, or the way a finger curls around a cup. And no one scans a letter so closely as a lover, searching for its small print, straining to hear its nuances, its gasps, its sighs and hesitations, poring over the secret messages that lie in every cadence. The difference between "Jane (whom I adore)" and "Jane, whom I adore," and the difference between them both and "Jane—whom I adore—" marks all the distance between ecstasy and heartache. "No iron can pierce the heart with such force as a period put at just the right place," in Isaac Babel's lovely words; a comma can let us hear a voice break, or a heart. Punctuation, in fact, is a labor of love. Which bring us back, in a way, to gods.

THE SANTA ANA

Joan Didion

Joan Didion is a novelist and a screen writer, but she is best known for her insightful essays on American culture and values. Her novels include River Run *(1963),* Play It As It Lays *(1971),* A Book of Common Prayer *(1977), and* Democracy *(1984). Her essays have been collected in* Slouching Towards Bethlehem *(1969), from which this selection is taken,* The White Album *(1979), and* Salvador *(1983).*

1   There is something uneasy in the Los Angeles air this afternoon, some unnatural stillness, some tension. What it means is that tonight a Santa Ana

will begin to blow, a hot wind from the northeast whining down through the Cajon and San Gorgonio Passes, blowing up sandstorms out along Route 66, drying the hills and the nerves to the flash point. For a few days now we will see smoke back in the canyons, and hear sirens in the night. I have neither heard nor read that a Santa Ana is due, but I know it, and almost everyone I have seen today knows it too. We know it because we feel it. The baby frets. The maid sulks. I rekindle a waning argument with the telephone company, then cut my losses and lie down, given over to whatever it is in the air. To live with the Santa Ana is to accept, consciously or unconsciously, a deeply mechanistic view of human behavior.

2   I recall being told, when I first moved to Los Angeles and was living on an isolated beach, that the Indians would throw themselves into the sea when the bad wind blew. I could see why. The Pacific turned ominously glossy during a Santa Ana period, and one woke in the night troubled not only by the peacocks screaming in the olive trees but by the eerie absence of surf. The heat was surreal. The sky had a yellow cast, the kind of light sometimes called "earthquake weather." My only neighbor would not come out of her house for days, and there were no lights at night, and her husband roamed the place with a machete. One day he would tell me that he had heard a trespasser, the next a rattlesnake.

3   "On nights like that," Raymond Chandler once wrote about the Santa Ana, "every booze party ends in a fight. Meek little wives feel the edge of the carving knife and study their husbands' necks. Anything can happen." That was the kind of wind it was. I did not know then that there was any basis for the effect it had on all of us, but it turns out to be another of those cases in which science bears out folk wisdom. The Santa Ana, which is named for one of the canyons it rushes through, is a *foehn* wind, like the *foehn* of Austria and Switzerland and the *bamsin* of Israel. There are a number of persistent malevolent winds, perhaps the best known of which are the mistral of France and the Mediterranean sirocco, but a *foehn* wind has distinct characteristics: it occurs on the leeward slope of a mountain range and, although the air begins as a cold mass, it is warmed as it comes down the mountain and appears finally as a hot dry wind. Whenever and wherever a *foehn* blows, doctors hear about headaches and nausea and allergies, about "nervousness," about "depression." In Los Angeles some teachers do not attempt to conduct formal classes during a Santa Ana, because the children become unmanageable. In Switzerland the suicide rate goes up during the *foehn,* and in the courts of some Swiss cantons the wind is considered a mitigating circumstance for crime. Surgeons are said to watch the wind, because blood does not clot normally during a *foehn.* A few years ago an Israeli physicist discovered that not only during such winds, but for the ten or twelve hours which precede them, the air carries an unusually high ratio of positive to negative ions. No one seems to know exactly why that should be; some talk about friction and others suggest solar disturbances. In any case the positive ions are there, and what an excess of positive ions does, in the simplest terms, is make people unhappy. One cannot get much more mechanistic than that.

4   Easterns commonly complain that there is no "weather" at all in Southern California, that the days and the seasons slip by relentlessly, numbingly bland. That is quite misleading. In fact the climate is characterized by infrequent but violent extremes: two periods of torrential subtropical rains which continue for weeks and wash out the hills and send subdivisions sliding toward the sea; about twenty scattered days a year of the Santa Ana, which, with its incendiary dryness, invariably means fire. At the first prediction of a Santa Ana, the Forest Service flies men and equipment from northern California into the southern forests, and the Los Angeles Fire Department cancels its ordinary nonfirefighting routines. The Santa Ana caused Malibu to burn the way it did in 1956, and Bel Air in 1961, and Santa Barbara in 1964. In the winter of 1966–67 eleven men were killed fighting a Santa Ana fire that spread through the San Gabriel Mountains.

5   Just to watch the front-page news out of Los Angeles during a Santa Ana is to get very close to what it is about the place. The longest single Santa Ana period in recent years was in 1957, and it lasted not the usual three or four days but fourteen days, from November 21 until December 4. On the first day 25,000 acres of the San Gabriel Mountains were burning, with gusts reaching 100 miles an hour. In town, the wind reached Force 12, or hurricane force, on the Beaufort Scale; oil derricks were toppled and people ordered off the downtown streets to avoid injury from flying objects. On November 22 the fire in the San Gabriels was out of control. On November 24 six people were killed in automobile accidents, and by the end of the week the Los Angeles *Times* was keeping a box score of traffic deaths. On November 26 a prominent Pasadena attorney, depressed about money, shot and killed his wife, their two sons, and himself. On November 27 a South Gate divorcee, twenty-two, was murdered and thrown from a moving car. On November 30 the San Gabriel fire was still out of control, and the wind in town was blowing eighty miles an hour. On the first day of December four people died violently, and on the third the wind began to break.

6   It is hard for people who have not lived in Los Angeles to realize how radically the Santa Ana figures in the local imagination. The city burning is Los Angeles's deepest image of itself: Nathanael West perceived that, in *The Day of the Locust;* and at the time of the 1965 Watts riots what struck the imagination most indelibly were the fires. For days one could drive the Harbor Freeway and see the city on fire, just as we had always known it would be in the end. Los Angeles weather is the weather of catastrophe, of apocalypse, and, just as the reliably long and bitter winters of New England determine the way life is lived there, so the violence and the unpredictability of the Santa Ana affect the entire quality of life in Los Angeles, accentuate its impermanence, its unreliability. The wind shows us how close to the edge we are.

WHAT ARE MANNERS?

Michael Korda

In addition to his role as an editor at the publishing company of Simon and Schuster, Michael Korda is also the author of several books of non-fiction, including the best-selling Power: How To Get It, How To Use It *(1975). This essay is an excerpt from* Success, *published in 1988.*

1   Almost all of us believe that we live in an age of uncouth manners, that things were better in some previous era. For example, the 18th century in England is known as a period of high refinement in social intercourse. We look back with nostalgia to the soft candlelight, the elaborate courtesies, the hand-kissing—unwilling to confront the brutal reality of a century in which dueling to the death was commonplace and gentlemen were expected to drink themselves under the table.

2   Manners change. In our day, it is considered good manners to be clean—indeed we spend billions of dollars on products designed to keep us "fresh." In the 18th century, by contrast, most doctors and church authorities frowned on bathing, and women's extravagant coiffures were often infested with lice.

3   The changeability of manners makes the whole subject difficult to approach. To take one example: It was not considered bad manners in the 18th century to wear your hat indoors. You would take it off to greet a lady, but then you'd put it right back on your head.

4   The reason for this is perfectly plain. In the first place, the hat served as a badge of rank throughout most of history, a visible mark of status; in the second place, you couldn't draw a sword easily if you were holding a hat in your hand.

5   There is a lesson to be learned from this. For the most part, manners are merely self-protective devices appropriate to the customs of a particular age. These customs sometimes become formalized and symbolic, but they invariably derive from some practical need. Thus, on meeting somebody, we commonly shake right hands—a formal custom of no present-day significance. But in an age when everybody carried weapons, it was a demonstration that one was prepared to converse without a weapon in one's hand, a sign of peace. What we think of as "good manners" was merely a way of saying, "I mean you no immediate violence, if you can show that your intention is the same."

6   In a similar spirit, the seat on the right hand of the host is the place of honor. One theory about the origin of this custom is that a right-handed man sitting on the host's right could not easily stab him. What had been the prudent place for a rival gradually became the honored seat for any important guest.

7   Caution lies behind manners, wherever we look. In days gone by, a host sampled the wine before serving it, not to check that the wine was all right but to prove to his guests that it wasn't poisoned. A wine steward used his polished silver wine server as a demonstration of the host's good will toward his guests. Silver was thought to neutralize poisons in wine.

8   Why do we stand aside and let someone older or more important go through the door first? One theory is that in medieval times it was sensible for the strongest man to leave the castle first, since there was always a possibility he would be met with armed opponents or the rebellious peasantry waving pitchforks and scythes. Gradually a certain honor descended upon this position. It was assumed that the most important person was also the strongest, and even if he wasn't, he could hardly deny it.

9   Manners are society's way of oiling the machinery. If you don't lubricate relationships, tempers rise and people fight unnecessary battles. Besides, it's worthwhile having good manners, if only so that when you drop them for a moment, people know you mean business. When Dwight D. Eisenhower, for example, turned red and swore, people ran for cover, because he was usually courteous to a fault.

10   People with good manners do better in most situations than those without. Most negotiations, for example, are impossible without good manners, which explains why diplomats are famed for their courtesy. The best lawyers, too, are usually exquisitely courteous. Beware of the man who never raises his voice and always treats you with courtesy—he could be going after the jugular.

11   In the 19th century, most of the great gunfighters of the American West were notorious for their florid good manners, being all too aware that if they let things get out of hand, they would have to draw and shoot. Good manners helped those men survive, since even the best gunfighter could win only so many gunfights before his luck ran out. They were not "big-talking men"; they were soft-spoken and courteous. It was said of "Wild Bill" Hickok that the moment he stopped smiling at you, you were dead, and John Wesley Hardin always did his best to persuade people who wanted to start a fight with him to have a drink on him instead and then go on home.

12   Despite mankind's reputation for violence, most people prefer to avoid confrontation, and avoiding confrontation is what manners are all about. Manners represent the triumph of civilization over barbarism, and the sensible application of enlightened self-interest. Manners are not a demonstration of weakness, but a sign of common sense.

13   In the end, there is no gain in being cruel to people, whether it is in the small failures of civility in daily life or in the larger ones. Manners are mankind's way of saying, "Let's not fight unless we have to"—and there may be no higher wisdom than that, in diplomacy, in business, in love and marriage, in the transactions of everyday life.

20

Exposition: Division/Classification

FRIENDS, GOOD FRIENDS, AND SUCH GOOD FRIENDS

Judith Viorst

Judith Viorst has published a collection of poems, It's Hard to Be Hip Over Thirty, and Other Tragedies of Married Life *(1970), and collections of prose,* Yes, Married: A Saga of Love and Complaint *(1972),* If I Were in Charge of the World and Other Worries *(1981), and* Love and Guilt and the Meaning of Life *(1984). She also writes children's books and is a contributing editor to* Redbook *magazine. This essay first appeared in that magazine in 1977.*

1   Women are friends, I once would have said, when they totally love and support and trust each other, and bare to each other the secrets of their souls, and run—no questions asked—to help each other, and tell harsh truths to each other (no, you can't wear that dress unless you lose ten pounds first) when harsh truths must be told.

2   Women are friends, I once would have said, when they share the same affection for Ingmar Bergman, plus train rides, cats, warm rain, charades, Camus, and hate with equal ardor Newark and Brussels sprouts and Lawrence Welk and camping.

3   In other words, I once would have said that a friend is a friend all the way, but now I believe that's a narrow point of view. For the friendships I have and the

friendships I see are conducted at many levels of intensity, serve many different functions, meet different needs and range from those as all-the-way as the friendship of the soul sisters mentioned above to that of the most nonchalant and casual playmates.

4   Consider these varieties of friendship:

5   1. Convenience friends. These are the women with whom, if our paths weren't crossing all the time, we'd have no particular reason to be friends: a next-door neighbor, a woman in our car pool, the mother of one of our children's closest friends or maybe some mommy with whom we serve juice and cookies each week at the Glenwood Co-op Nursery.

6   Convenience friends are convenient indeed. They'll lend us their cups and silverware for a party. They'll drive our kids to soccer when we're sick. They'll take us to pick up our car when we need a lift to the garage. They'll even take our cats when we go on vacation. As we will for them.

7   But we don't, with convenience friends, ever come too close or tell too much; we maintain our public face and emotional distance. "Which means," says Elaine, "that I'll talk about being overweight but not about being depressed. Which means I'll admit being mad but not blind with rage. Which means I might say that we're pinched this month but never that I'm worried sick over money."

8   But which doesn't mean that there isn't sufficient value to be found in these friendships of mutual aid, in convenience friends.

9   2. Special-interest friends. These friendships aren't intimate, and they needn't involve kids or silverware or cats. Their value lies in some interest jointly shared. And so we may have an office friend or a yoga friend or a tennis friend or a friend from the Women's Democratic Club.

10   "I've got one woman friend," says Joyce, "who likes, as I do, to take psychology courses. Which makes it nice for me—and nice for her. It's fun to go with someone you know and it's fun to discuss what you've learned, driving back from the classes." And for the most part, she says, that's all they discuss.

11   "I'd say that what we're doing is *doing* together, not being together," Suzanne says of her Tuesday-doubles friends. "It's mainly a tennis relationship, but we play together well. And I guess we all need to have a couple of playmates."

12   I agree.

13   *My* playmate is a shopping friend, a woman of marvelous taste, a woman who knows exactly *where* to buy *what,* and furthermore is a woman who always knows beyond a doubt what one ought to be buying. I don't have the time to keep up with what's new in eyeshadow, hemlines and shoes and whether the smock look is in or finished already. But since (oh, shame!) I care a lot about eyeshadow, hemlines and shoes, and since I don't *want* to wear smocks if the smock look is finished, I'm very glad to have a shopping friend.

14   3. Historical friends. We all have a friend who knew us when . . . maybe way back in Miss Meltzer's second grade, when our family lived in that three-room flat in Brooklyn, when our dad was out of work for seven months, when our brother Allie got in that fight where they had to call the police, when our

sister married the endodontist from Yonkers and when, the morning after we lost our virginity, she was the first, the only, friend we told.

15   The years have gone by and we've gone separate ways and we've little in common now, but we're still an intimate part of each other's past. And so whenever we go to Detroit we always go to visit this friend of our girlhood. Who knows how we looked before our teeth were straightened. Who knows how we talked before our voice got un-Brooklyned. Who knows what we ate before we learned about artichokes. And who, by her presence, puts us in touch with an earlier part of ourself, a part of ourself it's important never to lose.

16   "What this friend means to me and what I mean to her," says Grace, "is having a sister without sibling rivalry. We know the texture of each other's lives. She remembers my grandmother's cabbage soup. I remember the way her uncle played the piano. There's simply no other friend who remembers those things."

17   4. Crossroads friends. Like historical friends, our crossroads friends are important for *what was*—for the friendship we shared at a crucial, now past, time of life. A time, perhaps, when we roomed in college together; or worked as eager young singles in the Big City together; or went together, as my friend Elizabeth and I did through pregnancy, birth and that scary first year of new motherhood.

18   Crossroads friends forge powerful links, links strong enough to endure with not much more contact that once-a-year letters at Christmas. And out of respect for those crossroads years, for those dramas and dreams we once shared, we will always be friends.

19   5. Cross-generational friends. Historical friends and crossroads friends seem to maintain a special kind of intimacy—dormant but always ready to be revived—and though we may rarely meet, whenever we do connect, it's personal and intense. Another kind of intimacy exists in the friendships that form across generations in what one woman calls her daughter-mother and her mother-daughter relationships.

20   Evelyn's friend is her mother's age—"but I share so much more than I ever could with my mother"—a woman she talks to of music, of books and of life. "What I get from her is the benefit of her experience. What she gets—and enjoys —from me is a youthful perspective. It's a pleasure for both of us."

21   I have in my own life a precious friend, a woman of 65 who has lived very hard, who is wise, who listens well; who has been where I am and can help me understand it; and who represents not only an ultimate ideal mother to me but also the person I'd like to be when I grow up.

22   In our daughter role we tend to do more than our share of self-revelation; in our mother role we tend to receive what's revealed. It's another kind of pleasure—playing wise mother to a questing younger person. It's another very lovely kind of friendship.

23   6. Part-of-a-couple friends. Some of the women we call our friends we never see alone—we see them as part of a couple at couples' parties. And though we share interests in many things and respect each other's views, we aren't moved to deepen the relationship. Whatever the reason, a lack of time or —and this is more likely—a lack of chemistry, our friendship remains in the

context of a group. But the fact that our feeling on seeing each other is always, "I'm *so* glad she's here" and the fact that we spend half the evening talking together says that this too, in its own way, counts as a friendship.

24   (Other part-of-a-couple friends are the friends that came with the marriage, and some of these are friends we could live without. But sometimes, alas, she married our husband's best friend; and sometimes, alas, she *is* our husband's best friend. And so we find ourself dealing with her, somewhat against our will, in a spirit of what I'll call *reluctant* friendship.)

25   7. Men who are friends. I wanted to write just of women friends, but the women I've talked to won't let me—they say I must mention man-woman friendships too. For these friendships can be just as close and as dear as those that we form with women. Listen to Lucy's description of one such friendship:

26   "We've found we have things to talk about that are different from what he talks about with my husband and different from what I talk about with his wife. So sometimes we call on the phone or meet for lunch. There are similar intellectual interests—we always pass on to each other the books that we love—but there's also something tender and caring too."

27   In a couple of crises, Lucy says, "he offered himself, for talking and for helping. And when someone died in his family he wanted me there. The sexual, flirty part of our friendship is very small, but *some*—just enough to make it fun and different." She thinks—and I agree—that the sexual part, though small is always *some*, is always there when a man and a woman are friends.

28   It's only in the past few years that I've made friends with men, in the sense of a friendship that's *mine*, not just part of two couples. And achieving with them the ease and the trust I've found with women friends has value indeed. Under the dryer at home last week, putting on mascara and rouge, I comfortably sat and talked with a fellow named Peter. Peter, I finally decided, could handle the shock of me minus mascara under the dryer. Because we care for each other. Because we're friends.

29   8. There are medium friends, and pretty good friends, and very good friends indeed, and these friendships are defined by their level of intimacy. And what we'll reveal at each of these levels of intimacy is calibrated with care. We might tell a medium friend, for example, that yesterday we had a fight with our husband. And we might tell a pretty good friend that this fight with our husband made us so mad that we slept on the couch. And we might tell a very good friend that the reason we got so mad in that fight that we slept on the couch had something to do with that girl who works in his office. But it's only to our very best friends that we're willing to tell all, to tell what's going on with that girl in his office.

30   The best of friends, I still believe, totally love and support and trust each other, and bare to each other the secrets of their souls, and run—no questions asked—to help each other, and tell harsh truths to each other when they must be told.

31   But we needn't agree about everything (only 12-year-old girl friends agree about *everything*) to tolerate each other's point of view. To accept

without judgment. To give and to take without ever keeping score. And to *be* there, as I am for them and as they are for me, to comfort our sorrows, to celebrate our joys.

THE PLOT AGAINST PEOPLE

Russell Baker

Beginning his career as a journalist with the Baltimore Sun *in 1947, Russell Baker left in 1954 to become a reporter with the* New York Times. *Since 1967 he has written his columns, the "Observer" and the "Sunday Observer," for the* Times. *He has won the George Polk Award for Distinguished Commentary (1972) and the Pulitzer Prize for journalism (1979). His books include* All Things Considered *(1965) and* So This is Depravity *(1983). This essay originally appeared in the* New York Times *in 1968.*

1 Inanimate objects are classified into three major categories—those that don't work, those that break down and those that get lost.

2 The goal of all inanimate objects is to resist man and ultimately to defeat him, and the three major classifications are based on the method each object uses to achieve its purpose. As a general rule, any object capable of breaking down at the moment when it is most needed will do so. The automobile is typical of the category.

3 With the cunning typical of its breed, the automobile never breaks down while entering a filling station with a large staff of idle mechanics. It waits until it reaches a downtown intersection in the middle of the rush hour, or until it is fully loaded with family and luggage on the Ohio Turnpike.

4 Thus it creates maximum misery, inconvenience, frustration and irritability among its human cargo, thereby reducing its owner's life span.

5 Washing machines, garbage disposals, lawn mowers, light bulbs, automatic laundry dryers, water pipes, furnaces, electrical fuses, television tubes, hose nozzles, tape recorders, slide projectors—all are in league with the automobile to take their turn at breaking down whenever life threatens to flow smoothly for their human enemies.

6 Many inanimate objects, of course, find it extremely difficult to break down. Pliers, for example, and gloves and keys are almost totally incapable of breaking down. Therefore, they have had to evolve a different technique for resisting man.

7   They get lost. Science has still not solved the mystery of how they do it, and no man has ever caught one of them in the act of getting lost. The most plausible theory is that they have developed a secret method of locomotion which they are able to conceal the instant a human eye falls upon them.

8   It is not uncommon for a pair of pliers to climb all the way from the cellar to the attic in its single-minded determination to raise its owner's blood pressure. Keys have been known to burrow three feet under mattresses. Women's purses, despite their great weight, frequently travel through six or seven rooms to find hiding space under a couch.

9   Scientists have been struck by the fact that things that break down virtually never get lost, while things that get lost hardly ever break down.

10   A furnace, for example, will invariably break down at the depth of the first winter cold wave, but it will never get lost. A woman's purse, which after all does have some inherent capacity for breaking down, hardly ever does; it almost invariably chooses to get lost.

11   Some persons believe this constitutes evidence that inanimate objects are not entirely hostile to man, and that a negotiated peace is possible. After all, they point out, a furnace could infuriate a man even more thoroughly by getting lost than by breaking down, just as a glove could upset him far more by breaking down than by getting lost.

12   Not everyone agrees, however, that this indicates a conciliatory attitude among inanimate objects. Many say it merely proves that furnaces, gloves, and pliers are incredibly stupid.

13   The third class of objects—those that don't work—is the most curious of all. These include such objects as barometers, car clocks, cigarette lighters, flashlights and toy-train locomotives. It is inaccurate, of course, to say that they never work. They work once, usually for the first few hours after being brought home, and then quit. Thereafter, they never work again.

14   In fact, it is widely assumed that they are built for the purpose of not working. Some people have reached advanced ages without ever seeing some of these objects—barometers, for example—in working order.

15   Science is utterly baffled by the entire category. There are many theories about it. The most interesting holds that the things that don't work have attained the highest state possible for an inanimate object, the state to which things that break down and things that get lost can still only aspire.

16   They have truly defeated man by conditioning him never to expect anything of them, and in return they have given man the only peace he receives from inanimate society. He does not expect his barometer to work, his electric locomotive to run, his cigarette lighter to light or his flashlight to illuminate, and when they don't, it does not raise his blood pressure.

17   He cannot attain that peace with furnaces and keys and cars and women's purses as long as he demands that they work for their keep.

COLLEGE PRESSURES

William Zinsser

As a faculty member at Yale, William Zinsser designed and taught the first course in nonfiction writing offered at that University. Drawing on his experiences as a freelance writer and as a teacher, he wrote two popular books, On Writing Well: An Informal Guide to Writing Nonfiction *(1976), and* Writing with a Word Processor *(1982). He has also written books of social commentary, including* Pop Goes America *(1966) and* Willie and Dwike: An American Profile *(1984). He is currently executive editor of the Book-of-the-Month-Club. This essay was originally published in* Country Journal *in 1979.*

1   Dear Carlos: I desperately need a dean's excuse for my chem midterm which will begin in about 1 hour. All I can say is that I totally blew it this week. I've fallen incredibly, inconceivably behind.

2   Carlos: Help! I'm anxious to hear from you. I'll be in my room and won't leave it until I hear from you. Tomorrow is the last day for . . .

3   Carlos: I left town because I started bugging out again. I stayed up all night to finish a take home make-up exam & am typing it to hand in on the 10th. It was due on the 5th. P.S. I'm going to the dentist. Pain is pretty bad.

4   Carlos: Probably by Friday I'll be able to get back to my studies. Right now I'm going to take a long walk. This whole thing has taken a lot out of me.

5   Carlos: I'm really up the proverbial creek. The problem is I really *bombed* the history final. Since I need that course for my major . . .

6   Carlos: Here follows a tale of woe. I went home this weekend, had to help my Mom, & caught a fever so didn't have much time to study. My professor . . .

7   Carlos: Aargh! Nothing original but everything's piling up at once. To be brief, my job interview . . .

8   Hey Carlos, good news! I've got mononucleosis.

9   Who are these wretched supplicants, scribbling notes so laden with anxiety, seeking such miracles of postponement and balm? They are men and women who belong to Branford College, one of the twelve residential colleges at Yale University, and the messages are just a few of the hundreds that they left for their dean, Carlos Hortas—often slipped under his door at 4 A.M.—last year.

10   But students like the ones who wrote those notes can also be found on campuses from coast to coast—especially in New England and at many other private colleges across the country that have high academic standards and highly motivated students. Nobody could doubt that the notes are real. In their

urgency and their gallows humor they are authentic voices of a generation that is panicky to succeed.

11 My own connection with the message writers is that I am master of Branford College. I live in its Gothic quadrangle and know the students well. (We have 485 of them.) I am privy to their hopes and fears—and also to their stereo music and their piercing cries in the dead of night ("Does anybody *ca-a-are?*"). If they went to Carlos to ask how to get through tomorrow, they come to me to ask how to get through the rest of their lives.

12 Mainly I try to remind them that the road ahead is a long one and that it will have more unexpected turns than they think. There will be plenty of time to change jobs, change careers, change whole attitudes and approaches. They don't want to hear such liberating news. They want a map—right now—that they can follow unswervingly to career security, financial security, Social Security and, presumably, a prepaid grave.

13 What I wish for all students is some release from the clammy grip of the future. I wish them a chance to savor each segment of their education as an experience in itself and not as a grim preparation for the next step. I wish them the right to experiment, to trip and fall, to learn that defeat is as instructive as victory and is not the end of the world.

14 My wish, of course, is naive. One of the few rights that America does not proclaim is the right to fail. Achievement is the national god, venerated in our media—the million-dollar athlete, the wealthy executive—and glorified in our praise of possessions. In the presence of such a potent state religion, the young are growing up old.

15 I see four kinds of pressure working on college students today: economic pressure, parental pressure, peer pressure, and self-induced pressure. It is easy to look around for villains—to blame the colleges for charging too much money, the professors for assigning too much work, the parents for pushing their children too far, the students for driving themselves too hard. But there are no villains; only victims.

16 "In the late 1960s," one dean told me, "the typical question that I got from students was 'Why is there so much suffering in the world?' or 'How can I make a contribution?' Today it's 'Do you think it would look better for getting into law school if I did a double major in history and political science, or just majored in one of them?'" Many other deans confirmed this pattern. One said "They're trying to find an edge—the intangible something that will look better on paper if two students are about equal."

17 Note the emphasis on looking better. The transcript has become a sacred document, the passport to security. How one appears on paper is more important than how one appears in person. *A* is for Admirable and *B* is for Borderline, even though, in Yale's official system of grading, *A* means "excellent" and *B* means "very good." Today, looking very good is no longer good enough, especially for students who hope to go on to law school or medical school. They know that entrance into the better schools will be an entrance into the better law firms and better medical practices where they will make a lot of money. They also know that

the odds are harsh. Yale Law School, for instance, matriculates 170 students from an applicant pool of 3,700; Harvard enrolls 550 from a pool of 7,000.

18   It's all very well for those of us who write letters of recommendation for our students to stress the qualities of humanity that will make them good lawyers or doctors. And it's nice to think that admission officers are really reading our letters and looking for the extra dimension of commitment or concern. Still, it would be hard for a student not to visualize these officers shuffling so many transcripts studded with *As* that they regard a *B* as positively shameful.

19   The pressure is almost as heavy on students who just want to graduate and get a job. Long gone are the days of the "gentleman's C," when students journeyed through college with a certain relaxation, sampling a wide variety of courses—music, art, philosophy, classics, anthropology, poetry, religion—that would send them out as liberally educated men and women. If I were an employer I would rather employ graduates who have this range and curiosity than those who narrowly pursued safe subjects and high grades. I know countless students whose inquiring minds exhilarate me. I like to hear the play of their ideas. I don't know if they are getting *As* or *Cs,* and I don't care. I also like them as people. The country needs them, and they will find satisfying jobs. I tell them to relax. They can't.

20   Nor can I blame them. They live in a brutal economy. Tuition, room, and board at most private colleges now comes to at least $7,000, not counting books and fees. This might seem to suggest that the colleges are getting rich. But they are equally battered by inflation. Tuition covers only 60 percent of what it costs to educate a student, and ordinarily the remainder comes from what colleges receive in endowments, grants, and gifts. Now the remainder keeps being swallowed by the cruel costs—higher every year—of just opening the doors. Heating oil is up. Insurance is up. Postage is up. Health-premium costs are up. Everything is up. Deficits are up. We are witnessing in America the creation of a brotherhood of paupers—colleges, parents, and students, joined by the common bond of debt.

21   Today it is not unusual for a student, even if he works part time at college and full time during the summer, to accrue $5,000 in loans after four years— loans that he must start to repay within one year after graduation. Exhorted at commencement to go forth into the world, he is already behind as he goes forth. How could he not feel under pressure throughout college to prepare for this day of reckoning? I have used "he," incidentally, only for brevity. Women at Yale are under no less pressure to justify their expensive education to themselves, their parents, and society. In fact, they are probably under more pressure. For although they leave college superbly equipped to bring fresh leadership to traditionally male jobs, society hasn't yet caught up with this fact.

22   Along with economic pressure goes parental pressure. Inevitably, the two are deeply intertwined.

23   I see many students taking pre-medical courses with joyless tenacity. They go off to their labs as if they were going to the dentist. It saddens me because I know them in other corners of their life as cheerful people.

24   "Do you want to go to medical school?" I ask them.

25   "I guess so," they say, without conviction, or "Not really."

26   "Then why are you going?"

27   "Well, my parents want me to be a doctor. They're paying all this money and . . ."

28   Poor students, poor parents. They are caught in one of the oldest webs of love and duty and guilt. The parents mean well: they are trying to steer their sons and daughters toward a secure future. But the sons and daughters want to major in history or classics or philosophy—subjects with no "practical" value. Where's the payoff on the humanities? It's not easy to persuade such loving parents that the humanities do indeed pay off. The intellectual faculties developed by studying subjects like history and classics—an ability to synthesize and relate, to weigh cause and effect, to see events in perspective—are just the faculties that make creative leaders in business or almost any general field. Still, many fathers would rather put their money on courses that point toward a specific profession—courses that are pre-law, pre-medical, pre-business, or, as I sometimes heard it put, "pre-rich."

29   But the pressure on students is severe. They are truly torn. One part of them feels obligated to fulfill their parents' expectations; after all, their parents are older and presumably wiser. Another part tells them that the expectations that are right for their parents are not right for them.

30   I know a student who wants to be an artist. She is very obviously an artist and will be a good one—she has already had several modest local exhibits. Meanwhile she is growing as a well-rounded person and taking humanistic subjects that will enrich the inner resources out of which her art will grow. But her father is strongly opposed. He thinks that an artist is a "dumb" thing to be. The student vacillates and tries to please everybody. She keeps up with her art somewhat furtively and takes some of the "dumb" courses her father wants her to take—at least they are dumb courses for her. She is a free spirit on a campus of tense students—no small achievement in itself—and she deserves to follow her muse.

31   Peer pressure and self-induced pressure are also intertwined, and they begin almost at the beginning of freshman year.

32   "I had a freshman student I'll call Linda," one dean told me, "who came in and said she was under terrible pressure because her roommate, Barbara, was much brighter and studied all the time. I couldn't tell her that Barbara had come in two hours earlier to say the same thing about Linda."

33   The story is almost funny—except that it's not. It's symptomatic of all the pressures put together. When every student thinks every other student is working harder and doing better, the only solution is to study harder still. I see students going off to the library every night after dinner and coming back when it closes at midnight. I wish they could sometimes forget about their peers and go to a movie. I hear the clacking of typewriters in the hours before dawn. I see the tension in their eyes when exams are approaching and papers are due: *Will I get everything done?*

34   Probably they won't. They will get sick. They will get "blocked." They will sleep. They will oversleep. They will bug out. *Hey Carlos, help!*

35   Part of the problem is that they do more than they are expected to do. A professor will assign five-page papers. Several students will start writing ten-page papers to impress him. Then more students will write ten-page papers, and a few will raise the ante to fifteen. Pity the poor student who is still just doing the assignment.

36   "Once you have twenty or thirty percent of the student population deliberately overexerting," one dean points out, "it's bad for everybody. When a teacher gets more and more effort from his class, the student who is doing normal work can be perceived as not doing well. The tactic works, psychologically."

37   Why can't the professor just cut back and not accept longer papers? He can, and he probably will. But by then the term will be half over and the damage done. Grade fever is highly contagious and not easily reversed. Besides, the professor's main concern is with his course. He knows his students only in relation to the course and doesn't know that they are also overexerting in their other courses. Nor is it really his business. He didn't sign up for dealing with the student as a whole person and with all the emotional baggage the student brought along from home. That's what deans, masters, chaplains, and psychiatrists are for.

38   To some extent this is nothing new: a certain number of professors have always been self-contained islands of scholarship and shyness, more comfortable with books than with people. But the new pauperism has widened the gap still further, for professors who actually like to spend time with students don't have as much time to spend. They also are overexerting. If they are young, they are busy trying to publish in order not to perish, hanging by their finger nails onto a shrinking profession. If they are old and tenured, they are buried under the duties of administering departments—as departmental chairmen or members of committees—that have been thinned out by the budgetary axe.

39   Ultimately it will be the students' own business to break the circles in which they are trapped. They are too young to be prisoners of their parents' dreams and their classmates' fears. They must be jolted into believing in themselves as unique men and women who have the power to shape their own future.

40   "Violence is being done to the undergraduate experience," says Carlos Hortas. "College should be open-ended: at the end it should open many, many roads. Instead, students are choosing their goal in advance, and their choices narrow as they go along. It's almost as if they think that the country has been codified in the type of jobs that exist—that they've got to fit into certain slots. Therefore, fit into the best-paying slot.

41   "They ought to take chances. Not taking chances will lead to a life of colorless mediocrity. They'll be comfortable. But something in the spirit will be missing."

42   I have painted too drab a portrait of today's students, making them seem a solemn lot. That is only half of their story; if they were so dreary I wouldn't so thoroughly enjoy their company. The other half is that they are easy to like. They are quick to laugh and to offer friendship. They are not introverts. They are usually kind and are more considerate of one another than any student generation I have known.

43   Nor are they so obsessed with their studies that they avoid sports and extracurricular activities. On the contrary, they juggle their crowded hours to play on a variety of teams, perform with musical and dramatic groups, and write for campus publications. But this in turn is one more cause of anxiety. There are too many choices. Academically, they have 1,300 courses to select from; outside class they have to decide how much spare time they can spare and how to spend it.

44   This means that they engage in fewer extracurricular pursuits than their predecessors did. If they want to row on the crew and play in the symphony they will eliminate one; in the '60s they would have done both. They also tend to choose activities that are self-limiting. Drama, for instance, is flourishing in all twelve of Yale's residential colleges as it never has before. Students hurl themselves into these productions—as actors, directors, carpenters, and technicians —with a dedication to create the best possible play, knowing that the day will come when the run will end and they can get back to their studies.

45   They also can't afford to be the willing slave of organizations like the *Yale Daily News*. Last spring at the one-hundredth anniversary banquet of that paper —whose past chairmen include such once and future kings as Potter Stewart, Kingman Brewster, and William F. Buckley, Jr.—much was made of the fact that the editorial staff used to be small and totally committed and that "newsies" routinely worked fifty hours a week. In effect they belonged to a club; newsies is how they defined themselves at Yale. Today's student will write one or two articles a week, when he can, and he defines himself as a student. I've never heard the word newsie except at the banquet.

46   If I have described the modern undergraduate primarily as a driven creature who is largely ignoring the blithe spirit inside who keeps trying to come out and play, it's because that's where the crunch is, not only at Yale but throughout American education. It's why I think we should all be worried about the values that are nurturing a generation so fearful of risk and so goal-obsessed at such an early age.

47   I tell students that there is no one "right" way to get ahead—that each of them is a different person, starting from a different point and bound for a different destination. I tell them that change is a tonic and that all the slots are not codified nor the frontiers closed. One of my ways of telling them is to invite men and women who have achieved success outside the academic world to come and talk informally with my students during the year. They are heads of companies or ad agencies, editors of magazines, politicians, public officials, television magnates, labor leaders, business executives, Broadway producers, artists, writers, economists, photographers, scientists, historians—a mixed bag of achievers.

48   I ask them to say a few words about how they got started. The students assume that they started in their present profession and knew all along that it was what they wanted to do. Luckily for me, most of them got into their field by a circuitous route, to their surprise, after many detours. The students are startled. They can hardly conceive of a career that was not pre-planned. They can hardly imagine allowing the hand of God or chance to nudge them down some unforeseen trail.

21

Exposition:
Causal Analysis

WHY DO WOMEN WORK?

Gloria Steinem

Gloria Steinem is a writer, editor, lecturer, and leader of the women's movement. She was the founder and editor of Ms. Magazine, *for which she continues to write regularly. In 1972* McCall's *magazine named her Woman of the Year. In addition to numerous articles on women's issues, civil rights, and politics, Steinem has published* The Thousand Indias *(1957),* The Beach Book *(1963), and* Outrageous Acts and Everyday Rebellions *(1983), from which the following essay is taken.*

1   Toward the end of the 1970s, *The Wall Street Journal* devoted an eight-part, front-page series to "the working woman"—that is, the influx of women into the paid-labor force—as the greatest change in American life since the Industrial Revolution.

2   Many women readers greeted both the news and the definition with cynicism. After all, women have always worked. If all the productive work of human maintenance that women do in the home were valued at its replacement cost, the gross national product of the United States would go up by 26 percent. It's just that we are now more likely than ever before to leave our poorly rewarded, low-security, high-risk job of homemaking (though we're still trying to explain that it's a perfectly good one and that the problem is male society's refusal both

to do it and to give it an economic value) for more secure, independent, and better-paid jobs outside the home.

3   Obviously, the real work revolution won't come until all productive work is rewarded—including child rearing and other jobs done in the home—and men are integrated into so-called women's work as well as vice versa. But the radical change being touted by the *Journal* and other media is one part of that long integration process: the unprecedented flood of women into salaried jobs, that is, into the labor force as it has been male-defined and previously occupied by men. We are already more than 41 percent of it—the highest proportion in history. Given the fact that women also make up a whopping 69 percent of the "discouraged labor force" (that is, people who need jobs but don't get counted in the unemployment statistics because they've given up looking), plus an official female unemployment rate that is substantially higher than men's, it's clear that we could expand to become fully half of the national work force by 1990.

4   Faced with this determination of women to find a little independence and to be paid and honored for our work, experts have rushed to ask: "Why?" It's a question rarely directed at male workers. Their basic motivations of survival and personal satisfaction are taken for granted. Indeed, men are regarded as "odd" and therefore subjects for sociological study and journalistic reports only when they *don't* have work, even if they are rich and don't need jobs or are poor and can't find them. Nonetheless, pollsters and sociologists have gone to great expense to prove that women work outside the home because of dire financial need, or if we persist despite the presence of a wage-earning male, out of some desire to buy "little extras" for our families, or even out of good old-fashioned penis envy.

5   Job interviewers and even our own families may still ask salaried women the big "Why?" If we have small children at home or are in some job regarded as "men's work," the incidence of such questions increases. Condescending or accusatory versions of "What's a nice girl like you doing in a place like this?" have not disappeared from the workplace.

6   How do we answer these assumptions that we are "working" out of some pressing or peculiar need? Do we feel okay about arguing that it's as natural for us to have salaried jobs as for our husbands—whether or not we have young children at home? Can we enjoy strong career ambitions without worrying about being thought "unfeminine"? When we confront men's growing resentment of women competing in the work force (often in the form of such guilt-producing accusations as "You're taking men's jobs away" or "You're damaging your children"), do we simply state that a decent job is a basic human right for everybody?

7   I'm afraid the answer is often no. As individuals and as a movement, we tend to retreat into some version of a tactically questionable defense: "Womenworkbecausewehaveto." The phrase has become one word, one key on the typewriter—an economic form of the socially "feminine" stance of passivity and self-sacrifice. Under attack, we still tend to present ourselves as creatures

of economic necessity and familial devotion. "Womenworkbecausewehaveto" has become the easiest thing to say.

8   Like most truisms, this one is easy to prove with statistics. Economic need *is* the most consistent work motive—for women as well as men. In 1976, for instance, 43 percent of all women in the paid-labor force were single, widowed, separated, or divorced, and working to support themselves and their dependents. An additional 21 percent were married to men who had earned less than ten thousand dollars in the previous year, the minimum then required to support a family of four. In fact, if you take men's pension, stocks, real estate, and various forms of accumulated wealth into account, a good statistical case can be made that there are more women who "have" to work (that is, who have neither the accumulated wealth, nor husbands whose work or wealth can support them for the rest of their lives) than there are men with the same need. If we were going to ask one group "Do you really need this job?", we should ask men.

9   But the first weakness of the whole "have to work" defense is its deceptiveness. Anyone who has ever experienced dehumanized life on welfare or any other confidence-shaking dependency knows that a paid job may be preferable to the dole, even when the handout is coming from a family member. Yet the will and self-confidence to work on one's own can diminish as dependency and fear increase. That may explain why—contrary to the "have to" rationale— wives of men who earn less than three thousand dollars a year are actually *less* likely to be employed than wives whose husbands make ten thousand dollars a year or more.

10   Furthermore, the greatest proportion of employed wives is found among families with a total household income of twenty-five to fifty thousand dollars a year. This is the statistical underpinning used by some sociologists to prove that women's work is mainly important for boosting families into the middle or upper middle class. Thus, women's incomes are largely used for buying "luxuries" and "little extras": a neat doublewhammy that renders us secondary within our families, and makes our jobs expendable in hard times. We may even go along with this interpretation (at least, up to the point of getting fired so a male can have our job). It preserves a husbandly ego-need to be seen as the primary breadwinner, and still allows us a safe "feminine" excuse for working.

11   But there are often rewards that we're not confessing. As noted in *The Two-Career Couple,* by Francine and Douglas Hall: "Women who hold jobs by choice, even blue-collar routine jobs, are more satisfied with their lives than are the full-time housewives."

12   In addition to personal satisfaction, there is also society's need for all its members' talents. Suppose that jobs were given out on only a "have to work" basis to both women and men—one job per household. It would be unthinkable to lose the unique abilities of, for instance, Eleanor Holmes Norton, the distinguished chair of the Equal Employment Opportunity Commission. But would we then be forced to question the important work of her husband, Edward Norton, who is also a distinguished lawyer? Since men earn more than twice as much as women on the average, the wife in most households would be more likely to give

up her job. Does that mean the nation could do as well without millions of its nurses, teachers, and secretaries? Or that the rare man who earns less than his wife should give up his job?

13   It was this kind of waste of human talents on a society-wide scale that traumatized millions of unemployed or underemployed Americans during the Depression. Then, a one-job-per-household rule seemed somewhat justified, yet the concept was used to displace women workers only, create intolerable dependencies, and waste female talent that the country needed. That Depression experience, plus the energy and example of women who were finally allowed to work during the manpower shortage created by World War II, led Congress to reinterpret the meaning of the country's full-employment goal in its Economic Act of 1946. Full employment was officially defined as "the employment of those who want to work, without regard to whether their employment is, by some definition, necessary. This goal applies equally to men and to women." Since bad economic times are again creating a resentment of employed women—as well as creating more need for women to be employed—we need such a goal more than ever. Women are again being caught in a tragic double bind: We are required to be strong and then punished for our strength.

14   Clearly, anything less than government and popular commitment to this 1946 definition of full employment will leave the less powerful groups, whoever they may be, in danger. Almost as important as the financial penalty paid by the powerless is the suffering that comes from being shut out of paid and recognized work. Without it, we lose much of our self-respect and our ability to prove that we are alive by making some difference in the world. That's just as true for the suburban woman as it is for the unemployed steel worker.

15   But it won't be easy to give up the passive defense of "weworkbecausewe-haveto."

16   When a woman who is struggling to support her children and grandchildren on welfare sees her neighbor working as a waitress, even though that neighbor's husband has a job, she may feel resentful; and the waitress (of course, not the waitress's husband) may feel guilty. Yet unless we establish the obligation to provide a job for everyone who is willing and able to work, that welfare woman may herself be penalized by policies that give out only one public-service job per household. She and her daughter will have to make a painful and divisive decision about which of them gets that precious job, and the whole household will have to survive on only one salary.

17   A job as a human right is a principle that applies to men as well as women. But women have more cause to fight for it. The phenomenon of the "working woman" has been held responsible for everything from an increase in male impotence (which turned out, incidently, to be attributable to medication for high blood pressure) to the rising cost of steak (which was due to high energy costs and beef import restrictions, not women's refusal to prepare the cheaper, slower-cooking cuts). Unless we see a job as part of every citizen's right to autonomy and personal fulfillment, we will continue to be vulnerable to someone else's idea of what 'need' is, and whose 'need' counts the most.

18   In many ways, women who do not have to work for simple survival, but who choose to do so nonetheless, are on the frontier of asserting this right for all women. Those with well-to-do husbands are dangerously easy for us to resent and put down. It's easier still to resent women from families of inherited wealth, even though men generally control and benefit from that wealth. (There is no Rockefeller Sisters Fund, no J. P. Morgan & Daughters, and sons-in-law may be the ones who really sleep their way to power.) But to prevent a woman whose husband or father is wealthy from earning her own living, and from gaining the self-confidence that comes with that ability, is to keep her needful of that unearned power and less willing to disperse it. Moreover, it is to lose forever her unique talents.

19   Perhaps modern feminists have been guilty of a kind of reverse snobbism that keeps us from reaching out to the wives and daughters of wealthy men; yet it was exactly such women who refused the restrictions of class and financed the first wave of feminist revolution.

20   For most of us, however, "womenworkbecausewehaveto" is just true enough to be seductive as a personal defense.

21   If we use it without also staking out the larger human right to a job, however, we will never achieve that right. And we will always be subject to the false argument that independence for women is a luxury affordable only in good economic times. Alternatives to layoffs will not be explored, acceptable unemployment will always be used to frighten those with jobs into accepting low wages, and we will never remedy the real cost, both to families and to the country, of dependent women and a massive loss of talent.

22   Worst of all, we may never learn to find productive, honored work as a natural part of ourselves and as one of life's basic pleasures.

THE VIOLENCE IS FAKE, THE IMPACT IS REAL

Ellen Goodman

Ellen Goodman has written for Newsweek, *the* Detroit Free Press, *and the* Boston Globe. *Her popular newspaper column, "At Large," has been syndicated since 1976. She has won praise as a radio and television commentator, and in 1980 she won the Pulitzer Prize for distinguished commentary. Her essays have been collected in* Close to Home *(1979),* At Large *(1980),* Keeping in Touch *(1985), and* Making Sense *(1989). The following essay was first published in 1977.*

1   I don't usually think of television executives as being modest, shy and retiring. But for a decade or two, the same souls who have bragged about their success in selling products have been positively humble about their success in selling messages.

2   Yes indeed, they would tell advertisers, children see, children do . . . do buy candy bars and cereals and toys. But no, no, they would tell parents, children see, but children don't . . . imitate mangling and mayhem.

3   But now the government has released another study on TV and violence. The predictable conclusion is that "violence on television does lead to aggressive behavior by children and teenagers who watch the programs." After analyzing 2500 studies and publications since 1970, the "overwhelming" scientific evidence is that "excessive" violence on the screen produces violence off the screen.

4   Somehow or other, I feel like I have been here before. By now, the protestations of the networks sound like those of the cigarette manufacturers who will deny the link between cigarettes and lung disease to their (and our) last breath. By now, studies come and go, but the problem remains.

5   Today the average kid sits in front of the tube for 26 hours a week. The kids don't begin with a love of violence. Even today, one runaway favorite in the Saturday morning line-up is about the benign "Smurfs." But eventually they learn from grown-ups.

6   In the incredible shrinking world of kidvid, there is no regularly scheduled program for kids on any of the three networks between the hours of 7 A.M. and 6 P.M. A full 80 percent of the programs kids watch are adult television. For those who choose adventures, the broadcasters offer endless sagas of terror, chase, murder, rescue.

7   As Peggy Charren, who has watched this scene for a long time as head of Action for Children's Television, puts it: "Broadcasters believe that the more violent the problems, the more attractive the adventure to audiences in terms of sitting there and not turning it off. The ultimate adventure is doing away with someone's life. The ultimate excitement is death."

8   The government, in its report, listed some theories about why there is this link between violence on TV and violence in kids' behavior. One theory was that TV is a how-to lesson in aggression. Children learn "how to" hit and hurt from watching the way they learn how to count and read. Another theory is that kids who see a world full of violence accept it as normal behavior.

9   But I wonder whether violence isn't accepted because it is normalized— sanitized and packaged. We don't see violence on television in terms of pain and suffering, but in terms of excitement. In cartoons, characters are smashed with boulders, and dropped from airplanes only to get up unscathed. In adventure shows, people are killed all the time, but they are rarely "hurt."

10   As Charren put it, "There is no feeling badly about violence on television." We don't bear witness to the pain of a single gunshot wound. We don't see the broken hand and teeth that come from one blow to the jaw. We don't share the blood or the guilt, the anguish or the mourning. We don't see the labor of rebuilding a car, a window, a family.

11   Our television stars brush themselves off and return same time, same situation, next week without a single bruise. Cars are replaced. The dead are carted off and forgotten.

12   In Japan, I am told there is an unwritten rule that if you show violence on television, you show the result of that violence. Such a program is, I am sure, much more disturbing. But maybe it should be. Maybe that's what's missing.

13   In the real world, people repress aggression because they know the consequences. But on television, there are no consequences. In the end kids may be less affected by the presence of violence than by the absence of pain. They learn that violence is okay. That nobody gets hurt.

14   So, if the broadcasters refuse to curb their profitable adventures in hurting, their national contribution to violence, then let them add something to the mix: equal time for truth and consequences.

THE EFFECTS OF A NUCLEAR EXPLOSION
Jonathan Schell

Jonathan Schell is a staff writer for the New Yorker *magazine. This essay, on the effects of a bomb on New York City, was one of three articles originally published in the* New Yorker *and then collected into the book* The Fate of the Earth *(1982). Schell's other books include* The Village of Ben Suc *(1967),* The Time of Illusion *(1976), and* The Abolition *(1984), which proposes the end of nuclear weapons.*

1   One way to begin to grasp the destructive power of present-day nuclear weapons is to describe the consequences of the detonation of a one-megaton bomb, which possesses 80 times the explosive power of the Hiroshima bomb, on a large city, such as New York. Burst some 8,500 feet above the Empire State Building, a one-megaton bomb would gut or flatten almost every building between Battery Park and 125th Street, or within a radius of four and four-tenths miles, or in an area of 61 square miles, and would heavily damage buildings between the northern tip of Staten Island and the George Washington Bridge, or within a radius of about eight miles, or in an area of about 200 square miles.

2   A conventional explosive delivers a swift shock, like a slap, to whatever it hits, but the blast wave of a sizable nuclear weapon endures for several seconds and can surround and destroy whole buildings. People, of course, would be picked up and hurled away from the blast along with the rest of the debris.

Used with permission, Alfred A. Knopf, Inc.

Within the 61 square miles, the walls, roofs and floors of any buildings that had not been flattened would be collapsed, and the people and furniture inside would be swept down onto the street. (Technically, this zone would be hit by various overpressures of at least five pounds per square inch. Overpressure is defined as the pressure in excess of normal atmospheric pressure.)

3   As far away as 10 miles from ground zero, pieces of glass and other sharp objects would be hurled about by the blast wave at lethal velocities. In Hiroshima, where buildings were low and, outside the center of the city, were often constructed of light materials, injuries from falling buildings were often minor. But in New York, where the buildings are tall and are constructed of heavy materials, the physical collapse of the city would certainly kill millions of people.

4   The streets of New York are narrow ravines running between the high walls of the city's buildings. In a nuclear attack, the walls would fall and the ravines would fill up. The people in the buildings would fall to the street with the debris of the buildings, and the people in the street would be crushed by this avalanche of people and buildings.

5   At a distance of two miles or so from ground zero, winds would reach 400 miles an hour, and another two miles away they would reach 180 miles an hour. Meanwhile, the fireball would be growing, until it was more than a mile wide, and rocketing upward, to a height of over six miles. For ten seconds, it would broil the city below. Anyone caught in the open within nine miles of ground zero would receive third-degree burns and would probably be killed; closer to the explosion, people would be charred and killed instantly.

6   From Greenwich Village up to Central Park, the heat would be great enough to melt metal and glass. Readily inflammable materials, such as newspapers and dry leaves, would ignite in all five boroughs (though in only a small part of Staten Island) and west to the Passaic River, in New Jersey, within a radius of about nine and a half miles from ground zero, thereby creating an area of more than 280 square miles in which mass fires were likely to break out.

7   If it were possible (as it would not be) for someone to stand at Fifth Avenue and Seventy-second Street (about two miles from ground zero) without being killed instantly, he would see the following sequence of events. A dazzling white light from the fireball would illumine the scene, continuing for perhaps 30 seconds. Simultaneously, searing heat would ignite everything flammable and start to melt windows, cars, buses, lampposts, and everything else made of metal or glass. People in the street would immediately catch fire, and would shortly be reduced to heavily charred corpses.

8   About five seconds after the light appeared, the blast wave would strike, laden with the debris of a now nonexistent midtown. Some buildings might be crushed, as though a giant fist had squeezed them on all sides, and others might be picked up off their foundations and whirled uptown with the other debris. On the far side of Central Park, the West Side skyline would fall from south to north. The 400-mile-an-hour wind would blow from south to north, die down after a few seconds, and then blow in the reverse direction with diminished

intensity. While these things were happening, the fireball would be burning in the sky for the 10 seconds of the thermal pulse. Soon huge, thick clouds of dust and smoke would envelop the scene, and as the mushroom cloud rushed overhead (it would have a diameter of about 12 miles), the light from the sun would be blotted out, and day would turn to night.

9   Within minutes, fires, ignited by the thermal pulse and by broken gas mains, tanks of gas and oil, and the like, would begin to spread in the darkness, and a strong, steady wind would begin to blow in the direction of the blast. As at Hiroshima, a whirlwind might be produced, which would sweep through the ruins, and radioactive rain, generated under the meteorological conditions created by the blast, might fall.

10   Before long, the individual fires would coalesce into a mass fire, which, depending largely on the winds, would become either a conflagration or a firestorm. In a conflagration, prevailing winds spread a wall of fire as far as there is any combustible material to sustain it; in a firestorm, a vertical updraft caused by the fire itself sucks the surrounding air in toward a central point, and the fires therefore converge in a single fire of extreme heat. A mass fire of either kind renders shelters useless by burning up all the oxygen in the air and creating toxic gases, so that anyone inside the shelters is asphyxiated, and also by heating the ground to such high temperatures that the shelters turn, in effect, into ovens, cremating the people inside them.

11   In Dresden, several days after the firestorm raised there by Allied conventional bombing, the interiors of some bomb shelters were still so hot that when they were opened the inrushing air caused the contents to burst into flame. Only those who had fled their shelters when the bombing started had any chance of surviving. (It is difficult to predict in a particular situation which form the fires will take. In actual experience, Hiroshima suffered a firestorm and Nagasaki suffered a conflagration.)

12   In this vast theatre of physical effects, all the scenes of agony and death that took place at Hiroshima would again take place, but now involving millions of people rather than hundreds of thousands.

22

Argumentation

TEENAGERS WORK TOO SOON

Neal R. Peirce

Neal Peirce is a founder and contributing editor of the National Journal *and a former political editor of* Congressional Quarterly. *He writes a weekly syndicated column that appears in over 100 newspapers and is the author of 11 books, including* The Megastates of America *(1972) and* The Book of America: Inside Fifty States Today *(1983). This essay was published in 1987.*

1   The horror stories continue to mount—self-centered high-school students working excessive hours in the local fast-food joint or record store, centering their lives around the mall, designer jeans and status bars, anything but their studies.

2   Teachers complain of kids turning up dazed, bone weary for class. Principals tell of grades tumbling as students work as much as 20 to 40 hours a week, double what educators call a safe maximum.

3   Rarely have sociologists registered media attention to match Allen Greenberger's and Laurence Steinberg's recent book, "When Teen-agers Work." They clearly hit a tender nerve with their message that excessive juvenile work hours in uninspiring jobs ends up undermining schoolwork and breeding a generation of grasping materialists.

4   Two classic American values have crashed into each other. On the one hand, there's the work ethic. But there's another belief: Education means everything. On top of that, the nation has been in a paroxysm of concern about subquality education—not so much for fear youngsters will miss poetry or

literature or science, but to make sure the Japanese don't make impoverished fools of us.

5   So how do we strike a balance, for the kids' benefit and society's?

6   The teen-agers may not be the best judges. "Ask them," says Jeffrey Newman of the National Child Labor Committee, "and they say they love working. But so did the kids who came out of the mines in 1907. They were dead of black lung disease at 30, but at the age of 10 they were delighted to scrape their fingers bloody looking for coal. So did the 8-year-olds in the cotton mills of the South."

7   In those days, kids worked mostly to help put bread on the family table, not—as Greenberger and Steinberg note—to finance "the latest in headphones, or the newest style of cashmere sweater, or front-row seats to every concert in town."

8   Are government rules the answer? National law already limits work for youngsters under 16 to no more than three hours on any school day, plus six on the weekend, for a total of 18. Some states set even lower limits.

9   How about enforcing child-labor laws that exist? But as of now "Nobody pays any attention to the laws," Newman says, least of all the Reagan administration.

10   Solutions will have to come from parents, if they're not too hung up on materialistic acquisition themselves.

11   Right now, laments Amatai Etzioni, visiting professor at the Harvard Business School, "parents are mesmerized by the notion that if a teen-ager is working it's good for his character, he's off the streets, not watching TV."

12   "McJobs," as Etzioni calls the fast-food generation of work, "are more time consuming, less character building." Greenberger and Steinberg go so far as to suggest stressful jobs even lead young people to alcohol and marijuana— which the work, in turn, pays for.

13   And while everyone talks about how middle-class kids ought to curb their appetites for the non-essentials, vast numbers of children in inner cities are separated by miles and tortuous transit routes (if any) from most suburban fast-food and retail strips. Their jobless rate remains alarmingly high. And they're precisely the young people who often live in poverty. They and their families have genuine need of cash. Most could benefit the most from a positive work experience.

14   There's a chance necessity will drive more employers to cultivate the needy inner city teen-age worker pool. But that "solution" isn't likely to do more than brush at the problem of middle-class kids working too soon, too long, at shallow jobs for dubious ends.

ANIMALS IN RESEARCH:
THE CASE FOR EXPERIMENTATION
Frederick A. King

Frederick A. King earned his Ph.D. in psychology from John Hopkins and has taught psychiatry, neurosurgery, and physiology at Ohio State University and at the University of Florida. He is currently director of the Yerkes Primate Center, professor of anatomy, and associate dean of the medical school at Emory University. As an expert in the field of animal research, King presented his argument to counter the opposition to animal experimentation, a movement that has grown enormously in the past several years. This article was originally published in Psychology Today *in 1984.*

1   The Mobilization for Animals Coalition (MFA) is an international network of more than 400 animal-protectionist organizations that address themselves to a variety of issues, including hunting, trapping, livestock protection, vegetarianism and pets. Their primary concern, however, is an adamant opposition to animal research. Some groups within the movement want to severely curtail research with animals, but the most visible and outspoken faction wants to eliminate it.

2   The astonishing growth of this activist movement during the past three years has culminated this year in an intense attack on the use of animals in psychological research. This past spring, John McArdle of the Humane Society of the United States charged that torture is the founding principle and fundamental characteristic of experimental psychology, and that psychological experimentation on animals among all the scientific disciplines is "the ideal candidate for elimination. No major scientific endeavor would suffer by such an act." A recent pamphlet published by the MFA stated, "Of all these experiments, those conducted in psychology are the most painful, pointless and repulsive."

3   The following specific allegations have been made by the MFA: Animals are given intense, repeated electric shocks until they lose the ability even to scream in pain; animals are deprived of food and water and allowed to suffer and die from hunger and thirst; animals are put in isolation until they are driven insane or die from despair and terror; animals are subjected to crushing forces that smash their bones and rupture their internal organs; the limbs of animals are mutilated or amputated to produce behavioral changes; animals are the victims of extreme pain and stress, inflicted out of idle curiosity, in nightmarish experiments designed to make healthy animals psychotic.

4   Such irresponsible accusations of research cruelty have consistently characterized the publications of the MFA. However, a recent study by psychologists D. Caroline Coile and Neal E. Miller of Rockefeller University counters
these charges. Coile and Miller looked at every article (a total of 608) appearing
in the past five years in journals of the American Psychological Association
that report animal research. They concluded that none of the extreme allegations made by the MFA could be supported.

5   Coile and Miller admit that charges of cruelty may have gone unreported or
been reported elsewhere but, they say, if such studies did occur, "they certainly
were infrequent, and it is extremely misleading to imply that they are typical of
experimental psychology."

6   Furthermore, there are standards and mechanisms to ensure that research
animals are treated in a humane and scientifically sensible way. These mechanisms include the Federal Animal Welfare Act of 1966 (amended in Congress in
1970, 1976 and 1979); periodic inspection of all animal-research facilities by the
Department of Agriculture; visits by federal agencies that fund animal research
and are increasingly attentive to the conditions of animal care and experimental
procedures that could cause pain or distress; and a comprehensive document,
"Guide for the Care and Use of Laboratory Animals," prepared by the National
Academy of Sciences. In addition, virtually every major scientific society whose
members conduct animal research distributes guidelines for such research.
Above and beyond all of this, most universities and research institutes have
animal-care committees that monitor animal research and care.

7 The United States Public Health Service is revising its guidelines to require
institutions that do research with animals to designate even clearer lines of
authority and responsibility for animal care. This will include detailed information about how each institution complies with the new regulations as well as a
requirement that animal-research committees include not only the supervising
laboratory veterinarian and scientists but also a nonscientist and a person not
affiliated with the institution. These committees will review programs for animal care, inspect all animal facilities and review and monitor all research proposals before they are submitted to agencies of the United States Public Health
Service. The committees will also have the power to disapprove or terminate any
research proposal.

8   This is not to say that research scientists are perfect. There will be occasional errors, cases of neglect and instances of abuse—as is the case with any
human endeavor, whether it be the rearing of children, the practicing of a trade
or profession or the governing of a nation. But a high standard of humane
treatment is maintained.

9   The choice of psychological research for special attack almost certainly
stems from the fact that such research is viewed as more vulnerable than are
studies of anatomy, physiology or microbiology. In the minds of many, psychology
is a less well-developed science than the biological sciences and the benefits that
have accrued from psychological research with animals are less well known.

Hence, it is more difficult to grasp the necessity for animal research in behavioral studies than it is in biomedical studies.

10   Anyone who has looked into the matter can scarcely deny that major advances in medicine have been achieved through basic research with animals. Among these are the development of virtually all modern vaccines against infectious diseases, the invention of surgical approaches to eye disorders, bone and joint injuries and heart disease, the discovery of insulin and other hormones and the testing of all new drugs and antibiotics.

11   The benefits to humans of psychological research with animals may be less well known than those of medical research but are just as real. Historically, the application of psychological research to human problems has lagged considerably behind the applied use of medical research. Mental events and overt behavior, although controlled by the nervous system and biology of an organism, are much more difficult to describe and study than are the actions of tissues or organ systems. To describe the complex interplay of perceptions, memories, cognitive and emotional processes with a physical and social environment that changes from moment to moment, elaborate research designs had to be developed. Since even a single type of behavior, such as vocalization, has so many different forms, a wide variety of ways of measuring the differences had to be developed. Finally, because much psychological research makes inferences from behavioral observations about internal states of an organism, methods were needed to insure that the interpretations were valid. Such complexities do not make the study of animal or human behavior less scientific or important than other kinds of research, but they do make it more difficult and slow its readiness for clinical applications.

12 Basic psychological research with animals has led to important achievements in the interest of human welfare. Examples include the use of biofeedback, which had its origin in studies of behavioral conditioning of neuromuscular activities in rats and other animals. Today, biofeedback can be used to control blood pressure and hypertension and help prevent heart attacks. In the case of paralyzed patients, it can be used to elevate blood pressure, enabling those who would otherwise have to spend their lives lying down to sit upright. Biofeedback techniques also are used in the reduction and control of severe pain and as a method of neuromuscular control to help reverse the process of scoliosis, a disabling and disfiguring curvature of the spine. Biofeedback can also be a cost-effective alternative to certain medical treatments and can help avoid many of the complications associated with long-term drug use.

13   Language studies with apes have led to practical methods of teaching language skills to severely retarded children who, prior to this work, had little or no language ability. Patients who have undergone radiation therapy for cancer can now take an interest in nutritious foods and avoid foods that have little nutritional value, thanks to studies of conditioned taste aversion done with animals. Neural and behavioral studies of early development of vision in cats and primates—studies that could not have been carried out with children—have led to advances in pediatric ophthalmology that can prevent irreversible brain

damage and loss of vision in children who have cataracts and various other serious eye problems.

14   Behavioral modification and behavioral therapy, widely accepted techniques for treating alcohol, drug and tobacco addiction, have a long history of animal studies investigating learning theory and reward systems. Programmed instruction, the application of learning principles to educational tasks, is based on an array of learning studies in animals. These are but a few examples of the effectiveness and usefulness for humans of psychological research with animals.

15   Those opposed to animal research have proposed that alternatives to animal research, such as mathematical and computer models and tissue cultures, be used. In some cases, these alternatives are both feasible and valuable. Tissue cultures, for example, have been very effective in certain toxicological studies that formerly required live animals. For psychological studies, however, it is often necessary to study the whole animal and its relationship to the environment. Visual problems, abnormal sexual behavior, depression and aggression, for example, are not seen in tissue cultures and do not lend themselves to computer models. When human subjects cannot be used for such studies, animals are necessary if the research is to be done at all.

16 Extremists within the animal-rights movement take the position that animals have rights equal to or greater than those of humans. It follows from this that even if humans might benefit from animal research, the cost to animals is too high. It is ironic that despite this moral position, the same organizations condone—and indeed sponsor—activities that appear to violate the basic rights of animals to live and reproduce. Each year 10,000,000 dogs are destroyed by public pounds, animal shelters and humane societies. Many of these programs are supported and even operated by animal-protectionist groups. Surely there is a strong contradiction when those who profess to believe in animal rights deny animals their right to life. A similar situation exists with regard to programs of pet sterilization, programs that deny animals the right to breed and to bear offspring and are sponsored in many cases by antivivisectionists and animal-rights groups. Evidently, animal-rights advocates sometimes recognize and subscribe to the position that animals do not have the same rights as humans. However, their public posture leaves little room for examining these subleties or applying similar standards to animal research.

17   Within the animal-protectionist movement there are moderates who have confidence in scientists as compassionate human beings and in the value of research. Their primary aims are to insure that animals are treated humanely and that discomfort in animal experimentation is kept to a minimum. It is to this group that scientists and scientific organizations have the responsibility to explain what they do, why and how they do it and what benefits occur.

18   I believe that the values guiding contemporary animal research represent prevailing sentiment within the scientific community and, indeed, within society at large. And I believe that these values are congruent with those of the moderates within the animal-protectionist movement. As articulated by ethicist

Arthur Caplan, rights, in the most realistic sense, are granted by one group to another based on perceived similarities between the groups. Plainly, animals lack those characteristics that would allow them to share in the rights we grant to humans. We do not grant domestic animals the right to go where they wish or do what they want because they are obviously unable to comprehend the responsibilities and demands of human society. In fact, we do not as a society even grant all domestic animals and pets the right to live.

19   This does not mean, however, that we do not have a moral responsibility to animals. I believe, along with Caplan and the scientific research community at large, that we hold a moral stewardship for animals and that we are obliged to treat them with humane compassion and concern for their sentience. Many animal forms can and do feel pain and are highly aware of their environment. This awareness makes them worthy of our respect and serious concern. Caplan is certainly correct when he says that this moral obligation ought to be part of what it means to be a scientist today.

20   Science must proceed. The objective quest for knowledge is a treasured enterprise of our heritage and culture. Scientific inquiry into the nature of our living world has freed us from ignorance and superstition. Scientific understanding is an expression of our highest capacities—those of objective observation, interpretive reasoning, imagination and creativity. Founded on the results of basic research, often conducted with no goal other than that of increased understanding, the eventual practical use of this knowledge has led to a vastly improved well-being for humankind.

21   Extremists in the animal-rights movement probably will never accept such justifications for research or assurances of humane treatment. They may reject any actions, no matter how conscientious, that scientists take in realistically and morally reconciling the advance of human welfare with the use of animals. But, fortunately, there are many who, while deeply and appropriately concerned for the compassionate treatment of animals, recognize that human welfare is and should be our primary concern.

I HAVE A DREAM

Martin Luther King, Jr.

The Rev. Martin Luther King, Jr., president of the Southern Christian Leadership Conference, was the most well-known leader of the civil rights movement of the 1960s and the recipient of the 1964 Nobel Peace Prize. He was assassinated in 1968. King delivered this speech in 1963 at a celebration of the Emancipation

Proclamation, before a crowd of thousands who had marched to the Lincoln Memorial in Washington, D.C.

1   Five score years ago, a great American, in whose symbolic shadow we stand, signed the Emancipation Proclamation. This momentous decree came as a great beacon light of hope to millions of Negro slaves who had been seared in the flames of withering injustice. It came as a joyous daybreak to end the long night of captivity.

2   But one hundred years later, we must face the tragic fact that the Negro is still not free. One hundred years later, the life of the Negro is still sadly crippled by the manacles of segregation and the chains of discrimination. One hundred years later, the Negro lives on a lonely island of poverty in the midst of a vast ocean of material prosperity. One hundred years later, the Negro is still languishing in the corners of American society and finds himself an exile in his own land. So we have come here today to dramatize an appalling condition.

3   In a sense we have come to our nation's capital to cash a check. When the architects of our republic wrote the magnificent words of the Constitution and the Declaration of Independence, they were signing a promissory note to which every American was to fall heir. This note was a promise that all men would be guaranteed the unalienable rights of life, liberty, and the pursuit of happiness.

4   It is obvious today that America has defaulted on this promissory note insofar as her citizens of color are concerned. Instead of honoring this sacred obligation, America has given the Negro people a bad check; a check which has come back marked "insufficient funds." But we refuse to believe that the bank of justice is bankrupt. We refuse to believe that there are insufficient funds in the great vaults of opportunity of this nation. So we have come to cash this check—a check that will give us upon demand the riches of freedom and the security of justice. We have also come to this hallowed spot to remind America of the fierce urgency of *now*. This is no time to engage in the luxury of cooling off or to take the tranquilizing drugs of gradualism. *Now* is the time to make real the promises of Democracy. *Now* is the time to rise from the dark and desolate valley of segregation to the sunlit path of racial justice. *Now* is the time to open the doors of opportunity to all of God's children. *Now* is the time to lift our nation from the quicksands of racial injustice to the solid rock of brotherhood.

5   It would be fatal for the nation to overlook the urgency of the moment and to underestimate the determination of the Negro. This sweltering summer of the Negro's legitimate discontent will not pass until there is an invigorating autumn of freedom and equality. 1963 is not an end, but a beginning. Those who hope that the Negro needed to blow off steam and will now be content will have a rude awakening if the nation returns to business as usual. There will be neither rest nor tranquillity in America until the Negro is granted his citizenship rights. The whirlwinds of revolt will continue to shake the foundations of our nation until the bright day of justice emerges.

6   But there is something that I must say to my people who stand on the warm threshold which leads into the palace of justice. In the process of gaining our rightful place we must not be guilty of wrongful deeds. Let us not seek to satisfy our thirst for freedom by drinking from the cup of bitterness and hatred. We must forever conduct our struggle on the high plane of dignity and discipline. We must not allow our creative protest to degenerate into physical violence. Again and again we must rise to the majestic heights of meeting physical force with soul force. The marvelous new militancy which has engulfed the Negro community must not lead us to a distrust of all white people, for many of our white brothers, as evidenced by their presence here today, have come to realize that their destiny is tied up with our destiny and their freedom is inextricably bound to our freedom. We cannot walk alone.

7   And as we walk, we must make the pledge that we shall march ahead. We cannot turn back. There are those who are asking the devotees of civil rights, "When will you be satisfied?" We can never be satisfied as long as the Negro is the victim of the unspeakable horrors of police brutality. We can never be satisfied as long as our bodies, heavy with the fatigue or travel, cannot gain lodging in the motels of the highways and the hotels of the cities. We cannot be satisfied as long as the Negro's basic mobility is from a smaller ghetto to a larger one. We can never be satisfied as long as a Negro in Mississippi cannot vote and a Negro in New York believes he has nothing for which to vote. No, no, we are not satisfied, and we will not be satisfied until justice rolls down like waters and righteousness like a mighty stream.

8   I am not unmindful that some of you have come here out of great trials and tribulations. Some of you have come fresh from narrow jail cells. Some of you have come from areas where your quest for freedom left you battered by the storms of persecution and staggered by the winds of police brutality. You have been the veterans of creative suffering. Continue to work with the faith that unearned suffering is redemptive.

9   Go back to Mississippi, go back to Alabama, go back to South Carolina, go back to Georgia, go back to Louisiana, go back to the slums and ghettos of our northern cities, knowing that somehow this situation can and will be changed. Let us not wallow in the valley of despair.

10   I say to you today, my friends, that in spite of the difficulties and frustrations of the moment I still have a dream. It is a dream deeply rooted in the American dream.

11   I have a dream that one day this nation will rise up and live out the true meaning of its creed: "We hold these truths to be self-evident; that all men are created equal."

12   I have a dream that one day on the red hills of Georgia the sons of former slaves and the sons of former slaveowners will be able to sit down together at the table of brotherhood.

13   I have a dream that one day even the state of Mississippi, a desert state sweltering with the heat of injustice and oppression, will be transformed into an oasis of freedom and justice.

14   I have a dream that my four little children will one day live in a nation

where they will not be judged by the color of their skin but by the content of their character.

15   I have a dream today.

16   I have a dream that one day the state of Alabama, whose governor's lips are presently dripping with the words of interposition and nullification, will be transformed into a situation where little black boys and black girls will be able to join hands with little white boys and white girls and walk together as sisters and brothers.

17   I have a dream today.

18   I have a dream that one day every valley shall be exalted, every hill and mountain shall be made low, the rough places will be made plain, and the crooked places will be made straight, and the glory of the Lord shall be revealed, and all flesh shall see it together.

19   This is our hope. This is the faith with which I return to the South. With this faith we will be able to hew out of the mountain of despair a stone of hope. With this faith we will be able to transform the jangling discords of our nation into a beautiful symphony of brotherhood. With this faith we will be able to work together, to pray together, to struggle together, to go to jail together, to stand up for freedom together, knowing that we will be free one day.

20   This will be the day when all of God's children will be able to sing with new meaning

> My country, 'tis of thee,
> Sweet land of liberty,
>   Of thee I sing:
> Land where my fathers died,
> Land of the pilgrims' pride,
> From every mountain-side
>   Let freedom ring.

21   And if America is to be a great nation this must become true. So let freedom ring from the prodigious hilltops of New Hampshire. Let freedom ring from the mighty mountains of New York. Let freedom ring from the heightening Alleghenies of Pennsylvania!

22   Let freedom ring from the snowcapped Rockies of Colorado!

23   Let freedom ring from the curvaceous peaks of California!

24   But not only that; let freedom ring from Stone Mountain of Georgia!

25   Let freedom ring from Lookout Mountain of Tennessee!

26   Let freedom ring from every hill and molehill of Mississippi. From every mountainside, let freedom ring.

27   When we let freedom ring, when we let it ring from every village and every hamlet, from every state and every city, we will be able to speed up that day when all of God's children, black men and white men, Jews and Gentiles, Protestants and Catholics, will be able to join hands and sing in the words of the old Negro spiritual, "Free at last! free at last! thank God almighty, we are free at last!"

23

Description

PICTURES OF MY PARENTS

Maxine Hong Kingston

Maxine Hong Kingston teaches creative writing at the University of Hawaii. She is the author of The Woman Warrior: Memoirs of a Girlhood Among Ghosts *(1976), a collection of autobiographical essays about growing up as a Chinese-American in California. She has also published another collection of essays,* China Men *(1980), and a novel,* Tripmaster Monkey *(1989). This essay is from* The Woman Warrior.

1   Once in a long while, four times so far for me, my mother brings out the metal tube that holds her medical diploma. On the tube are gold circles crossed with seven red lines each—"joy" ideographs in abstract. There are also little flowers that look like gears for a gold machine. According to the scraps of labels with Chinese and American addresses, stamps, and postmarks, the family airmailed the can from Hong Kong in 1950. It got crushed in the middle, and whoever tried to peel the labels off stopped because the red and gold paint came off too, leaving silver scratches that rust. Somebody tried to pry the end off before discovering that the tube pulls apart. When I open it, the smell of China flies out, a thousand-year-old bat flying heavy-headed out of the Chinese caverns where bats are as white as dust, a smell that comes from long ago, far back in the brain. Crates from Canton, Hong Kong, Singapore, and Taiwan have that smell too, only stronger because they are more recently come from the Chinese.

2   Inside the can are three scrolls, one inside another. The largest says that in the twenty-third year of the National Republic, the To Keung School of Midwifery, where she has had two years of instruction and Hospital Practice, awards its Diploma to my mother, who has shown through oral and written examination her Proficiency in Midwifery, Pediatrics, Gynecology, "Medecine," "Surgary," Therapeutics, Ophthalmology, Bacteriology, Dermatology, Nursing and Bandage. This document has eight stamps on it: one, the school's English and Chinese names embossed together in a circle; one, as the Chinese enumerate, a stork and a big baby in lavender ink; one, the school's Chinese seal; one, an orangish paper stamp pasted in the border design; one, the red seal of Dr. Wu Pak-liang, M.D., Lyon, Berlin, president and "Ex-assistant étranger à la clinique chirugicale et d'accouchement de l'université de Lyon"; one, the red seal of Dean Woo Yin-kam, M.D.; one, my mother's seal, her chop mark larger than the president's and the dean's; and one, the number 1279 on the back. Dean Woo's signature is followed by "(Hackett)." I read in a history book that Hackett Medical College for Women at Canton was founded in the nineteenth century by European women doctors.

3   The school seal has been pressed over a photograph of my mother at the age of thirty-seven. The diploma gives her age as twenty-seven. She looks younger than I do, her eyebrows are thicker, her lips fuller. Her naturally curly hair is parted on the left, one wavy wisp tendrilling off to the right. She wears a scholar's white gown, and she is not thinking about her appearance. She stares straight ahead as if she could see me and past me to her grandchildren and grandchildren's grandchildren. She has spacy eyes, as all people recently from Asia have. Her eyes do not focus on the camera. My mother is not smiling; Chinese do not smile for photographs. Their faces command relatives in foreign lands—"Send money"—and posterity forever—"Put food in front of this picture." My mother does not understand Chinese-American snapshots. "What are you laughing at?" she asks.

4   The second scroll is a long narrow photograph of the graduating class with the school officials seated in front. I picked out my mother immediately. Her face is exactly her own, though forty years younger. She is so familiar, I can only tell whether or not she is pretty or happy or smart by comparing her to the other women. For this formal group picture she straightened her hair with oil to make a chinlength bob like the others'. On the other women, strangers, I can recognize a curled lip, a sidelong glance, pinched shoulders. My mother is not soft; the girl with the small nose and dimpled underlip is soft. My mother is not humorous, not like the girl at the end who lifts her mocking chin to pose like Girl Graduate. My mother does not have smiling eyes; the old woman teacher (Dean Woo?) in front crinkles happily, and the one faculty member in the western suit smiles westernly. Most of the graduates are girls whose faces have not yet formed; my mother's face will not change anymore, except to age. She is intelligent, alert, pretty. I can't tell if she's happy.

5   The graduates seem to have been looking elsewhere when they pinned the rose, zinnia, or chrysanthemum on their precise black dresses. One thin girl

wears hers in the middle of her chest. A few have a flower over a left or a right nipple. My mother put hers, a chrysanthemum, below her left breast. Chinese dresses at that time were dartless, cut as if women did not have breasts; these young doctors, unaccustomed to decorations, may have seen their chests as black expanses with no reference points for flowers. Perhaps they couldn't shorten that far gaze that lasts only a few years after a Chinese emigrates. In this picture too my mother's eyes are big with what they held—reaches of oceans beyond China, land beyond oceans. Most emigrants learn the barbarians' directness—how to gather themselves and stare rudely into talking faces as if trying to catch lies. In America my mother has eyes as strong as boulders, never once skittering off a face, but she has not learned to place decorations and phonograph needles, nor has she stopped seeing land on the other side of the oceans. Now her eyes include the relatives in China, as they once included my father smiling and smiling in his many western outfits, a different one for each photograph that he sent from America.

6   He and his friends took pictures of one another in bathing suits at Coney Island beach, the salt wind from the Atlantic blowing their hair. He's the one in the middle with his arms about the necks of his buddies. They pose in the cockpit of a biplane, on a motorcycle, and on a lawn beside the "Keep Off the Grass" sign. They are always laughing. My father, white shirt sleeves rolled up, smiles in front of a wall of clean laundry. In the spring he wears a new straw hat, cocked at a Fred Astaire angle. He steps out, dancing down the stairs, one foot forward, one back, a hand in his pocket. He wrote to her about the American custom of stomping on straw hats come fall. "If you want to save your hat for next year," he said, "you have to put it away early, or else when you're riding the subway or walking along Fifth Avenue, any stranger can snatch it off your head and put his foot through it. That's the way they celebrate the change of seasons here." In the winter he wears a gray felt hat with his gray overcoat. He is sitting on a rock in Central Park. In one snapshot he is not smiling; someone took it when he was studying, burred in the glare of the desk lamp.

7   There are no snapshots of my mother. In two small portraits, however, there is a black thumbprint on her forehead, as if someone had inked in bangs, as if someone had marked her.

8   "Mother, did bangs come into fashion after you had the picture taken?" One time she said yes. Another time when I asked, "Why do you have fingerprints on your forehead?" she said, "Your First Uncle did that." I disliked the unsureness in her voice.

9   The last scroll has columns of Chinese words. The only English is "Department of Health, Canton," imprinted on my mother's face, the same photograph as on the diploma. I keep looking to see whether she was afraid. Year after year my father did not come home or send for her. Their two children had been dead for ten years. If he did not return soon, there would be no more children. ("They were three and two years old, a boy and a girl. They could talk already.") My father did send money regularly, though, and she had nobody to spend it on but herself. She bought good clothes and shoes. Then she decided

to use the money for becoming a doctor. She did not leave for Canton immediately after the children died. In China there was time to complete feelings. As my father had done, my mother left the village by ship. There was a sea bird painted on the ship to protect it against shipwreck and winds. She was in luck. The following ship was boarded by river pirates, who kidnapped every passenger, even old ladies, "Sixty dollars for an old lady" was what the bandits used to say. "I sailed alone," she says, "to the capital of the entire province." She took a brown leather suitcase and a seabag stuffed with two quilts.

Ode to Thanksgiving

Michael J. Arlen

Michael J. Arlen is a television critic and staff writer for The New Yorker *magazine. He won the Screen Directors' Guild for television criticism in 1968 and the National Book Award for contemporary affairs in 1976. Arlen is the author of numerous books, including* Living-Room War *(1969) and* Passage to Ararat *(1975). This essay is from* The Camera Age *(1981), a collection of some of his* New Yorker *articles.*

1   It is time, at last, to speak the truth about Thanksgiving, and the truth is this. Thanksgiving is really not such a terrific holiday. Consider the traditional symbols of the event: Dried cornhusks hanging on the door! Terrible wine! Cranberry jelly in little bowls of extremely doubtful provenance which everyone is required to handle with the greatest of care! Consider the participants, the merrymakers: men and women (also children) who have survived passably well throughout the years, mainly as a result of living at considerable distances from their dear parents and beloved siblings, who on this feast of feasts must apparently forgather (as if beckoned by an aberrant Fairy Godmother), usually by circuitous routes, through heavy traffic, at a common meeting place, where the very moods, distempers, and obtrusive personal habits that have kept them all happily apart since adulthood are then and there encouraged to slowly ferment beneath the cornhusks, and gradually rise with the aid of the terrible wine, and finally burst forth out of control under the stimulus of the cranberry jelly! No, it is a mockery of a holiday. For instance: *Thank you, O Lord, for what we are about to receive.* This is surely not a gala concept. There are no presents, unless one counts Aunt Bertha's sweet rolls a present, which no one does. There is precious little in the way of costumery: miniature plastic turkeys and those

witless Pilgrim hats. There is no sex. Indeed, Thanksgiving is the one day of the year (a fact known to everybody) when all thoughts of sex completely vanish, evaporating from apartments, houses, condominiums, and mobile homes like steam from a bathroom mirror.

2   Consider also the nowhereness of the time of year: the last week or so in November. It is obviously not yet winter: winter, with its death-dealing blizzards and its girls in tiny skirts pirouetting on the ice. On the other hand, it is certainly not much use to anyone as fall: no golden leaves or Oktoberfests, and so forth. Instead, it is a no-man's-land between the seasons. In the cold and sobersides northern half of the country, it is a vaguely unsettling interregnum of long, mournful walks beneath leafless trees: the long, mournful walks following the midday repast with the dread inevitability of pie following turkey, and the leafless trees looming or standing about like eyesores, and the ground either as hard as iron or slightly mushy, and the light snow always beginning to fall when one is halfway to the old green gate—flecks of cold, watery stuff plopping between neck and collar, for the reason that, it being not yet winter, one has forgotten or not chosen to bring along a muffler. It is a corollary to the long, mournful Thanksgiving walk that the absence of this muffler is quickly noticed and that four weeks or so later, at Christmastime, instead of the Sony Betamax one had secretly hoped the children might have chipped in to purchase, one receives another muffler: by then the thirty-third. Thirty-three mufflers! Some walk! Of course, things are more fun in the warm and loony southern part of the country. No snow there of any kind. No need of mufflers. Also, no long, mournful walks, because in the warm and loony southern part of the country everybody drives. So everybody drives over to Uncle Jasper's house to watch the Cougars play the Gators, a not entirely unimportant conflict which will determine whether the Gators get a Bowl bid or must take another post-season exhibition tour of North Korea. But no sooner do the Cougars kick off (an astonishing end-over-end squiggly thing that floats lazily above the arena before plummeting down toward K. C. McCoy and catching him on the helmet) than Auntie Em starts hustling turkey. Soon Cousin May is slamming around the bowls and platters, and Cousin Bernice is oohing and ahing about "all the fixin's," and Uncle Bob is making low, insincere sounds of appreciation: "Yummy, yummy Auntie Em, I'll have me some more of these delicious yams!" Delicious yams? Uncle Bob's eyes roll wildly in his head. Billy Joe Quaglino throws his long bomb in the middle of Grandpa Morris saying grace, Grandpa Morris speaking so low nobody can hear him, which is just as well, since he is reciting what he can remember of his last union contract. And then, just as J. B. (Speedy) Snood begins his ninety-two-yard punt return, Auntie Em starts dealing everyone second helpings of her famous stuffing, as if she were pushing a controlled substance, which it well might be, since there are no easily recognizable ingredients visible to the naked eye.

3   Consider for a moment the Thanksgiving meal itself. It has become a sort of refuge for endangered species of starch: cauliflower, turnips, pumpkin, mince (whatever "mince" is), those blessed yams. Bowls of luridly colored yams, with

no taste at all, lying torpid under a lava flow of marshmallow! And then the sacred turkey. One might as well try to construct a holiday repast around a fish—say, a nice piece of boiled haddock. After all, turkey tastes very similar to haddock: same consistency, same quite remarkable absence of flavor. But then, if the Thanksgiving *pièce de résistance* were a nice piece of boiled haddock instead of turkey, there wouldn't be all that fun for Dad when Mom hands him the sterling-silver, bone-handled carving set (a wedding present from her parents and not sharpened since) and then everyone sits around pretending not to watch while he saws and tears away at the bird as if he were trying to burrow his way into or out of some grotesque, fowl-like prison.

4   What of the good side to Thanksgiving, you ask. There is always a good side to everything. Not to Thanksgiving. There is only a bad side and then a worse side. For instance, Grandmother's best linen tablecloth is a bad side: the fact that it is produced each year, in the manner of a red flag being produced before a bull, and then is always spilled upon by whichever child is doing poorest at school that term and so is in need of greatest reassurance. Thus: "Oh, my God, *Veronica,* you just spilled grape juice [or plum wine or tar] on Grandmother's best linen tablecloth!" But now comes worse. For at this point Cousin Bill, the one who lost all Cousin Edwina's money on the car dealership three years ago and has apparently been drinking steadily since Halloween, bizarrely chooses to say: "Seems to me those old glasses are always falling over." To which Auntie Meg is heard to add: "Somehow I don't remember receivin' any of those old glasses." To which Uncle Fred replies: "That's because you and George decided to go on vacation to Hawaii the summer Grandpa Sam was dying." Now Grandmother is sobbing, though not so uncontrollably that she can refrain from murmuring: "I think that volcano painting I threw away by mistake got sent me from Hawaii, heaven knows why." But the gods are merciful, even the Pilgrim-hatted god of cornhusks and soggy stuffing, and there is an end to everything, even to Thanksgiving. Indeed, there is a grandeur to the feelings of finality and doom which usually settle on a house after the Thanksgiving celebration is over, for with the completion of Thanksgiving Day the year itself has been properly terminated: shot through the cranium with a high-velocity candied yam. At this calendrical nadir, all energy on the planet has gone, all fun has fled, all the terrible wine has been drunk.

5   But then, overnight, life once again begins to stir, emerging, even by the next morning, in the form of Japanese window displays and Taiwanese Christmas lighting, from the primeval ooze of the nation's department stores. Thus, a new year dawns, bringing with it immediate and cheering possibilities of extended consumer debt, office-party flirtations, good—or, at least, mediocre— wine, and visions of Supersaver excursion fares to Montego Bay. It is worth noting, perhaps, that this true new year always starts with the same mute, powerful mythic ceremony: the surreptitious tossing out, in the early morning, of all those horrid aluminum-foil packages of yams and cauliflower and stuffing and red, gummy cranberry substance which have been squeezed into the refrigerator as if a reenactment of the siege of Paris were shortly expected. Soon afterward,

the phoenix of Christmas can be observed as it slowly rises, beating its drumsticks, once again goggle-eyed with hope and unrealistic expectations.

THE MAN IN THE WATER

Roger Rosenblatt

During the 1970's Roger Rosenblatt served as director of expository writing at Harvard University. He later became literary editor of The New Republic *and served on the editorial board of the* Washington Post, *where he was also a columnist. He has published* Black Fiction *(1974),* Children of War *(1983), and* Witness: The World Since Hiroshima *(1985). A senior writer for* Time *magazine until 1988, he is now an editor for* U.S. News & World Report. *The following selection appeared in* Time *in 1982, following the crash of an Air Florida plane into the freezing waters of the Potomac River in Washington, D.C.*

1   As disasters go, this one was terrible, but not unique, certainly not among the worst on the roster of U.S. air crashes. There was the unusual element of the bridge, of course, and the fact that the plane clipped it at a moment of high traffic, one routine thus intersecting another and disrupting both. Then, too, there was the location of the event. Washington, the city of form and regulations, turned chaotic, deregulated, by a blast of real winter and a single slap of metal on metal. The jets from Washington National Airport that normally swoop around the presidential monuments like famished gulls are, for the moment, emblemized by the one that fell; so there is that detail. And there was the aesthetic clash as well—blue-and-green Air Florida, the name a flying garden, sunk down among gray chunks in a black river. All that was worth noticing, to be sure. Still, there was nothing very special in any of it, except death, which, while always special, does not necessarily bring millions to tears or to attention. Why, then, the shock here?

2   Perhaps because the nation saw in this disaster something more than a mechanical failure. Perhaps because people saw in it no failure at all, but rather something successful about their makeup. Here, after all, were two forms of nature in collision: the elements and human character. Last Wednesday, the elements, indifferent as ever, brought down Flight 90. And on that same afternoon, human nature—groping and flailing in mysteries of its own—rose to the occasion.

3   Of the four acknowledged heroes of the event, three are able to account for their behavior. Donald Usher and Eugene Windsor, a park police helicopter

team, risked their lives every time they dipped the skids into the water to pick up survivors. On television, side by side in bright blue jumpsuits, they described their courage as all in the line of duty. Lenny Skutnik, a 28-year-old employee of the Congressional Budget Office, said: "It's something I never thought I would do"—referring to his jumping into the water to drag an injured woman to shore. Skutnik added that "somebody had to go in the water," delivering every hero's line that is no less admirable for its repetitions. In fact, nobody had to go into the water. That somebody actually did so is part of the reason this particular tragedy sticks in the mind.

4   But the person most responsible for the emotional impact of the disaster is the one known at first simply as "the man in the water." (Balding, probably in his 50s, an extravagant mustache.) He was seen clinging with five other survivors to the tail section of the airplane. This man was described by Usher and Windsor as appearing alert and in control. Every time they lowered a lifeline and flotation ring to him, he passed it on to another of the passengers. "In a mass casualty, you'll find people like him," said Windsor. "But I've never seen one with that commitment." When the helicopter came back for him, the man had gone under. His selflessness was one reason the story held national attention; his anonymity another. The fact that he went unidentified invested him with a universal character. For a while he was Everyman, and thus proof (as if one needed it) that no man is ordinary.

5   Still, he could never have imagined such a capacity in himself. Only minutes before his character was tested, he was sitting in the ordinary plane among the ordinary passengers, dutifully listening to the stewardess telling him to fasten his seat belt and saying something about the "no smoking sign." So our man relaxed with the others, some of whom would owe their lives to him. Perhaps he started to read, or to doze, or to regret some harsh remark made in the office that morning. Then suddenly he knew that the trip would not be ordinary. Like every other person on that flight, he was desperate to live, which makes his final act so stunning.

6   For at some moment in the water he must have realized that he would not live if he continued to hand over the rope and ring to others. He *had* to know it, no matter how gradual the effect of the cold. In his judgment he had no choice. When the helicopter took off with what was to be the last survivor, he watched everything in the world move away from him, and he deliberately let it happen.

7   Yet there was something else about the man that kept our thoughts on him, and which keeps our thoughts on him still. He was *there,* in the essential, classic circumstance. Man in nature. The man in the water. For its part, nature cared nothing about the five passengers. Our man, on the other hand, cared totally. So the timeless battle commenced in the Potomac. For as long as that man could last, they went at each other, nature and man; the one making no distinctions of good and evil, acting on no principles, offering no lifelines; the other acting wholly on distinctions, principles and, one supposes, on faith.

8   Since it was he who lost the fight, we ought to come again to the conclusion that people are powerless in the world. In reality, we believe the reverse,

and it takes the act of the man in the water to remind us of our true feelings in this matter. It is not to say that everyone would have acted as he did, or as Usher, Windsor and Skutnik. Yet whatever moved these men to challenge death on behalf of their fellows is not peculiar to them. Everyone feels the possibility in himself. That is the abiding wonder of the story. That is why we would not let go of it. If the man in the water gave a lifeline to the people gasping for survival, he was likewise giving a lifeline to those who observed him.

9   The odd thing is that we do not even really believe that the man in the water lost his fight. "Everything in Nature contains all the powers of Nature," said Emerson. Exactly. So the man in the water had his own natural powers. He could not make ice storms, or freeze the water until it froze the blood. But he could hand life over to a stranger, and that is a power of nature too. The man in the water pitted himself against an implacable, impersonal enemy; he fought it with charity; and he held it to a standoff. He was the best we can do.

24

Narration

38 WHO SAW MURDER
DIDN'T CALL THE POLICE

Martin Gansburg

Martin Gansburg has been a reporter and editor for The New York Times since 1942 and has also written for such magazines as Diplomat, Catholic Digest, and Facts. This article was published in The New York Times in 1964, shortly after the murder of Kitty Genovese.

1   For more than half an hour 38 respectable, law-abiding citizens in Queens watched a killer stalk and stab a woman in three separate attacks in Kew Gardens.

2   Twice the sound of their voices and the sudden glow of their bedroom lights interrupted him and frightened him off. Each time he returned, sought her out and stabbed her again. Not one person telephoned the police during the assault; one witness called after the woman was dead.

3   That was two weeks ago today. But Assistant Chief Inspector Frederick M. Lussen, in charge of the borough's detectives and a veteran of 25 years of homicide investigations, is still shocked.

4   He can give a matter-of-fact recitation of many murders. But the Kew Gardens slaying baffles him—not because it is a murder, but because the "good people" failed to call the police.

5   "As we have reconstructed the crime," he said, "the assailant had three chances to kill this woman during a 35-minute period. He returned twice to

complete the job. If we had been called when he first attacked, the woman might not be dead now."

6   This is what the police say happened beginning at 3:20 A.M. in the staid, middle-class, tree-lined Austin Street area:

7   Twenty-eight-year-old Catherine Genovese, who was called Kitty by almost everyone in the neighborhood, was returning home from her job as manager of a bar in Hollis. She parked her red Fiat in a lot adjacent to the Kew Gardens Long Island Rail Road Station, facing Mowbray Place. Like many residents of the neighborhood, she had parked there day after day since her arrival from Connecticut a year ago, although the railroad frowns on the practice.

8   She turned off the lights of her car, locked the door and started to walk the 100 feet to the entrance of her apartment at 82–70 Austin Street, which is in a Tudor building, with stores on the first floor and apartments on the second.

9   The entrance to the apartment is in the rear of the building because the front is rented to retail stores. At night the quiet neighborhood is shrouded in the slumbering darkness that marks most residential areas.

10   Miss Genovese noticed a man at the far end of the lot, near a seven-story apartment house at 82–40 Austin Street. She halted. Then, nervously, she headed up Austin Street toward Lefferts Boulevard, where there is a call box to the 102nd Police Precinct in nearby Richmond Hill.

"He Stabbed Me"

11   She got as far as a street light in front of a bookstore before the man grabbed her. She screamed. Lights went on in the 10-story apartment house at 82–67 Austin Street, which faces the bookstore. Windows slid open and voices punctuated the early-morning stillness.

12   Miss Genovese screamed: "Oh, my God, he stabbed me! Please help me! Please help me!"

13   From one of the upper windows in the apartment house, a man called down: "Let that girl alone!"

14   The assailant looked up at him, shrugged and walked down Austin Street toward a white sedan parked a short distance away. Miss Genovese struggled to her feet.

15   Lights went out. The killer returned to Miss Genovese, now trying to make her way around the side of the building by the parking lot to get to her apartment. The assailant stabbed her again.

16   "I'm dying!" she shrieked. "I'm dying!"

A City Bus Passed

17   Windows were opened again, and lights went on in many apartments. The assailant got into his car and drove away. Miss Genovese staggered to her feet. A city bus, Q-10, the Lefferts Boulevard line to Kennedy International Airport, passed. It was 3:35 A.M.

18   The assailant returned. By then, Miss Genovese had crawled to the back of the building, where the freshly painted brown doors to the apartment house held out hope of safety. The killer tried the first door; she wasn't there. At the second door, 82–62 Austin Street, he saw her slumped on the floor at the foot of the stairs. He stabbed her a third time—fatally.

19   It was 3:50 by the time the police received their first call, from a man who was a neighbor of Miss Genovese. In two minutes they were at the scene. The neighbor, a 70-year-old woman and another woman were the only persons on the street. Nobody else came forward.

20   The man explained that he had called the police after much deliberation. He had phoned a friend in Nassau County for advice and then he had crossed the roof of the building to the apartment of the elderly woman to get her to make the call.

21   "I didn't want to get involved," he sheepishly told the police.

Suspect Is Arrested

22   Six days later, the police arrested Winston Moseley, a 29-year-old business-machine operator, and charged him with homicide. Moseley had no previous record. He is married, has two children and owns a home at 133-19 Sutter Avenue, South Ozone Park, Queens. On Wednesday, a court committed him to Kings County Hospital for psychiatric observation.

23   When questioned by the police, Moseley also said that he had slain Mrs. Annie May Johnson, 24, of 146–12 133d Avenue, Jamaica, on Feb. 29 and Barbara Kralik, 15, of 174–17 140th Avenue, Springfield Gardens, last July. In the Kralik case, the police are holding Alvin L. Mitchell, who is said to have confessed that slaying.

24   The police stressed how simple it would have been to have gotten in touch with them. "A phone call," said one of the detectives, "would have done it." The police may be reached by dialing "O" for operator or SPring 7-3100. . . .

25   Today witnesses from the neighborhood, which is made up of one-family homes in the $35,000 to $60,000 range with the exception of the two apartment houses near the railroad station, find it difficult to explain why they didn't call the police. . . .

26   A housewife, knowingly if quite casually, said, "We thought it was a lover's quarrel." A husband and wife both said, "Frankly, we were afraid." They seemed aware of the fact that events might have been different. A distraught woman, wiping her hands in her apron, said, "I didn't want my husband to get involved."

27   One couple, now willing to talk about that night, said they heard the first screams. The husband looked thoughtfully at the bookstore where the killer first grabbed Miss Genovese.

28   "We went to the window to see what was happening," he said, "but the light from our bedroom made it difficult to see the street." The wife, still apprehensive, added: "I put out the light and we were able to see better."

29   Asked why they hadn't called the police, she shrugged and replied: "I don't know."

30   A man peeked out from a slight opening in the doorway to his apartment and rattled off an account of the killer's second attack. Why hadn't he called the police at the time? "I was tired," he said without emotion. "I went back to bed."

31   It was 4:25 A.M. when the ambulance arrived to take the body of Miss Genovese. It drove off. "Then," a solemn police detective said, "the people came out."

A HANGING

George Orwell

George Orwell is the pseudonym of Eric Blair, well-known British novelist and essayist. Two of his most popular books are Animal Farm *(1945), a political satire, and* 1984 *(1949), a novel depicting life in a totalitarian society under the watchful eye of "Big Brother." This narrative is included in* Shooting an Elephant and Other Essays *(1950).*

1   It was in Burma, a sodden morning of the rains. A sickly light, like yellow tinfoil, was slanting over the high walls into the jail yard. We were waiting outside the condemned cells, a row of sheds fronted with double bars, like small animal cages. Each cell measured about ten feet by ten and was quite bare within except for a plank bed and a pot for drinking water. In some of them brown silent men were squatting at the inner bars, with their blankets draped around them. These were the condemned men, due to be hanged within the next week or two.

2   One prisoner had been brought out of his cell. He was a Hindu, a puny wisp of a man, with a shaven head and vague liquid eyes. He had a thick, sprouting moustache, absurdly too big for his body, rather like the moustache of a comic man on the films. Six tall Indian warders were guarding him and getting him ready for the gallows. Two of them stood by with rifles and fixed bayonets, while the others handcuffed him, passed a chain through his handcuffs and fixed it to their belts, and lashed his arms tight to his sides. They crowded very close about him, with their hands always on him in a careful, caressing grip, as though all the while feeling him to make sure he was there. It was like men handling a fish which is still alive and may jump back into the water. But he stood quite unresisting, yielding his arms limply to the ropes, as though he hardly noticed what was happening.

Used with permission, Harcourt, Brace, Jovanovich.

3   Eight o'clock struck and a bugle call, desolately thin in the wet air, floated from the distant barracks. The superintendent of the jail, who was standing apart from the rest of us, moodily prodding the gravel with his stick, raised his head at the sound. He was an army doctor, with a grey toothbrush moustache and a gruff voice. "For God's sake hurry up, Francis," he said irritably. "The man ought to have been dead by this time. Aren't you ready yet?"

4   Francis, the head jailer, a fat Dravidian in a white drill suit and gold spectacles, waved his black hand. "Yes sir, yes sir," he bubbled. "All iss satisfactorily prepared. The hangman iss waiting. We shall proceed."

5   "Well, quick march, then. The prisoners can't get their breakfast till this job's over."

6   We set out for the gallows. Two warders marched on either side of the prisoner, with their rifles at the slope; two others marched close against him, gripping him by arm and shoulder, as though at once pushing and supporting him. The rest of us, magistrates and the like, followed behind. Suddenly, when we had gone ten yards, the procession stopped short without any order or warning. A dreadful thing had happened—a dog, come goodness knows whence, had appeared in the yard. It came bounding among us with a loud volley of barks, and leapt round us wagging its whole body, wild with glee at finding so many human beings together. It was a large woolly dog, half Airedale, half pariah. For a moment it pranced round us, and then, before anyone could stop it, it had made a dash for the prisoner and, jumping up, tried to lick his face. Everyone stood aghast, too taken aback even to grab at the dog.

7   "Who let that bloody brute in here?" said the superintendent angrily. "Catch it, someone!"

8   A warder, detached from the escort, charged clumsily after the dog, but it danced and gambolled just out of his reach, taking everything as part of the game. A young Eurasian jailer picked up a handful of gravel and tried to stone the dog away, but it dodged the stones and came after us again. Its yaps echoed from the jail walls. The prisoner, in the grasp of the two warders, looked on incuriously, as though this was another formality of the hanging. It was several minutes before someone managed to catch the dog. Then we put my handkerchief through its collar and moved off once more, with the dog still straining and whimpering.

9   It was about forty yards to the gallows. I watched the bare brown back of the prisoner marching in front of me. He walked clumsily with his bound arms, but quite steadily, with that bobbing gait of the Indian who never straightens his knees. At each step his muscles slid neatly into place, the lock of hair on his scalp danced up and down, his feet printed themselves on the wet gravel. And once, in spite of the men who gripped him by each shoulder, he stepped slightly aside to avoid a puddle on the path.

10   It is curious, but till that moment I had never realized what it means to destroy a healthy, conscious man. When I saw the prisoner step aside to avoid the puddle I saw the mystery, the unspeakable wrongness, of cutting a life short when it is in full tide. This man was not dying, he was alive just as we

are alive. All the organs of his body were working—bowels digesting food, skin renewing itself, nails growing, tissues forming—all toiling away in solemn foolery. His nails would still be growing when he stood on the drop, when he was falling through the air with a tenth-of-a-second to live. His eyes saw the yellow gravel and the grey walls, and his brain still remembered, foresaw, reasoned—reasoned even about puddles. He and we were a party of men walking together, seeing, hearing, feeling, understanding the same world; and in two minutes, with a sudden snap, one of us would be gone—one mind less, one world less.

11   The gallows stood in a small yard, separate from the main grounds of the prison, and overgrown with tall prickly weeds. It was a brick erection like three sides of a shed, with planking on top, and above that two beams and a crossbar with the rope dangling. The hangman, a grey-haired convict in the white uniform of the prison, was waiting beside his machine. He greeted us with a servile crouch as we entered. At a word from Francis the two warders, gripping the prisoner more closely than ever, half led half pushed him to the gallows and helped him clumsily up the ladder. Then the hangman climbed up and fixed the rope round the prisoner's neck.

12   We stood waiting, five yards away. The warders had formed in a rough circle round the gallows. And then, when the noose was fixed, the prisoner began crying out to his god. It was a high, reiterated cry of "Ram! Ram! Ram! Ram!" not urgent and fearful like a prayer or cry for help, but steady, rhythmical, almost like the tolling of a bell. The dog answered the sound with a whine. The hangman, still standing on the gallows, produced a small cotton bag like a flour bag and drew it down over the prisoner's face. But the sound, muffled by the cloth, still persisted, over and over again: "Ram! Ram! Ram! Ram! Ram!"

13   The hangman climbed down and stood ready, holding the lever. Minutes seemed to pass. The steady, muffled crying from the prisoner went on and on. "Ram! Ram! Ram!" never faltering for an instant. The superintendent, his head on his chest, was slowly poking the ground with his stick; perhaps he was counting the cries, allowing the prisoner a fixed number—fifty, perhaps, or a hundred. Everyone had changed color. The Indians had gone grey like bad coffee, and one or two of the bayonets were wavering. We looked at the lashed, hooded man on the drop, and listened to his cries—each cry another second of life; the same thought was in all our minds: oh, kill him quickly, get it over, stop that abominable noise!

14   Suddenly the superintendent made up his mind. Throwing up his head he made a swift motion with his stick. "Chalo!" he shouted almost fiercely.

15   There was a clanking noise, and then dead silence. The prisoner had vanished, and the rope was twisting on itself. I let go of the dog, and it galloped immediately to the back of the gallows; but when it got there it stopped short, barked, and then retreated into a corner of the yard, where it stood among the weeds, looking timorously out at us. We went round the gallows to inspect the prisoner's body. He was dangling with his toes pointed straight downwards, very slowly revolving, as dead as a stone.

16   The superintendent reached out with his stick and poked the bare brown body; it oscillated slightly. "*He's* all right," said the superintendent. He backed out from under the gallows, and blew out a deep breath. The moody look had gone out of his face quite suddenly. He glanced at his wrist-watch. "Eight minutes past eight. Well, that's all for this morning, thank God."

17   The warders unfixed bayonets and marched away. The dog, sobered and conscious of having misbehaved itself, slipped after them. We walked out of the gallows yard, past the condemned cells with their waiting prisoners, into the big central yard of the prison. The convicts, under the command of warders armed with lathis, were already receiving their breakfast. They squatted in long rows, each man holding a tin pannikin, while two warders with buckets marched round ladling out rice; it seemed quite a homely, jolly scene, after the hanging. An enormous relief had come upon us now that the job was done. One felt an impulse to sing, to break into a run, to snigger. All at once everyone began chattering gaily.

18   The Eurasian boy walking beside me nodded towards the way we had come, with a knowing smile: "Do you know, sir, our friend (he meant the dead man) when he heard his appeal had been dismissed, he pissed on the floor of his cell. From fright. Kindly take one of my cigarettes, sir. Do you not admire my new silver case, sir? From the boxwalah, two rupees eight annas. Classy European style."

19   Several people laughed—at what, nobody seemed certain.

20   Francis was walking by the superintendent, talking garrulously: "Well, sir, all hass passed off with the utmost satisfactoriness. It was all finished—flick! like that. It iss not always so—oah, no! I have known cases where the doctor wass obliged to go beneath the gallows and pull the prissoner's legs to ensure decease. Most disagreeable!"

21   "Wriggling about, eh? That's bad," said the superintendent.

22   "Ach, sir, it iss worse when they become refractory! One man, I recall, clung to the bars of hiss cage when we went to take him out. You will scarcely credit, sir, that it took six warders to dislodge him, three pulling at each leg. We reasoned with him. 'My dear fellow,' we said, 'think of all the pain and trouble you are causing to us!' But no, he would not listen! Ach, he wass very troublesome!"

23   I found that I was laughing quite loudly. Everyone was laughing. Even the superintendent grinned in a tolerant way. "You'd better all come out and have a drink," he said quite genially. "I've got a bottle of whisky in the car. We could do with it."

24   We went through the big double gates of the prison into the road. "Pulling at his legs!" exclaimed a Burmese magistrate suddenly, and burst into a loud chuckling. We all began laughing again. At that moment Francis' anecdote seemed extraordinarily funny. We all had a drink together, native and European alike, quite amicably. The dead man was a hundred yards away.

BEAUTY: WHEN THE OTHER
DANCER IS THE SELF

Alice Walker

A poet, essayist, and scholar, Alice Walker is best known for her novel The Color Purple, *which won both the Pulitzer Prize and the American Book Award in 1982 and was later made into a popular film. Some of her other writings include* Langston Hughes, American Poet *(1973),* Love & Trouble *(1973),* You Can't Keep A Good Woman Down *(1981), and* A Temple of My Familiar *(1989). The following selection comes from her 1983 collection of essays,* In Search of Our Mothers' Gardens.

1   It is a bright summer day in 1947. My father, a fat, funny man with beautiful eyes and a subversive wit, is trying to decide which of his eight children he will take with him to the county fair. My mother, of course, will not go. She is knocked out from getting most of us ready: I hold my neck stiff against the pressure of her knuckles as she hastily completes the braiding and then beribboning of my hair.

2   My father is the driver for the rich old white lady up the road. Her name is Miss Mey. She owns all the land for miles around, as well as the house in which we live. All I remember about her is that she once offered to pay my mother thirty-five cents for cleaning her house, raking up piles of her magnolia leaves, and washing her family's clothes, and that my mother—she of no money, eight children, and a chronic earache—refused it. But I do not think of this in 1947. I am two and a half years old. I want to go everywhere my daddy goes. I am excited at the prospect of riding in a car. Someone has told me fairs are fun. That there is room in the car for only three of us doesn't faze me at all. Whirling happily in my starchy frock, showing off my biscuit-polished patent-leather shoes and lavender socks, tossing my head in a way that makes my ribbons bounce, I stand, hands on hips, before my father. "Take me, Daddy," I say with assurance: "I'm the prettiest!"

3   Later, it does not surprise me to find myself in Miss Mey's shiny black car, sharing the back seat with the other lucky ones. Does not surprise me that I thoroughly enjoy the fair. At home that night I tell the unlucky ones all I can remember about the merry-go-round, the man who eats live chickens, and the teddy bears, until they say: that's enough, baby Alice. Shut up now, and go to sleep.

4   It is Easter Sunday, 1950. I am dressed in a green, flocked, scalloped-hem dress (handmade by my adoring sister, Ruth) that has its own smooth satin

petticoat and tiny hot-pink roses tucked into each scallop. My shoes, new T-strap patent leather, again highly biscuit-polished. I am six years old and have learned one of the longest Easter speeches to be heard that day, totally unlike the speech I said when I was two: "Easter lilies / pure and white / blossom in / the morning light." When I rise to give my speech I do so on a great wave of love and pride and expectation. People in the church stop rustling their new crinolines. They seem to hold their breath. I can tell they admire my dress, but it is my spirit, bordering on sassiness (womanishness), they secretly applaud.

5   "That girl's a little *mess*," they whisper to each other, pleased.

6   Naturally I say my speech without stammer or pause, unlike those who stutter, stammer, or, worst of all, forget. This is before the word "beautiful" exists in people's vocabulary, but "Oh, isn't she the *cutest* thing!" frequently floats my way. "And got so much sense!" they gratefully add . . . for which thoughtful addition I thank them to this day.

7   *It was great fun being cute. But then, one day, it ended.*

8   I am eight years old and a tomboy. I have a cowboy hat, cowboy boots, checkered shirt and pants, all red. My playmates are my brothers, two and four years older than I. Their colors are black and green, the only difference in the way we are dressed. On Saturday nights we all go to the picture show, even my mother; Westerns are her favorite kind of movie. Back home, "on the ranch," we pretend we are Tom Mix, Hopalong Cassidy, Lash LaRue (we've even named one of our dogs Lash LaRue); we chase each other for hours rustling cattle, being outlaws, delivering damsels from distress. Then my parents decide to buy my brothers guns. These are not "real" guns. They shoot "BBs," copper pellets my brothers say will kill birds. Because I am a girl, I do not get a gun. Instantly I am relegated to the position of Indian. Now there appears a great distance between us. They shoot and shoot at everything with their new guns. I try to keep up with my bow and arrows.

9   One day while I am standing on top of our makeshift "garage"—pieces of tin nailed across some poles—holding my bow and arrow and looking out toward the fields, I feel an incredible blow in my right eye. I look down just in time to see my brother lower his gun.

10   Both brothers rush to my side. My eye stings, and I cover it with my hand. "If you tell," they say, "we will get a whipping. You don't want that to happen, do you?" I do not. "Here is a piece of wire," says the older brother, picking it up from the roof; "say you stepped on one end of it and the other flew up and hit you." The pain is beginning to start. "Yes," I say. "Yes, I will say that is what happened." If I do not say this is what happened, I know my brothers will find ways to make me wish I had. But now I will say anything that gets me to my mother.

11   Confronted by our parents we stick to the lie agreed upon. They place me on a bench on the porch and I close my left eye while they examine the right. There is a tree growing from underneath the porch that climbs past the railing

to the roof. It is the last thing my right eye sees. I watch as its trunk, its branches, and then its leaves are blotted out by the rising blood.

12   I am in shock. First there is intense fever, which my father tries to break using lily leaves bound around my head. Then there are chills: my mother tries to get me to eat soup. Eventually, I do not know how, my parents learn what has happened. A week after the "accident" they take me to see a doctor. "Why did you wait so long to come?" he asks, looking into my eye and shaking his head. "Eyes are sympathetic," he says. "If one is blind, the other will likely become blind too."

13   This comment of the doctor's terrifies me. But it is really how I look that bothers me most. Where the BB pellet struck there is glob of whitish scar tissue, a hideous cataract, on my eye. Now when I stare at people—a favorite pastime, up to now—they will stare back. Not at the "cute" little girl, but at her scar. For six years I do not stare at anyone, because I do not raise my head.

14   Years later, in the throes of a mid-life crisis, I ask my mother and sister whether I changed after the "accident." "No," they say, puzzled. "What do you mean?"

15   *What do I mean?*

16   I am eight, and, for the first time, doing poorly in school, where I have been something of a whiz since I was four. We have just moved to the place where the "accident" occurred. We do not know any of the people around us because this is a different county. The only time I see the friends I knew is when we go back to our old church. The new school is the former state penitentiary. It is a large stone building, cold and drafty, crammed to overflowing with boisterous, ill-disciplined children. On the third floor there is a huge circular imprint of some partition that has been torn out.

17   "What used to be here?" I ask a sullen girl next to me on our way past it to lunch.

18   "The electric chair," says she.

19   At night I have nightmares about the electric chair, and about all the people reputedly "fried" in it. I am afraid of the school, where all the students seem to be budding criminals.

20   "What's the matter with your eye?" they ask, critically.

21   When I don't answer (I cannot decide whether it was an "accident" or not), they shove me, insist on a fight.

22   My brother, the one who created the story about the wire, comes to my rescue. But then brags so much about "protecting" me, I become sick.

23   After months of torture at the school, my parents decide to send me back to our old community, to my old school. I live with my grandparents and the teacher they board. But there is no room for Phoebe, my cat. By the time my grandparents decide there *is* room, and I ask for my cat, she cannot be found. Miss Yarborough, the boarding teacher, takes me under her wing, and begins to teach me to play the piano. But soon she marries an African—a "prince," she says—and is whisked away to his continent.

24   At my old school there is at least one teacher who loves me. She is the teacher who "knew me before I was born" and bought my first baby clothes. It is she who makes life bearable. It is her presence that finally helps me turn on the one child at the school who continually calls me "one-eyed bitch." One day I simply grab him by his coat and beat him until I am satisfied. It is my teacher who tells me my mother is ill.

25   My mother is lying in bed in the middle of the day, something I have never seen. She is in too much pain to speak. She has an abscess in her ear. I stand looking down on her, knowing that if she dies, I cannot live. She is being treated with warm oils and hot bricks held against her cheek. Finally a doctor comes. But I must go back to my grandparents' house. The weeks pass but I am hardly aware of it. All I know is that my mother might die, my father is not so jolly, my brothers still have their guns, and I am the one sent away from home.

26   "You did not change," they say.

27   *Did I imagine the anguish of never looking up?*

28   I am twelve. When relatives come to visit I hide in my room. My cousin Brenda, just my age, whose father works in the post office and whose mother is a nurse, comes to find me. "Hello," she says. And then she asks, looking at my recent school picture, which I did not want taken, and on which the "glob," as I think of it, is clearly visible. "You still can't see out of that eye?"

29   "No," I say, and flop back on the bed over my book.

30   That night, as I do almost every night, I abuse my eye. I rant and rave at it, in front of the mirror. I plead with it to clear up before morning. I tell it I hate and despise it. I do not pray for sight. I pray for beauty.

31   "You did not change," they say.

32   I am fourteen and baby-sitting for my brother Bill, who lives in Boston. He is my favorite brother and there is a strong bond between us. Understanding my feelings of shame and ugliness he and his wife take me to a local hospital, where the "glob" is removed by a doctor named O. Henry. There is still a small bluish crater where the scar tissue was, but the ugly white stuff is gone. Almost immediately I become a different person from the girl who does not raise her head. Or so I think. Now that I've raised my head I win the boyfriend of my dreams. Now that I've raised my head I have plenty of friends. Now that I've raised my head classwork comes from my lips as faultlessly as Easter speeches did, and I leave high school as valedictorian, most popular student, and *queen,* hardly believing my luck. Ironically, the girl who was voted most beautiful in our class (and was) was later shot twice through the chest by a male companion, using a "real" gun, while she was pregnant. But that's another story in itself. Or is it?

33   "You did not change," they say.

34   It is now thirty years since the "accident." A beautiful journalist comes to visit and to interview me. She is going to write a cover story for her magazine

that focuses on my latest book. "Decide how you want to look on the cover," she says. "Glamorous, or whatever."

35   Never mind "glamorous," it is the "whatever" that I hear. Suddenly all I can think of is whether I will get enough sleep the night before the photography session: if I don't, my eye will be tired and wander, as blind eyes will.

36   At night in bed with my lover I think up reasons why I should not appear on the cover of a magazine. "My meanest critics will say I've sold out," I say. "My family will now realize I write scandalous books."

37   "But what's the real reason you don't want to do this?" he asks.

38   "Because in all probability," I say in a rush, "my eye won't be straight."

39   "It will be straight enough," he says. Then, "Besides, I thought you'd made your peace with that."

40   And I suddenly remember that I have.

41   *I remember:*

42   I am talking to my brother Jimmy, asking if he remembers anything unusual about the day I was shot. He does not know I consider that day the last time my father, with his sweet home remedy of cool lily leaves, chose me, and that I suffered and raged inside because of this. "Well," he says, "all I remember is standing by the side of the highway with Daddy, trying to flag down a car. A white man stopped, but when Daddy said he needed somebody to take his little girl to the doctor, he drove off."

43   *I remember:*

44   I am in the desert for the first time. I fall totally in love with it. I am so overwhelmed by its beauty, I confront for the first time, consciously, the meaning of the doctor's words years ago: "Eyes are sympathetic. If one is blind, the other will likely become blind too." I realize I have dashed about the world madly, looking at that, storing up images against the fading of the light. *But I might have missed seeing the desert!* The shock of that possibility—and gratitude for over twenty-five years of sight—sends me literally to my knees. Poem after poem comes—which is perhaps how poets pray.

ON SIGHT

I am so thankful I have seen
The Desert
And the creatures in the desert
And the desert itself.

The desert has its own moon
Which I have seen
With my own eye.

There is no flag on it.

Trees of the desert have arms
All of which are always up
That is because the moon is up
The sun is up

Also the sky
The stars
Clouds
None with flags.

If there *were* flags, I doubt
the trees would point.
Would you?

45   *But mostly, I remember this:*

46   I am twenty-seven, and my baby daughter is almost three. Since her birth, I have worried about her discovery that her mother's eyes are different from other people's. Will she be embarrassed? I think. What will she say? Every day she watches a television program called "Big Blue Marble." It begins with a picture of the earth as it appears from the moon. It is bluish, a little battered-looking, but full of light, with whitish clouds swirling around it. Every time I see it I weep with love, as if it is a picture of Grandma's house. One day when I am putting Rebecca down for her nap, she suddenly focuses on my eye. Something inside me cringes, gets ready to try to protect myself. All children are cruel about physical differences, I know from experience, and that they don't always mean to be is another matter. I assume Rebecca will be the same.

47   But no-o-o-o. She studies my face intently as we stand, her inside and me outside her crib. She even holds my face maternally between her dimpled little hands. Then, looking every bit as serious and lawyerlike as her father, she says, as if it may just possibly have slipped my attention: "Mommy, there's a *world* in your eye." (As in, "Don't be alarmed, or do anything crazy.") And then, gently, but with great interest: "Mommy, where did you *get* that world in your eye?"

48   For the most part, the pain left then. (So what, if my brothers grew up to buy even more powerful pellet guns for their sons and to carry real guns themselves. So what, if a young "Morehouse man" once nearly fell off the steps of Trevos Arnett Library because he thought my eyes were blue.) Crying and laughing I ran to the bathroom, while Rebecca mumbled and sang herself off to sleep. Yes indeed, I realized, looking into the mirror. There *was* a world in my eye. And I saw that it was possible to love it: that in fact, for all it had taught me of shame and anger and inner vision, I *did* love it. Even to see it drifting out of orbit in boredom, or rolling up out of fatigue, not to mention floating back at attention in excitement (bearing witness, a friend has called it), deeply suitable to my personality, and even characteristic of me.

49   That night I dream I am dancing to Stevie Wonder's song "Always" (the name of the song is really "As," but I hear it as "Always"). As I dance, whirling and joyous, happier than I've ever been in my life, another bright-faced dancer joins me. We dance and kiss each other and hold each other through the night. The other dancer has obviously come through all right, as I have done. She is beautiful, whole and free. And she is also me.

Index

"A Dying Art: The Classy Exit Line,"
    346–348
"A Hanging," 416–419
Abbreviations, 331–332
Abstraction, 110, 111, 148, 224
Accuracy, 121–122, 159
Adjectives:
    errors with, 299, 303–304, 305
    faulty comparison, 304
Adverbs:
    conjunctive, 313–314
    errors with, 303–304, 305
Advertising, 126, 162, 220, 226
    conflicting views, 230
Allen, Woody, 130
American Psychological Association (APA),
    281
Analysis, 10, 12
"Androgynous Male, The" (Perrin), 188–191
Anger, 124
"Animals in Research: The Case for
    Experimentation," 396–400
APA documentation style, 281–283
Apology, 77
Apostrophe, 320–321
Argumentation, 12, 78, 126, 143
    anticipate opposing views, 214
    audience, 214
    developing your essay, 213–222
    emotional appeals, 220
    evidence, 221
    examples, 219
    logic in, 219, 220
    logical fallacies, 222–225
    organization, 216, 218
    Pro-and-Con Sheet, 215, 218
    problems to avoid, 222
    professional essays 230, 233, 234–235
    revision worksheet, 235–236
    Rogerian technique, 222
    student essay, 228–229
    working thesis, 216
Arlen, Michael J., 407–410
"Attitude," 354–357
Attitude(s), 18, 124
Audience, 16, 17, 24(9), 26, 77, 85, 90, 124,
    125, 126, 173, 183–184, 194, 214, 242
Awkwardness, 77, 103, 112

Baker, Russell, 377–378
"Ban those books!" 226
"Battle of Progress, The," 243–245
"Beauty: When the Other Dancer Is the Self,"
    420–425
Beginnings, 74–82
Berry, Wendell, 363–365
Bias, 267
Bibliography:
    card entry (sample), 274
    note-taking, 264–265
    "References" list, 282
    works cited list, 277–281
"Blind Paces," 186–188
Body:
    of the essay, 41
    paragraphs, 41–73, 85, 145
    see also Paragraphs
Boredom, 18, 109
Brackets, 325
Brady, James, 230
Brainstorming, 262
"Breatharianism," 20
"Bringing back the joy of Market Day," 175–177
Britt, Suzanne, 361–363
Brown University, 110
Browsing, 264
Buckley, Jr., William F., 341–346
Bureaucratic jargon (recipe), 139–140
Burke, Kenneth, 13

Calhoun, John C., 3
Capitalization, 81, 330–331
Card catalog (library), 262
Carson, Johnny, 87
"Case against Boxing Reforms, The," 286–288
Catch-22, 251
"Catching Garage Sale Fever," 161–164
Catton, Bruce, 177–180
Causal analysis:
    cause/effect relationship, 201
    development by, 201–212
    limit your essay, 202
    organization, 202–203
    problems to avoid, 204
    revision worksheet, 211–212
    sample student essay, 205–207
    thesis statement, 202

Cause and effect, 220
Checklist, for effective essays, 91–92
Choppiness, 87, 116–117, 173–174
Chronological order, 62–63, 158, 251
Circular definitions, 185
Citations, *see* Bibliography; Documentation
Clarity, 4, 28, 31–32, 40, 87, 95, 96–102, 109, 120, 132, 159, 183–184, 268
Classification and Division:
  classification described, 193
  comparison of c. and d., 193
  developing your essay, 192–201
  dividing a subject into its parts, 192–193
  problems to avoid, 195
  professional essay (Lebowitz), 198–200
  revision worksheet, 201
  sample student essay, 196–197
Clauses, 104, 111, 116–118, 312, 314
Clemens, Samuel, 359–360
"Clever Animals," 339–341
Clichés, 87, 112, 125, 130, 136
Clustering, 10
Coherence, 44, 62–71, 151, 160
Colette, 83
College campus, 5
"College Pressures," 379–384
Colloquial language, 123, 259
Colon, 318–319
Comma(s), 312–317
Comma splice, 306–307, 313, 318
Commitment, 3–4
Common knowledge, 271
Communication, 3, 26, 120
  four types (modes), 143–144
  goal of writing, 4
Comparison and contrast, 10, 12, 77, 220, 225
  block, 172
  choppy essay, 173–174
  clear and distinct description, 173
  development by, 170–181
  point by point, 171
  problems to avoid, 172–174
  professional essay (Catton), 177–180
  revision worksheet, 181
  "so-what" thesis, 172–173
  student essay, 175–177
  thesis statement, 171
Complaint, 77
Compound words, 326
Compromise, 222
Computers, 88–89
Conciseness, 87
Conclusion(s), 49, 76, 78–80, 153, 160, 164, 177, 188, 197, 207, 229, 244, 255, 270, 288

Confucius, 121
Confusion, 19, 29, 62, 87, 99, 121–122
Conjunctions:
  coordinating, 115, 313
  subordinating, 116
Conjunctive adverbs, 313–314
Connotation (words), 126–127
Conrad, Joseph, 3, 56, 240–241
Content, questions on, 96–97,156, 168–169, 180, 191, 200, 210, 233, 235, 247–248, 259
Contractions, 320–321
Coordination:
  equally weighted ideas, 115 (note)
  of sentences, 115
Creativity, 24(5), 81
Cubing, 10

Dangling modifier, 100–101, 304
Dash(es), 324, 325–326
Daybook, *see* Journal
Deadwood constructions, 87, 102–104, 108
Deception, 220
Deductive order, 63–64
Deep-structure revision, 88
Definition:
  arguing by, 220
  circular, 185
Definition, Extended, 181–192
  clarity and your audience, 183–184
  developing your essay, 183–184
  methods of defining terms, 184
  problems to avoid, 184–185
  reasons for, 182–183
  revision worksheet, 192
  sample student essay, 186–188
Denotation (words), 126
Description, 10, 12, 25, 143, 173, 237–249, 251
  appropriate details, 239
  change in perspective, 242
  dominant impression, 239
  figurative language, 241
  objective, 237
  problems to avoid, 242
  professional essay (Selzer), 245–247
  purpose, 237
  revision worksheet, 248–249
  sensory details, 240
  specific details, 238
  student essay, 243–245
  subjective, 237
  vividness, 240
  see also Modifiers
Details, 19, 41, 54, 55, 73, 87, 97, 150, 168(4), 173, 237, 238, 239, 251, 252

Development (of or by), 52–56, 85–86, 87, 144, 145
    argumentation, 213–236
    causal analysis, 201–212
    classification and division, 192–201
    comparison and contrast, 170–181
    definition, 181–192
    example, 146–157
    paragraphs, 52–57
    process analysis, 157–170
Dialogue, 252, 259, 316(10)
Dictionary, 182, 185
Didion, Joan, 368–370
Diminutives, 135
Directional process analysis, 157
Directions, 157
Direct quotations, *see* Quotations
Discovery, 28, 40
"Discus Thrower, The," (Selzer), 245–247
Disorder, 19
Documentation:
    paraphrased or summarized ideas, 267
    parenthetical, 275, 282
    plagiarism and, 271–272
    style, 275–277
Dominant impression, 239
"Dorm Life," 92–93
Double negative, 297
Drafts:
    basics of the short essay; ten rules, 141–142
    first, 44, 84–85
    revisions, 83–94
    saving rough drafts, 88
    second, 85–86
    third, 87
Drama: dramatizing the subject, 13–15

Effect:
    questions asked by, 202
    see also Causal analysis
"Effects of a Nuclear Explosion, The," 391–393
Elbow, Peter, 8 (note)
Ellipsis marks, 328
Emotion(s), 18, 124, 125, 126
    argument *ad populum*, 224
    argumentation, 220
    arousing positive feelings, 128
Emphasis, 114, 118, 315, 325
Ending, 74–82
    Hemingway's *A Farewell to Arms,* 83
    see also Conclusion
Endnote form, 281
Enthusiasm, 4
Essay map, 36–38, 40, 228

Essay:
    basics; ten rules for drafts, 141–142
    effective; checklist, 91–92
    parts (three), 74
et al. usage, 282–283
Euphemisms, 132–134, 169(8)
Examples, 41, 153, 173, 219, 287
    coherence lacking in, 151
    development by, 146–157
    enough to be persuasive, 150
    relevant, 150
    revision worksheet, 157
    weakness: lack of specific detail, 150–151
    well chosen, 150
Exclamation point, 312
Exit, definition of, 131
Experience, personal, 5, 148, 221
Exposition, 143, 145–212
    causal analysis, 201–212
    classification and division, 192–201
    comparison and contrast, 170–181
    definition, 145
    definition essays, 181–192
    example, 145, 146–157
    process analysis, 157–170
    strategies of, 145–212
Extended definition, *see* Definition, Extended

Fallacies, *see* Logical fallacies
Fatigue, 84
Fiction, 250
Figurative language, 135–136, 225
    in description, 241
Fillers, 103
First impression, 74
First person, 112
Flashback, 251
Flippancy, 125
Focus, 5–15, 24, 31, 85, 110–111
    topic sentence, 47–48
    works like a camara, 6
Footnote form, 281
Foreign words, 327
Formal language, 123
Formal writing, 332
Fragments (sentences), 306
Free association, 10, 12
Freedom: proper use of language, 134
Freewriting, 7–8
Friend, 90
"Friends, Good Friends, and Such Good Friends," 373–377

Gender, 134–135
Generalities, 54, 55, 87, 146, 185, 221,
    222–223, 238
Getting started, 3–4
Gillmore, Robert, 234–235
Gobbledygook, 139–140
"Good Scythe, The," 363–365
Goodman, Ellen, 389–391
Graffiti, 182 (note)
Grammar, 87
    errors in, 293–310
    see also Adverbs; Adjectives; Apostrophe;
        Colon; Nouns; Pronouns; Quotation
        marks; Semicolon; Verbs
Gransburg, Martin, 413–416
"Grant and Lee: a Study in Contrasts,"
    177–180
"Great American Cooling Machine, The"
    (Trippett), 207–210
Gregory, Dick, 256–259

Handbook to grammar, punctuation, and
    mechanics, 291–336
He/she generic pronoun problem, 134
Heller, Joseph, 251
Hemingway, Ernest, 83, 182
Hiccup syndrome, 111
Hoover, Herbert, 111
Horace, 84
"How to Write and "F" Paper: Fresh Advice for
    Students of Freshman English," 357–358
However (usage), 314
Humor, 95, 194
Hurley, Dan, 266
Huxley, Aldous, 134
Hyperbole, 241
Hyphen, 326–327
Hypostatization, 224

"I Have a Dream," 400–403
"I" usage, 112
ibid. (usage), 281
Idea hook, 72
Ideas, 26, 84, 86, 90
    basic, to writing, 3
    confidence in, 4
    note-taking, 265
    saving, 23–24
    verbalizing, 89
Idiomatic phrases, 122–123
Images, 220
Impression:
    dominant, 239
    first, 74

"In Praise of the Humble Comma," 366–368
"Indian era at Mesa Verde," 196–197
Inductive order, 64
Infinitive:
    phrases, 104
    split, 296–297
Informal language, 123
Informative process analysis, 158
Intention: four modes of communication, 143
Interest, 4, 6, 19, 26, 40, 74, 97, 103, 109, 120
Interrupters (parenthetical elements),
    316–317
Interviews, 12–13, 280–281
Introduction(s), 41, 48, 49, 74–76, 103, 152,
    161, 186, 196, 205, 228, 243, 254, 286,
    314
Invective, 124
Inversion, for emphasis, 114
Irony, 124–125, 322
Italics, 327–328
"It's Simply Not Worth It," 205–207
Iyer, Pico, 366–368

Jargon, 87, 106, 110, 131, 132
Journal, 15, 22–25, 26
    uses, 23–25

Keillor, Garrison, 354–357
Kennedy, John F., 123
Kerr, Jean, 3
Key words: repetition, 66
King, Frederick A., 396–400
King Kong, 117, 118
King, Martin Luther, Jr., 220, 400–403
Kingston, Maxine Hong, 404–407
Knowledge: your subject and your audience,
    17
Korda, Michael, 371–372

Language:
    levels of, 123–124
    sensitivity to, 25(12)
Lead-ins, 74–78
Lebanon, 133
Lebowitz, Fran, 198–200
Length of paragraphs, 56–57
"Let's make a deal," 90
Levels of language, 123–124
Libraries, 262
    special collections, 263–264
Listing ideas, 6–7
Logical fallacies:
    argument *ad hominem,* 223
    argument *ad populum,* 224

bandwagon appeal, 224
begging the question, 223
circular logic, 204
faulty analogy, 225
hasty generalization, 222–223
hypostatization, 224
non sequitur, 223
one right, one wrong, 224
post hoc, ergo propter hoc, 204
quick fix, 225
red herring, 223
straw man, 224–225
Looping, 8–9

Magazines, 278
"Man in the Water, The," 410–412
Mapping, 10
Marx Brothers, 99
Meaning: connotation and denotation, 126
Mechanics, guide to, 330–336
abbreviations, 331–332
capitalization, 330–331
errors in, 87
numbers, 332–333
spelling, 334–336
Medicare, 126
Metaphor(s), 135, 225, 241
Miscommunication, 130
Misplaced modifier, 95, 99–101, 107, 305
Mitford, Jessica, 164–168
Mixed constructions, 101–102
Mixed structure (sentences), 308–309
MLA documentation style, 275–277
Modern Language Association of America
(MLA), 275
Modes of communication, *see* Communication;
Strategies
Modifier(s):
dangling, 100–101, 304
misplaced, 95, 99, 305
specific, precise, 110
vague, 129
Modifying phrases, errors in, 304–305
Morrow, Lance, 346–348
Motivation, for writing, 3–4

Names:
connotations, 126
generic consistency, 135
proper, 330
Narration (narratives): 143, 250–260
believable characters, 251–252
brief, 250
details, 251

dialogue, 252
extended, 250
insignificant detail, 252–253
limit scope, 252
logical time sequence, 251
point of view, 251
problems to avoid, 252–253
professional essay, 256–259
revision worksheet, 255–256
student essay, 254–255
subject choice, 252
writing effective n., 250–253
Narrowing a subject, 5, 31, 36, 195, 227, 286
National Rifle Association, 230
Newspapers, 279
Nicaragua, 133
Nixon, Richard, 225
Nominalizations, 131
Non sequitur, 223
North, Oliver, 133
Note-taking, 264–265
Nouns:
collective, 294
errors with, 298–299
vague, 129
Number(s), 332–333
singular/plural forms, 293–295

Obscenity, 124
Observation, 23
"Ode to Thanksgiving," 407–410
"Of" phrases, 104
Omission (. . .), 328
Opinions, 213
forcefulness, 33
"Oranges," 349–354
Order:
deductive, 63–64
inductive, 64
of information, 62–64
process analysis, 158
of words, 99–101, 114
Organization, 44, 85, 145, 150, 159, 171, 202,
216, 218, 242
Originality, 80
Orwell, George, 416–419
Outline, 37, 42–44
Oversimplification, 204
Overuse:
lead-ins, 77
of similar constructions, 111–112

Pacing, 253
Padding, 96

Paragraphs:
    coherence, 62–71, 151
    concluding, 78–80
    development, 44, 52–56
    exercises, 57, 68–71
    first sentence, 72
    organizing, 44
    planning the essay, 41–44
    sequence, 71–72
    summary, 73
    topic sentence, 45–52
    transitions, 64–65
    underdeveloped, 37
    unity, 58–62
    vague generalities, 54
Parallelism, 66–67, 307
Paraphrase, 265–266
Parentheses, 325–326
Parenthetical elements (interrupters), 316–317
Parker, Dorothy, 137
Passive voice verbs, 105–106, 297
Pattison, Joseph C., 357–358
Peirce, Neal R., 394–395
Period(s), 311–312
Periodical indexes, 263
Perrin, Noel, 188–191
Personification, 241, 244
Persuasion, 125, 126, 150
Phrases, 104, 111, 314
    idiomatic, 122–123
"Pictures of My Parents," 404–407
Plagiarism, 265, 271–273
    unintentional, 272
Point of view, 112, 222, 244, 251
Politicians, 125
    use of connotation, 126
Pomposity, 126, 131
Possessive case, 298–299
Pratt, John Clark, 273 (note)
Preachiness, 126, 221, 251
Precision, 128
Predication, faulty, 101–102, 308
Prefixes, spelling of, 335
Prepositions, 122
Pretentiousness, 19, 106, 125, 127, 131
Prewriting, 3–26, 221
    analyze audience before drafting, 18–20
    summary, 26
Pro-and-Con Sheet, 215, 218
Process analysis, 157–170
    conclusion, 160
    development of, 158–160
    kinds: directional and informative, 157
    linking words in, 159–160

    professional essay (Mitford), 164–168
    revision worksheet, 170
    sample student essay, 161–164
    thesis statement, 160
Profanity, 124
Professional essays (Part Two):
    argumentation (Swift), 230, 233; (Gillmore), 234–235
    causal analysis (Trippett), 207–210
    classification and division (Lebowitz), 198–200
    comparison and contrast (Catton), 177–180
    definition essay (Perrin), 188–191
    description (Selzer), 245–247
    example (Strick), 154–158
    narration (Gregory), 256–259
    process analysis (Mitford), 164–168
    See also Part Four
Progress report, 25(11)
Pronouns:
    errors with, 294, 299–302
    generic problem, 134
    incorrect case, 301
    shift in, 300
    substituted for key nouns, 66
    vague reference, 300
Proofreading, 94, 335–336
Propaganda, 126
Prose, four basic types of, 143
Punctuation, 87, 252
    apostrophe, 320–321
    brackets, 325
    colon, 318–319
    commas, 312–317
    dash, 325–326
    ellipsis mark, 328
    exclamation point, 312
    guide to, 311–329
    hyphen, 326–327
    italics (underlining), 327–328
    parentheses, 323–324
    periods, 311–312
    question marks, 312, 321–322
    quotations, 270
    semi-colon, 318
Purpose, 4, 5–6, 56, 85, 143, 145, 194, 250, 251, 253

Question marks, 312
Quick fix, 225
Quotations, 79, 39–40
    direct, 264–265
    material longer than five typed lines, 276

overuse of, 269
punctuation, 270, 321–322
varied sentence pattern, 269–270

Readers:
identifying, 17–20
think about them as you write, 20
Reagan, Ronald, 230
Recipe (bureaucratic jargon), 139–140
Red herring, 223
Redundancy, 105
Relaxation, 91
Repetition, of key words, 66
Research paper, 221, 261–289
balanced treatment, 267
biased sources, 267
borrowed material as "window," 272–273
choosing sources, 267–268
current sources, 268
difference: use of documented sources, 261
incorporating source material, 268–270
logical use of sources, 268
note-taking, 264–265, 285
persuasive writing, 270
reliability of sources, 267
searching for topic, 261–264
series of small parts, 89
supplementary notes, 284–285
up-to-date reports, 268
validity of sources, 267–268
see also Bibliography; Plagiarism
Revision, 83–94, 120
key to effective word choice, 137
necessity, 83
summary, 94
thinking process, 83
Rhetorical question, 79
"River rafting teaches worthwhile lessons,"
152–153
Rogers, Carl, 221–222
Rosenblatt, Roger, 410–412
Roosevelt, Franklin, 106
Rough draft, *see* Drafts
Run-on sentences, 307

"Santa Ana, The," 368–370
Sarcasm, 124–125
Schell, Jonathan, 391–393
Semicolon, 318
Senses, 240–241
Sensitivity, 25(12)
Sentences:
average number of words in, 87
beginning with transition word, 65

center-of-gravity (example), 9
choppy, 116–117
clarity problems, 95
comma splice, 306–307
concise style, 102–104
content, 96–97
coordination, 115
effective, 95–120
exercises, 119–120
summary, 120
exercises, 107–108
false predication, 308
faulty construction, 306–309
faulty parallelism, 307
fragments, 306
identically constructed, 111
mixed construction, 101–102
mixed structure, 308–309
repeating patterns, 111
run-on, 307
simple, 98–99
specific, 97–98
subordinate clauses, 116–118
word selection and, 106
Sentimentality, 125
Sexist language, 134–135
"Shame", 256–259
She/He generic pronoun problem, 134
sic (usage), 264
Similes, 135, 241
Simplicity, 98–99
Sketching, 12
Slang, 130–131
Slogans, 220, 225
"So What's So Bad about Being So-So?,"
154–158
"Sound of Music: Enough Already,"
(Lebowitz), 198–200
Sources, *see* Documentation; Research papers
Space, order of, 63
Specialized language, 131
Specificity, 97–98
Spelling, 87
guide to mechanics, 334–336
Split infinitive, 296–297
Split-page entry, 24(6)
Springsteen, Bruce, 12
Statistics, 268
Steinem, Gloria, 385–389
Stereotyping, 134
Strategies, of exposition, 145–212
argumentation, 213–236
causal analysis, 201–212
classification and division, 192–201

comparison and contrast, 170–181
definition, 181–192
example, 146–157
patterns of development, 144
process analysis, 157–170
Straw man, 224–225
Strick, Lisa Wilson, 154–158
Structure, questions on, 156, 168–169, 180, 191, 200, 210, 233, 235, 247–248, 259
Student essays (texts):
    causal analysis, 205–207
    classification and division, 196–197
    comparison and contrast, 175–177
    definition, 186–188
    description, 243–245
    effective essays, 92–94
    essays developed by example, 152–153
    extended definition, 186–188
    looping, 9
    narration essay, 254–255
    process analysis, 161–164
    sample of MLA style, 285–289
Style:
    clear, 96–102
    concise, 102–104
    emphatic, 114–118
    lively, 109–114
    questions on, 120, 156, 168–169, 180, 191, 200, 210, 233, 235, 247–248, 259
    varying sentences, 111
Subject, 30, 78, 84, 124, 252
    audience knowledge of, 17
    caring about, 4
    dramatizing, 13–15
    process analysis, 158
    selecting, 30
        enthusiasm, 4
        narrowing a large subject, 5
        personal experience, 4–5
        start early, 4
        strong interest, 4–5, 26
Subjunctive (verb), 296
Subordination, 116–118
Suffixes, 335
Summarizing (note-taking), 265–266
Supplementary notes, 284–285, 288
Swift, Al, 230, 233
Synecdoche, 241

Tack-on words, 132
"Teenagers Work Too Soon," 394–395
Tense shift, 296
Textbook: write your own, 25(13)

"That Lean and Hungry Look," 361–363
"The Plot Against People," 377–378
Thesis statement, 27–40, 74, 145, 160, 171, 173, 202, 254, 255
    errors in, 33–34
    essay map, 37
    exercises, 35
    express in one sentence, 29
    function, 27, 40
    lead-in introducing, 77
    limited to fit assignment, 31
    location (paragraph), 32
    one main idea, 29, 40
    qualities of a good thesis, 28–34
    specific terms, 31–32
    time of discovering, 33, 40
    universalizing, 30
    working thesis and, 28
Thing (the word), 129(note)
Thomas, Lewis, 339–341
Time:
    avoiding pressure, 89
    order of, 62–63
    shifts in, 251
"38 Who Saw Murder Didn't Call the Police," 413–416
Title(s), 82, 134, 321, 331
    presenting; two basic rules, 81
"To be," 104
"To Bid the World Farewell," 164–168
Tone, 81, 123–125, 126, 168(6), 221
Topic, see Subject
Topic sentence, 45–52, 58, 151
    exercise, 49–52
    focus, 47–48
    functions, 45
    placing, 48–49
    recasting, 47
    sample, 45
    specific language, 45
    support for your essay, 46
Transition, 151, 159–160, 173–174, 253
    overuse of words and phrases, 65
    paragraphs, 64–65, 72–73
    variety of devices, 67
Trash, 90
Trendy expressions, 130
Trippett, Frank, 207–210
Triteness, 80
Twain, Mark, 20, 268
"Two Ways of Viewing the River," 359–360
Typed papers, 88

"Ultimate in Diet Cults: Don't Eat Anything at All," 20–22
Underlining, 327–328
Understatement, 241
Unity, 44, 58–62, 160

Vagueness, 129
Verbs, 132
  double negative, 297
  faulty agreement, 293–295
  passive voice, 105–106, 297
  specific, descriptive, 109–110
  split infinitive, 296–297
  subjunctive, 296
  tense shift, 296
  vague, 129
Viewpoints, 213
"Violence Is Fake, the Impact Is Real, The," 389–391
Viorst, Judith, 373–377
Vividness, 87, 148, 240, 251
Voice, 19, 251

Walker, Alice, 420–425
"We Don't Need a Uniform Poll-Closing" (Gillmore), 234–235
"We Need a Uniform Poll-Closing Time" (Swift), 230, 233
"What Are Manners?," 371–372
"Why Do Women Work?," 385–389
"Why Don't We Complain?," 341–346
Williams, Robin, 182

Wittig, Susan, 36 (note)
Wolfe, Thomas, 27
Word processors, 88–89
Wordiness, 102, 131, 137
Wordplay, 81
Words:
  choice of, 20, 106, 121
    revision the key to, 137
    summary, 141
  confused, 121–122
  connotation and denotation, 126
  logic of, 121–141
    exercises, 127–128
  order, 99–101
    emphasis, 114
  per sentence, 87
  precise, 128
  selecting the best, 128–137
  simple and direct, 131, 132
  unfamiliar, 19–20
  see also Transition
Working bibliography, *see* Bibliography
Working thesis statement, 15, 27–28, 40, 76, 216
  see also Thesis statement
Works cited list, 277–281, 289
Writer's block, 15, 44, 84
  suggestions for minimizing, 89–91
Writing, only for yourself, 19

X, 84

Zinsser, William, 379–384